Municipal
Bonds

Municipal
Bonds

The Comprehensive Review of Tax-Exempt Securities and Public Finance

Robert Lamb & Stephen P. Rappaport

McGraw-Hill Book Company

New York St. Louis San Francisco Auckland Bogotá
Hamburg Johannesburg London Madrid Mexico
Montreal New Delhi Panama Paris São Paulo
Singapore Sydney Tokyo Toronto

Library of Congress Cataloging in Publication Data
Lamb, Robert B
   Municipal bonds.

   Includes index.
    1. Municipal finance—United States.
2. Municipal bonds—United States. 3. Securities,
Tax-exempt—United States. I. Rappaport, Stephen P
joint author. II. Title.
HJ9145.L35   336.3'1   79-27105
ISBN 0-07-036082-0

The editors for this book were Kiril Sokoloff and Chet Gottfried; the
designer was Mark E. Safran, and the production supervisor was Sally
Fliess. It was set in Baskerville by The Heffernan Press Inc.

It was printed and bound by R. R. Donnelley & Sons Company.

To Our Parents,
Robert Keen Lamb and Helen Boyden Lamb,
in memoriam; and
Dr. Bernard Francis Rappaport and Claire Ruth Rappaport

Contents

Contents

Foreword

The last ten years have been momentous times for the nation's municipal securities industry and for investors in the securities issued by federal agencies, and state and local governments throughout the nation. The growth in the volume of municipal financing and the great increase in the number of investors in municipal securities give ample proof of the increasing importance of municipal finance.

The decade also has been marked by increased demands for municipal and other governmental services, by budgetary struggles, by serious financial problems experienced by a number of cities and other issuers—all problems shared by citizens, municipal employees, professional advisers, institutional and individual investors alike. New standards of disclosure, new oversight techniques and the increased involvement of federal, regulatory and legislative authorities have raised serious questions regarding such basic matters as the historic separation of federal and state government and the overall future course of government finance. Both the practical and the very philosophical economic and national policy issues have been brought to the forefront of the national and securities and banking industry consciousness in this last decade.

It is surprising that, in a field as important to so many as is the business of municipal finance, there is relatively little in the way of resource material of genuine educational value.

Municipal Bonds: The Comprehensive Review of Tax-Exempt Securities and Public Finance by Robert Lamb and Stephen P. Rappaport stands as a genuine contribution to filling a real need. It represents a comprehensive review as well as an excellent insight into the important field of municipal finance and will be a valuable source for those working actively in the field—underwriters, counsel and government officials, as well as investors in municipal bonds who wish to know more about this vital subject.

Edward I. O'Brien
President
Securities Industry Association

March 3, 1980

Acknowledgments

This book was written with the advice of many individuals whose day-to-day work involves municipal bond finance. While the authors take full responsibility for the contents of this volume, we would like to take this opportunity to thank certain individuals whose advice we sought.

Although we cannot list all of those who in one way or another provided such help, there are nonetheless a great number of individuals who must be acknowledged as our principal sources of unfailing support, both moral and substantive.

High on this list were Edward O'Brien and Robert Royer of the Securities Industry Association; Peter Harkins of the Dealer Bank Association; Donald Beaty and Robert Doty of the Municipal Finance Officers Association; Albert Gordon Sr., and Duncan Gray of Kidder, Peabody & Co.; Brenton Harries, John Dailey, and Richard Huff, Standard and Poor's Corporation; the late Jackson Phillips of Moody's Investors Service; Raymond Lauber of Chase Manhattan Bank; Herman Charbonneau of Chemical Bank; William McCarthy, Blyth Eastman Paine Webber; John DeJung, National Securities and Research Corporation; Sylvan Feldstein of Smith Barney, Harris Upham; David Darst of Goldman, Sachs; and Kevin Collins of The First Boston Corporation.

Other members of the investment banking community who contributed were Richard Ackerman, Merrill Lynch, Pierce, Fenner and Smith, Inc.; Lawrence Caffrey and Joan Camens, Paine, Webber, Jackson & Curtis; Alan Weeden, Weeden & Co.; John Tamagni, Lazard Frères; Edward Kresky, Wertheim & Co.; Richard Jenrette, Donaldson, Lufkin and Jenrette; John Noonan, Michael Hernandez, Albert Haiback, and Tamara Bund, Kidder, Peabody; Donald Patterson, Blyth Eastman Paine Webber; Morgan Murray, William Gibson, and George Friedlander, Smith Barney, Harris Upham; Peter Loeb, Sherman Lewis, and David Troob, Shearson Loeb Rhoades; Arthur Petersen, formerly of

Acknowledgments

Blyth Eastman Dillon; William Deegan, L. F. Rothschild, Unterberg, Tobin; Daniel Lingenfelter, Underwood, Neuhaus; Robert Martin and Dick Joseph, Dain Bosworth Inc.; Giles Brophy, First Penco Securities; Robert Stovall, Dean Witter Reynolds; William Hough of William R. Hough & Co.

Other members of the commercial banking community who were extremely helpful include: John Vella and Michael LaTorre, Bank of America; James Thompson, North Carolina National Bank; Larry Clyde and Roy Nahas, Crocker National Bank; John Rowe, First National Bank of St. Louis; Continental Bank; R. C. Johannesman, Mercantile Trust Company; George Casey, Wells Fargo Bank; Amos Beason, Frederic Rosenbauer and Peter Merrill, Morgan Guaranty Trust Company.

Many other professional associations and individuals provided much support and aid in accumulating material and statistics. In addition to the Municipal Finance Officers Association, the Dealer Bank Association, and the Securities Industry Association cited earlier, those providing the most assistance included: Alex Radin, American Public Power Association; Eric Johnson, American Water Works Association; W. A. Rusch, International Bridge, Tunnel, and Turnpike Association; Raymond Long, National Association of State Budget Officers; Mark Keane, International City Management Association; David Herlinger and William Johnston, Council of State Housing Agencies; Gerald Esser, Municipal Finance Officers Association; Bernard Hillenbrand, National Association of Counties; John Gunther, U.S. Conference of Mayors; and William Cassella, National Municipal League.

Among those who provided much encouragement in the early stages of the manuscript were Philip Fahey, Howard Whitman, John Cooper, Gene Mahon, Jack Kelly, Donald Scalley, Alfred Allen, Neal Sullivan, Bruce Deichle, and Bruce Treitler, all of Thomson McKinnon Securities Inc. In addition, Julian Smerling, Peter Vlachos, and Richard Moynihan of the Dreyfus Corporation provided much interest and enthusiasm for the project throughout all stages.

At Bache Halsey Stuart Shields, the following individuals provided much encouragement during the period when the manuscript was in its final stages: William Marlin, the late Edwin Bueltman, Theodore Swick, Samuel Plaia, James Glynn, Ernest Dubin, James Perry, and Ethan Deinard.

Other individuals whose advice we sought include John Winders and Joan Lulkovich, of the *The Daily Bond Buyer* and *The Weekly Bond Buyer*; Christopher Taylor, formerly of the Municipal Securities Rulemaking Board; John Butler of the Municipal Bond Insurance Association; Mathew Malone, Richard Cacchione, and Thomas Cacchione of Fitch Investors Service; and former Standard and Poor's staff members:

Preston Miller and Robert Margolies; and Robert White Jr. of White's Rating Service. John Brenner and Freda Stern Ackerman of Moody's are also acknowledged.

Members of New York University's Graduate School of Business Administration who provided insightful comments were: Wassily Leontief, William Silber, Robert Lindsay, Robert Kavesh, Lawrence Ritter, Arnold Sametz, Ernest Bloch, Edward Altman, Ingo Walter, William Guth, William Berliner, William Dill, Oscar Ornati, David Rogers, Hrach Bedrosian, Jeremy Weisen, George Sorter, Barbara Coe, Lawrence Rosenberg, and Peter Dubno.

Colleagues who responded with enthusiasm for the book include: Demetrios Caraley, Douglas Chalmers, Richard Pious, Charles Hamilton, and Robert Connery, all of Columbia University; Robert Gilmour, University of Connecticut; Douglas Rogers, Kidder, Peabody; Walter Stursberg, Reavis and McGrath, Esqs.; Bernard Axelrod, Esq.; and Richard Schmaltz, Morgan Stanley & Co.

Other writers on finance are also acknowledged here: Lenox Moak, James Van Horne, John Petersen, Alan Rabinowitz, and Wade Smith.

We are grateful to all those individuals cited here and to the many others, especially the municipal bond attorneys and accountants.

Three individuals who contributed enormously to the production of this book were: Melvin Simensky, of Gersten, Sherer & Kaplowitz, Esqs.; editor Thomas Rosenbaum; and Research Assistant, Lynn Togut.

Finally, we would like to acknowledge the support of the following organizations, some of whose names have changed as a result of mergers:

The American Public Power Association
Bache Halsey Stuart Shields Incorporated
Bank of America N.T. & S.A.
Blyth Eastman Dillon & Co.
The Chase Manhattan Bank, N.A.
Chemical Bank
Continental Illinois National Bank and Trust Company of Chicago
Council of State Housing Agencies
Crocker National Bank
Dain Bosworth Inc.
The Dealer Bank Association
Dean Witter Reynolds Inc.
Donaldson, Lufkin & Jenrette Securities Corporation
The First Boston Corporation
First National Bank in St. Louis
First Penco Securities Inc.

Acknowledgments

Fitch Investors Service, Inc.
William R. Hough & Co.
The International Bridge, Tunnel, and Turnpike Association
Kidder, Peabody & Co., Incorporated
Lazard Frères & Co.
Loeb Rhoades, Hornblower & Co.
Mercantile Trust Company N.A.
Merrill Lynch, Pierce, Fenner & Smith Inc.
Municipal Bond Insurance Association
North Carolina National Bank
Paine, Webber, Jackson & Curtis Incorporated
L. F. Rothschild, Unterberg, Towbin
The Securities Industry Association
Smith Barney, Harris Upham & Co. Incorporated
Standard & Poor's Corporation
Thomson McKinnon Securities, Inc.
Underwood, Neuhaus & Co., Inc.
Weeden & Co., Incorporated
Wells Fargo Bank, N.A.
Wertheim & Co., Inc.

Robert Lamb
Stephen P. Rappaport

March 15, 1980

Municipal
Bonds

part1

Introduction

chapter1

The Growth of Municipal Debt and Investment

Introduction

The most dynamic area of the investment industry today, as for the past decade, remains largely untouched in academic or trade literature: the market for municipal securities, which help to finance state and local government functions through the issuance of debt. Indeed, the largest number of securities issuers in the entire world are the federal, state, and local governmental entities. Taken altogether, the dollar volume of debt issued from 1970 to 1978 by municipalities was about double the total issuance of all corporate debt.

A major portion of this increase in municipal debt was issued to supply the critical needs for both urban and rural services, such as electric power, housing, transportation, education, hospitals, and pollution control. These debt securities were issued not only by cities, states, and counties but also by a growing number of public revenue authorities. One such authority is the Port Authority of New York and New Jersey, whose annual budget and general indebtedness each exceed those of many states; its budget even exceeds that of many countries.

The magnitude of this development in municipal finance over the past decade cannot be understated. Yet it took a crisis involving New York City and New York State to make the business, academic, and investor communities aware of the importance of credit analysis and volume of governmental debt at all levels. Similarly, the technical default in 1975 of the New York State Urban Development Corporation (UDC; once purported to be the most innovative state housing, finance, and construction agency) demonstrated the far-reaching impact that these newly created governmental entities could have on the U.S. economy, the investment community, and the various basic needs of Americans, such as housing.

To a considerable degree since World War II, state and local governments have forgone pay-as-you-go financing for certain basic services. As a result, highways, hospitals, housing, power facilities, waste disposal systems, transportation systems, and port facilities are among the services that people use daily, but whose successful financing depends on the underwriting and distribution of tax-exempt bonds by the investment banking firms and brokerage industry as well as by several hundred commercial banks which have dealer departments.

In a similar way, the increase of the federal government's debt, which has come in the form of the issuance of Treasury and federal agency obligations, is intimately related to the municipal market and plays a vital role in the liquidity structures of institutional investors, such as commercial banks and life insurance companies. It also has had a tremendous impact on private investors. These federal securities have recently been used to finance both conventional and government-backed residential housing, university dormitories, and hospitals.

Intergovernmental relationships have received very little attention from schools and departments of business at most U.S. universities. Moreover, it seems clear that as government and the investment industry become involved in providing the financing for more and more of the social needs of Americans, the financing will take the form of public debt and bonds.

The explosive growth in state and municipal debt has resulted in a substantial increase in the number of financial analysts engaged in this work. In a drastic shift of emphasis, commercial banks, investment banking firms, corporations, and insurance companies have developed new groups or departments within their finance departments to deal with this expanding debt market. This development is partly the result of the sharp decline in investor interest in the corporate equity markets, following losses during most of the 1970s. It also resulted because the major profits of brokerage houses and underwriters have been coming from underwriting and dealing in the debt issues of state and local governments. The major commercial banks and investment banking firms on Wall Street have dramatically increased their government and municipal departments, composed of traders, salespeople, researchers, and underwriters, over the last 10 years. At the same time the American Express Company, like other corporations, has also had to hire a whole range of specialists to manage its over $3 billion of holdings in state and local municipal bonds.

While the credit analysis area has been growing dramatically, there has been little literature on it that is comprehensive and up to date. The small amount of material written on municipal securities was, for the most part, published before 1939. More recent brief notes and pamphlets that firms use to train their employees have been quite limited in scope and do not fully describe the municipal marketplace.

The municipal securities industry with its attendant issues, such as credit analysis, debt insurance, and disclosure, will continue to be an important part of Wall Street and of each regional market of the nation. Therefore, this volume is the focus of an expanding literature that will bring together the issues and impacts of all public debt with which Americans, particularly the investment community, must wrestle on a daily basis. As a consequence, educational programs in the business of municipal and government securities will now become a necessity for the future wave of trainees, business students, and interested investors who have to cope with these rapidly expanding and changing markets.

Municipal Finance

The Tax Exemption

The key feature of municipal securities, and one that may account for their substantial growth in this past decade, is their tax-exempt status. Not only are holders of municipal bonds not required to pay federal income tax on their "coupon" (interest) income, but their interest is also frequently exempt from most state and local taxes. (For example, residents of New York are exempt from state and local taxes on interest from their New York State bonds.) This crucial feature was generally granted them first by an important Supreme Court case, *McCulloch v. Maryland* (1819).

This tax exemption of municipal bonds was reaffirmed by the federal government through section 103D of the Internal Revenue code, which, in effect, has enabled municipalities to come to the capital markets and obtain funds at a lower rate of interest than those prevailing in the commercial marketplace. With inflation rates pushing middle-class income earners into higher tax brackets, it is becoming ever more attractive to invest in tax-exempt municipal bonds whose yields, while lower than those of corporate bonds in absolute terms, usually are higher on a net aftertax basis because of this exemption from federal tax. Table 1-1 illustrates the importance of this unique tax-exempt feature. Investors in most tax brackets (30 percent or better) can receive greater returns from municipal securities than may be available on an aftertax basis from all other comparable types of investments. Obviously the higher an individual's tax bracket, the greater the advantage of this tax-exempt feature.

The role of the Internal Revenue Service (IRS) is extremely important in the municipal bond market. At times, a bond issue cannot even come

TABLE 1-1   Tax-Free vs. Taxable Income

Under federal income tax rates effective after Dec. 31, 1978, here are the comparable yields. This table gives the approximate yields which taxable securities must earn in various income brackets to produce, after tax, yields equal to those on tax-free bonds yielding from 5.50% to 8.50%. (Yields on tax-free bonds rose well above 8.50% in 1980.) The table is computed on the theory that the taxpayer's highest bracket tax rate is applicable to the entire amount of any increase or decrease in his or her taxable income resulting from a switch from taxable to tax-free securities, or vice versa.

(Taxable income in thousands)

Joint return	$16 to $20	$20 to $24	$24 to $30	$30 to $35	$35 to $46	$46 to $60	$60 to $80	$85 to $109	$109 to $162	$162 to $215	$215 to Over
% Bracket	24	28	32	37	43	49	54	59	64	68	70
5.50	7.24	7.64	8.09	8.73	9.65	10.78	11.96	13.41	15.28	17.19	18.33
5.60	7.37	7.78	8.24	8.89	9.82	10.98	12.17	13.66	15.56	17.50	18.67
5.70	7.50	7.92	8.38	9.05	10.00	11.18	12.39	13.90	15.83	17.81	19.00
5.80	7.63	8.06	8.53	9.21	10.18	11.37	12.61	14.15	16.11	18.13	19.33
5.90	7.76	8.19	8.68	9.37	10.35	11.57	12.83	14.39	16.39	18.44	19.67
6.00	7.89	8.33	8.82	9.52	10.53	11.76	13.04	14.63	16.67	18.75	20.00
6.10	8.03	8.47	8.97	9.68	10.70	11.96	13.26	14.88	16.94	19.06	20.33
6.20	8.16	8.61	9.12	9.84	10.88	12.16	13.48	15.12	17.22	19.38	20.67
6.30	8.29	8.75	9.26	10.00	11.05	12.35	13.70	15.37	17.50	19.69	21.00
6.40	8.42	8.89	9.41	10.16	11.23	12.55	13.91	15.61	17.78	20.00	21.33
6.50	8.55	9.03	9.56	10.32	11.40	12.75	14.13	15.85	18.06	20.31	21.67
6.60	8.68	9.17	9.71	10.48	11.58	12.94	14.35	16.10	18.33	20.63	22.00
6.70	8.82	9.31	9.85	10.63	11.75	13.14	14.57	16.34	18.61	20.94	22.33
6.80	8.95	9.44	10.00	10.79	11.93	13.33	14.78	16.59	18.89	21.25	22.67
6.90	9.08	9.58	10.15	10.95	12.11	13.53	15.00	16.83	19.17	21.56	23.00
7.00	9.21	9.72	10.29	11.11	12.28	13.73	15.22	17.07	19.44	21.88	23.33
7.25	9.54	10.07	10.66	11.51	12.72	14.22	15.76	17.68	20.14	22.66	24.17
7.50	9.87	10.42	11.03	11.90	13.16	14.71	16.30	18.29	20.83	23.44	25.00
7.75	10.20	10.76	11.40	12.30	13.60	15.20	16.85	18.90	21.53	24.22	25.83
8.00	10.53	11.11	11.76	12.70	14.04	15.69	17.39	19.51	22.22	25.00	26.67
8.25	10.86	11.46	12.13	13.10	14.47	16.18	17.93	20.12	22.92	25.78	27.50
8.50	11.18	11.81	12.50	13.49	14.91	16.67	18.48	20.73	23.61	26.56	28.33

SOURCE: Financial Government and Public-Affairs, Inc., Washington, D.C., 1978 data.

to market because bond counsel does not feel comfortable giving a decision on the tax-exempt status of the bonds on the federal, state, or local level. In the case of federal exemption, however, bond counsel will sometimes request a specific ruling from the IRS. When the IRS gives a ruling and grants exemption, it is not intended to be a blanket ruling; it is only a ruling on that particular case. Nevertheless, in requesting a ruling, bond counsel cites precedent of similar approved issues, which may ultimately cause the IRS to change its rules and regulations. The IRS is concerned with three factors regarding the tax exemption: (1) that the bonds are being issued for a governmental purpose, (2) that the revenue authority is not dealing simply with a paper entity, and (3) that the power of condemnation and governmental authority are maintained.

For example, for the $302-million New Jersey Sports and Exposition Authority bonds, there was a request for certain IRS rulings in regard to the issuance of the bonds. At issue, specifically, was the involvement of the state of New Jersey in the creation of the authority and what the state's involvement was with regard to the revenues from the authority. The question here was what was to be the "public purpose" of the New Jersey Sports and Exposition Authority. The answer was that the state would be sharing in surplus revenues from the project. As a result, the effect upon the rate of taxation in the state of New Jersey would benefit the citizens of that state. History has proved this to be a correct assumption.

The Growth of Municipal Debt

On New Year's Day, 1978, in the "Business and Finance" section of *The New York Times*, the lead headline read: "Municipal Bonds: The Star of 1977." Indeed, that year was surely the year of municipal bonds. New issues of state and local securities jumped to a record high of $45 billion in long-term bonds and $66 billion in total new issues, and numerous investment bankers on Wall Street greatly expanded their municipal departments while other firms founded new ones. Perhaps the most significant indication of the size of the municipal investment business is contained in Table 1-2.

By 1970 the total volume of new municipal issues (totaling $35.6 billion) exceeded corporate issues (totaling $25.6 billion) by 39 percent. By 1973 the total volume of new municipal issues increased while corporate issues declined, and by 1977 the municipal new issue volume was more than twice that of corporate bonds. In 1978 the total volume of new municipal issues reached $68 billion while corporate issues declined to $22 billion. Municipal issues maintained their relatively strong substantial lead in 1979.

Another significant indication of the difference between the municipal and corporate securities markets lies in the statistics that while there are 40,000 issuers of municipal securities and approximately 1.3 million issues outstanding, there are only 33,000 corporate issuers and only 63,000 issues of corporate securities. Because of the heavy financial requirements of state and local governments, the total outstanding of state and municipal debt at the end of 1977 rose to almost $258 billion, which is quadruple the amount that was outstanding in 1960. With the

TABLE 1-2 Totals and Volumes for Municipal and Corporate Debt Issues*

| | Municipal Issues | | | | | | Corporate Issues | | | | | |
| | Long-term | | Short-term | | Total | | Bonds | | Preferred bonds | | Total | |
Year	Number	Vol.†	Number	Vol.†	Number	Vol.†	Number	Vol.†	Number	Vol.†	Number	Vol.†
1970	4701	17.8	2903	17.9	7604	35.6	549	24.3	55	1.3	604	25.6
1971	5461	24.4	3350	26.3	8811	50.7	598	25.6	77	2.2	675	27.8
1972	5103	22.9	3317	25.2	8420	48.2	469	18.9	78	2.3	547	21.2
1973	4741	23.0	3406	24.7	8147	47.6	264	13.4	54	2.4	318	15.8
1974	4287	22.8	3414	29.0	7701	51.9	376	27.3	57	1.7	433	29.0
1975	4724	29.3	3383	29.0	8107	58.3	526	37.0	86	3.0	612	40.0
1976	4768	33.8	2613	21.9	7381	55.7	383	25.2	69	2.4	452	27.6
1977	5130	45.0	2240	21.3	7370	66.4	351	22.0	60	2.4	418	24.4
1978	5061	46.2	2002	21.6	7063	67.9	319	20.1	56	2.3	377	22.4

* Because of rounding, figures may not add up to totals.

† In $ billions.

SOURCES: "A Decade of Municipal Financing," *The Daily Bond Buyer*, July 6, 1979, p. 5, and "Total Underwritten Public Financing," *Investment Dealers Digest* (various issues).

most significant increases coming in the revenue bond market for the purposes cited in Table 1-4.

There has been concern, in the wake of New York City's fiscal crisis and the 1975 default of the New York State UDC, that the possibility of municipal bond defaults is increasing. Since investors in tax-exempt municipal bonds are generally conservative and do not like surprises, it may not be reassuring to note the national default statistics in Table 1-5.

But 4770 of the 6195 defaults occurred in the 1930s, and in terms of total dollars, municipal defaults have been very small, especially in light of the fine repayment record of municipalities as compared to corporations that declared bankruptcy following the Great Depression.

Nevertheless, the record since the Depression has not been spotless. There were 79 municipal defaults in the 1940s, even during the boom production of the war years. There were 112 defaults during the 1950s and nearly 300 in the economic expansion years of the 1960s. Default, or bankruptcy, by municipalities, states, cities, and public authorities was known to be a possibility even before New York's experiences. While the Depression years account for the overwhelming bulk of these municipal debt defaults with 4770, the safeguards built in by "New Deal" legislation following the Great Depression by no means prohibited the possibility of a municipal default. The fact that three times as many municipalities defaulted in the 1960s, during what was thought to be an economic boom period, as defaulted in the 1950s and 1940s makes it more apparent that credit, or risk, analysis of municipal securities is of vital importance to anyone entering this investment field. The latest figures for the 1970s show that far from the possibility of fiscal crises disappearing, they have begun to involve larger and more important debt issuers, such as New York City and New York State agencies (as, for example, UDC). Thus today it is vitally important that risk analysis of municipal debt be both as up to date and as practical as possible. This book takes, as its major focus, a definitive approach to risk analysis of all types of municipal debts.

Definition of Municipal Securities

A critical distinction to be made in municipal finance is that between securities that are general obligations of a state or local government which are secured by taxing power and those that are in a broad category called revenue bonds. General obligation (GO) bonds are backed by a pledge of the full faith and credit, i.e., the taxing power of the issuing governmental entity, and, as such, for decades were considered to be the most secure of all the municipal issues because governments have the

TABLE 1-3 State and Local Debt Outstanding by Character, in $ Millions

(Full faith and Nonguaranteed)

Year	Gross state and local debt	Character state long-term			State short-term	Total state debt	Character local long-term			Local short-term	Total local debt
		Total	Full faith	Non-guaranteed			Total	Full faith	Non-guaranteed		
1977	$257,532	$87,184	$42,913	$44,271	$3,016	$90,200	$156,963	$94,837	$62,126	$10,369	$167,332
1976	240,086	78,368	38,421	39,947	6,011	84,379	142,941	92,222	50,718	12,766	155,707
1975	221,224	67,548	33,736	33,812	4,580	72,127	133,890	81,836	52,054	15,206	149,096
1974	206,616	61,697	30,855	30,842	3,599	65,296	128,256	80,095	48,161	13,064	141,320
1973	188,485	55,701	28,443	27,258	3,674	59,375	116,905	74,502	42,403	12,205	129,110
1972	174,502	50,542	25,228	25,314	3,912	54,453	108,239	70,585	37,654	11,810	120,049
1971	158,827	44,321	21,502	22,819	3,472	47,793	99,296	62,523	36,773	11,738	111,034
1970	143,570	38,903	17,736	21,167	3,104	42,008	92,512	57,601	34,911	9,051	101,563
1969	133,548	36,906	16,183	20,724	2,647	39,553	86,560	54,694	31,866	7,436	93,995
1968	121,158	33,622	14,698	18,923	2,045	35,666	79,109	50,380	28,730	6,382	85,492
1967	114,614	31,185	13,558	17,627	1,287	32,472	76,436	49,204	27,232	5,706	82,142
1966	107,051	28,504	12,709	15,795	1,060	29,564	72,497	47,091	25,405	4,991	77,487

Year											
1965	99,512	26,235	11,819	14,415	800	27,034	67,969	44,598	23,371	4,509	72,478
1964	92,222	24,401	11,147	13,254	641	25,041	63,126	42,119	21,007	4,055	67,181
1963	87,452	22,751	10,658	12,093	424	23,176	60,399	40,046	20,353	3,876	64,276
1962	81,288	21,612	10,313	11,300	411	22,023	55,931	38,008	17,923	3,334	59,265
1961	75,023	19,529	9,521	10,009	464	19,993	52,011	35,143	16,869	3,019	55,030
1960	69,955	18,128	8,912	9,216	415	18,543	48,673	32,738	15,935	2,739	51,412
1959	64,110	16,421	8,211	8,210	509	16,930	44,706	31,052	13,654	2,474	47,180
1958	58,187	15,065	7,349	7,716	329	15,394	40,672	28,495	12,177	2,122	42,793
1957	52,733	13,522	6,490	7,032	216	13,738	37,013	26,210	10,803	1,982	38,995
1956	49,161	12,643	6,213	6,430	247	12,890	34,424	25,895	8,529	1,846	36,271
1955	44,267	10,950	5,929	5,022	248	11,198	31,322	24,611	6,711	1,747	33,069
1954	38,931	9,317	5,770	3,547	283	9,600	27,581	22,483	5,098	1,750	29,331
1953	33,781	7,505	5,158	2,347	320	7,824	24,499	20,322	4,177	1,458	25,957
1952	30,100	6,640	4,926	1,714	235	6,874	22,080	18,480	3,601	1,146	23,226

SOURCE: Joan Lulkovich, research editor, *Statistics on State and Local Government Finance*, The Bond Buyer, New York, 1979, p. 8. Compiled by "The Daily Bond Buyer" from bulletins issued by the Bureau of the Census entitled "Governmental Finances." Because of rounding, details may not add to totals. Figures from this source differ from comparable figures issued by the Treasury Department.

TABLE 1-4 State and Municipal Bonds Sold by Purposes, 1969 to 1978, in $1000s

	1978	1977	1976	1975	1974	1973	1972	1971	1970	1969
School	$ 6,239,540	$ 5,136,350	$ 5,177,240	$ 4,455,535	$ 4,999,513	$ 4,806,911	$ 5,348,943	$ 5,723,009	$ 4,983,101	$ 3,174,829
Water and sewer*	4,469,944	4,459,140	3,307,591	2,461,694	2,120,119	2,296,073	2,841,441	3,617,497	2,329,706	1,357,049
Highway, bridge and tunnel	1,876,918	1,350,479	1,552,089	1,095,391	980,813	1,453,415	2,082,267	2,717,903	1,497,392	1,571,846
Gas and electric†	5,991,730	5,750,819	4,457,366	2,181,465	1,521,757	1,558,387	—	—	—	—
Hospital	3,138,494	4,734,054	2,725,976	1,959,019	1,292,409	—	—	—	—	—
Industrial	586,076	463,816	356,909	517,801	339,970	269,762	470,695	219,510	47,593	24,020
Pollution control†	3,482,361	3,868,146	2,664,358	2,526,046	2,179,005	2,093,512	—	—	—	—
Public housing authority	—	—	—	—	460,985	1,029,240	958,960	1,000,435	130,790	397,885
Veterans aid	1,155,000	592,000	621,500	745,830	672,615	414,000	259,700	307,300	213,000	147,000
Other	19,274,698	18,705,663	12,981,524	13,383,445	8,326,779	9,031,345	10,978,836	10,783,880	8,560,061	4,787,622
Total	$46,214,763	$45,060,469	$33,844,556	$29,326,229	$22,823,968	$22,952,646	$22,940,843	$24,369,536	$17,761,645	$11,460,251

* Figure revised for the year 1975.
† Figures revised for the years 1973–1975.
‡ Includes industrial and nonindustrial financing.

SOURCE: Joan Lulkovich, research editor, *Statistics on State and Local Government Finance*, The Bond Buyer, New York, 1979, p. 8. Statistics compiled by "The Daily Bond Buyer."

TABLE 1-5 Recorded Defaults, by Type of Local Government Unit and Geographic Region, 1839 to 1969

	1839–1849	1850–1859	1860–1869	1870–1879	1880–1889	1890–1899	1900–1909	1910–1919	1920–1929	1930–1939	1940–1949	1950–1959	1960–1969	Total defaults	Number of local governments in 1967[a]
By type of unit:															
Counties and parishes		7	15	57	30	94	43	7	15	417	5	12	24	727	3.049
Incorp. munics.	4	4	13	50	30	93	51	17	39	1434	31	31	114	1911	18.048
Unincorp. munics.		4	9	45	31	50	33	5	10	88	7	4	26	313	17.105
School districts				4	5	9	11		14	1241	5	23	60	1372	21.782
Other districts				2	1	12	11	7	107	1590	30	42	70	1872	21.254
By geographic region:															
New England states[b]	1				2		1	1	1	7	1		4	18	3.045
Middle Atlantic states[c]		5	6	19	11	13	13	4	4	251	9	4	10	350	10.437
Southern states[d]	1	1	32	29	36	25		9	51	1863	16	33	76	2172	9.478
Midwestern states[e]	2	9	28	54	46	89	68	6	18	1152	18	34	76	1530	37.359
Southwestern states[f]			1	19	7	79	27	5	24	707	25	36	112	1042	9.558
Mountain states[g]					2	17	2	8	17	270	5	4	3	329	4.289
Pacific states[h]			1	2	3	22	14	3	70	520	5	1	13	654	7.052
Totals	4	15	37	159	97	258	149	36	185	4770	79	112	294	6195	81.248

[a] The number of local government units has changed rapidly. For example, in 1932 there were 127,108 school districts, 8580 other districts, and 175,369 state and local government units.
[b] Connecticut, Maine, Massachusetts, New Hampshire, Rhode Island, and Vermont.
[c] Delaware, District of Columbia, Maryland, New Jersey, New York, and Pennsylvania.
[d] Alabama, Arkansas, Florida, Georgia, Kentucky, Louisiana, Mississippi, North Carolina, South Carolina, Tennessee, Virginia, and West Virginia.
[e] Illinois, Indiana, Iowa, Michigan, Minnesota, Missouri, Nebraska, Ohio, North Dakota, South Dakota, and Wisconsin.
[f] Arizona, Kansas, New Mexico, Oklahoma, and Texas.
[g] Colorado, Idaho, Montana, Nevada, Utah, and Wyoming.
[h] Alaska, California, Hawaii, Oregon, and Washington.

SOURCE: U.S. Advisory Commission on Intergovernmental Relations, *City Financial Emergencies: The Intergovernmental Dimension*, 1976, p. 10.

power to levy taxes to meet the debt service (principal and interest) on the bonds. For instance, taxes that most Americans pay include those on property, sales, and personal income. These are the revenue sources upon which municipalities and states can draw and which they can increase to pay for services or debt service on bonds. One of the paradoxical problems facing New York City and New York State in 1975 was their need to increase levies on a variety of taxes for financing additional services, with the resultant possibility that tax increases would drive out industry and people from the state, thus reducing the number of taxpayers.

In the last 20 years, the issuance of tax-supported GO bonds has declined relative to revenue bonds from over 70 percent to under 40 percent of the total new issues from the municipal bond market. GO bonds will continue to be an important financing vehicle for such municipal capital improvements as schools, streets, and municipal buildings, but their share is likely to continue to decline. Out of a total of $45 billion of long-term tax-exempt bonds sold in 1977, only about $17.9 billion, or just under 40 percent, were GO bonds. The same was true in 1978.

The tremendous growth in the revenue-backed municipal debt issued since World War II has been helped by the growth of revenue authorities. The Port Authority of New York and New Jersey, created in 1921, was the first major user of the municipal public authority device in the United States and is one of the nation's largest public agencies. These revenue authorities are generally designed to contract debts that are payable through user fees and service charges. These bond obligations do not constitute debt of the municipalities or state in which they are located.

State laws govern whether a municipal entity must use GO debt or can use revenue bonds. (This will be discussed in Chapter 13.) However, when municipalities have a choice of issuing either GO or revenue bonds and desire to have *only* the users of facilities pay for their financing and *not* the entire citizenry of a community, revenue bond financing is used. When voter approval of GO bonds cannot be obtained, revenue bonds are also sometimes used. Because they may not be subject to statutory or constitutional debt limitations, revenue bonds may be the most convenient means for financing a capital program that benefits several government jurisdictions. Although they were originally used to finance canals and turnpikes, today's revenue bonds include those for sewers, gas service, telephone systems, parking, airports, ports, rapid transit, stadiums and other recreation facilities, solid waste disposal systems, college dormitories, student loans, and special tax and tax increment bonds. The municipal issuers of these revenue bonds may include one community or several communities' combinations of incorporated and unincorporated areas, and authorities which in some instances even cross state lines.

The issuance of revenue bonds was originally developed to finance utility projects. Later, under federal sponsorship, such debt was broadened to provide for local public housing projects. As recently as 1957, the bulk of all local revenue bonds outstanding had been incurred for these two purposes. The early 1960s, however, saw the beginning of a rapid extension in the use of revenue bonds to finance types of projects traditionally financed by GO full faith and credit borrowing. For example, many of today's public schools and office buildings with debt service paid from "rentals" derived from taxes or other general government revenue (and various projects with debt service payable from the yield of earmarked nonproperty taxes, i.e., gasoline, sales, utility, or hotel taxes, or other specific revenue sources) were, during earlier years, full faith security.

With the creation of the Port Authority of New York and New Jersey in 1921 and the Triborough Bridge and Tunnel Authority in the early Forties, it was clearly established that not only were political subdivisions entitled to exemption from federal income taxation on bond interest but so also were special district governments with wide functional and territorial jurisdictions. Such special districts have played a vital role in the development of areawide metropolitan facilities.

By the mid-1950s almost every state had some sort of enabling legislation for revenue bond financing, and an estimated $59.5 billion of revenue bonds, utilized to finance revenue-producing projects by over 1000 municipalities, counties, special districts, states, and state agencies, remained outstanding.

Perhaps the most controversial bond ever to emerge on the investment banking scene has been the "moral obligation" bond. This security is issued by revenue authorities, but the state provides a moral pledge of payment in the event that an authority is unable to make timely debt service. However, unlike the GO pledge, the moral obligation bond does not require voter approval and does not have the state's official pledge of its full faith and credit. The most famous moral obligation bond was issued by the UDC, which defaulted on $104.5 million in bond anticipation notes (including interest) on February 25, 1975. Although New York State created the Project Finance Agency as a financing device to redeem the UDC obligations, the state also appropriated money to enable the UDC to make principal and interest payments. Consequently, because of the UDC crisis, moral obligation bonds, which had been issued by public authorities in 35 states, demanded the immediate attention of credit analysts in both the government and the investment industry. It should be added that when New York State ultimately did honor its moral obligation bond pledge to UDC on its notes, it was regarded as an important precedent by the financial community for future moral obligation bond pledges of state support. (In order to give a balanced picture of moral obligation bonds it should be mentioned that few moral obligation public authorities in America have ever defaulted.)

As noted earlier, there is a wide variety of projects financed by revenue bonds, and an occasional debate has arisen as to the desirability, capability, and willingness of states to make good on their public authority debts regardless of whether they are backed by a state's moral pledge. Furthermore, significant attention has been focused on these revenue agencies concerning their inability or ability to solve metropolitan problems and to provide better service delivery in light of what some people consider to be their semiautonomous status "once removed" from control by the voters. All these issues have substantial bearing on the credit analysis of these governmental enterprises. The tools provided in this book should aid in their analysis.

One significant use of the authority device by government corporations has been the lease-backed arrangements whereby municipal bonds are issued by an authority to finance the construction of a facility, which is then leased to a municipal entity at a rental calculated to be sufficient to pay interest and principal on the bonds.

In addition, there is a wide variety of other revenue bonds—for example, the bonds that in effect are secured by federal government authority (actually they are annual-contribution payments which include debt service payments). There are also government-corporation combinations, such as industrial revenue bonds and pollution control bonds. A municipal entity issues bonds that are backed by the credit of private corporations through the use of leases. These bonds have traditionally been considered tax-exempt because they meet public purpose objectives. More important, there also exists an equally large variety of municipal securities that are backed by combinations of user fees and charges or rents. These are bonds issued to finance public power projects, water and sewer systems, housing projects, hospitals, transportation facilities, and industrial revenue bonds.

Since the early 1970s, several hybrid types of municipal bonds have emerged in which debt service charges are payable primarily from pledged revenues or from limited or special taxes, but for which the issuing unit also pledges its full faith and credit (i.e., its taxing power) if the primary revenues fall short. In discussing such "hybrids," most analysts have tended to group them with GO bonds.

Small Volume Issues of Municipal Bonds   Several types of municipal bonds that used to be important factors in the market, such as bonds for toll roads, bridges, and tunnels, are less so today. Because of space limitations these and other small volume municipal issues, such as bonds for garages, airports, and sports complexes and education revenue bonds, are dealt with in separate studies in the appendixes at the end of this book.

Municipal Notes   Although this book deals only with municipal bonds, it should be stressed that municipal notes, such as tax anticipation notes (TANs), bond anticipation notes (BANs), and revenue anticipation notes (RANs), increased in volume dramatically between 1969 and 1974 and then decreased between 1974 and 1975. They now have stabilized at twice their 1969 level. In brief, communities are using more than $20 billion in short-term notes as well as more than $40 billion in long-term bonds. In part, erratic growth in the volume of short-term debt has occurred because of the very high prevailing rates of interest that municipalities must pay for bonds. Municipalities would often rather not lock into a very high interest cost by selling 20- to 40-year bonds if they believe interest rates over the next year or two may come down. They could then fund their debt needs more cheaply by issuing long-term bonds when rates decrease.

This movement toward the issuance of more municipal notes and other types of short-term municipal debt has a good side and a bad side. It enables municipalities to smooth out their financial operations and their payrolls. The bad side is that there is a danger of continually funding a short-term operating deficit in such a way that the underlying financial shortfall is not corrected.

Who Holds Municipal Securities?

The purchase of state and local government securities has been cyclical, as shown in Table 1-6. In 1950 households and commercial banks held equal shares in the municipal markets—both totaled approximately one-third of all issues. By 1960 individual holdings of municipal securities totaled 44 percent, while commercial banks only held 25 percent. However, the position of the commercial banks had almost reversed by 1970, whereby banks held 48 percent of the outstanding municipal securities and households had dropped to 32 percent.

Perhaps the most significant shift in holdings by any financial institution came in the mid-1970s—immediately preceding and in the wake of the New York City crisis in the municipal bond market—when some commercial banks and some insurance companies started decreasing

TABLE 1-6   Ownership of Outstanding State and Local Government Securities

(Year-end, selected years from 1950 to 1975)*

	1950	1955	1960	1965	1970	1975
	(Millions of Dollars)					
Commercial banks	8.4	13.1	17.7	38.9	70.2	103.1
Households	9.0	19.2	30.8	36.4	45.6	81.6
Non-life insurance companies	1.1	4.2	8.1	11.3	17.8	35.8
Other financial intermediaries	1.6	2.9	4.7	4.3	4.4	6.7
Nonfinancial corporate business	0.7	1.2	2.4	4.6	2.2	4.5
State and local governments	3.6	5.2	7.2	4.8	4.3	4.5
Total outstanding	24.4	45.9	70.8	100.3	144.5	235.4
	(Percent)					
Commercial banks	34.5	28.6	25.0	38.8	48.6	43.8
Households	36.9	41.8	43.5	36.3	31.6	34.7
Non-life insurance companies	4.7	9.1	11.4	11.3	12.3	14.9
Other financial intermediaries	6.6	6.4	6.6	4.3	3.1	2.8
Nonfinancial corporate businesses	2.7	2.7	3.4	4.6	1.5	1.9
State and local governments	14.7	11.3	10.1	4.8	3.0	1.9

* Because of rounding, figures may not add up to totals.
SOURCE: Board of Governors of the Federal Reserve System, *Flow of Funds Accounts.*

their portfolios of municipal securities, in part to lower their risk as a buffer against local default. Obviously a few banks also cut back because their losses on loans and losses on real estate investment trusts meant they did not need as much income tax shelter from tax-free municipal bonds. This cutback may have been made not simply because of the fiscal problems of cities but because lease financing of foreign credits to underdeveloped countries became, in some instances, a better tax-avoidance mechanism.

The Municipal Market

The market for municipal securities has two parts: (1) the *primary market* and (2) the *secondary market*. The primary market, or new issue market, exists for securities when they are first issued. As greater demands are made upon state and local governments to raise the money needed for building and replacing, investors will have a continuing choice of new bonds that will finance educational facilities, mass transit, pollution control, housing, and urban redevelopment, to cite only a few examples.

The secondary market, or trading market, in municipal securities—although it begins even before the securities are issued in the "when-issued" trades—really refers to the market in which older, seasoned issues are bought and sold before their final maturity. This nationwide market is made up of dealers and brokers who are in contact via telephone and wire networks. This system offers a trading market for municipal securities and enables one to buy or sell municipal securities comparatively easily. The existence of the secondary market allows investors to change their portfolios in terms of the types of bonds they own, their maturities, and their ratings. In addition, the secondary market allows them to take tax losses or gains when appropriate because of changes in the investors' tax bracket.

The Issue of Credit Analysis

While the methods of credit analysis for municipal securities are dealt with in Chapter 3, "The Rating Agencies: Their Role in the Municipal Marketplace," the vital importance of sharpening and improving these tools as shown in this book cannot be overemphasized. Unlike that of corporate securities, the creditworthiness of municipal bonds and other forms of government debt depends on a whole range of complicated factors: the fiscal policies of the issuing body, budgeting procedures used in a specific city, legal restrictions, and principles of financial solvency that simply are not encountered in the corporate field. This detailed knowledge is harder to come by than in the corporate securities market, and hence a comparatively small group of municipal specialists strongly influences the credit ratings of state and local governments. The rapid expansion in the issuance of municipal bonds, which occurred after 1975, and the shrinkage of the equity market have led to a vast new interest in municipal bonds and in tools for analyzing their strengths and weaknesses. In this rush to obtain municipal securities, the nonspecializing firms have often acquired and then relayed the opinions of the specialists.

Perhaps the most far-reaching influence that the New York City fiscal crisis and the UDC default had on the investment community was largely in the field of credit analysis: a field that had been the exclusive domain of the rating agencies of Moody's and Standard & Poor's. The upshot of the crises was that investment bankers and investors alike suggested that the ratings just were not good enough as indexes of bond security. With GO bonds, the problem—spearheaded by the New York City fiscal crisis—was largely that the ratios used previously as the indicators of creditworthiness were no longer applicable to the budget problems and revenue-raising capacities of the states, cities, and other municipal entities. The property tax, for example, which for a long period had been the mainstay of city revenues, decreased proportionally to such an extent that the debt valuation ratios were no longer valid. Moreover, for almost every city in the nation there was a different method of analysis because of the different legal constraints on each issue. Thus for comparative purposes, the ratings which really indicate bond security in terms of the relationship to other issues and issuers were questionable.

As cities became urban areas of decay, federal funds began to be pumped into these areas, and the traditional ratios used in credit analysis simply did not take into account the new federal infusion of funds. This problem was made worse because much of the money went directly to individuals through food stamps, poverty programs, aid to dependent children, welfare, etc., so that the important ratio of net overall debt as a percentage of total personal income also became a meaningless evaluation tool. Another problem was the relationship of GO debt to overlapping and special debt incurred by public authorities. The post–World War II period and, in particular, the years after 1960 saw a tremendous increase in the number of authorities that were issuing bonds for a wide variety of public purposes. With the issuance of these new securities came an increase in the complexity of these bonds, and new questions arose as to (1) the backing of these securities and (2) their relation to the debt of the underlying municipality.

Proposition 13 and the Effect of the Tax Revolt on Analyzing Municipal Credits

On June 6, 1978, California voters, in one of the most popular actions in recent election history, sought to cut their property taxes by more than half and proclaimed a thundering outcry against big and more expensive government. Their Proposition 13, otherwise known as the Jarvis-Gann initiative, was approved by the voters as an amendment to the state of California constitution (Article XIII A). It passed by a substantial two-to-one majority and was immediately seen as a dramatic forecast of growing concern among voters across the country against the ever rising tide of taxes.

Because of Proposition 13, every credit analyst of municipal bonds, whether at rating agencies or in financial organizations, realized that increased emphasis must be placed upon evaluating the political process of municipalities and conducting region-by-region analyses of the mood of the electorate.

There is little question that taxpayers are frustrated and angry across the nation because of their perception that government fails to deliver services at reasonable cost. Many counties, cities, and other local governments show evidence of mismanagement and waste. Many taxpayers feel that garbage is seldom collected on schedule, law enforcement is lax, schools fail to teach children how to read, street potholes seem to multiply, fire alarms go unanswered, traffic congestion makes driving an ordeal, and at times city hall seems incapable of answering even the most elementary questions.

Underlying this public disaffection with inadequate government performance is the view that as government performance decreases, taxes increase. Thus it is no surprise that taxpayers do show increasing signs of being incensed, and the tax revolt fever *is* spreading to other states where the property tax burden is the heaviest.

To get a clear picture in dollars and cents of what the tax revolt is all about, it is helpful to note that in fiscal year 1977, California collected $465 per capita in property taxes. New York State was fourth on the list with $446 per capita, trailing Massachusetts at $490 per capita and New Jersey at $464 per capita. In terms of a percentage of all personal income, Massachusetts led all the states with 7.4 percent of personal income going for property taxes; California, with 6.5 percent, was second; and New York and New Jersey were tied at 6.3 percent. It is always important to reflect that this local tax burden comes on top of substantial taxes at other levels. The property tax referendum, like the school bond vote, is the one time the general public is given a chance to vote directly on all taxes taken together. Many analysts have argued that any federal tax, indeed any other program if put to a vote (like the local school bond issue), would be voted down and would have been during any time within the last 20 years. The present tax revolt, therefore, is simply the first time taxpayers have seen an opportunity to register their opinions clearly.

It should thus come as no surprise that measures to limit taxation or government spending appeared on the ballots of 16 states on November 7, 1978, and in 12 states such measures were successful. Nevada, Arizona, Hawaii, Illinois, Michigan, Texas, Alabama, Missouri, North Dakota, and South Dakota adopted constitutional amendments somewhat similar to that enacted in California. In addition, Tennessee and New Jersey have enacted legislation that tied government spending to economic growth. Yet, although a crucial test may not have arrived in these states, the effect thus far on current bonds outstanding in those states has been quite comforting to their bondholders. The 12 elections will neither immediately nor drastically impair the security of their outstanding bonds.

In summary, proposals of the Proposition 13 type became law in only one other state (Idaho), and spending ceiling measures became law in only four states. Four of the twelve successful measures addressed relatively narrow tax and spending problems, and one dictates a personal income tax reduction. These latter would appear to have negligible adverse effects on bond security.

An initial surprise from the passage of the California proposition is that it appears to be working so well. However, only the existence of a $5-billion California state budget surplus made many layoffs and cutbacks unnecessary. In fact, preliminary figures indicate that despite the rollback in assessed values, California will this year and again next year generate another large surplus.

However, the long-term effect of Proposition 13 on California issues and on outstanding municipal bonds and notes in other states will probably not be known for several years. In New York, if local revenues were suddenly cut by a Jarvis-Gann type of amendment, the state would find it difficult, if not impossible, to fill the gap. As a result of the 1978 election, Idaho will be substantially affected because, unlike California, it lacks a budget surplus with which to cushion the impact of the property tax rollback that was adopted. Consequently, all existing Idaho municipal bonds secured by property taxation could well be adversely affected.

It is too early to conclude, as some municipal analysts did, that with the sole exception of Idaho, municipal bond holders emerged "almost unscathed" from the first major post-Proposition 13 battle of the taxpayers revolt. It is true that Oregon and Michigan voters, contrary to expectations, refused to follow the California example. It is also fair to state that the spending and collection limitations which were adopted in several states were moderate measures. Their primary effect, nevertheless, will be to slow the growth of the public sector and cut out many municipal GO bonds and revenue bonds.

One of the dangers of amendments of the Proposition 13 type across the entire country was to make local jurisdictions even more dependent on federal and state grants and programs. There will almost undoubtedly be a further loss of local control. Increased dependency over the last 20 years upon state, county, and federal revenues to meet not only extraordinary but also ordinary day-to-day operations is already leading to a steady lessening of local financial self-reliance, and this trend after Proposition 13 is expected to increase sharply. To counter this trend, priorities will have to be established, and the public will then perhaps begin to pay more attention to how well its many and various governments perform against specific yardsticks. Elected officials across the country are arguing with their constituents that soaring costs confront government with only three alternatives: (1) increase taxes, (2) cut services, or (3) both.

Among the expected long-term effects of Proposition 13 on municipal finance is the growing conviction that we may well find that our municipal governments will be relegated to nondiscretionary funding of programs in public safety and roads. Special districts may be formed for specific programs and purchases. And it is also almost certain that new regional agencies will have to be created.

The most powerful consequences will be a reduction in GO borrowing and a trend toward user charges for activities such as those related to adult and special education, libraries, sanitation, water and sewer services, electric power, and recreational facilities. In line with this, we can, therefore, expect even greater reliance upon revenue bond financing, which need not be backed by the voters or even submitted for their approval.

Risks and Returns of Municipal Bonds

Risks

While it is certainly true that municipal bonds have, on the whole, been relatively safe investments over the years and their default record, even during the Great Depression, was far less than that for corporate bonds, it is not true that municipal bonds are risk-free. Like virtually all other types of securities, municipal bonds have certain risks associated with them, and of necessity some municipal bonds have more risks than others. Therefore, it may be important for investors and bond analysts to consider the comparative risks of certain types of municipal bonds versus certain other municipal bonds, as we will do in the following chapters. And it may also be important to weigh this range of risks of municipal bonds in comparison with risks on government bonds, government agency bonds, international bonds, or corporate bonds or stocks.

On the whole municipal bonds have far more risks than government securities that are backed by the federal government, with its power to print money, but municipal bonds have far fewer risks than corporate stocks, which can fluctuate enormously. All municipal bonds have certain common types of risks; nevertheless, different categories of municipal bonds have different specific risks associated with them in particular. Eight kinds of risks that can be associated with municipal bonds are listed. Several are interrelated, possibly because, in part, they involve the loss or change in value of the bond's principal or the loss or change in value of its interest payments.

1. Default. If a municipality goes bankrupt, it might not pay back the principal and interest on its bonds.

2. Delayed payments or delinquency. Although technically this is a kind of default, if payment quickly resumes, it is not a full-scale default.

3. Loss resulting from a rating change. This is the risk of changing credit quality.

4. Liquidity. This risk would be due to an investor's inability to obtain cash immediately or quickly in exchange for the bonds.

5. Marketability. There may not be any buyers.

6. Call. Loss may result when bonds are "called" or paid back long before their maturity or expiration date.

7. Loss of asset value. This occurs when the inherent value of the bonds' principal falls. (A bond's price goes down when the yields on current prevailing bonds go up.)

8. Loss of interest. If investors have to sell during periods of lower interest rates and if they cannot reinvest principal at as high an interest rate as before, they lose interest. (It is the same as risk of call except that the investor—not the issuer—initiates the sale.)

For certain individual or institutional investors certain risks (for example, credit quality or default) will be of greater concern than others (for example, liquidity). It should also be noted that some buyers are prohibited from investing in certain securities that carry certain types and degrees of risks. Lawyers, accountants, bankers, brokers, dealers, and investors in the bond market have quite different perceptions of what is and is not a risk.

While, obviously, different individuals have different "risk profiles" (some try to avoid risk entirely, others try to avoid certain risks only, and some seek or welcome risk), we cannot catalog every individual's perception of risks. Nevertheless, we can bracket several types of risk profiles and identify the types of bonds each would perhaps choose or avoid.

Bond dealers' perceptions of risk, for example, are strongly colored by the fact that they are 80 to 90 percent leveraged at all times. They would, therefore, tend to worry about making any serious mistake and tend to turn over their portfolios very rapidly. Long-term risks would thus be less important to such dealers, whereas avoiding the liquidity risk would be vital.

Institutional investors might well view risk from the standpoint of their fiduciary relationship to clients' investments and would almost certainly avoid investing in municipal bonds that lacked sufficient rating or credit quality (as, for example, those below investment grade, unrated securities, defaulted securites, or discount bonds). Marketability risk would be important for institutional buyers who buy in large blocks and who, therefore, must be concerned about buying unfamiliar credits or small issues of local bonds.

Returns

Strange as it may seem, there is no general agreement on what "yield" really means. Therefore, the meaning of any given calculation of yield, or rate of return, is related to specific situations and the specific techniques employed for its measurement. "Yield to maturity," "yield to call," "net interest cost," "Canadian interest cost," "running yield," and other terms denote some of the different measurements of overall return that are employed by different buyers, dealers, brokers, underwriters, etc.

Each different class of participants in the municipal bond market may use a different set of yield calculations and measurements of return because of the participants' quite different needs. For an ordinary investor the simplest method of calculating yield, or return, is probably best, but for institutions or funds more complex measures are needed. Certain market participants are forced by law to use a specific measure of yield. For example, underwriters of bonds are usually required by state laws to use net interest cost. This is because the municipal issuer of the bonds is in many states required by law to select, from among the competing underwriters, bids that have the lowest net interest cost.

In effect, net interest cost (NIC) is a technique for reducing bids from all different underwriters to a common standard of measurement. NIC is relatively simple and can be computed with a pencil and paper. (Today's more complicated measurements of yield and return must be figured on computers.)

Although the total NIC of a new bond issue is a fixed measure, it can result from many different individual yields on the various bonds in a new offering. For example, a long-term bond has more impact on the NIC calculation than a short-term bond because it generates more cash than a short-term bond. The trick, therefore, is to put the high coupons on the short-term bonds and lower coupons on the longer maturities, which results in a lower NIC. By thus manipulating which yields they will offer on which maturities, underwriters seek to select a low enough total NIC to win the bidding, but not one that is so low that they will lose money on the underwriting.

The NIC measurement has recently come under criticism because it fails to take explicit account of the time value of money, and thus other techniques which do acknowledge this factor have begun to gain a following, e.g., the Canadian interest cost.

Whereas underwriters are forced to think in terms of NIC, in contrast, bond traders and investors tend to think in terms of "yield to maturity." The calculation of yield to maturity was long thought to be simple and accurate; however, it is in fact very deceptive, as Sidney Homer and Martin Leibowitz's *Inside the Yield Book: New Tools for Bond Market Strategy*[1] demonstrated a decade ago. This is because the actual yield to maturity always depends upon the interest rate at which one can reinvest the coupons when they are received. If one cannot get as high a rate of interest for the coupons as the original yield rate on the bonds, then the actual yield to maturity will be lower than the stated yield to maturity. If one can get a higher interest rate at which to reinvest the coupons, then the actual yield to maturity will be far higher. The range of yields to maturity on exactly the same bond is quite considerable.

These two most popular measures of yield, the net interest cost and yield to maturity, have no necessary relationship as far as we can determine.

"Running yield" or "Current yield" is another popular measure of return and is simply the coupon rate divided by the price of the bond. It is a useful measure of a bond's current value if the investor wants current income. However, for a long-term investor, yield to maturity might provide a better guide to long-term return.

"Yield to call" is yet another measure of a bond's return. Many municipal bonds, especially newer ones, are callable, and some may have more than one call provision. A "call" is a payment of the principal back to the bondholder at a time well in advance of the maturity date printed on the bond. As already noted, if the bond is called, the investor has the problem of reinvesting the principal at a rate of return equivalent to or better than the rate of return received under the old bond. The current rate of interest may be lower than the rate the investor was getting on the bond, which is one primary reason why bonds are called and why refunding of bonds has become so popular.

Note to Chapter 1

[1] Sidney Homer and Martin Leibowitz, *Inside the Yield Book: New Tools for Bond Market Strategy*, Prentice-Hall, Englewood Cliffs, N.J., and New York Institute of Finance, New York, 1972.

chapter 2

The Municipal Bond Market: Buyers and Sellers

This chapter will briefly summarize all the operations and major facts about the buying and selling of municipal bonds in the United States today. The first half will concentrate on the buyers of municipal bonds in both the primary and the secondary market. The role of individual investors and intermediaries for individual investors will be contrasted with the role of major institutional investors, such as commercial banks and insurance companies. The functions of brokers, dealers, and various types of bond funds will also be discussed. The second half of the chapter will cover the selling of municipal bonds. We will examine syndication of bond offerings and the different forms of underwriting arrangements by competitive sale and negotiation. The small localized sales of municipal bonds will be contrasted with the large deals in the national market. The role of regional investment firms and regional banks in both national and local sales will be explained.

We can split each of the many bond markets into its participants: its buyers and sellers. Whether we analyze the market for general obligation bonds or revenue bonds or those of states, cities, school districts, or public authorities, the roles of the different participants in those markets will bear certain similarities but also reveal many crucial differences. This is partly because the nearly infinite variety of municipal bonds, which are unquestionably more diverse and heterogeneous than corporate securities, creates a quite distinct market within each narrow type of bond and within each range of price, yield, quality, and maturity.

Within each group of buyers and sellers of each of these securities, one can look at the *primary market*, meaning the creation and placing of new securities, in contrast to the trading of existing securities in what is known as the *secondary market*. Indeed, among these groups as well we must reduce each to investors, dealers, and brokers; break these still further into bank or nonbank and by size of portfolio; and then specify whether each is exclusively a specialist in municipal bonds or is more diversified. And, finally, among the dealers we must look at the role of individual underwriters and syndicates.

These different breakdowns are all quite important to the way the unified municipal bond market functions, and, therefore, each individual investor or new trainee in this field should be well aware of how these different players interact.

The Small Municipal Bond Bought by the Local Bank

Numerically, the vast majority of all new municipal issues in the United States are really small- to moderate-sized loans to municipalities for such things as a fire engine, school bus, or bridge. These bonds might not ever truly enter the national public bond market at all. In a small community, especially when buying some specific piece of capital equipment with a definite estimable life, the town managers will simply ask a local commercial bank to provide a loan in order to purchase the equipment. Working together, they will structure the loan as a collection of tax-exempt municipal bonds by negotiating directly the terms and rate of interest. These bonds will probably never be resold or leave the community, the state, or indeed the bank's vault at all, for they were tailor-made for that particular bank customer in order to secure the loan to that municipality. (Occasionally local banks will sell these bonds in order to be able to keep buying new local bond issues.) Other local investors will also buy small bond issues to hold until maturity. The very special nature of local bonds, with their very limited liquidity and marketability by the standard of other nationally sold bonds, makes it clear that this small-issue municipal bond market is of a totally different nature from the large-scale national and regional municipal bond markets with which this book is primarily concerned. It should never be forgotten, however, that this local market has always existed and to some degree or other will certainly continue.

The Buyers

In 1979 the United States state and local debt outstanding totaled approximately $270 billion. Each year approximately 8000 issues come to market from the 70,000 government units that are permitted to issue federally tax-exempt debt. These issues stretch in maturity from only a few months to 30 years or more.

Because of the extraordinary variety of municipal bonds, which are infinitely more diverse than corporate bonds, the individual or institutional investor can pinpoint exactly the type, yield, price, risk, quality, and length of maturity of the bond desired. And while it is true that during the Great Depression there were 3000 defaults, the overall risk for all municipal bonds issued from 1929 to 1979 has been remarkably slight.

In the United States in 1979 by far the largest holders of municipal bonds were still the commercial banks who owned nearly half of all state and local debt outstanding. Municipal bonds are bought by commercial banks not only because of their track record of safety, but also because of their federal tax exemption and their yield and to ensure that the institutions are seen to be supporting local communities.

Individuals owned approximately one-third of all municipal bonds, and they have been strong participants in this market over the past decade. During this period commercial bank investments in municipal bonds have grown but have remained far more stable as a percentage of the total purchase of new bonds.

Among the other buyers of municipal bonds, the fire and casualty insurance companies are followed by corporations, life insurance companies, and foreigners.

It should be stressed, however, that yearly totals do not reflect the constant buying and selling by some participants in this market and the steady unchanging ownership of the same bonds for decades which characterizes others as noted below.

As Table 2-1 demonstrates, the buying side of the municipal bond market has for decades been dominated by three groups which together have over 90 percent of all outstanding municipal bonds: individuals, commercial banks, and non-life or fire and casualty insurance companies. Their shares move up and down over time, so that while individuals were the largest net buyers during the period 1971–1979, they were net sellers from 1969 to 1971, during which period banks were substantial net buyers.

The bond ownership shifts that the numbers in Table 2-1 indicate should be clarified. Banks and insurance companies are both buying and selling bonds during any particular period, and, therefore, the same yearly total may in no way give a clear picture of how they are constantly adjusting their holdings to take advantage of many perceived investment opportunities in many different types of municipal securities during any one month. A second key point is that an individual's bonds are often actually held, bought, and sold by bank trust departments and other financial managers, such as investment banking firms, that make many of the crucial market decisions. Finally, investment bankers and banks

TABLE 2-1 Year-End Holders of Outstanding Municipal Securities, in $1000s

	1972		1975	
	Amount	Percent	Amount	Percent
Total outstanding	177.3	100.00	230.5	100.00
Households	47.1	26.57	74.2	32.19
Commercial banks	90.0	50.76	102.8	44.60
Non-life insurance companies	26.5	14.94	34.3	14.88
Other	13.7	7.73	19.2	8.33

SOURCE: From data in Joan Lulkovich, research editor, *Statistics on State and Local Government Finance,* The Bond Buyer, New York, 1977, p. 22.

are among the major bond dealers, and so they are constantly buying and selling municipal bonds for others. Therefore, while these gross movements by giant institutions are easy to spot, the underlying range and variety of transactions that actually cause these gross shifts are not as easy to identify.

Institutional Investors and the Municipal Bond Market

Most organizations owning portfolios of municipal bonds are not run exclusively for the purpose of buying municipal bonds. Instead, they are run as part of a larger profit-making enterprise which is only incidentally or partly an investor in tax-exempt bonds. Obviously, major exceptions to this generalization would be the closed-end and open-end municipal bond funds. However, to take two examples from among the major buyers of municipal bonds, neither insurance companies nor banks regard buying municipal bonds as their central reason for existence. Therefore, inevitably, their decisions to buy and sell municipal bonds are governed by many considerations based on factors that frequently have little or nothing to do with supply, demand, price, or other changes in the municipal bond market itself.

What then are the major reasons for, and patterns of, such institutional purchases of bonds? First, the different ways in which banks and insurance companies are taxed determine to a considerable extent their purchases and sales of tax-exempt municipal bonds. As Hendershott's lectures for the Salomon Brothers Center at NYU demonstrate, these types of institutions receive tax shelters for their total profit-making activities from their municipal bonds, but they need such tax protection at different times, often for different reasons, and in response to different cyclical trends.

Large commercial banks whose primary purpose is to make loans are only residual users of funds for the most part. In other words, if they *cannot* make loans and they *can* anticipate taxable profits, then they will tend to buy municipal bonds. Their buying is therefore residual, or leftover, and occurs after they have either met their loan demand or reached a level of loan demand that they find acceptable. They are more likely to sell municipal bonds to make loans than vice versa. Only over the long run are banks net municipal bond buyers, but in the short term their rate of municipal bond sales changes, and can change more rapidly and more frequently than does that of insurance companies.

The pattern of insurance company buying is partly governed by what their actuaries believe is the acceptable level of insurable risks. They need only to keep readily available enough funds to cover that level of insurance claims. The rest of their funds will tend to be constantly invested. For this reason insurance companies are virtually always net investors in the municipal bond market, except in cases of catastrophic losses or during a severe economic downturn. Their municipal bond sales, therefore, tend to be primarily for the purpose of reinvesting in higher-yielding securities, among municipal bonds or elsewhere.

The pattern of insurance company securities purchases is partly governed by what Hendershott calls the "underwriting cycle," so that when their insurance underwriting is going well, they tend to buy municipal bonds, but when their insurance income is small or their losses are large, they tend to buy taxable bonds instead.

What is important to note about the large institutional players in these markets is that they provide a kind of price leadership both because of the size of their transactions and because of their high visibility. The hefty volume of their buying and selling gives them a strong bargaining leverage in any given negotiation, especially so because in municipal bond deals, for many types of bonds, the most common issuance is only for $10 million to $20 million or less. Therefore, a major institution in certain instances can effectively influence the price by taking a large fraction of the issue.

Among America's 100 largest banks, the top 10 in 1975 held portfolios of municipal bonds of approximately $11 billion in total: nearly 5 percent of the value of all municipal bonds outstanding. These annual figures compiled by the *American Banker* also showed that these 100 banks together in 1975 held $32.1 billion or 13.9 percent of the total supply. Today, Citibank, Bank of America, and Continental Illinois National Bank & Trust Company each holds over $2 billion.

The annual reports of the nation's casualty insurance companies clearly indicate that the very largest hold even larger portfolios than banks. What is clear from even a glance at the annual reports of major insurance companies is that their volume of buying and selling is so high that one firm alone literally can and does, by itself, increase or decrease the total buying and selling of all municipal bonds by 1 to 2 percent in any one year. For example, Allstate Insurance, a branch of Sears, Roebuck, states in the 1977 Sears annual report that it has holdings of $3.4 billion in state and municipal bonds. Thus it had increased by $600 million in that one year which is a figure equivalent to over 1 percent of all sales of municipal bonds publicly sold.

Individuals

In total, the number of individual investors in municipal bonds is so large that some place the figure as high as 8 or 10 million. We have classified this group of investors in Table 2-2 as far as gross holdings by tax bracket is concerned.

But what is crucial to understand is that the actual level, amount, and type of transaction engaged in by all these individuals—on their own or through their investment bankers, broker/dealers, financial advisers, or bank trust officers—simply cannot be fully documented. It is secret—hidden—and the tax-free income need not be reported. It is significant despite the secrecy, however, that some municipal bond holdings and trading of individuals are larger than those of many of the smaller institutions. And even more important is the collective impact of these 8 million individuals whose municipal bond transactions during a year can outstrip the movement of institutions, particularly in their ability to create sharp up or down trends in markets.

Among individual investors it has been estimated that fully 70 percent of all municipal bonds are held by those individuals with marginal tax rates of 50 percent, but the remaining 30 percent of municipal bond

TABLE 2-2   Cumulative Percentage of Households' Holding of Tax-Exempt Bonds by Marginal Federal Income Tax Rate

Marginal tax rate, %	Cumulative % of holdings
20	4.7
30	15.2
40	24.3
50	30.6
60	62.4
70	100.0

SOURCE: Harvey Galper and George E. Petersen, "The Equity Effects of a Taxable Bond Subsidy," *National Tax Journal,* December 1973, p. 617.

buyers include perhaps 2 million investors below the 30 percent tax bracket. Table 2-2 indicates the ownership patterns of individuals by tax bracket over the years.

Obviously, as inflation has pushed salaries higher with the cost of living, more and more Americans have been escalated into higher tax brackets. Thus with each year a whole new layer of wage earners is confronted with a higher tax charge for the same effective purchasing power. It is these groups to whom the new benefits of tax-free municipal bonds hold an ever more appealing allure as the governmental tax bite worsens.

Institutional Bond Funds for Individuals

Since individuals' accounts in various types of funds are frequently handled and actively managed by banks and financial institutions, it is important to see how these players as buyers and sellers affect the market. While some funds turn over constantly, several times each year, most do not. Chase Manhattan Bank's municipal fund is perhaps typical of the average turnover. That fund had a turnover rate of 70 to 80 percent with an average maturity of 21 years. On the other hand, unit trust funds of municipal bonds created in 1961 by law do not and cannot change their portfolio of bonds once the bonds are bought. Hence they have occasionally become victims of souring interest rates, which cause them to lose asset principal. These unit trust fund investment companies are registered with the Securities and Exchange Commission (SEC), but their individual investors are not taxed as a corporation. Individuals can buy units of small amounts and get the advantages of diversification of risk as if they held many. While individuals may sell all or a portion of their unit, they cannot substitute new bonds. When all the units are retired at expiration or when all are sold ahead of expiration, the trust simply disappears as a legal entity.

The major disadvantage of these unit trust funds for investors is that because they cannot exchange, sell, or trade bonds declining in market value, they tend to be hit very hard during periods of soaring interest rates, as we have experienced during this last decade. Also, since they are locked into a portfolio from a previous time, the individuals who *must* sell before the redemption date can lose a large portion of their asset principle because of a depressed market.

The unit trust funds were created by many of the major bond dealers over the past 20 years (whose buying departments accumulate the portfolios for a trustee). The unit trust funds were split into two groups: those retailed for a sales charge by registered sales representatives and those issued as "no load" funds which were sold via direct mail and carry no sales charge to individuals. Because a typical fund is only $50 million, it is when hundreds of funds are clustered under one firm that the magnitude of this municipal buying and selling can be appreciated.

The goal of all such unit trust funds is to provide a reasonably stable stream of income that is tax-free over a long period of time. Two other specialized types of unit trust funds exist which concentrate on bonds of only one state or one intermediate maturity to benefit particular types of investors, who, for example, can frequently avoid state and local taxes. Also, a California resident may know that state's municipal credits better than those elsewhere and feel more comfortable investing there.

In addition to the several billion dollars of bonds in these unit trust funds, there developed in late 1976, as a result of an alteration in the federal law, the creation of new open-ended tax-exempt municipal bond funds that, unlike unit trust funds, could allow active management or trading of the bonds in the portfolio. Like unit trust funds, these are also split into two groups: those that charge a commission and those that do not. They are also split into those that are extremely actively managed, turned over, or traded versus those that anticipate holding most bonds till maturity. Once again, the major advantage to investors is argued to be that they can enter this market with a fractional share of $100 or $250, far smaller than the $5000 cost of the typical municipal bond. Investors also gain the advantages of diversification of a portfolio of bonds instead of the risk of putting all their eggs in one basket.

Dealers

Dealers both underwrite new issues and make over-the-counter markets for holders of tax-exempt municipal bonds. In the United States today, there is an ongoing dealer market for every type of municipal bond (including markets for defaulted issues). Yet what must be stressed is that this entire dealer market is largely unknown, and has been for decades.

The one clear handle that gives an insight into this dealer market is *The Blue List*, which shows most new issues and secondary markets of the best-known credits. It is commonly held that *The Blue List* at any given time shows between 50 and 75 percent or more of the total dealer inventory in both new and old bonds.

In the past two decades the number of dealers has risen by 16 percent—largely made up of new bank dealers, whose number has quadrupled from 50 to nearly 200. Since many firms, including perhaps

30 percent of *The Blue List* firms, have gone out of business and others have merged or been acquired, this dealer market should not be seen as unchanging but as participating in the larger financial shifts taking place on Wall Street and elsewhere.

While the failure rate of financial brokerage firms has been spectacular, the truly significant occurrence has been (1) the sudden start of municipal departments and divisions by practically every financial firm and (2) the dramatic increase in staff of those firms that already had a municipal department or division. Thus, in total, the sales growth of municipal bonds has been responsible for keeping large segments of the securities business alive and for employing a large portion of the stockbrokers, underwriters, and traders, who were forced out of business by the failures, mergers, and acquisitions of firms in the past.

Dealers can be divided between bank and nonbank or between those which are exclusively municipal dealers and those which are wings of larger firms or banks. It has been noted that the smaller dealers have the following key characteristics: most are corporations that hold no long-term debt but usually have huge short-term debt to finance an extraordinarily highly leveraged position. Because of their heavy potential expenses if they hold any bonds for long, most dealers hold particular bonds to maintain a position only for the minimum time it takes to sell the bonds to an institution or an individual (who will frequently hold onto the investment for the life of the security).

The larger, more diversified dealers at banks or large brokerage firms trade, swap, and otherwise exchange municipal bonds and even corporate securities with the federal government and federal agencies so that they can maintain an active market in each. They are constantly looking for the slight edge or fractionally undervalued security into which they will move. This movement into and out of the tax-exempt market is frequently influenced not so much by what is happening in it as what is happening in other quite separate securities markets.

Dealers in tax-exempt bonds may also be ordered by the higher management of their firm to act in their trading in such a way as to maximize the firm's total position regardless of the current position of the tax-exempt market, or to act for the current tax benefit of those receiving the firm's profits rather than for the long term.

What is crucial but rarely understood is that despite the very heavy leverage or bank borrowings required by dealers in the tax-exempt market, the interest on those borrowings used to finance tax-exempt purchases is not usually a tax-deductible item (or if it is so used, the income from the coupon accrual is not tax-exempt).

Although banks are prohibited by law, under the Glass-Steagall Banking Reform Act of 1933, from underwriting most revenue bonds still, they are currently pushing very hard in Washington to have that law amended. Nevertheless, they can act as agents for buying revenue bonds and engage in sales of revenue bonds for their customers' portfolios.

Sales Trading and Back Office

The three separate operations engaged in by all municipal dealers and brokerage firms are sales, trading, and back office technical work. These are all quite separate from the work of underwriters, which will be discussed later in this chapter. The larger the dealer firm, the more people in each operation and the greater the likelihood that they will be spread apart or regionalized. In the largest firms, interconnected microphones in front of every trader and salesperson in different parts of the country enable constant communication.

Nevertheless, despite this contact there remains frequently an underlying conflict between salespeople and traders because salespeople are often paid by commission, try to always satisfy their customers, and only make money when deals are being completed, whereas traders must report the best overall profit for each period and so wait and hold out, or manipulate their position in their markets. In most firms, not only are there always more salespeople than traders, but sales earnings tend to dominate.

Brokers

In contrast to dealers, bond brokers do not trade on their own behalf but exclusively for customers among bond dealers, from whom they get commissions. Not only are there far fewer brokers than dealers, but the very largest brokerage firm only employs a staff of 100.

J. J. Kenny, which is fully specialized and automated, handles 500 or more separate bonds on any given day and must be aware of all the credit information that is up to the minute and pertinent to all these different securities. J. J. Kenny's brokers must be able to make virtually instant decisions about the best times to buy and sell during a day's trading.

Risk

Over the years, municipal bonds have come to be generally regarded as extremely safe investments. High-grade bonds are frequently considered safe, and medium-grade bonds have a large margin of safety to satisfy even conservative buyers. What many point to is the strong track record displayed by even the lowest 10 to 15 percent during depressions and recessions. Chapter 13, "Legal Protection, Disclosure, and Liability," goes into detail analyzing risks, defaults, and credits, but the fact is that even during the Great Depression the vast majority of municipalities kept afloat financially, a remarkable feat considering the corporate and bank experience of the same period. Thus, relative to other securities, tax-free municipal bonds have performed well, and the number of defaults has, except during the Great Depression, been quite minimal. This is not to say that there is no risk in buying municipal bonds or that one's asset principal will not drastically change in value during the life of a bond before it is redeemed. Current markets fluctuate considerably in response to a whole range of factors we will touch upon.

In examining the day-to-day risks and performance of bonds in the trading market, it is clear that the daily participants are constantly looking at that strange rubber sheet that encompasses the whole municipal bond universe of prices, yields and credits, long and short terms, and searches for the undervalued securities. Just as with any other bond, the key factors are liquidity, or closeness to cash; the marketability, or ready range of buyers; the credit name, or familiarity to buyers; and above all, the official ratings by the two major rating services. The prices and yields of all other securities at that moment in the broader municipal and other securities markets are closely examined by all municipal analysts because they supply the range of immediate alternative investments. Just as with corporate bonds, the credit name and rating are the most critical factors; indeed, these factors are far more critical than for corporations because of the vast number of municipal bonds. In fact, because there are 1,000,000 municipal bonds issued, compared to only 10,000 corporate bonds, and the unusual and unfamiliar credits among municipal bonds are many, both the individual and institutional investor are far more dependent on the rating services for guidance in obtaining municipal bonds than for obtaining corporate bonds. Also, since neither Moody's nor Standard & Poor's (S&P) rates even 40 percent of all municipal bonds, most of the large institutional investors are unable or unwilling to invest in the unrated bonds at all. Moreover, only those issues that trade in giant volume can accommodate the large institutional investors. Thus there is something akin to follow-the-leader kinds of pressures that develops among those funds that actively manage or frequently swap, trade, or turn over their portfolio of municipal bonds. Because there is an abiding question about whether interest rates can be forecast, there is an ongoing dispute between those who argue that "managing" a municipal portfolio to get the best interest rate is totally impossible and those who argue that it is essential. This dispute gained added fire in this last decade due to soaring interest rates, dramatically changing bond yields and prices, and the entrance into this municipal bond market in force of the new funds and institutions. Also important were masses of individuals ricocheting from their painful experience of getting burned in the stock market to municipal bonds for the first time, expecting them to provide a safer haven. With so many newcomers to this municipal market, among both investors and fund managers, there were bound to be certain tendencies that were mistakenly carried over from stock market investing or corporate bond investing into the municipal market before participants learned how very different, indeed unique, this market is.

Price Characteristics of Municipal Bonds

General market bonds which cross state lines in search of buyers on the national or regional scale must obviously be priced in relation to one another. But countless small municipal bond issues are bought and held locally and never leave the municipality. Their characteristics often are less uniform than those of general market bonds. In general, however, local bonds of the large populous states, such as New York, California, etc., do move in price and yield quite closely to price levels in the general market because the same individual and institutional investors look at them as they look at other alternative securities and, consequently, force considerable uniformity. Thus it is in the less populous states, cities, and regions that deviations start to occur from the general levels of bond prices and yields. There, the difference between the unknown name and the better-known credit becomes critical. As a result, higher prices become required in order to justify these variations in relative marketability of these unknown bonds.

The effect on bond prices and trading behavior caused by a new issue's size is difficult to gauge for the buyer and seller. For in evaluating the pricing level, most sellers of a $50-million issue know it is frequently the fate of the last $10 million that determines whether the syndicate makes a profit. For the buyer it is the size of this issue that can affect the presence or absence of an aftermarket. Whereas standard borrowings by large states that are regularly in the market for a set amount are considered easy to price and evaluate, it is the *extra-large* issues that can pose a problem. Especially small issues can also result in bond prices that are out of line with the average. This "size leverage," as it is sometimes dubbed, is noted by many participants, but in general it is significant that there are not wider variations in bond prices given the variety of differences involved within this multiplicity of bonds.

Like the various stock markets and the corporate bond market, the municipal bond market tends to move together. While some bonds of different grades also tend to move together, there are strong tendencies for the highest-grade bonds to act as market leaders and let others follow. Leads and lags of different particular securities are watched daily, even hourly, but for the most part the participants' expectations that different groups of bonds will be bid and traded in line with the general trend tend to be fulfilled.

What is significant is not the minor variations, which must of necessity always occur in such sectional lags and leads, but rather the basic underlying trend, which is for the high-grade credits to maintain their price stability better than the lower-grade credits. A result of this could be that when the whole market slides down in level 30 basis points, the high-grade bonds might hardly change, while the lower-rated bonds will slide away far deeper on the downside. Likewise—in the opposite direction—when the market is rising, the reverse happens as the low-grade bonds make up for their decline by rising faster.

Prices of Revenue Bonds

Revenue bonds, as noted by Wilson White, Jr., in *White's Ratings*, tending by nature to be not as predictable in price as GO bonds, have eight vital characteristics:

1. As a class, they are not as broadly secured and do not have as wide a margin of safety. As a result, they have, for the most part, higher yields, and for this reason more investors have gone into revenue bonds in the last decade than into GO bonds.

2. In the past revenue bonds had a greater infrequency of new issues upon which to base ratings or trading experience. This is far less true today, however.

3. Revenue fluctuations are more possible. They can affect the safety factor and, consequently, the market more quickly and drastically than in the case of municipal tax collections.

4. The creation of junior liens seals off prior liens.

5. There is a frequent use of term bonds, which cannot be compared with serial issues. Also, a combination of serial and term bonds makes them difficult to compare exactly with prices of GO bonds.

6. The gradual retirement of a substantial part of an issue can place an inordinately high value upon the outstanding balance. This can be sharply reversed by a new flotation.

7. An earning's lack or lag on a construction project may be reflected in high yield, which can be sharply altered when earnings start to flow freely.

8. In the case of seasoned issues, a secondary market, which is thinner than that of general obligation bonds, tends to make prices, yields, and *White's Ratings* less accurate.

Both new, unsold issues and old, outstanding municipal bonds are brought into the secondary market for sale. They are advertised in what is known as *The Blue List*, which since 1935 has been a daily publication (on blue-tinted paper) that lists 50 to perhaps 75 percent of the dollar volume of all the outstanding secondary issues for sale in the United States. Until *The Blue List* was created and a central listing service established, the selling of bonds was strictly a door-to-door operation. It has been noted that major trust departments in New York banks, for example, had long benches on which bond salespeople would sit, waiting their turn to talk to each investment manager who did the bond trading. Their firms' position was carried on scraps of paper, which they carried in their coat pocket. Today, by contrast, salespeople, traders, and dealers in many firms are constantly on the phone and interconnected loudspeaker systems; they are involved in a very sophisticated communications network.

Investors, bond analysts, or municipal issuers who are interested in knowing the size of the municipal bond market should start with the total par value of all bonds listed for one day at the back of *The Blue List*. Then, by adding the total of these outstanding issues to *The Daily Bond Buyer's* total of the list of the "30-day visible supply" of new issuers, they will have a good guess as to the size of the total municipal bond market at any one moment.[1] They will then be well able to gauge whether it is rising or falling, and therefore whether it is a good time to buy bonds or, if they are issuers, to sell bonds if they are concerned about the degree of competition at the moment from other issues coming to market.

The Sellers

Underwriting and Syndication

The simplest form of selling municipal bonds is discussed at the beginning of this chapter: a municipality asks its local bank to structure a loan for a specific piece of equipment in the form of a set of tax-exempt bonds. While such sales remain the most numerous, the overwhelming dollar volume comes from bond sales transacted between bond issuers and dealers in the primary, or new issue, market via a system known as underwriting and syndication.

Underwriting is a common practice throughout the municipal markets whereby investment bankers and commercial banks join in a syndicate contract with a bond issuer to buy the entire new bond issue at a set price (whether reached competitively or through negotiation) and then resell that issue in smaller wholesale or retail pieces to the public. Although both investment bankers or securities dealers and commercial banks underwrite GO bonds, by law, under the famous Glass-Steagall Banking Reform Act of 1933, commercial banks are not permitted to underwrite municipal revenue bonds. Despite some furious lobbying activity over a considerable period, it is uncertain whether this law will be changed.

The underwriting of massive blocks of bonds sold by municipalities, in amounts of over $25 million and up to $500 million and more in one issue, cannot be handled exclusively by one dealer or bank. This is not only because of capital limitations but also because each bulk buyer of bonds wishes to carefully spread, or diversify, its risk to make sure it does not have all its eggs in one basket should this issue, for whatever reasons, not be readily salable at the intended reoffering scale.

These bulk transactions between municipalities and bond dealers in this new issue market are of two types: competitive or negotiated. Since the financial managers of cities, towns, and states are often required by law to do so, they request competitive bids for their municipalities' bonds rather than relying on negotiation with only one underwriter or one group. However, when money is tight in the nation's debt markets and large bond issues are hard to sell, a negotiated sale may well be the best solution for the issuer. In other cases—where the bond issue is very large or of an entirely new type, where an entirely new market must be developed, or where a new issuer is coming to market for the first time—a negotiated sale (where only one underwriter or one syndicate is dealt with by the issuer) can make great sense.

If a municipality decides to do a negotiated underwriting, it contacts a number of leading managing underwriters and asks them to submit a presentation of their credentials. It then selects the firm or management team it believes, for a combination of reasons (capital, distributing ability, management record, municipal finance expertise), will be the most competent and achieve the lowest net interest cost marketing the issue.

The selected managers assist in structuring the issue, performing due diligence in the preparation of the official statement, conducting a premarketing sales campaign, and, finally, negotiating in good faith the terms of the sale. Critics will argue that, this municipality squandered its assets unnecessarily by simply opting for the first or only bid submitted. It is certainly true that competitive bids might tend to result in a lower net interest cost. Nevertheless, those in favor of the negotiated sale argue that such underwritings usually involve the performance of many extra tasks for the municipality which justify a management fee and possibly a slightly higher net interest cost, all other things being equal.

In most states the law explicitly requires that issuers sell GO bonds by competitive bidding, usually by submission of a sealed bid. It is for this reason that most bond issues still come to market via competitive bids. GO bonds tend to be easier to sell on the whole than revenue bonds and to need less explanation in order to be sold. They do not require the extra care and services that many revenue bonds require. GO bonds have no holding restrictions as to ownership, while revenue bonds do. Nor are there any limitations as to the type of investment dealer who can bid to underwrite them.

In contrast, revenue bonds tend to come to market via negotiated transactions with an underwriter or a single syndicate for the following reasons. The infrequency of coming to market was in the past a primary reason why most revenue issues were negotiated. Only a limited number of dealers were willing to assume liability for such new untested issues, and a vast amount of legal and financial groundwork was needed before financing was possible. Underwriters were understandably reluctant to give their guarantee of purchase to such bond issues regardless of the state of the bond market. Today these conditions are changing somewhat with the far more substantial size of the revenue bond issues, but a large number still tend to come the negotiated route because of these factors and others, such as tradition or ability to find a market "window" or to have a pre-sale effort.

Revenue bonds often come to market in a single-term issue, while GO bonds come to market in serial form over a span of years. Since it may be more difficult to find a large number of buyers for an issue of bonds all maturing in one year, say 2013, the sale of these bonds may take more time. Each buyer of a brand-new and unknown revenue issue (such as a joint action power agency combining several municipalities together for the first time under a power supply contract) will require time to evaluate the sources of future earnings, sinking fund provisions, the cash flow of the authority, the cost of the power to the users, the quality of the management, and the level of debt coverage. All these factors account for some of the newest issuers coming to market via negotiation.

However, many of the best-known names come to market via negotiation, such as Power Authority of the State of New York, New York State Housing Finance Agency, Nebraska Public Power District, Salt River Project, and many other frequent issuers. Uncertainty in different bond markets at different times is pointed to as the reason why they chose negotiated sales, but other key factors would include the unusually large size of an issue which may be difficult to sell in total to retail customers, especially when many issues are coming to market at one particular time.

The dollar volume of negotiated issues has risen over recent years compared with that of negotiated sales. Both competitive bidding and negotiated sales are usually quite constrained by local legal requirements in state constitutions and statutes as well as in local town or city statutes. For these legal reasons peculiar to the locality, the generalized description of competitive bidding and underwriting procedures, which follows, will vary somewhat from one municipality to another.

The exact method of advertising a forthcoming bond sale by a municipality is usually set down in local laws, and it involves not only a public notice in *The Daily Bond Buyer* or some other financial publication but also a list of details concerning the bond issue:

- Date, time, and place of sale
- Amount of issue, maturity schedule, and call feature (if any)
- Manner in which bid is to be made (sealed or oral)
- Authority for sale
- Type of bond (revenue, GO, etc.)
- Limitation as to interest rates plus the payment dates of the interest
- Denominations and registration privileges
- Amount of bid (at par or better or discount allowed)
- Amount of good faith check
- Names of approving attorneys and a statement to the effect that these attorneys will furnish an unqualified legal opinion approving the legality of the bonds and also a certificate that no litigation is pending which will affect the issuance of the bonds
- Bid form
- Method and place of settlement for the bonds
- The right to reject any or all bids
- Manner of obtaining a copy of the official statement or prospectus

The Syndicate

Whereas a negotiated bid is sought by an issuer's proposal to an underwriter or single group of underwriters to enter a bid, in contrast, competitive deals will be advertised by the issuing municipality in *The Daily Bond Buyer* a week or more before the day set for the award of the bonds to the winning underwriting syndicate. Competitive deals and negotiated ones begin with investment bankers and/or commercial banks joining together into groups which are called municipal securities' "dealing accounts," or "syndicates," to make bids on these new bonds being offered for sale. In an informal manner these syndicates have formed over time. Because of traditional associations they usually bid in substantially the same groups as they did for some previous issue of bonds for this same issuer. This is not to say that there are not shifts among those belonging to these groups over time. Some dealers leave the proposed syndicate on a new issue because they feel that (1) the bond price the other syndicate partners have agreed upon is too high or too low or (2) the profit spread is inadequate. Other syndicate members are dropped from the syndicate when they have not in the past shown themselves able to sell their whole allocation of bonds.

Within syndicates the largest dealers have a better capacity to handle the mechanical operations of the syndicate as a whole, and they become known as the managing underwriters. Although some deals are "comanaged," others of the very largest dealers will usually be designated "joint managers." Then, there follows a clear bracketing of the different members in the syndicate into tiers depending on what share of the loan issue they are able to underwrite. This clear-cut status is very important in maintaining the "pecking order" within the syndicate and is watched very closely. The order of the names of the syndicate members printed in financial publications' advertisements, known as "tombstones," is first by bracket, then by the size of each member's share of participation in the issue, and finally alphabetically within each bracket. Underwriters have been known to resign from syndicates rather than appear behind what they deem lesser firms, and so the manager must be quite careful to be aware of the objections of different members.

For large states or cities that come into the debt markets one, two, or three times every year, it would be relatively impractical for underwriting syndicates to regroup into different partnerships each time. Firms that have bid together as a syndicate, therefore, in one state, say California, are expected to join together for the next syndicate offering of municipal bonds by the state. It definitely conflicts with standard underwriting practice for firms to repeatedly shift back and forth between syndicates, and most syndicates stay relatively intact for some time.

The syndicates sometimes merge when an especially large issue is being brought to market. They also can split up for smaller issues. But there tends to be a good deal of continuity of syndicate membership because of the crucial need for absolute trust, cooperation, and honesty. Dependability and, especially, familiarity on a personal basis with the individuals with whom you work in the syndicate are the basic reasons that syndicates endure. Even when a firm drops from the syndicate on one deal, because of overpricing or some other reason, it will remain a member of the next syndicate unless it "is asked to find another home." Because there are so many municipal issues offered for sale during any particular year or month, it is not uncommon for syndicate members who are working together on one deal to be competitors at the same time on another deal where they, for whatever reasons, are part of separate syndicates.

The syndicate manager, upon seeing a municipal bond advertisement in *The Daily Bond Buyer* for a new issue, contacts former members of the syndicate and arranges a meeting to discuss a bid. The manager also circulates to all the account members actual written contracts requiring that they be bound by the rules of the account. This does not mean that they cannot drop out of the account after signing. They can drop out right up until the very last minute before the syndicate makes its final offer, but once the syndicate has won the bid, all members are bound to the terms of participation that they have contracted for in advance.

The legal syndicate letter sent by the managing underwriter directly to each member of the syndicate spells out the duties and obligations of each to the other for the time that the syndicate lasts (usually 30 days—however, 45- and 60-day agreements are sometimes found). While this may appear to be a kind of partnership, the letter spells out specifically that it is not. Instead, it is a form of joint venture in which the liability of each member is detailed in a special fashion.

The manager can borrow funds, advertise, pledge securities, submit the bid, and otherwise act as the official agent for the whole syndicate. The manager's mistakes, except for ones that result from "want of good faith," usually will not result in any legal action by other syndicate members.

The price ideas of the different members of the syndicate, which are shared in their first meeting, reflect each participant's assessment of the bond markets, interest rate levels, and general economic outlook of the municipal and national economy at that moment. From this general-pricing discussion emerges a scale of proposed prices for each broad 5-year period in the new bond issue. With these 5-year "spots" running until the final maturity of the bonds, the manager is easily able to scale all the intervening years' prices and hence develop a full schedule of prices, yields, and profit spreads for the entire issue. The manager always tries to secure from the syndicate's membership a bid that is high enough to be profitable but low enough to be competitive against the bids being submitted by other syndicates.

The next meeting of the syndicate occurs the following day, approximately an hour before the time the bonds are to be sold. This is usually a meeting of all members in person, although sometimes it is held in "conference call" by phone. The lead manager at this final meeting announces the interest rates at which the members generally feel investors will be attracted to the issue. Those who disagree with the interest rates generally agreed on for the whole issue have the right to drop out of the syndicate. Each member firm's name is read out, and each firm's opinions are sought with regard to the rate and whether it wishes a larger or smaller "participation," or share, of the total underwriting—or whether it will "drop." The critical problem for the manager is then to determine whether there are enough dealers left at the agreed-upon price to fully underwrite the loan to the municipality.

The manager can decide that not enough members remain at this price, and hence the rate of interest must be increased to attempt to win back into the account some of the members who have dropped. Alternatively, the manager can decide that too many members wish to increase their participation. The rate of interest must be too high and, therefore, must be lowered in order to ensure that it is truly competitive and retains a chance of being the winning bid in the competition in 1 hour's time.

In these hectic minutes just before submission of the final bid, the manager's computer is used during the meeting to determine the very best coupon rates to use for the bid, given a whole variety of factors. The computer projections of prices, coupon rates, yields to maturity, and profit spread are all added together in various combinations to find a net interest cost figure that will be relayed to the issuer at the last possible moment. Usually, the bid is phoned to a contact near the issuer to make sure these last-minute negotiations of the members at the manager's office can proceed with all the very latest market information before the bid is transmitted to the issuer. Since sometimes hundreds of millions of dollars are at stake in one offering, it is understandable that these last minutes are somewhat tense as each partner assesses its degree of risk or exposure in pricing too high or too low and thereby suffering a loss.

Sizable losses on underwriting are certainly frequent enough, today as in the past, to give each of the underwriters pause. For this reason, the pressure is quite strong for members of the syndicate to come up with realistic rates of interest when bidding. No underwriter wants an unsalable issue on its hands.

Finally, at the designated time and place the municipal issuer opens the bids from the different competing syndicates, and they are compared. Usually the award is made to the account which promised to pay the lowest net interest cost. Recently, this method of awarding the sale of bonds has been attacked on the ground that it fails to explicitly take into account the actual time value of money. Nevertheless, this remains the predominant method of awarding underwriting contracts.

The winning syndicate, as part of its original computation of its bid, agreed upon a reoffering price for these bonds—for every bond in every maturity. Therefore, the instant the winning bid has been accepted by the municipality, the selling departments of the syndicate members start making telephone calls or sending teletype messages around the country to all their normal or special customers to announce the details of the new offering.

In advance of the final actual bid these same customers have usually been contacted at least once for their interest in buying. However, no customer is definitely committed until the syndicate has won the bid. The result is that often certain eager buyers who expressed interest accept right away and agree to buy a certain number of bonds, while others say the final agreed-upon rate is too expensive and they will pass this issue by. During these first hours, known as the "order period," if the underwriting is very successful, all orders are gathered together, the whole issue is sold, and the syndicate will close.

If the syndicate manages to sell the underwriting in a period of but a few days, its members will usually be able to profit from their risk taking in this venture, and this is another reason that widespread canvassing of customers in advance is so thorough and why timing is of the essence.

Yet if the U.S. Federal Reserve Bank intervenes in the bond market, if the bond markets as a whole encounter a bad time, or if many, many other issues come to market at this very same time with better rates of interest, then by the end of the first week all the bonds in this particular issue may well not be resold by the syndicate. It will be forced to "break" and sell the bonds for whatever lower price the general prevailing bond market will now require to "unload" these bonds. At the point at which the syndicate breaks, the manager sends out bills to the members reminding them of their original share participation and asking them to pay up for the loss on the account. They must then buy their share of bonds at their agreed-upon price regardless of the price at which they can now resell the bonds. The bonds that are left will be prorated among all the members of the syndicate.

These remaining bonds will be advertised in *The Blue List* and either sold at the lower market rates or held by the former syndicate's members in their own account until a later time when they find an acceptable buyer. The two final alternatives can each be quite expensive and are the two situations in which underwriters incur substantial losses.

The member firms of the underwriting syndicate are subject to two separate types of assessment: the "western, or divided, account" versus the "eastern, or undivided, account."

Today, most accounts or syndicates are undivided as to liability because most dealers do not wish to take on the risks inherent in divided accounts. Many will not even bid on the underwriting of divided accounts. In brief, the distinction between these two types of accounts and the liability of member firms are as follows: In an undivided account each syndicate member's sale of its underwriting participation reduces its liability. In a divided account it does not because each member's liability is broken down by brackets of particular types of bonds. For example, the first 10-year bonds, which are generally easier to sell, are shared by all members of the syndicate, and one firm's sale of all of them does not reduce its liability for the sale of the more difficult last 30-year maturities. In this scheme, a single firm's sales reduce somewhat the total liability of others in the syndicate but may not discharge that firm's total liability.

Regional Investment Firms

Among the less well publicized aspects of the municipal bond market is the role of the regional investment firms. They serve as local underwriters and brokerage institutions and in some regions still dominate the municipal market.

The range of local investors is frequently better known by regional firms than by firms in New York or even a national organization. For this reason it has been common for major national underwriters to ask important regional firms, such as Dain Bosworth Inc. of Minneapolis or Robinson-Humphrey of Atlanta, to join an underwriter syndicate as a comanager or major-bracket partner in a new underwriting for a municipality in their state or region. Major regional banks may also be asked to join particular national syndicates for the same reason. Municipal bond selling (unlike the selling or underwriting of corporate securities) tends to require so much more on-the-spot local knowledge of a particular town, school system, public facility, or public authority that the regional firm has an advantage over the New York investment firms in knowing a specific municipality, its economic and debt trends, its financial position, and the caliber of management.

From 1973 to 1976, many national brokerage firms joined in especially powerful syndicates to go after new regional underwritings, and they became known as "barracuda accounts." Because they were then thought to threaten the existence of the regional investment firms, there developed a tense rivalry between New York and the regional firms. While the outright tension has decreased somewhat, the pressure from the New York firms, which have been expanding their branch offices across the country and out into the regions, has continued as they have bought up weaker (and some stronger) regional firms in order to gain hefty regional distribution for their new issues. Because such national brokerage firms have a whole network of regional and national offices and such a wide range of financial services, they increasingly have put new pressure on the smaller regional firms.

This regional versus national competition should be seen as part of the larger battle between many investment institutions today. The failures, mergers, and acquisitions which have occurred during the last decade are widely expected to continue in the next decade as the various investment organizations attempt to enlarge their capital base, computerize their back office operations, offer a full range of financial services, and put down ever stronger regional roots to ensure their sales distribution systems. While a number of regional firms will continue to do well because of their strong local roots and depth of local relations, it is likely in this ongoing and intensively competitive period that a number of weaker regional firms as well as weaker national firms may be acquired or go out of business.

Conclusion to the Underwriting Process

While most competitive offerings attract several bids which may result in "close covers," or bids very near the winning one, it is very unusual ever to hear of a "tie" bid. Underwriters of the winning syndicate as well as customers they contact are especially pleased if there was a close cover or very near alternative bid by another syndicate because it is a clear indication that the price of these bonds is very competitive, indeed. Usually, the further away the next bid is, the harder it will be to sell the issue. These bids and their range are published in *The Daily Bond Buyer*. The dispersion of the many bids can usually be greater than 10 basis points or 0.1 percent; nevertheless, the closest cover bid is usually less distant than 0.05, suggesting that the underwriting market is quite competitive.

Studies of how competitive, in fact, this new issue municipal bond market is have been engaged in by a number of analysts. Reuben Kessel in the early 1970s found, using Stigler's theory of economics of information, that more bidders would lower the market-reoffering prices and lower the profit spreads.[2] That assertion is being hotly debated today. This critical issue has recently had so much attention because of the renewed effort by commercial banks to have the federal laws changed to discontinue the Glass-Steagall Banking Reform Act, which prohibited them from underwriting almost all revenue bonds. Although the larger debate on this question has continued for over 35 years, the argument made by these new analysts, researchers, and lobbying groups is that *if* there were more underwriters making different competitive bids on the same issue, it would force down the profit spread and result in lower interest cost to the issuing municipalities throughout the United States. Opponents of this view can cite contrasting evidence drawn from other research studies which indicate that little or no savings in the underwriting costs of municipal bonds would occur if commercial banks were free to compete.[3]

Notes to Chapter 2

[1] *The Daily Bond Buyer* is the most comprehensive source of all statistics on bonds available. *The Weekly Bond Buyer*, which they also publish, is a summary of the week's bond activity.

[2] For these studies see Rueben Kessel, "A Study of the Effects of Competition in the Tax-Exempt Bond Market," *Journal of Political Economy*, vol. 79, no. 4, July–August 1971, pp. 706–738. More recent studies include one by Michael Mussa of the Graduate School of Business, University of Chicago, for the SIA (*Competition in Borrowing Costs in the Municipal Revenue Bond Market: An Appraisal of the Evidence*, Securities Industry Association, New York, January 1979.

[3] See also pp. 314–315 of this text.

chapter 3

The Rating Agencies: Their Role in the Municipal Marketplace

Over the last four decades, the rating of municipal bonds by independent analysts has grown from next to negligible importance into a
central and, in many cases, controlling factor in whether an investor or
institution will buy a municipal bond. Yet, the degree of faith attached by
the individual and institutional investor to a rating on a municipal bond
issue is matched only by their lack of knowledge about how a rating is
reached. This occurred partly because, until very recently, little or nothing had been written or publicized about the rating process.

Due to this vacuum, this chapter grew out of lengthy discussions with
analysts at the Standard & Poor's Corporation, Moody's Investors Service, Fitch Investors Service, and White's Ratings—four advisory services
in the United States whose systems of ratings for municipal bonds are
used throughout the country. Policy discussions were also held about the
role of ratings with representatives, senators, and regulators, and with
the rating agency directors Brenton Harries of Standard & Poor's, the
late Jackson Phillips of Moody's, Richard Cacchione of Fitch Investors
Service, and Wilson White, Jr., of White's Ratings.

Despite the faith of most institutions and individual investors in ratings, many other observers of the municipal bond business, especially in
government, are by no means as positive in their appraisal of the rating
agencies. One critic went so far as to argue that given the number of
municipal bonds and the number of rating analysts, the average bond
rating would only take 20 seconds. While this figure is undoubtedly an
exaggeration, it is true that overworked analysts must obviously take
such a wide range of factors into account in all cases that they cannot
always have adequate time to reach an objective judgment. Many observers argue that "split ratings," or differences in ratings, by the services is
demonstrable proof that ratings are overly subjective and inadequate as

a standard of objective fact. Others maintain that they are inaccurate or misleading and point to the New York City notes and the Urban Development Corporation's notes; each had received investment-grade ratings from Moody's just days before their fiscal problems surfaced.

On the whole, the rating agencies have performed remarkably well, and their status as "all powerful" is enhanced by carping critics. Those critics claim that with the flick of a pencil the agencies can ruin a municipality's credit standing and add millions to the cost of borrowing through higher interest payments. Indeed, with the recent increase in public resentment against higher-tax burdens, as evidenced by the passage of Proposition 13 in California and a number of other such resolutions, it is clear that the power and authority of the rating agencies to accurately assess the credit of municipalities will become even more important. In fact, a few members of Congress and members of the Securities and Exchange Commission (SEC) have now concluded that as ratings are such a vital piece of information for each investor, at least two ratings should be required to be published by all municipalities and corporations in all their official statements and prospectuses.

The Meaning of a Rating on a Municipal Bond

The concept of a rating is simple. What is the probability of the timely repayment of principal and interest? While the following pages cannot give all the details of how ratings are reached—primarily because of the number, diversity, and complexity of the variables involved—they will spell out the fundamental credit analysis conducted by the major rating agencies.

The sheer size of today's public market for corporate and municipal debt, involving huge reservoirs of money through insurance companies, savings banks, trusts, mutual funds, profit sharing plans, pension plans, and so on, has made the traditional word-of-mouth assessments of credit values totally insufficient. Therefore, independent rating agencies developed to help investors by providing an easily recognizable set of symbols (i.e., A,B,C) which grade, on the same scale, a range of issuers of debt stretching from Consolidated Widget to Exxon; to foreign governments, such as Japan; and to municipal issuers, as varied as New York State and the Pinellas County, Florida, Water and Sewer District. The simplicity of the rating symbol is especially important because many issuers sell bonds with varying security pledges ranging from first-mortgage bonds and sinking fund debentures to bonds that are callable, convertible, or double- or triple-barreled in their backing; in short, the range is extremely complex.

As the number of municipal bond issues has multiplied each year, ratings of bonds by these agencies have increased in importance and complexity. Also, since ratings affect the eligibility of bonds for purchase by institutional investors, they can influence the interest rate a community must pay on its bonds. Due to federal and state regulations, many institutional investors, particularly banks and pension funds, can only buy bonds of a specified quality. Most trusts and estates today are guided by what is called the "prudent person" rule in buying their investment bonds. A high rating for a given bond issue will broaden the market for that bond and should reduce the net interest cost to the issuer.

Basic Similarities and Differences of the Rating Agencies

Moody's Investors Services Inc. and Standard & Poor's Corporation are the two major municipal rating services.[1] They rate bonds on request by the issuer, for a set fee based upon time and effort; they continue to maintain and renew the rating until the bond has been redeemed. Prior to 1968 (S&P), 1970 (Moody's), and 1974 (Fitch), the agencies derived all their income from the sale of publications which provided information on municipal bond issues for the benefit of the financial community and investors. The research for ratings was done at no charge to the municipality whose bonds were being rated. The crippling financial expense of doing free analysis and the growing complexity and volume in the municipal financing field caused them to change to a fee policy.

The above can be made clear by citing the simplest of statistics. Moody's began its rating service in 1918 when there were $1.2 billion of municipal bonds issued; today over $40 billion worth are underwritten each year. Furthermore, the technical aspects of the rating of municipal bonds—population growth and movement as well as industrial growth and change—have made the analysis of each issue more difficult.

The rating agencies rate virtually all types of GO and revenue bonds, encompassing bonds of states, counties, cities, school districts, and special-purpose taxing districts. Both limited- and unlimited-tax GO bonds of these issuers are rated. In addition, all three rate the following revenue bonds: *enterprise systems*, such as electric, water, sewer, gas, airports, parking, ports, toll facilities, solid waste disposal, transit, hospitals, housing, race tracks (under certain conditions), stadiums (if additionally secured), telephone, marinas, and auditoriums; *special tax revenue bonds*, such as sales, franchise, hotel, utility, cigarette, business license, and fuel; *special revenue bonds*, such as higher education (tuition, etc.), student loan, tax increment, special assessment (if additionally secured), lease-rental obligations, debt service makeups, and insured bonds.

There are, however, fundamental differences of philosophy and policy between Moody's and Standard & Poor's that dictate fundamental differences in their approaches to rating municipal bonds. For example, while Moody's rates municipal short-term notes, Standard & Poor's does not. Since such notes now account for $21 billion in new financing each year, they represent an enormous public market. This difference in policy between the two agencies in this dispute is not just an academic one or simply a storm in a teacup. While Moody's believes that Standard & Poor's is not fulfilling its job as a rating agency by its refusal to provide the investor with adequate rating judgment on notes, Standard & Poor's argues,

> In our opinion, they [short-term notes] have a variety of inherent weaknesses which could leave the investor exposed to financial loss. For example, we will not rate Bond Anticipation Notes, the repayment of which by definition depends upon the issuer's ability to borrow at some future date. By far the largest defaults on municipal securities in recent history were the short-term notes of New York City and the Urban Development Corporation (N.Y.), neither of which was rated by S&P.[2]

Rating agencies are thought to be remarkably similar with regard to bonds in four vital aspects: independence, symbols, general criteria, and warning.

Independence   Each believes that its ratings are of value only so long as it is considered totally objective, independent, and disinterested, i.e., credible. That credibility is very fragile, and so each is cautious to have no corporate or governmental influence.

Symbols   While their symbols have slight differences, they are virtually identical. Table 3-1 compares Moody's symbols with Standard & Poor's and includes S&P's definitions of its symbols.

In addition to the rating categories, the symbols A-1 and Baa-1 are used by Moody's to identify those bonds in the A and Baa groups which possess the strongest investment attributes. Standard & Poor's uses + and − (for all categories from BB to AA) to indicate, respectively, extra strengths and weaknesses.

General Criteria   Each bases its ratings in varying degrees on the following considerations: (1) Likelihood of default—capacity and willingness of the obligator as to the timely payment of interest and repayment of principal in accordance with the terms of the obligation, (2) nature and provisions of the obligation, and (3) protection afforded by , and relative position of, the obligation in the event of bankruptcy, reorganization, or some other arrangement under the laws of bankruptcy and other laws affecting creditor's rights.

TABLE 3-1   Municipal Bond Symbols and Definitions

Moody's	Standard & Poor's	
Aaa	AAA	Bonds rated AAA have the highest rating assigned by Standard & Poor's to a debt obligation. Capacity to pay interest and repay principal is extremely strong.
Aa	AA	Bonds rated AA have a very strong capacity to pay interest and repay principal and differ from the highest-rated issues only to a small degree.
A	A	Bonds rated A have a strong capacity to pay interest and repay principal, although they are somewhat more susceptible to the adverse effects of changes in circumstances and economic conditions than bonds in higher-rated categories.
Baa	BBB	Bonds rated BBB are regarded as having an adequate capacity to pay interest and repay principal. While they normally exhibit adequate protection parameters, adverse economic conditions or changing circumstances are more likely to lead to a weakened capacity to pay interest and repay principal for bonds in this category than for bonds in higher-rated categories.
Ba B Caa Ca C	BB B CCC CC	Bonds rated BB, B, CCC, and CC are regarded, on balance, as predominantly speculative with respect to capacity to pay interest and repay principal in accordance with the terms of the obligation. BB indicates the lowest degree of speculation and CC the highest degree of speculation. While such bonds are likely to have some quality and protective characteristics, these are outweighed by large uncertainties or major risk exposures to adverse conditions.
D	C	The rating C is reserved for income bonds on which no interest is being paid.

SOURCE: S&P's symbols and definitions are from Standard & Poor's Corporation, *Municipal and International Bonds: An Overview,* p. 72.

Warning   All three rating services warn that a rating is not a recommendation to purchase, sell, or hold a security. This is because the rating agency does not comment as to the market price or suitability for a particular investor of a particular bond. Also, the rating does not mean the rating agency has performed an audit. Nor does it attest to the authenticity of the information given to the agency by the issuer and on which the agency bases its ratings. Ratings of all three agencies can be changed, suspended or withdrawn as a result of changes in information or a municipality's refusal to provide information. The agencies also attempt to make it clear that they are not saying that one bond issue is better than another; their rating is simply an assessment at a single point in time of the nature of the security underlying the specific bond issue.

Once a decision has been made that an issue will be sold, whether competitively or by negotiation, a rating request to one of the rating agencies is initiated by the issuer or its authorized representatives. The events that follow the initation of a typical Standard & Poor's rating process and which ultimately result in the assignment of a rating are depicted in Figure 3-1.

It is important to remember that while there are a number of parties involved in the sale and purchase of a bond, the rating agencies are not themselves involved with the actual structuring of a given issue. That is the function and responsibility of the issuer, the investment banker, legal bond counsel, and accountants, who all stand in what Standard & Poor's calls "the inner circle," whereas rating agencies stand in "the outer circle" of investors, fiduciaries, and financial publishers as the recipient and user of material prepared by those in a position to attest to their accuracy and completeness.

Prior to the assignment of many ratings, the agencies meet with representatives of the issuing entity at their offices or on the site and give the issuer an opportunity to make a presentation. The purpose of the meeting is to resolve questions and uncertainties concerning the proposed bond issue; it will also allow the rating agencies the opportunity to assess the quality of the management of the issuing body.

Each of the rating agencies aims to determine whether the issue is investment grade or speculative grade. The term "investment grade" was originally used by various regulatory bodies to connote obligations which are eligible for investment by various institutions, such as banks, insurance companies, and savings and loan associations. Over time this term has gained widespread usage throughout the investment community. Issues rated in the four highest categories—AAA, AA, A, and BBB—are generally recognized as investment grade. Securities rated below BBB are generally referred to as "speculative securities."

Once established, municipal bond ratings remain in effect for as long as financial information is furnished regularly or until the next bond sale. For most issues the rating agencies need annual audits and budget documents on an ongoing basis. For revenue bond ratings involving construction financing, they also need at least quarterly progress reports covering the project involved. In a lease-rental situation, where the lease-rental payment is dependent upon the completion and/or acceptance of the project by the leasee, they request a copy of a "certificate of completion." For Standard & Poor's, Moody's, and Fitch the failure, by municipalities, to supply all the above information on a timely basis

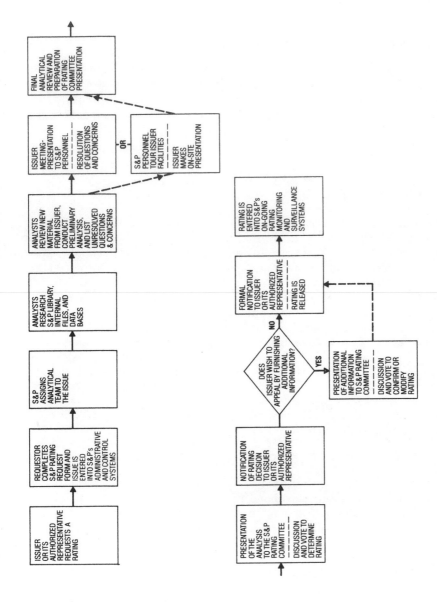

Figure 3-1 S&P municipal bond rating process—generalized flow diagram. (SOURCE: Standard & Poor's Corporation, *Municipal and International Bond Ratings: An Overview*, p. 7. Reprinted by permission.)

necessitates a suspension or withdrawal of the rating, inasmuch as their first rule is that a rating must be based upon all the adequate facts.

Moody's Rating of General Obligation Bonds

While Standard & Poor's and Moody's share four basic criteria in analyzing municipal bonds (examining the entity's debt, economic base, finances, and management of the municipality), a fundamental difference exists in their approach. According to Moody's, debt and the debt ratios that follow from it are the first and most crucial factors to analyze: "The first question asked in the analysis leading to the rating is what has the debtor pledged to pay."[3] On the other hand, for Standard & Poor's *the economic base* is the first and most important factor.

For example, Moody's states:

> The analyst is concerned with the total impact of all debt obligations on the reasonable ability of the taxpayers of the issuing unit to meet them. To this end, his central and first task is to derive a measure of the debt burden. In simplest terms, this is the relationship between the total debt burden on the tax base in the governmental unit and the wealth located there.
>
> The overall net debt is related to the broadest and most generally available measure of the wealth of the community, which is the assessed valuation of all taxable property adjusted to reflect market value as nearly as possible. The adjustment is made through application of an equalization ratio, which generally reflects a state government's appraisal of local assessment practices and which is widely necessitated by grants-in-aid which require measures of local wealth. Empirical evidence indicated that there is good reason to expect difficulty in meeting debt obligations when the debt burden exceeds the 12% range and when an exogenous factor, such as an economic recession, comes into play.[4]

In contrast, Standard & Poor's states:

> We consider an issuer's economic base the most critical element in our determination of municipal bond ratings. It is axiomatic that a community's fiscal health derives from its economic health. Virtually all revenue sources, from sales and income taxes, to permits and property taxes, are affected by economic conditions.[5]

The Standard & Poor's approach will be discussed in the following section.

Moody's analysis, concentrating on debt and debt ratios, is the more established and more traditional approach. Moody's spells out its own debt analysis in the following list:

Debt Analysis:

1. Debt policy: the uses, purposes, and planning of debt issuance, as well as the type of instruments used.

2. Debt structure: adequacy of plans for debt retirement, the relation between rate of retirement and purpose of debt, resources of the community, and existing and future debt needs.

3. Debt burden: gross and net debt related to resources and a comparison with other communities, overlapping debt and pyramiding.

4. Debt history and trend: the record as to defaults, refunding of maturing bonds and funding of operating deficits, rapidity of debt growth relative to purposes for which it has been incurred.

5. Prospective borrowing: authorized and uninsured bonds, adequacy of capital programming, obsolescence or inadequacy of capital plant, existing debt structure.[6]

The Moody's analyst also examines the structure of the debt and how the issuer plans to reduce it. Unnecessary deferral of debt payment raises questions, and as a general rule, the analyst prefers payment to be reasonably related to the life of the improvement that the debt is used to finance. The payment of one-half of the debt of a community over the ensuing 10 years is generally recognized as being prudent; it accounts theoretically for some depreciation, besides maintaining capacity to borrow in the future. Another aspect of debt structure the analyst seeks to determine is irregularities and any special problems which might be incurred in meeting them.

Other aspects of the analyst's appraisal of the debt of a community include examining the community's debt history, the reasons as to how and why the community issues debt to meet both its needs and resources, and the probabilities of future borrowing by the community. The latter factor is of utmost importance. It involves an assessment of a city's capital planning relative to its own position in history. For a deteriorating older city or for a rapidly growing newer city, future borrowing policy dictates particular and careful planning. While turning to other factors in the analysis, the analyst must bear in mind the possible future debt policies of the borrowing unit.

Economic Base of Municipal Bonds According to Standard & Poor's

Among the factors Standard & Poor's considers in evaluating the economic base are income levels and the rate of income growth. Both per capita and per household income levels and growth rate are measured against those for the region in which the community is located, its standard metropolitan statistical area (SMSA), the state, and the nation.

Next Standard & Poor's analyzes the employment mix to isolate areas of potential vulnerability compared with state, regional, and national trends, considering both short- and long-term aspects. While unemployment figures can be useful in some cases, the stress at Standard & Poor's is on the growth of the labor force. These figures give a real indication of the expansion or contraction of the local economy and are a measure of its economic viability.

Then Standard & Poor's analyzes population growth using a four-decade trend as well as recent estimates, the age of the population (under 18 and over 65 are considered "dependent" population requiring more costly services), and educational attainment levels as they relate to wage-earning capacity.

The leading employers and taxpayers are weighed carefully in relation to the types of industry involved, their commitment to the area, expansion plans, etc. Any significant shifts in taxpayers or employers are analyzed for their impact on the economic base. Building activity is another good indicator of economic vitality and of course translates into assessments and revenues from higher property taxes. Standard & Poor's looks carefully at the mix of building activity (residential versus commercial and industrial) and the effects of various economic conditions on building activity. Other economic indicators include the age and composition of the housing stock, retail sales activity (which indicates whether a community is a locally, regionally, or nationally important center), and bank deposits.

In summary, communities with higher income levels and diverse economic bases, which provide protection against economic fluctuations, clearly demonstrate a stronger capacity to pay the long-term bondholder. As we previously stated, assessments of the economic viability of a community must take a long-term perspective because the issuer's ability to meet debt service is a long-term consideration. Economic change is generally slow but persistent, and a high capacity to pay at present may not translate into a long-term trend.

Financial Analysis of Municipal Credits

Both Moody's and Standard & Poor's use much the same techniques for their financial analysis of a municipality's credit. Historical budget and audit report analyses are conducted with an emphasis on the issuer's revenue structure and how well it responds to various economic conditions. The translation of resources into revenues to pay expenses, including debt service, requires periodic and constant examination of the issuer's accounts.

Their examination of the financial operations of the community for the latest period available serves to confirm its performance under existing conditions. Current account analysis includes examination of the absolute size of the current budget, the trend in budget growth related to growth in population tax base, and the revenue/expenditure balance or imbalance over a period of years.

For analyzing the municipality's current account, the rating agencies concentrate on the main operating funds which are basically tax-supported, such as the general fund, debt service fund, and road or welfare fund. The special revenue fund would be included if federal revenue-sharing monies were used primarily for operating rather than for capital purposes. The municipality's reliance on outside federal and state aids or on short-term borrowing or any other sign that the community's tax calendar is not geared to its rate of expenditures is taken as a signal that cash flow problems are likely because the community is counting on outsiders to constantly bail it out of temporary or permanent imbalance.

Next, the rating agencies analyze all the major revenue sources, their changing importance as part of the entire revenue picture, and the suitability of these revenue sources considering the economic base. Expenditure trends and categories are analyzed, as is the balance sheet, to determine the accumulative effect of each year's revenue and expenditure scorecard. Comparing this year's budget with actual operations is a key test of both financial and managerial strengths.

Critical to all rating agencies is the analysis of the revenue system to determine the reliance on the community's property tax, the trend of assessed valuation, and tax delinquencies. All the agencies concur that a balanced composition of revenues sufficiently diversified so that the community is not unduly reliant on one or two big taxpayers or outside financing sources is necessary to give the issuer of municipal bonds the necessary flexibility to meet all its obligations.

Evaluating the Municipalities' Managers

The rating agencies give great weight to an assessment of the management of the municipality, but they employ a rather subjective and impressionistic approach to it. They meet with the managers personally to size up their knowledge and professionalism and are especially concerned with the availability of adequate financial documents, annual budgets, reports, and planning for land use, capital expenditure, and future income and expenditure projections. Cost controls and management systems zoning are each signs of professional management. They indicate that management is thinking about how services are to be provided in the future to perpetuate the municipality's growth and strength.

Obviously, managers are restricted somewhat in their ability to plan by charter, statutory, or constitutional limitations on tax rates, levies, and bases of assessment, and so a knowledge of the governmental structure and traditions of the municipality is essential for the rating analyst. Intergovernmental relations are today an increasingly significant key in assessing the cooperation and competition between this municipality and others.

In general, the range and level of services in relation to the communities' ability to provide such services (and the sharing of responsibility with other overlapping governmental bodies) are the central focus in the assessment of managers by the rating agencies. Their ability to deal with possible litigation, labor relations, and tax collection in a future recession or depression are all evaluated by the rating agents.

For each of the rating agencies, the crucial problem is how the separate analyses of the economic base, debt, finance, and management are blended together and weighed in order to arrive at a single rating, e.g., BBB. Each agency warns against a rigid mathematical formula or blanket rule for making this final rating determination. Moody's insists, "There is no way to cram them all into a single formula which invariably produces the right answer. The stumbling block is weighing."[7]

The conclusion of Moody's is that *ability to pay* is the crucial part of a good rating. Moody's says its analysts "are well down the road to reaching a judgment on this by an examination of the debt burden as it relates to the wealth of the community."[8] The second "accepted principal" for reaching a rating judgment is *willingness to pay*. Moody's concedes that "probably, most disagreements on ratings spring from different analysts."[9]

The approach of a rating agency to the different types of municipal bonds obviously varies according to the category and credit involved. While the major differences in rating approaches are between GO and revenue bonds, even within GO bonds there are different methods of analysis that depend upon whether a district is a state, county, city, or school district or a special district. This is because although the conceptual analysis is the same, state governments have sovereign powers or unique fiscal options that must be reflected in the creditworthiness of state GO bonds. Since states can unilaterally establish funding levels for certain local programs, e.g., education, they have an increased control over expenditure levels. Funding levels are usually statutorily, not constitutionally, determined, with the result that the statute sets the limits.

Political practicality, however, dictates that once a given level of funding is reached, the bureaucratic law of incrementalism usually makes it difficult to cut the level—and nearly impossible to decrease it. Because of states' unique powers they have great discretion in setting, establishing, or changing due dates for taxes and major-disbursement dates for state aid. This discretionary power can immediately and favorably impact the cash flow calendar of a state.

While the same broad areas of analysis (including debt, economic base, management, and finance) are important for almost all municipal bonds, the difference between the rating analyses of GO and revenue bonds centers on the former's general taxing power of the community, as opposed to the latter's specific credit backing of the revenues. When an issuer sells a GO bond secured by its full faith, credit, and taxing power, it is attaching to that issue its broadest pledge, encompassing such things as its ability to levy an unlimited ad valorem property tax or other revenue taxes, such as sales or income taxes.

In contrast, in its simplest terms a revenue bond security almost always involves an enterprise where the debt is related to the earnings of that enterprise. Therefore, revenue bond analysis is usually far simpler than the analysis of GO bonds, involving a closed system with a fixed and limited number of variables which are more amenable to simple quantification and comparison. The enterprise provides a community benefit, such as a water system, sewer service, a toll bridge, or a road, but it is a benefit that depends upon consumer usage. Therefore, the crucial points for the analysis of a revenue bond are the bond's demand and its legal protections for the bondholder in case the user demand declines.

There are specific types of analysis that must be performed on revenue-producing enterprises, such as engineers' appraisals of the soundness of the physical plant and system; special consideration of the secular, cyclical, and operating characteristics of the industry in which the enterprise is operating; and an examination of the particular system being built. The legal protections are far more important for revenue bonds because you do not have the backing of the taxing power, in most cases, to fall back on.

How Specific Types of Bonds Are Rated

For examining both revenue and GO bonds, Moody's and Standard & Poor's employ the same five general criteria: finance, debt, economic base, management, and legal analysis. However, in addition to their differences in weighing these five factors, which have already been discussed, each rating agency focuses on a number of specialized aspects of each type of revenue bond that force their rating analysis to break down by category. This has led to specialization among the rating experts, who usually handle only a given type of bond—e.g., housing, public power, hospital—or, for GO bonds, a given area. Each agency has one individual who handles California, one who handles Texas, etc.

The specialized aspects of the bond ratings for electric utilities will serve as an example of what the rating agencies' analysts specifically look at. Within utility systems, analysts must start by clearly distinguishing four different types: (1) the self-generating system where the public utility has its own plant; (2) the distribution system where power is purchased from a wholesaler and the public utility only needs transmission lines; (3) the wholesale system, which is large and uses straight-debt leverage to construct power generation units; and (4) the combination system, which has aspects of the first three types. In addition to determining whether a utility is a wholesale or retail operation, the rating agents must consider the service area (urban, rural, or suburban), the type of power (nuclear, hydroelectric, coal, or gas), the type of fuel mix, and cost and price projections. Most important, they must analyze the relationship between small utilities and large public and private systems because many utilities are not large enough to meet all load requirements on their own and, therefore, must rely on nearby power authorities that are outside their jurisdiction.

The other kinds of revenue bonds have similar types of specific key rating factors that must be taken into account by each of the agencies in making an evaluation. For example, water and sewer revenue bonds have some of the same characteristics as electric utility bonds but are essentially always monopoly operations. Many people believe there are simply no risks at all in buying these bonds because the population must have water and sewer facilities and so must pay their rates. On the contrary, it has been shown by sad experience that there are many risks in start-up stages where a new community, a new development, or a new zone is being created or added to because all revenues are based on projections. Projections of a new population influx frequently are somewhat different from the actual numbers. Another key aspect that rating analysts focus on is how much water leaks out of the system and never reaches the customers, although the ratepayers must pay for it anyway. Next, is the supply of water guaranteed within the region or dependent upon outsiders? Are the system's pipes, buildings, filters, etc., up to date or antiquated? Perhaps the prime concerns today in analyzing a water and sewer system are the type of sewerage treatment and whether it now meets or will meet by 1983 the strict federal, state, and municipal antipollution guidelines.

Again, each type of revenue bond has a specific type of rating analysis requirement. For toll roads, it is computing both current and future traffic trends and fuel costs. For port bonds, it is determining import/export tonnage and trends in types of cargo.

Two new types of municipal bonds issued are for housing and hospitals, and they require far more detailed analysis because of their greater complexity. For example, until quite recently, hospitals relied on philanthropy, but in the space of the last 10 years hospital revenue bonds have skyrocketed in terms of both the number of issues and dollar volume. The hospital bond rating begins with submission to the agency of many different types of documents by the hospital management, by lawyers, and by financial advisers and accountants. Since several hospital bonds were among those that have failed, Standard & Poor's no longer rates start-up situations. This is an important point, since this is where the investor needs the most help.

Next, a field trip to visit and observe the facilities, the management, and the doctors is invariably called for. Also, the nature of the project, its need and timing, and the nature of competing hospitals and facilities are vital. Usually, the feasibility study and all forecasts must be examined in detail for *5-year trends* in admission and discharges, average length of stay, patient days, number of beds in service, and average occupancy. The financial analysis must consider the reimbursement by third-party insurance schemes, statements of revenues and expenses, balance sheets, cash flow, and statements of changes in fund balances. "Medical staff characteristics" is a special category of analysis that each of the rating agencies goes into in great detail. The rating analyst checks the doctors' university affiliations, state board certifications, and malpractice insurance not only to ascertain the quality of the medical personnel but also to determine whether they can actually supply the patient needs to fund the hospital's new debt. The legal analysis is especially difficult with hospital finance because the rating agencies must assess what a mortgage on a set of hospital buildings and equipment is worth if the hospital were to go into default. For this reason Standard & Poor's uses a very elaborate and detailed method to analyze the characteristics of the medical staff and the hospital as an institution as well as the hospital's market position, management, finance, and economics.

Housing bonds, which represent by far the largest type of revenue bond, are also extremely complex and require a variety of types of analysis. For example, some programs provide financing for specific projects, while others involve a portfolio of projects. They must also be broken down into programs for single-family or multifamily apartments or condominiums, housing for the aged, housing for the poor, housing for middle-income groups, etc. The rating agent begins by analyzing the various types of revenue bond issues for housing. They fall into four major groups: (1) direct loan program issues by which a state housing finance agency provides a direct mortgage loan; (2) mortgage purchase issues, which provide mortgage money for single-family homes; (3) Section 8-11(b) local housing authority issues, which are federally subsidized and are for low- and moderate-income groups and for elderly people; and (4) the loans to lenders programs, which are analogous to mortgage-backed bonds but have become less popular recently.

Each different type of housing bond requires a different type of rating analysis and a different set of factors to consider and weigh carefully. Direct loan program bonds, by far the simplest, are issued by a state housing finance agency and are generally secured by and payable from mortgage loan repayments, federal subsidy payments, and, sometimes, state moral obligation appropriations.

Perhaps the two most complex are the mortgage purchase revenue bonds and the Section 8-11(b) housing revenue bonds. The first group has so many variations that the analysis, argues S&P, must be "tailored to the specific characteristics of the issue."[10] For example, programs often involve a large pool of geographically diversified mortgages on all different types of property in new construction and old colonials on all different types of property in different geographic and economic regions and vastly contrasting socioeconomic communities. Therefore, an actuarial approach itself would be insufficient without a more detailed analysis. The quality of the portfolio of mortgages is a central focus of attention of the analysis, as is the asset protection. Both tests require rather severe restrictions on the types of mortgages involved so that the best possible and high-equity mortgages on single-family dwellings which are detached and owner-occupied. Such restrictions frequently run directly counter to the public purpose doctrine of these programs, according to the government standards, and to the reason for their tax exemption. Also the mortgage pool must be enlarged to meet the public purpose requirements, but this adds an additional likelihood of default, which must be met by providing some additional asset protection of the bondholders. Therefore, supplementary protection of the bonds becomes crucial; it includes the provision for mortgage reserve funds, insurance, and backup financial support.

Next, the cash flow analysis is perhaps the most complicated analysis that the rating agents must go through, principally because they never can be certain how much prepayment of mortgages will occur. It is necessary to assume that some percentage will prepay throughout the life of the bonds, but the crux of the problem is *when*? The vast majority of the mortgages may be prepaid in a lump sum during one year or a very few years. Statistically, the prepayment schedules on different housing bonds vary considerably.

Since the ultimate responsibility for the housing projects' success or default must rest on the executives of the local housing authority, rating analysts must deal closely with them and assess their figures, information, and management. This involves a field trip and meetings with the issuer, sponsor, or developer; the management and marketing agents; the underwriters and/or financial consultant; and the feasibility consultant or market analyst.

After doing all the homework and compiling as much data as possible in reference to the particular bond issue, the particular projects, and the particular community, the rating analyst goes to a rating committee of the agency. This committee consists of the analyst and three to five other people. Together they weigh the mass of information and decide upon a rating.

Key Ratios for Revenue Bond Analysis

Because of the range and varieties of revenue bonds issued for a multitude of public purposes and the myriad of factors which analysts and investors must watch for, there are certain key ratios that are commonly employed to test creditworthiness:

$$\text{Operating ratio (\%)} = \frac{\text{Operating and maintenance expenses}}{\text{Operating revenues}}$$

$$\text{Interest coverage } (x) = \frac{\text{Net revenues}}{\text{Interest payments required}}$$

$$\text{Debt service coverage } (x) = \frac{\text{Net revenues}}{\text{Debt service required}}$$

$$\text{Debt service safety margin (\%)} = \frac{\text{Gross revenues } minus \text{ operating and maintenance expenses } minus \text{ current debt service}}{\text{Gross revenues}}$$

$$\text{Debt ratio (\%)} = \frac{\text{Net debt}}{\text{The sum of working capital plus plant}}$$

$$\text{Net takedown (\%)} = \frac{\text{Net revenues}}{\text{Gross revenues}}$$

The Smaller Rating Services: Fitch and White's

Two other smaller rating services should be looked at. Fitch Investors Service, while employing methods similar to those of Moody's and Standard & Poor's, tends to specialize in hospital ratings and may do more of these than any other service. Fitch maintains an office in Denver from which most of the hospital ratings originate and another in the Wall Street area from which all other ratings are done. Because Fitch tends to specialize, it only employs seasoned rating analysts who have received their training in one speciality elsewhere. This is in contrast to the practice of the two major rating firms, which engage in extensive training programs for their new recruits.

The other quite unique rating service is White's Ratings. White's, in contrast to the traditional credit research method of Fitch, Moody's, and Standard & Poor's, uses a system of analysis based on the study of the trading market, e.g., how bonds actually are priced and find their level in the market. White's uses a relative market value index that lets *the bond market* be the rater of each bond. It does this by translating each yield into a scaled number from 1 to 100 and listing them. As Wilson White, Jr., has stated for years in his famous annual book: "These ratings have nothing to do with what I think of the various credits, but are geared to their market assessment."[11] Each bond is scaled to 0.05 of its yield and given a "White's rating" that changes with its performance periodically in the actual bond market.

Just as Standard & Poor's and Moody's have increased their municipal staffs (S&P more than doubled its municipal analysts) since 1974, so has each of these two smaller rating services, thus demonstrating an across-the-board growth in this field. While the number of bonds issued has soared in the past 5 years, the growth of the rating analysts far exceeds the increasing number of bond issues and thus reflects the rating services' need to take on more specialists to supply more in-depth coverage of municipal bonds. This is an assessment with which they each concur. Each of the four rating services now hires, in addition to new trainees, specialists with extra credentials and detailed training in law, accounting, finance, municipal governments, etc., unlike the generalists whom they hired primarily in the past.

The Power of the Rating Agencies

While the rating services insist that ratings are no more than approximate guides of relative bond values, and *not* absolutes, ratings are definitely viewed by many as being *absolutes*. This is a crucial point because not only do many individual investors see ratings from this perspective, but the federal government insists upon making the ratings of Moody's and Standard & Poor's a cornerstone for bank portfolio audits. The critical distinction between investment-grade securities (unlike speculative-grade securities), such as those with ratings from AAA to BBB, therefore, is not simply linguistic, but is in fact a legal category as to what banks, other financial institutions, and legal fiduciaries may invest in for trusts and other portfolios. This investment-grade rating is taken as a stamp of assurance that these bonds will not default, and the federal government, therefore, allows them to be counted *at cost*, rather than at market value, during day-to-day trading, when computing the solvency of a particular bank or financial institution. While the federal government could some day change this ruling, it appears that the participants in most municipal bond markets assume that it will not, for two reasons: (1) the banks are the major holders of municipal bonds in this country and (2) it might disrupt the whole market to change the ruling.

The power of the rating agencies thus extends far beyond their budgets and personnel. The rating agencies have an influence upon the entire bond market, upon the fate of particular cities, and upon the cost of capital for municipalities of all kinds. And, ultimately, they affect our national economy.

A rating change can, some say, put a municipality or an authority into receivership. During the 1974–1975 New York City and New York State crises, the fear that all New York credits would be downgraded as a result was a mounting concern in the debt market as a whole (although this was *not* being stated by Moody's or S&P). Many municipal investors and analysts anticipated that a New York City default would cause the state to default, that together the defaults would have a domino effect on all New York credits, and that this would inevitably snowball into a national financial crisis. That the government stepped in with loan guarantees for New York City but not for some other municipalities in difficult circumstances has been cited by some observers as proof that this was indeed the case.

A different kind of storm among municipal issuers occurred in 1978 when Moody's withdrew ratings on almost 500 small issuers who had not provided current data. While this might appear to be a storm in a teacup because the amount of bonds was small, the decision of Moody's to withdraw, or downgrade, a rating from "investment grade" is a potent force among bond investors who regard ratings, to some degree, as absolute criteria.

Ratings Influence the Cost of Borrowing: The Lower the Rating, the Higher the Interest Cost

A substantial number of studies during the past 20 years have concluded that interest cost, or the cost of capital, definitely varies directly with the rating: (1) the higher the rating, the lower the interest cost and (2) the lower the rating, the higher the interest cost to the municipality. Yet despite the unanimity of these studies, it remains uncertain just how much influence this rating effect will have on any particular bond during any particular period or on any particular type of market. This is because these (rating–interest cost) relationships are not static; they change according to the business cycle and the particular sector of the economy that the bonds relate to. Overall it has been concluded by Petersen, Kessel, Moody's, and others that 20-year bonds rated BBB and AAA averaged a 1 percent difference in yield just after World War II. That gap narrowed to 50 basis points or 0.5 percent in the 1950s, stretched to nearly 70 basis points in 1971, and has shrunk to 50 basis points again. What has also been documented by these studies is that lower-grade bonds have far greater price volatility and so are rightfully considered to have far greater risk associated with them.

Risk is an important concept in municipal bond analysis, yet what is not generally realized is that credit risk is not just the chance of outright default or the delay of timely interest payments. Instead, risk for the investor involves the consequences of financial changes in value during the whole life of the bond. In other words, if the market value of the bond drops substantially at some point in the future just when the investor has to sell the bond in a hurry, long before the bond's expiration date, the investor is faced with a loss, an unforeseen cost, a risk. For this reason ratings have been called by John Petersen, in *The Rating Game*, a report card to gauge the future secondary market performance of the bond over its entire life, not just its immediate or long-term chance of default.[12]

It is clear that there are many other factors besides a bond's rating that can impact upon the bond's price. Among these factors, the most important are the bond's name, its issuer's familiarity in the market, and the geographic region. However, in all studies ratings were shown to have the most consistent effect on bond prices of any single factor.

The Rating Standards

Although most bonds are rated in the top four categories that constitute investment grade, a large new group of municipalities requesting ratings tends to fall right at the bottom of the investment grade. This might suggest that municipalities which formally went unrated are now feeling the pressure to obtain a rating in order to secure credit in the public markets. It might further suggest that a tougher standard is now being applied to newly rated issues than in the past.

By examining the categories today, one sees clearly that Moody's reduced the number of Aaa, Aa, and Baa ratings. Thus the investment grade is harder to get into today than it was 10 years ago. Two facts seem to accompany this stiffening of standards. First, in the 1950s members of Congress and the SEC began investigating the rating services. They did so again in the early 1970s. Later, Moody's introduced the 1 after specific ratings and Standard & Poor's the + and − as a way to add another notch to a rating without changing a full grade.

Are these general changes in rating standards important, and are changes in particular ratings significant in the overall bond market? These questions have been analyzed by many studies in response to the prevailing view today that market participants fully anticipate these changes in advance and discount or revalue bonds ahead of time. Nevertheless, the moment that a rating change is announced the market price of that bond experiences a jolt. After a change the yields on upgraded bonds decrease, and those on downgraded bonds rise. Changes in yields come faster and in a more pronounced fashion than could be accounted for by change in the perceived credit of the municipality itself.

Not only do municipal bond ratings affect yields, they also directly affect the costs of marketing a bond issue because an underwriting firm's profits directly reflect ratings on bonds. Petersen, in *The Rating Game*, concludes that an Aaa bond's average cost for an underwriting is $3.10 less per bond than the cost for a Baa; similarly an Aaa is $1.80 cheaper and an A is 96 cents cheaper.[13] Thus the higher the rating, the lower the profit; the riskier the bond, the higher the charge for underwriting. This is partly a self-fulfilling prophecy, for far more underwriters tend to bid on Aaa securities, scrambling all over to join syndicates and compete, whereas far fewer will tend to bid on most Baa bonds, which are considered quite risky. The lack of competition among underwriters also raises the price the municipality must pay to obtain underwriters.

The authors will not take sides in the ongoing dispute between those who argue that Moody's ratings are better than Standard & Poor's ratings and those who argue the opposite. It is, however, important for bond analysts and investors to realize that there are key reasons for this dispute. Today Standard & Poor's is viewed by many as the most innovative and creative rating service. Yet in the past and to some extent still today, Moody's has been viewed as the primary rating service for two reasons: (1) it is older and has a longer experience with ratings and (2) it covers a significantly larger group of credits including municipal notes which, as we have already stressed, Standard & Poor's refuses to rate.

While only 30 percent of all municipal issues are rated because of the many tiny local issuances, 60 percent of the dollar volumes of all municipal bonds are rated by both services, and this includes all the major issuers. Of those remaining, 35 percent were rated only by Moody's and 5 percent only by Standard & Poor's. A split rating however, of more than one grade is extremely rare (e.g., an A from one service and an AAA from the other), suggesting that within a narrow range there is a good deal of continuity between the two firms in the outcomes of their evaluation process.

In conclusion, the crucial point of all this is that ratings have a very important effect on a bond's price in the market, and this is widely realized. Because of this, key trading decisions are based upon it. Second, because it is the new bond issues which receive constant rating surveillance, most research and investigation tends to follow or to react to the rating services. Therefore, the older outstanding credits tend to get less attention. Less information is available on them, and this ultimately has an effect on their market.

Notes to Chapter 3

[1] Moody's is a wholly owned subsidiary of Dun and Bradstreet, Inc. Standard & Poor's is a wholly owned subsidiary of McGraw-Hill, Inc., having been acquired in 1966.

[2] Standard & Poor's Corporation, *Municipal and International Bond Ratings: An Overview*, pp. 6, 8.

[3] Moody's Investors Services Inc., *Pitfalls in Issuing Municipal Bonds*, 1977, p. 13.

[4] Ibid., p. 16.

[5] S&P, op. cit., p. 12.

[6] Moody's, op. cit., p. 14.

[7] Ibid.; interview with Dr. Jackson Phillips, vice president, Municipal Bond Reports, Moody's Investors Services, Sept. 12, 1978.

[8] Ibid.

[9] Ibid.

[10] S&P, op. cit., p. 46.

[11] Wilson White, Jr., *White's Tax-Exempt Bond Market Ratings,* International Data Corporation, 1976.

[12] John E. Petersen, *The Rating Game,* The Twentieth Century Fund, 1975.

[13] Ibid., p. 75.

part2

General Obligation Bonds

chapter 4

State and Local Revenues and Expenditures

So intricately entwined are state, local, and federal financial systems today that an interrelated analysis of all three systems is essential for an accurate picture of their fiscal operations. It was not always so. Traditionally, for the first 150 years of our nation, the American system of government functioned so that there existed three separate tiers of government financial systems, namely, the federal, the state, and the local. The financial operations of each tier were seen to be separate and distinct. And in reality, during the early years of the American Republic, there was little movement of funds from one tier to the other, as governments of each tier found it neither financially necessary nor morally incumbent upon them to provide monies as well as financial services for the other governments. This early picture was aptly dubbed the "layer cake" model of federal-state-local fiscal relations.

As the character or, perhaps more accurately, the mission of the American government changed in the years following the Great Depression, so did the fiscal relations among the three governmental tiers. The federal government virtually reversed its position of noninvolvement in the economic affairs of the nation and also to a degree reversed its noninvolvement with state and city finances. With increases in income taxes as well as other revenue sources and with the establishment of major social programs, such as welfare, aid to education, and social security, the government of the United States began to discharge its constitutional obligation to promote the general welfare.

To be sure, the federal government was not alone in funding such general welfare programs: Funding was, in fact, undertaken on a cooperative basis between the federal and state governments. More often than not, the federal government provided "grants-in-aid" and "matching grants," so that the state governments were required to pay their proportionate share for the governmental programs and services that their own populace would receive. The federal government, under the American Constitution, could not legally "mandate" such programs for states and municipalities because the Constitution confers certain powers on the federal government, and it reserves many powers for the states. Nonetheless, federal involvement resulted from the federal power to "tax and spend for the general welfare." With the United States providing matching grants and "seed monies" to the states, and with the states, in turn, providing funds in those ways to their localities, which were in essence "creatures of the states," the carrot-and-stick approach actually brought forth a new era in fiscal relations in American government. As a result, the layer cake model of American finance neatly gave way to what was termed the "marble cake" theory.

It cannot be overstressed that here was the first major change in the pattern and the philosophy of American governmental finance. It came suddenly and with great force. The laissez faire policy of the eighteenth and nineteenth centuries that pervaded American economic affairs gave way to the image of a veritable federal octopus. Yet this virtual "about-face" in economic philosophy came to fruition without violence.

The marble cake picture of fiscal relations among the tiers of government laid the basis for the next and final metamorphosis in governmental financial affairs. This change was accomplished through the issuance of tremendous amounts of debt via new fiscal entities, created at all three levels of government, that were known as "revenue authorities," or "public authorities." Many states developed, for example, public housing authorities following the U.S. Housing Act of 1937. Public power authorities, turnpike authorities, port authorities, and many other varieties sprang up and multiplied in number and in complexity. In the 1960s a state form of public authority with a "moral obligation" pledge by the state was introduced, and it added further complexity to the already confusing array of revenue authorities.

What is important is that since World War II, a large part of the dramatic growth in the issuance of state and local debt can be attributed to these various sorts of revenue authorities. The increase in revenue bond underwritings since 1945, for example, has been almost *eightyfold*.

Public authorities had been operating in America since the nineteenth century when, after a series of cyclical depressions, states adopted constitutional restrictions on the borrowing powers of their legislatures and the use of state credit. Beginning with the early canal companies, these revenue enterprises were designed to circumvent the prohibitions by borrowing outside the purview of state responsibility, that is, by borrowing without the backing of state funds to deliver the governmental services to which most Americans were becoming accustomed.

However, the proliferation of these revenue enterprises on a large scale was spawned by the "New Deal" in the 1930s. The national government, as noted earlier, virtually mandated, in fine federalistic fashion, the establishment of local public authorities for such services as housing and transportation.

The establishment of revenue authorities, endowed with almost limitless debt-creating ability, brought forth a quasicorporate financial mechanism for issuing public debt that changed the nature of federal-state-local fiscal relations. In some cases, federal and state funds were funneled to these debt-creating mechanisms for such services as housing, transportation, public power, and even education. In this way, the marble cake analogy of interlocking levels of government finance gave way to a "mixed marble cake" of overlapping, frequently changing, and often conflicting government service financing. As a result, finding the security behind many municipal bonds today has been said to resemble tracing a New York subway line to its origin.

How then does the ordinary investor or bond analyst go about the task of evaluating municipal bonds if these new fiscal interrelationships of states and municipalities with the federal government *and* with revenue authorities are so complex?

One approach to this problem is to analyze each revenue category and each expense category (in order to spot the largest or the most important trends). A second approach is to see if they balance. In other words, is the state or municipality accruing a surplus or is it incurring a deficit?

State and Local Budget Surpluses

The year 1977 was the fifth year since 1950 that state and local revenues outstripped expenditures, resulting in budget surpluses.[1] When taken together, states and localities compiled budget surpluses totaling $13.7 billion in 1977, compared to the $4.1 billion in budget surpluses aggregated in 1976. Furthermore, within recent years, short-term financing used to cover budget deficits has fallen significantly for a number of states, and for others, such financing has leveled off since 1975. Recent surveys indicate that of the 24 states that registered budget deficits in 1976, only 6 ran deficits in 1977.

As a result of these surpluses, and as will be discussed later, many states are debating long-term ways of returning these tax dollars to the taxpayers and methods of reducing tax rates on a variety of revenue sources. The surpluses recorded in 1976 and 1977 reflected current trends: rising revenues through inflation, increased taxes, and limitations on expenditure growth or fiscal restraint exercised by states in the wake of the well-known financial woes of some states and munici-

TABLE 4-1 State-Local Deficit or Surplus on General Accounts
(In $ Billions Based on the National Income and Product Figures)

Fiscal year	Deficit or surplus
1950	−1,876
1955	+2,651
1960	−1,372
1965	−546
1966	+193
1967	−2,153
1968	−977
1969	−2,228
1970	−3,985
1971	−3,808
1972	−5,614
1973	+4,129
1974	−2,013
1975	−6,222
1976	+3,908
1977	+13,700

SOURCE: Adapted from Elsie M. Watters, *The Financial Outlook for State and Local Governments to 1980*, The Tax Foundation, Inc., New York, 1973, p. 96, and private interview in 1973.

palities. They key question, however, is: Which state revenue systems were capturing inflation-generated revenues most efficiently?

Some recent empirical studies have isolated the effects of inflation on state and local budgets.[2] On the one hand, the studies point to the conclusion that even during the comparatively mild inflation that occurred between 1967 and 1972, the revenue systems of most local governments captured additional revenues as a result of inflation. Moreover, such revenues grew at a faster rate than the inflation-induced expenditures. However, on the other hand, the data showed further that during the same period, some *states* were forced to bear expenditure increases as a result of inflation, and these increases were greater than increases registered by revenues. From 1972 through 1974, when inflation ran rampant, revenue growth resulting from inflation *did not* keep pace with inflation-induced expenditures at either the state or the local level. It has been calculated that between 1972 and 1974, the net purchasing power index of states fell to 90.6 and that of localities fell to an average of 90.2, on the basis index of 100. (This basis index of 100 indicates that revenues and expenditures increased commensurably. Consequently, the real purchasing power of the governments with 100 as their basis index would remain unchanged.)

Yet, it is interesting to note that state and local governments were still in a much better financial position in the year 1973–1974 than they had been in for many preceding years. In isolating the reasons, especially in light of inflationary periods, one study concluded that the firmer financial position of state and local budgets resulted from extensive tax increases in the late 1960s and the early 1970s.[3] Of course, economic growth and inflation automatically generated revenues, but these revenues did not equal expenditure increases. To ward off budget deficits, statutory tax increases were taken *in advance*. It was disclosed that between 1965 and 1971 states and localities almost doubled their revenues from charges, fees, and miscellaneous sources. Moreover, this increase was accompanied by a reduction in the rate of expenditures.

State and Local Revenues: The Property Tax

Wealth emanates from the land, wrote many early political economists. Yet any cursory evaluation of the American political scene today shows that not only has the property tax, over the past 50 years, become less significant as a revenue source for both state and local governments, but it also is under attack throughout the nation. Property assessments have been increasing dramatically and straining the taxpayers' budgets well beyond what many of them consider reasonable. Put differently, although the property tax has declined in significance as the source of staple government revenue, present tax rates are so high that a nation-wide backlash has developed with a potential for reducing the property tax to an even less significant portion of total government revenue. If other revenue sources do not make up for the gap created by the future limiting of property assessment rates, then fewer government services will be provided.

It is interesting to note that it appears that taxpayers' views, in the last 50 years, have finally come full circle—moving slightly back toward a laissez faire philosophy. This may not take the form of radical limitations on the property tax rate that the nation has seen in California through the enactment of Proposition 13, which amended the California constitution. The heart of the measure was the limitation of ad valorem real property taxes to 1 percent of the market value of property based on the property owner's 1975–1976 tax bill, with the possibility of increases that would not exceed 2 percent annually. At the time of passage, property tax rates in California averaged approximately 2 percent of full market value. As a result, although outstanding GO debt, which was approved by local voters, was exempt from the 1 percent limit, additional GO bonds secured by ad valorem property taxes were effectively limited.

How significant is this property tax revolt for the municipal bond market as a whole?

There are a number of ways to chart the development of the property tax as a revenue source for state and local governments over the past half century. In 1932 the property tax, the mainstay of local revenue, accounted for over 97 percent of all local revenue from any source at the local level of government. By 1978 only 80 percent of total local government revenues accrued from property taxes. The property tax, however, varies in importance as a revenue source in terms of both government and area. Town governments and school districts rely most heavily on the property tax. The tax makes up over 60 percent of the revenues of townships nationwide and over 45 percent of the revenues of school districts. For counties and other municipalities, the property tax is only one-third of the available revenues. As a percentage of all taxes, however, the property tax is still overwhelmingly important. On the average for school districts and townships, the property tax as a percentage of all taxes totals 98 and 96 percent, respectively. Counties use the property tax to the extent of approximately 85 percent of all taxes, and other municipalities derive 65 percent of their revenue from the property tax.

As will be discussed in Chapter 6, "Regional Differences in State and Local Finance," there are great regional disparities in the revenue and expenditure patterns of states and localities, as well as regional differences in broad economic and financial indicators. At this time, it may be appropriate to mention the regional differences in the use of the local property tax as a revenue source. When property taxes are measured as a percentage of total revenue by region, it is found that New England makes the greatest use of them. The property tax makes up approximately 65 percent of the total revenue of states in New England. The northeastern Central and the northwestern Central states make the second greatest use of the property tax, which accounts for approximately 45 percent of the total general revenue in those regions. In contrast, South Atlantic and southeastern Central states make the least use of the property tax; revenues from taxation on property constitute only 29 percent of the total general revenue. Moreover, there is substantial variation in the use of the property tax in the Mountain and Pacific states. In those states, revenues from the tax vary from 20 to over 60 percent of the total general revenue.

The Property Tax Debate

The property tax has only recently become the subject of widespread and extensive public policy debates and initiatives aimed at questioning its inherent economic inequities and limiting it as a revenue source.

Previously, there has been much attention devoted to the property tax in academic literature by economists, political scientists, and jurists. Taking their lead from differing court rulings, these academic investigators have tended to concentrate their analysis on whether the use of the property tax as a basis for public school financing was just or unjust.

In the famous case of *Serrano v. Priest* (1970) the Supreme Court held that the use of the property tax to support local public schools resulted in unequal education. Thus it appeared possible that the Supreme Court might at one stroke disallow the most important object of local public finance. However, the Supreme Court in the case of *Rodriguez v. San Antonio School District* (1970) held that the present method of financing public education in the San Antonio school district did not run counter to the equal protection clause of the U.S. Constitution by simply allowing wealthier districts to provide more monies to their school districts (through the property tax) than less wealthy districts. Nonetheless, a number of state courts, notably in California and New Jersey, have held that the inequalities caused by the differing abilities of local school districts to support public education through the property tax are indeed unconstitutional when applied to state constitutions. Consequently, the matter may now be a more difficult problem than ever before, and state solutions will vary.

During the 1970s, as a result of debate over the financing of public education with property taxes, a variety of other larger issues emerged concerning the status of the property tax as the major source of local governmental revenue. Proponents argue that the tax is one that is inherently stable, providing consistent revenues during times of economic difficulty. In contrast, sales, income, and other nonproperty taxes are much more subject to cyclical economic conditions. In addition, they argue that the wealthier individuals who hold more property must bear a substantially greater share of the tax than less fortunate individuals.

However, detractors of the property tax suggest that it discourages improvements on property, lest the property be taxed at a higher rate. Second, during periods of inflation, assessments, which are usually made at the local level, are not raised commensurately with the theoretical changes in the value of property. Thus the property tax is more inflexible than other sources of revenue. It is likely that the debates and sophisticated academic studies on the property tax will continue.

State Revenue Response to Inflation

There are distinct state and regional patterns in the contribution that each revenue source makes to the entire state or local revenue system. For example, the states of the Northeast and Midwest relied more heavily on the property tax than did the other regions of the nation. Such revenue-raising statistics are important in determining which states are able to capture additional revenues as a result of inflation or in discerning which states must cap expenditures and exercise fiscal restraint when inflation-induced revenues are comparatively low.

In general, although the personal income tax and the local property tax both are capable of adding unanticipated revenues to budgets during inflationary periods, the personal income tax is the most reliable revenue source. As a result, those state or local tax structures that rely more heavily on the progressive income tax, as opposed to sales or property taxes, have more resilience during times of inflation. States that do not rely on it must resort to fiscal austerity measures to keep pace with inflation and to stockpile budget surpluses.

Table 4-2 includes the 39 states that rely to a significant extent on the progressive income tax as a revenue source. It ranks them as to both the degree of reliance on the tax and the degree of progressivity of the tax. The states that tend to benefit most from their ability to capture additional income tax revenues during inflation *are not* in the Northeast, except, of course, for New York State. Four Northeastern states did not rely heavily enough on the income tax even to appear on the table.

Newer State and Local Revenues

For decades the property tax in this country was thought to be insensitive to the business cycle and to be an ironclad support for municipal securities. Therefore, in the 1950s, Philadelphia's bonds were considered somewhat suspect because the city was dependent upon wage and sales taxes that would fluctuate with the business cycle. Many credit analysts of that period were still reacting to fears from the Great Depression of the 1930s; these fears colored their interpretation of each factor in GO bond evaluation. This perspective tended to warn them against any municipal tax, revenue, or support mechanism which was overly dependent upon the business cycle. This bias tended to lead to higher credit ratings for municipalities that were exclusively dependent upon property taxes and lower credit ratings for municipalities that were overly dependent upon other sources of income that would, in turn, be overly dependent upon the business cycle.

Today, in contrast, confidence has waned in the property tax as an unquestioned support of GO bonds, whereas income tax and sales tax revenues of states and municipalities, which are pegged to the rate of inflation and the growth of the gross national product, are considered stronger revenue supports than they once were.

TABLE 4-2   The Progressive Income Tax States Ranked According to Degree of Progressivity and Reliance on the Personal Income Tax

		Income tax progressivity*		
		High	Medium	Low
State personal income tax as a percentage of state tax revenue†	High	Colorado Delaware Hawaii Minnesota *New York* Oregon Virginia	Alaska Maryland *Massachusetts* Wisconsin	Iowa Montana
	Medium	California Georgia Idaho Michigan Missouri Nebraska North Dakota Oklahoma South Carolina Utah	Alabama Arizona Arkansas Kansas North Carolina *Rhode Island* *Vermont*	Illinois Indiana Kentucky West Virginia
	Low	Louisiana *Maine* Mississippi New Mexico Ohio		

* Progressivity is measured by the ratio of the effective tax rate for a family of four at $25,000 to the effective rate of $7500. A tax has high progressivity if the ratio is at least 3, medium if from 2 to 3, and low if below 2. As a comparison, the same ratio for the federal personal income tax in 1974 was 2.5 before the tax rebate and 3.2 after the tax reduction.

† Low, 0–15 percent; medium, 15–30 percent; high, above 30 percent.

SOURCE: U.S. Advisory Commission on Intergovernmental Relations, *Federal-State-Local Finances: Significant Features of Fiscal Federalism,* 1975 ed., pp. 8, 30.

Nonproperty taxes may be divided into four *major* categories: (1) individual income tax, (2) corporate income tax, (3) sales and gross receipts taxes, and (4) motor vehicle tax. The individual and corporate income taxes need no further explanation here, but it is sufficient to state that the individual income tax constitutes almost 30 percent of all revenues from local nonproperty taxes. The sales and gross receipts taxes, however, account for over 50 percent of all the nonproperty tax revenues of local governments. This tax category may be divided into two broad subcategories: the general sales tax and the selective sales tax. The general sales tax supplies the larger portion of the revenues from sales and gross receipts, accounting for approximately 35 percent of the nonproperty tax revenues of local governments. The selective sales tax accounts for almost 20 percent of all nonproperty tax revenues of local governments and is composed of taxes on such items as motor fuel, public utilities, and tobacco products. Motor vehicle and license taxes include almost 3 percent of all nonproperty tax revenues of local governments. In addition, nontax revenues account for about 15 percent of the nonproperty tax revenues. Nontax revenues cover a wide variety of service charge items, including parking fees, educational expenses, hospital charges, park and recreation fees, water and transportation charges, and certain other special assessments. Taken separately, each accounts for only a small portion of the total nontax revenues, but taken together, they are an ever growing source of revenues for both state and local governments.

Intergovernmental revenues were touched on earlier in this chapter when federal aid to states and localities was discussed. Here, however, it must be made crystal clear that a growing revenue source for almost all local governments is state aid. By the mid-1970s, state aid to local governments accounted for almost 35 percent of all local government revenues. There is, of course, a variety of kinds of state aid provided to localities, and there are a myriad of methods through which such aid is administered. Detailed analyses of these methods and of specific state programs have been provided by a plethora of books and research articles in recent years.

What is most important to realize about all such programs and such aid is that in one form or another they have become an integral part of the American federal, state, and local systems of government finance. For the investor or bond analyst, the extent to which such aid constitutes a significant part of a single state's or municipality's total revenue, however, is a critical dimension in analyzing its credit. A detailed discussion of this aspect of intergovernmental aid will be covered in some of the following chapters in those specific cases where it is most significant to a certain type of bond's credit evaluation (e.g., New Jersey school bonds). In the wake of Proposition 13 types of movements in over 20 states and the threat of limitations they pose for the taxing and spending powers of local municipalities, it appears clear that state and federal aid will continue to be an important source of local revenue for many years to come.

In general, it can be argued that municipal GO bonds are riskier today than they used to be because of the increasing numbers of examples in which many municipalities are dependent on outside governmental funds. While grants, subsidies, matching grants, cost-share programs, and revenue-sharing programs of all sorts do not necessarily cause financial destabilization of a municipality, they tended to have that effect in a number of cases. This destabilizing force occurs because the external financial dependence is not usually a guarantee as to what other levels of government will do over the long-term life of 20-, 30-, or 40-year bonds that are being issued by municipalities. And for this reason credit analysts of municipal GO bonds have sometimes felt awkward when forced to look beyond the single municipal entity for the long-term security *of certain municipal bonds.* Since the analysts have frequently lacked any absolute guarantee that these external funds would be forthcoming throughout the life of the bonds, they have had to make a guess about or an estimate of whether those external payments would be secure and would be made in a timely fashion over the next 20 to 40 years.

Most federal and state grants and transfer payments to a municipality are looked upon as fiscal leverage that gives great financial support to the municipality. However, this may be very deceptive. If a state government or the federal government says it will give $8 for every $2 that a municipality supplies, the general impression is that the municipality's income will be stronger and more secure. Yet if the municipality fails to earn that $2 because of lost property taxes (for example, when businesses, industries, or individual taxpayers leave), lost sales taxes, or any other traditional revenues that may suddenly evaporate, the result is to reduce that municipality's total revenues by $10—not just by $2.

This situation is one of the simpler reasons why it is hard for many of the older cities to balance their finances, for they have frequently already overcommitted their locally generated revenues. It may also be a reason why outside government funding and grants have sometimes had a destabilizing effect upon certain municipalities' finances.

Virtually no federal or state grants cover 100 percent of the costs of the projects or programs they support. (Even grants labeled as 100 percent almost never include total overhead expenses.) Most grants are partial, frequently matching what a municipality puts up, and thus cover only the start-up costs, marginal costs, basic costs, or capital costs, but almost never the *full costs.* Since some of these federal programs (e.g., environmental and pollution control standards for water and sewage treatment plants) are in effect mandated or forced upon municipalities, it is possible for a municipality to find itself strained by the financial costs of accepting federal and state grants. While subsidies and grants definitely help a municipality to adjust its cash flow (and certainly they supply vitally important revenues for municipalities today), these external funds do not come free, as many observers assume, but, instead, can carry considerable hidden costs.

In addition to this problem of dependence upon federal and state revenues, certain municipalities have experienced difficulties because of their dependence upon surplus earnings from certain of their revenue authorities. As we will show in more detail in Chapter 12, "Municipal Accounting," a number of surplus funds from various revenue-producing enterprises and revenue authorities (for public power, water and sewer facilities, parking garages, etc.) were occasionally funneled into the "general fund" for supporting the general operating expenses and the general obligations of the city. Indeed, because of the long-term drop in the cost of electric power, for 40 years many municipalities used municipal electric revenues as part of their general funds. Towns and cities, in many cases, became dependent upon these revenues as sources to cover their operating expenses. Today, however, because of the recent sharp increases in fuel costs and other expenses as well as new, more stringent legal protections for holders of revenue bonds, the surplus from municipal electric utilities and water and sewer authorities has shrunk or dried up. In some cities and towns, severe cash flow problems have been incurred or have been intensified because of the declining profitability from the generation of electricity.

General Expenditures by State and Local Governments

As shown in Table 4-3, expenditures by state and local governments have soared in dollar volume and by function over a period of 25 years. Expenditures for education since 1950 have been and still are by far the largest single item of state and local governments. For 1975 it was projected that education would take $81 billion of the $215 billion in total general expenditures. In that same year, public welfare expenditures, at $27 billion, ranked second in terms of dollar volume, with expenditures for highways totaling $23 billion and following close behind.

Today, although spending for education still remains the largest expenditure of state and local governments, the percentage increases registered by the functions of health and hospitals and by miscellaneous functions (including police, fire, general administration, sanitation and sewage, housing and urban renewal, public welfare, and interest on a general debt) have outstripped the percentage increase of expenditures for education. Expenditures for education by state and local governments were projected to increase by 121.7 percent between 1970 and 1980, while expenditures for health and hospitals, miscellaneous functions, and public welfare were expected to increase by 209.4 percent, 174.7 percent, and 168.8 percent, respectively.

Nevertheless, as a percentage of total general expenditures as shown

TABLE 4-3 General Expenditures by Major Function of State and Local Governments
(Actual and Projected, Selected Fiscal Years, 1950 to 1980)

Fiscal year	Total general	Major function				
		Education	Highways	Public welfare	Health and hospitals	All other
		In $ millions				
Actual:						
1950	22,787	7,177	3,803	2,940	1,743	7,119
1960	51,876	18,719	9,428	4,404	3,794	15,531
1970	131,332	52,718	16,427	14,679	9,668	37,840
1980	320,021	116,877	29,810	39,460	29,914	103,960
		Percent increase, selected intervals				
1950–1955	48.0	65.9	69.7	7.8	44.4	35.9
1955–1960	53.8	57.2	46.1	39.0	50.3	60.6
1960–1970	153.2	181.6	74.2	233.3	154.8	143.6
1970–1980	143.7	121.7	81.5	168.8	200.4	174.7

SOURCE: Adapted from Elsie M. Watters, *The Financial Outlook for State and Local Governments to 1980*, The Tax Foundation, Inc., New York, 1973, p. 76.

in Table 4-3, education expenditures have constituted approximately 40 percent of all expenditures since 1960. This fact is important for two reasons: (1) education remains the most important expenditure item, with expenditures far exceeding the monies spent for every other government service, and (2) this stability stands in contrast to the decreasing growth rate for highway expenditures, on the one hand, and the increasing rate of growth for public welfare expenditures, on the other hand.

Indeed, as a percentage of total expenditures by state and local governments, monies spent for highways have been cut in half since 1960. At that time, expenditures for highways constituted over 18 percent of the total general expenditures for all government services. By 1980 this percentage should hover at approximately 9.3 percent. Expenditures for public welfare, however, have shown the opposite trend. In 1960 monies spent on public welfare constituted only about 8.5 percent of the total state and local general expenditures. By 1980 public welfare expenditures should constitute about 12.3 percent of total expenditures. For the past 20 years the rate of growth in public welfare expenditures has outstripped the rate of growth in monies spent on education, sanitation, highways, police, or administration in the United States.

The Effect of Curbs on Borrowing, Curbs on Taxes, Curbs on Expenditures

As recently as 10 years ago, GO bonds represented approximately 75 percent of all municipal bonds. Largely because of investor concern after the New York City financial crisis that some municipalities were neither well managed nor financially accurate in their accounts, GO bond representation dropped precipitously to 40 percent of all newly issued bonds in 1978. In fact, since that 40 percent figure was compiled before the full impact of Proposition 13 was known and before the tax revolt had spread its full distance from California, it appears quite likely that the GO bond share of the total municipal market will continue to decline during this coming decade.

This decline will result partly from new state laws that prevent the issuing of new bonds or the raising of new taxes; set ceilings on bonded indebtedness, limits on spending, or limits on capital appropriations; or demand balanced budgets.

Nevertheless, what is crucial to realize is that a great many GO bonds will continue to be issued for schools, municipal buildings, police and fire protection, etc., despite these various new legal restrictions. No doubt a weariness among certain municipal managers will lead them to seek out revenue bond alternatives to issuing GO bonds that require taxpayer or voter approval, but not all municipal financing needs can be met by revenue bonds.

Therefore, it appears clear that among these new municipal GO bonds certain bargains may be available because of the comparative difficulty of issuing them; but also some cities will issue new bonds that will carry more risk than the amount attached to comparable bonds issued in previous years. The reason for this latter likelihood is that a municipality's pledge of "full faith and credit," i.e., its taxing power, may well have meant more before these new laws restricted it.

This uncertainty is one crucial reason why the credit analysis of GO bonds is more important now than in the past for the private investor and institutional bond analyst. In many cases, there is comparatively less backup credit or taxing power to fall back on, and it is possible that two communities pledging "full faith and credit" may mean two entirely different pledges of security.

The following chapter will provide a framework for analyzing GO bonds and determining just what a specific municipality's full faith and credit (taxing power) is really worth. And obviously, in that framework for analysis, each municipality's credit must rest upon its balance of revenues and expenses, which we have evaluated in this chapter.

Conclusion

A range of regional, economic, and financial data is compiled annually by the U.S. Department of Commerce, various other federal agencies, the Brookings Institution, and various other private research organizations. Their findings add an important factual backdrop to the currents of rumors and speculations about regional strengths and weaknesses that flow constantly back and forth through the financial community.

These studies point up the continuing economic and financial strength of regions that are often considered dangerous to invest in, including the Northeast, Atlantic, and Midwest states. The clearest trend these studies reveal is a pronounced convergence among all regions in terms of per capita income. The importance of this finding is that the era of financial and economic dominance of certain regions and subservience or obvious weakness of others is giving way to an evening out of both individual and corporate incomes as well as costs of and standards of living.

For this convergence to have taken place, obviously certain regions, such as the South, have certainly had to have been improved. However, while growth in the rate of income per capita is generally thought to have been far greater in the South and West than in the Northeast, in fact the Northeast has to a considerable measure held its own. It is therefore only when we break down in more detail those various components of income and components of growth that we see which factors in particular are most significant in regional terms for investment decisions. Government spending, for example, has continued to be strong in the Northeast, as it has been in the South. But the composition of that government spending has meant a shift of military procurement budgets to the South, the Pacific states, and the Mountain states and away from the Atlantic states and Great Lakes areas. Simultaneously, other government spending for welfare, transfer payments, and other noninvestment spending have continued to be strong or have even increased in the Northeast and in the Atlantic states. It is this composition of the government spending which may be considered significant—more so than the total dollar amounts of spending.

Growth is another key factor in regional analysis beyond absolute current strength. That is, various growth measures indicate how a region, a state, or a municipality may tend to change over the decades, and this change will have important consequences with regard to whether a particular portfolio of municipal credits in one region has a greater tendency to improve or decline or remain stable. On this score it appears likely that the Northeast credits have a tendency to remain stable in contrast to the credits of certain Southern or Pacific area municipalities which sometimes show a slightly greater inclination toward improvement. Yet municipal bonds of the Northeast, will probably show no greater tendency to default, and thus in today's prevailing climate of preference for the South, it may well be possible to find a range of stable and secure credits in the Northeast that are slightly underpriced because of this regional stigma. Alternatively, certain municipalities in the South may well have a greater tendency to improve over time so that a Baa on the average in that region has a slightly greater tendency to improve in credit strength to an A than a comparable credit in the Northeast.[4]

Notes to Chapter 4

[1] Certain state surplus figures are somewhat misleading because they include pension payments, which are really an ongoing expense and which go into trust funds. California's surplus is quite unique.

[2] David Graytak and Bernard Jump, "The Effect of Inflation on State and Local Government Finances; 1967–1974," Occasional Paper No. 25 of the Metropolitan Studies Program of the Maxwell School of Citizenship and Public Affairs, Syracuse University, Syracuse, 1975, pp. 32–37.

[3] Elsie M. Watters, *The Financial Outlook for State and Local Governments to 1980,* The Tax Foundation, Inc., New York, 1973, p. 11.

[4] See also Chapter 6, "Regional Differences in State and Local Finance," for a discussion of regional finance based on detailed financial variables.

chapter 5

General Obligation Bonds: A Framework for Analysis*

If there has been one single event that has changed the nature of municipal credit analysis, it was the fiscal crisis of New York City in 1975. Prior to this event, aside from the rating agencies, there was far less analysis done either on Wall Street or by the large institutional bond purchasers than there is today. GO bonds secured by the full faith and credit and taxing powers of the issuers were rarely really questioned beyond their credit ratings by either Moody's or Standard & Poor's. If Wall Street firms, bank trust departments, and insurance company portfolio managers did have in-house analysts of municipal bonds, these analysts tended to focus only on municipal revenue bonds and oftentimes carried out the corporate bond evaluations as well.

The New Interest in General Obligation Bond Analysis

The notion that states and cities could default on their GO debt was, of course, known because of the defaults during that Great Depression. However, modern bond defaults by cities and states were generally thought to be so remote a possibility that they were usually considered only in reference to a deeply depressed national economy, such as that of the early 1930s. And, as many bond salespeople were quick to point out,

* By Sylvan G. Feldstein, Robert Lamb, and Stephen P. Rappaport. Sylvan G. Feldstein has a B.S., M.Phil., and Ph.D. from Columbia University and is a municipal bond analyst and officer at Smith Barney, Harris Upham & Company, Inc. He is on the membership committee of the Municipal Analyst Group of New York (MAG) and is the founding editor of the *New Jersey Municipal Bond News*.

even during the Great Depression the repayment records of municipal bond defaults were far better than those of corporations. There seemed little reason for Wall Street underwriters and institutional purchasers to invest sizable staff resources to evaluate GO bonds. In fact, because of the legal right of communities to levy a property tax and other taxes without limitation as to rate or amount, GO bonds were long considered to be one of America's safer and less volatile investments.

However, the near bankruptcy in 1975 of New York, the nation's largest city, and the resulting liberalization in federal procedures for municipal bankruptcy catapulted GO bond analysis to the forefront of importance in the fixed-income investment community. In 1975, the New York City bondholders and noteholders were, from a legal standpoint, first in line to get paid, but they unhappily realized that a GO bond issuer would not, in order to pay noteholders and bondholders, forgo providing municipal services which were demanded by strong political constituencies. The credit analysis of GO bonds today springs largely from this realization.

Methods of Credit Analysis of General Obligation Bonds

As we have shown in Chapter 3, "The Rating Agencies: Their Role in the Municipal Marketplace," there are several different approaches to the credit analysis of GO bonds. There are those who follow Standard & Poor's concentration on the socioeconomic base of a community, and, in contrast, there are those who follow Moody's concentration on the debt burdens and ratios. Since GO credit analysis involves the same four main factors: (1) debt burden, (2) economic base, (3) administration, and (4) local government revenues, the differences between the credit analyses of any particular GO bond tend to stem from the relative emphases placed on each of these four categories.

Subtle Differences between the Standard & Poor's and Moody's Approaches

The late Jackson Phillips, former head of Moody's municipal credit rating department, believed that the credit analysis of GO bonds centered on two issues: (1) the municipality's ability to pay and (2) its willingness to pay its bonded indebtedness in a timely fashion.[1] His approach to municipal bonds, therefore, centered on the debt ratios of each municipality, which were used to determine a municipality's past, present, and future debt payment. He focused on debt trends over a 10-year period, whether rising, falling, or holding constant, and he undertook an elaborate analysis of debt ratios that compared the rate of borrowings with trends in other factors, such as property assessments, property tax collections, personal incomes, and budget operations. From these he assessed how well a community had been paying its debt and its potential ability and willingness to pay off new debt issues.

The Moody's analysis of a state bond would, for example, concentrate on the state's debt issuance, debt burden, debt history, and debt payout schedule over the life of each past, present, and presently known future bond. The ratio of debt to wealth would be an important ratio to be compared with the ratios of other states. Strong emphasis would be placed on the state's statutory debt limits and the strength of its budget operations. Finally, an effort would be made to make sure the term of the bonded debt matched the useful life of the facility being funded by the new bond.

In contrast, the credit analysis of Standard & Poor's for the same state bond would tend to emphasize socioeconomic factors of the state's population and income: "We consider an issuer's economic base the most critical element in our determination. . . . It is axiomatic that a community's fiscal health derives from its economic health. Virtually all revenue sources, from sales and income taxes to permits and property taxes, are affected by economic forces."[2] In looking at exactly the same bond that Moody's is analyzing, Standard & Poor's would concentrate on the per capita growth trends and total personal income and would use these measures to compare one state with another or with the national averages. Also of critical importance to the firm's credit judgment would be the employment rate and employment mix of the state, trends of employment and population influx or exit, and the actual age and makeup of the population. For municipalities, school districts, and counties, local building activity, the age of the housing stock, and its composition would be explored in detail along with (1) trends in property assessments and (2) trends in the mix of industrial, commercial, and residential properties. To undertake such an analysis, great reliance would be placed on documents from the Bureau of the Census, the Department of Labor, and the Department of Commerce, and their statistics would be vital sources quite distinct from those supplied by the issuer.

From Standard & Poor's perspective it is the bond issuer's social factors and economic base which pay off its debt. From Moody's perspective a bond is a debt, and, therefore, the debt and budget characteristics of the issuer must be emphasized. Although each rating agency would obtain many of the same pieces of background information about the municipal bond issuer, they tend to weigh them differently in terms of the credit risks.

This difference is evident from their respective credit ratings of the GO bonds of Allegheny County, Pennsylvania. Standard & Poor's rates the bonds AA, but Moody's rates the same bonds only Baa-1. Standard & Poor's credit rating of AA would be based on the following factors: (1) steady growth of the economy since 1969 and wealth variables above the national medians, (2) a good industrial mix with decreasing dependence on steel production, (3) improving budget operations with accounting procedures being developed to conform to generally accepted accounting principles (GAAP) in 2 years, and (4) a rapid schedule of debt retirement which mitigates the impact of future bond sales. Moody's credit rating of Baa-1 appears to be based primarily upon four budget-related factors: (1) high debt load, with more bonds expected to be issued for highway and bridge repairs and for the building of a new hospital; (2) unfunded pension liabilities; (3) unorthodox budgetary practices of shifting tax revenues from the county tax levy to the county institution district levy; and (4) an archaic procedure for property assessment (which is the basis of several court cases).[3]

Recent Developments in Credit Analysis

Our own method of credit analysis of GO bonds overlaps Moody's and Standard & Poor's approaches, but it also raises additional potential questions favored by a number of municipal bond analysts on Wall Street and by major investment firms, banks, and insurance companies. We, too, will look at a bond issuer's debt structure and economic base, but along with these factors we emphasize the management capability, the political and legal settings, and the revenue and budget characteristics of the local government. These latter considerations are especially important today because they reveal (1) the degree to which a bond issue is independent of or overdependent on outside revenue sources and (2) the degree to which the issuer is willing and able politically to maintain genuinely balanced budgets.

Reviewing the value of intergovernmental aid programs is quite complex. The investment community has the traditional viewpoint that any local government overly dependent upon outside sources of income is in a less desirable position than one that pays its own way. Yet, the budget operations of a municipality may be significantly strengthened by that outside support. For example, the school districts in Newark and Hoboken in New Jersey in 1978 received approximately 75 percent of their revenues from the state. In these two instances it is a state constitutional provision and a resulting state law which ensure that if those cities lose their property tax revenues, the state will make up the difference. As the property assessments decline, under state law, the amount of state aid increases. Therefore, does this clear dependence on state aid make the GO bonds of Hoboken and Newark stronger credit risks or poorer ones?

Another area of new concern is whether or not the community presents clear, complete, and timely accounting records. Full disclosure in footnotes and explanations of any and all changes in accounting procedures are simple tests of financial and managerial competence. Noting whether the municipality uses or does not use a certified public accounting firm and whether its reports are stated to be in conformance with GAAP and local laws are other easy and quick checks on the financial competence of the municipality's managers.

Another relatively simple test of a municipality's health is to compare the projected budget with the actual performance of operations for the previous year. Such a comparison shows how reliable the municipality's managers are in managing their finances. A final, quite useful check can be made of the tax-supported operating funds, such as the general fund and debt service fund, which can easily be compared with the capital fund and special revenue fund to determine whether or not there is a clear segregation of these monies and if the local government is indeed living within its means.

Two critical factors included by both Standard & Poor's and Moody's and which we stress in particular are (1) the actual political structure of the municipality and (2) its management's ability and willingness to maintain balanced budgets. Although full-scale systems of management administered by professionals were absent in most American cities, counties, and school districts until recently, such professional management is becoming a necessity now. The presence or absence of professional managers will directly influence such credit analysis questions as the updating of property valuations and assessment trends. Likewise, it will have an effect upon the direction of tax collections, delinquencies, and levies. The presence or absence of long-range land use, industrial planning, clear management control systems, and zoning standards will also give a quick indication of the professional caliber of a municipality's management. The political strength of the governing body's members, their length of tenure, and the rate of turnover are usually readily obtained facts that indicate governmental continuity. Also important is management's ability to resolve labor disputes: How forceful has the political leadership been in dealing with collective-bargaining issues?

Basic Questions to Ask When Analyzing a General Obligation Bond

We must point out that there is no universally accepted method or theory of credit analysis. To a considerable extent it remains more an art than a science. It requires individual judgment and personal interpretation of a range of important factors. We hope the following material will provide some simple, clear guidelines for the investor or bond analyst to consider when reviewing a GO bond.

Information relating to the analysis of GO bonds may be grouped into four categories: (1) debt, (2) budget, (3) revenues, and (4) the economics of the community.

These four categories, with slight modifications, may be applied to the GO bonds issued by states, counties, school districts, towns, or cities.

Information Related to the Debt

First, ask what is the total amount of GO debt outstanding. This figure would include all bonds and notes secured by the general taxing powers, "limited" and "unlimited," of the issuer.

Several issuers have limited-tax GO bonds outstanding. These bonds are secured by the limited power of the issuer to raise taxes. For example, while King County, Washington, issues unlimited-tax GO bonds, it also issues limited-tax bonds. The limited-tax bonds, although they are general obligations, are secured only by the revenues generated by a property tax that cannot exceed $1.80 per $1000 of assessed value in the county. Nonetheless, when calculating the issuer's true total GO debt, the limited-tax bonds and the unlimited ones, which are secured by the full taxing powers of the issuer, are initially combined.

Next, information is also required on the GO debt trend for the previous 5 years. These figures show whether or not the issuer has been using debt to an increasing degree, possibly during periods of local economic adversity and decline when capital improvements are not required. An increase in debt is not automatically negative, however, if one takes into consideration the impact of inflation and the genuine needs of the community. On the one hand, many growing suburban communities have shown rapid increases in debt as they financed the construction of water and sewer systems, new roads, and schools. On the other hand, some declining areas (such as New York City) have turned to GO debt as a way of financing budget deficits and priming the local economy. While determining the GO debt trend for 5 years, one also must be consistent in reporting the GO notes issued. If the record of debt outstanding at the end of the issuer's fiscal year is used, one could overlook the notes that were issued and redeemed during the course of the year. To avoid this omission one must determine the bonds outstanding at the year-end and must also indicate the notes sold during the course of the year.

The Security for General Obligation Debt The security behind the GO bonds sold by states, counties, school districts, and municipalities usually includes a pledge that the issuer will use its full taxing powers to see that the bondholder receives bond principal and interest when due. Under various state and local government constitutions and charters, providing such security usually involves the levy of unlimited taxes on property, a first claim by the bondholder to monies in the issuer's general fund, and the legal duty of the governing body to pass any legislation needed to increase revenues. In order to enhance further the security for their bond issues, some states (such as Wisconsin) have formally waived their rights to immunity from suits by bondholders, thereby making it easier for the bondholder to seek a mandamus against the state.

The Double-barreled Bonds While most GO bonds are secured by only the general taxing powers of the issuer, and perhaps by whatever monies are available in the issuer's general fund, some bonds are also secured by earmarked revenues which flow outside the general fund. For example, the state of Illinois issued GO Transportation, Series A bonds. These bonds are general obligations of the state and are secured by the gasoline taxes in the state's transportation fund. Because, as a matter of actual practice, debt service is paid from monies in the transportation fund, the bonds are considered to have a "double-barreled" security. We believe that if all other factors are equal, bonds having a double-barreled security should be considered a stronger credit than the issuer's straight GO bonds.

Net General Obligation Debt In order to determine the debt ratios it is necessary to determine the amount of the issuer's GO bonds that is not double-barreled, or supported by earmarked revenues. To obtain this figure one has to review the accounting reports of the issuer. While certain funds outside the issuer's general fund may be used to pay debt service, the source of monies in the specific fund will determine whether the bonds are operationally double-barreled or just straight GOs. For example, New York State has issued GO bonds for housing that are secured by monies in the state's housing fund. Although the annual debt service on these bonds is indeed paid out of the housing fund, the bonds are not genuinely self-supporting (or double-barreled). This peculiarity arises because most of the monies in the fund are appropriated by the state for grants to local governments; these monies are credited to the fund by the state comptroller for payments owed the fund by the local governments.

The net GO figure should include all those bonds that require monies from the general fund to pay debt service, for the purpose of the figure is to show the amount of GO debt that the general taxing powers of the issuer (as characterized by the general fund) support. Moody's would deduct from this figure the amount of monies at year-end in any sinking funds or debt reserves. Since it is not always certain what these reserves are invested in, we would tend not to deduct these amounts from the debt figures.

Overlapping and Underlying Debt   Still another debt figure necessary for the analyst to determine is the total amount of GO debt for which the issuer's taxpayers are responsible. If the issuer is a municipality, the overlapping debt would include the GO debt of its county, school district(s), and special districts such as water and sewage authorities which have issued GO bonds secured by unlimited property taxes. In determining how much of a county's outstanding GO debt must be included in the municipality's overlapping debt, one must determine the percentage of the real estate property values of the municipality vis-à-vis that of the county. That percentage represents the county's overlapping debt that pertains to the municipality's real property taxpayers. Similar approaches are used to determine the overlapping debt of school districts and special districts applicable to the municipality's taxpayers.

When the issuer is a county government, the same procedure is used to determine the applicable GO debt of other jurisdictions. Here, however, the debt is known as "underlying" debt and not "overlapping" debt, though the concept is the same.

One must be careful in determining what overlapping, or underlying, debt the taxpayer is indeed responsible for paying. For example, while Baltimore County, Maryland, physically surrounds the city of Baltimore, its jurisdiction stops at the city's borders. And the city is not legally considered to be within the county's jurisdiction. Therefore, taxpayers in the city of Baltimore are not responsible for the county's GO bonds, and the county taxpayers are not legally responsible for the city's GO bonds.

State Debt   Normally, when determining the overlapping, or underlying, debt of school districts, counties, or municipalities, the GO debt of their state is not considered. This is because states, unlike local governments, have broader revenue sources and potential powers under their constitutions to pay debt service on their GO bonds without reverting to property taxes, which are the major revenue sources of most local governments. Delaware is the one state where one should not exclude the overlapping GO debt from the local debt figure. Because of the state's small size and because the state provides many of the services (such as highway and school construction) which in other states are provided by local governments, the Delaware state debt is used in determining the overlapping debt figure for the local units of government.

Special Debt Besides the net GO debt and the overlapping, or underlying, GO debt, there are also three other debt obligations that many states, counties, and municipalities incur and which should be considered part of the issuer's debt load. They are outstanding leases, moral obligation commitments, and unfunded pension liabilities.

Lease Debt Many states and local governments have entered into leases or lease/purchase agreements for the construction of new buildings, highway repairs, and rentals for office space and data processing computers. The rental payments come from various sources, including general fund revenues, earmarked tax revenues, student tuition, patient fees, and amusement park fees. In some instances, such as lease/rentals of computer equipment, the leases are also secured by the equipment itself. This area of borrowing has become increasingly important in the last 20 years. As examples of the magnitude of this debt, in 1978 alone New York City's lease payments, just for office space, totaled $78 million, and the total lease/rental debt of New York State was over$3.7 billion. While they are leaders in the issuance of such debt, most GO debt issuers have lease/rental debt outstanding. Since this debt usually has a legal claim to the general revenues of the issuer, analysts should include it in their overall debt figures as well.

Moral Obligation Debt During the last 15 years many states have been issuing moral obligation municipal bonds, which were introduced in Chapter 1. These bonds, structured as revenue bonds with 1-year debt reserves, carry a potential state liability for making up deficiencies in their debt reserves, should any occur. Under most state laws, if a draw down of the reserve occurs, the bond trustee must report the amount used to the governor and state budget director. The state legislature, in turn, may appropriate the requested amount, though there is no legally enforceable obligation to do so. Bonds with this makeup provision are the so-called moral obligation bonds.

Here is a typical example of the legal language which explains this procedure:

> In order further to assure the maintenance of such urban rental debt service reserve funds, there shall be annually apportioned and paid to the agency for deposit in each urban rental debt service reserve fund such sum, if any, as shall be certified by the chairman of the agency to the

governor and director of the budget as necessary to restore such reserve fund to an amount equal to the maximum amount of principal and interest maturing and becoming due and sinking fund payments required to be made in any succeeding calendar year on the urban rental project bonds of the agency then outstanding and secured by such reserve fund. The chairman of the agency shall annually, on or before December first, make and deliver to the governor and director of the budget his certificate stating the sums, if any, required to restore each such urban rental debt service reserve fund to the amount aforesaid, and the sum so certified, if any, shall be apportioned and paid to the agency during the then current state fiscal year.

Under the Constitution of the State of New York, all monies apportioned and paid to the agency pursuant to the above quoted provision of the New York State Housing Finance Act, prior to the payment thereof, are subject to appropriation by the State legislature for such purpose. Accordingly, such provision of the New York State Housing Finance Act does not constitute a legally enforceable obligation upon the part of the State of New York nor create a debt on behalf of the State of New York enforceable against the State.[4]

Since 1960 over 20 states have issued bonds with this unique security feature. The first state was New York State with its housing finance agency (HFA) "moral obligation" bonds. This feature was developed by a well-known bond attorney, John Mitchell, who had extensive experience and knowledge of state constitutions and laws.

In the history of moral obligation financing, most of this debt has been self-supporting—no state financial assistance has been required. However, in all the instances where the moral pledge was called upon, the respective state legislatures responded by appropriating the necessary amounts of monies. This occurred in Pennsylvania with the bonds and notes of the Pennsylvania HFA; in New Jersey with the bonds of the South Jersey Port Authority; and in New York State with the bonds and notes of the UDC and with the nonprofit housing bonds of the HFA.

Unfunded Pension Liabilities Still another special debt figure that the analyst must develop is the current unfunded pension liability of the issuer. That is, what is the difference between the expected assets of the public employee pension system at current annual contribution rates and the future benefits to be paid out to the issuer's employees? In assessing this figure the analyst must determine when the pension system was last audited, who performed the audit, and what the auditor's assumptions were concerning, among other factors, the average age of public employee entry and retirement. The credit analyst should also determine whether the issuer has a plan in operation to reduce the unfunded liability and, if so, how long it will take (10, 20, or 50 years, for example) to eliminate the liability. Still another question to raise concerning pensions is their legal basis. That is, can pension benefits unilaterally be reduced by the local governments? Such reduction is allowed in some jurisdictions but not in others. An example of the latter would be New York State, where the state constitution prevents the reduction of pension benefits once they are granted to the public employees. Therefore, the unfunded pension liabilities of local governments in New York must be taken much more seriously than in states where such guarantees do not exist.

For purposes of determining the special debt figure, which represents the potential debt liability in a worst-case environment, the lease obligations, the moral obligations, and the unfunded pension liabilities are combined, and one figure is used.

Straight Revenue Debt   Besides the general obligation, special lease, moral obligation, and pension liability, many governing bodies have also issued revenue bonds which are secured solely by the monies generated by the revenue-producing enterprises. Municipalities have issued water and sewer revenue bonds, and many states have issued toll road revenue bonds, most of which do not have a legal claim to the general taxing powers of the respective municipality or state. Nonetheless, the credit analyst should tabulate the issuer's outstanding revenue debt. Though this debt is not factored into the debt ratios, it is important to know the total borrowing activities of the issuer.

Future Bond Financings   While some GO issuers have small amounts of debt outstanding, they may be required to borrow significant amounts of money in the future. In order to factor this possibility into the credit assessment, the analyst must learn what the future financing plans are. As an example, a municipality that will have to issue large amounts of GO bonds to finance the construction of mandatory federal improvements for pollution control is of weaker quality than one that has already met the standards.

However, not all large-scale programs of capital construction are in themselves undesirable. Issuers that are borrowing heavily today to construct their physical infrastructures, such as new roads, schools, and water systems, may be better long-term investments than those issuers who have postponed making improvements and, as a result, have much less GO debt outstanding. The latter may very well face the prospect of extensive capital expenditures, somewhere down the road, in order to remain attractive for continued economic development and just to meet the service demands of the taxpayers.

As an example, in the early 1960s the GO bonds of Newark, New Jersey, and Parsippany-Troy Hills, New Jersey, were rated by Moody's as

A and Baa, respectively; Standard & Poor's gave the rating BBB for both. Newark was seen as a mature, developed community with little need for additional borrowing. In contrast, Parsippany-Troy Hills, a growing, youthful suburban community, had relatively higher borrowing needs in order to finance new streets and schools. Thus at the time Moody's considered Parsippany-Troy Hills to be a weaker credit than Newark, but Standard & Poor's considered both communities comparable. Yet today Moody's and Standard & Poor's credit ratings for Newark are Baa and BBB, respectively, and their credit ratings for Parsippany-Troy Hills are A-1 and A+, respectively. The credit analyst must make a qualitative judgment on the future of the issuer 10 to 15 years later—no matter how difficult or speculative it is to do so, and regardless of how sizable the financing plans for current or future bonds appear to be.

Debt Limits   For many years credit analysts viewed debt limits as major safeguards for the bondholder. Those GO debt limits which are restricted by the need for electoral approvals before bonds can be sold are still meaningful checks on excessive borrowing. However, debt limits which are tied to percentages of the issuer's real estate wealth have become less significant. This has resulted from the experience of New York City in 1974–1975. In spite of state constitutional debt limits, the city had sold, over many years, amounts of GO bonds which were beyond its financial means and yet several billion dollars below its debt limits. The experience of New York City reveals the weakness of debt limits as a real safeguard for the bondholder.

Information Related to the Budget

The second general category of information required by the analyst is related to the budget. Here, we are concerned about questions of executive powers, budgetary control, public services, accounting history, and the potential impacts of taxpayer revolts.

Powers of the Chief Executives   Learning the form of government of the GO bond issuer is very important to the analyst. Governments that have strong executive systems (i.e., strong governors, strong county executives, or strong mayors) are, in general, preferred to those that do not. This preference results because strong centralized executive systems have the potential to deal quickly and efficiently with unforeseen budgetary and economic problems. Perhaps the importance of this is best seen in the city of Cleveland. Cleveland has a weak chief executive who has very little power beyond his access to the press. His limitations include the need for electoral approval for increasing property and personal income taxes that are above the state-allowed levels; no control over many of the city's essential services; limited appointment and removal powers; and a term of office which is only 2 years, so that he must consistently focus on reelection strategies rather than policy directives. As a result of this fact and the city's overall economic and political problems, the city defaulted in 1978 on its GO notes and is expected to be a continuing investment risk.

In the 1970s the cities of Detroit, Baltimore, Newark, and Boston all had similar economic problems—in the cases of Newark and Detroit, economic problems far more serious than those of Cleveland—but they all managed to avoid defaults. One possible reason why these cities have been able to manage their problems is that they have strong executive forms of government, whereas Cleveland does not.

There are three basic components of a strong executive, regardless of whether the chief executive is a governor, county executive, or mayor. First, the chief executive must have at least a 4-year term of office with the right to seek reelection without limit. Second, the chief executive must control three aspects of the annual budgetary process: (1) the preparation of the budget, which is presented to the legislative body for approval; (2) line-item veto powers over the approved budget; and (3) control over the implementation of the budget, including the power to determine allotment periods, to fill personnel lines, and to award contracts. The third component is the ability to control the bureaucracy through extensive personnel appointment and removal authority.

Services Directly Provided In order to project future budgetary demands it is necessary to determine the services which are provided by the issuer. In general, issuers that provide a full range of services have a weaker credit quality than those which provide only basic minimum services. For a municipality basic services include utilities (such as water and sewage treatment), garbage pickups, street maintenance, police and fire protection, and recreational programs. Large municipalities that provide additional services, including extensive welfare programs, hospital care, housing, mass transportation, and higher education, usually have bureaus and departments that are captives of pressure groups which demand these services without regard to budgetary consequences.

General Budget Appropriations by Function While many issuers provide the same services, quantitative distinctions should be made in order to determine what the budgetary priorities of the issuer really are. This is best done by determining the general budget appropriations in the current fiscal year by function, amount, and percentage of the total budget appropriation.

Accounting Procedures and Funds The most desirable accounting system is known as a "modified accrual system." In general, in this system revenues are only considered received when they are physically in the issuer's general fund. At the same time, expenditures are deemed to have occurred when contracts and other legal liabilities are entered into by the issuer, even though warrants for payment of these obligations may not have been made yet. The modified accrual system is the most honest and fiscally conservative accounting system. Many issuers, however, prefer other accounting systems which allow their governing bodies to have greater flexibility in the budgetary process. For example, for issuers who define "revenues" to include monies that are due but not necessarily received, a budget can quickly be balanced: The governing body levies a new tax or increases projected revenues from existing taxes and then adds the new amount to the revenue side of the budget. On the expenditure side, those issuers that use "cash expenditure accounting" can easily close their fiscal year with a budget surplus by just delaying actual payments until after the new fiscal year has begun.

Audit Procedures　Auditing is yet another important area of concern for the investor and bond analyst. The best auditing procedure is for the issuer to be audited annually by an outside certified public accountant (CPA) who applies generally accepted accounting principles, using the modified accrual system of accounting. For sound cost-related reasons, however, many issuers (states, in particular) do not have such audits performed.

If no audit by an outside CPA is commissioned, the next best safeguard for the bondholder is to have the issuer's accounts annually audited by a public official who is politically independent of the chief executive. Many states and municipalities have treasurers and comptrollers who are also elected public officials or appointees of the legislative branch. The institutional rivalry and competition between these elected public officials can provide checks and balances in the accounting areas.

Budget Trends　In order to determine the overall budgetary soundness of the issuer, it is necessary for the analyst to determine the revenues and expenditures of the issuer's general fund and all operating funds for at least a 3-year period. In this way one can see whether the issuer has balanced budgets, budget surpluses, or budget deficits. Clearly, those communities that have yearly budget deficits (for example, New York City has had them in one form or another since at least 1965) are serious investment risks, regardless of how positive the other analytical variables may appear to be.

Still another related question to ask is: What was the cash fund balance in the issuer's general fund at the end of the most recent fiscal year? While some issuers may show budget deficits during the previous 3-year period, the deficits may be planned in order to reduce a fund balance surplus. Surpluses sometimes accumulate in state governments which have elastic revenue structures made up of income and sales taxes. During expansions in the local economies or during inflationary periods, these revenues will greatly increase. Many states, such as California and Minnesota, build substantial budget surpluses during such periods. They can then draw upon these surpluses either to meet revenue shortfalls caused by recessions or to meet increased wage and salary demands caused by inflation.

Short-Term Debt as a Percentage of the General Fund Receipts of the Prior Year   In order to determine how well the issuer matches revenue flows to expenditure flows, it is necessary to determine the percentage of short-term debt in relation to the issuer's general fund revenues of the prior year. The short-term debt does not include the issuer's bond anticipation notes (BANs) but does include both tax anticipation notes (TANs) and revenue anticipation notes (RANs). Issuers that are committed to policies that require them to borrow large amounts of money to meet expenditure schedules are clearly less attractive than issuers that have coordinated their expenditure flow with their revenue flow so as to minimize the need for issuing annual short-term debt.

Budgets and Taxpayer Revolts   In looking at budget trends one must also assess the potential impacts of newly enacted or anticipated budget and tax limitation measures. Examples of these include (1) the 5 percent "Cap" laws in New Jersey, which since 1976 have limited the annual budget increases of the local government to not more than 5 percent, and (2) Proposition 13 in California, which significantly restricted local property tax revenue growth, the issuance of new GO bonds, and other functions. While each measure must be carefully reviewed, in general, it can be said that taxpayer attempts to reduce taxes and government expenditures on the local levels by these measures have positive benefits for GO bonds. At the same time, these measures may have negative consequences for the overlapping GO bonds of the state governments. On the local level such restrictions on budget expenditures and tax collections can result in reductions in some municipal services; these restrictions can also provide governing bodies and budget directors with the legal weapons and supportive political climates for resisting constituent demands for increased services and for bargaining with their local organized public employees—i.e., with the unions representing fire fighters, police, schoolteachers, etc. In the last 10 years, the militancy of these unions has been very costly. Since approximately two-thirds of the annual expenditures by local governments are for salaries, pensions, and related purposes, curbs in these areas can be very beneficial in slowing down the escalating costs of local governments.

While the political activities and effectiveness of public employee unions and other pressure groups are lessened at the local government level, they may be correspondingly increased at the state government level. This pressure results from their attempts to have the states provide increased state aid to local governments or to have the state governments begin to finance and operate public programs that were originally the responsibility of the local governments. An example of this development is in California. Since the enactment of Proposition 13 and as a result of increased political pressures, the funds that the state has raised are replacing the funds that localities are no longer permitted to raise. One result is that the percentage of certain local government budgets financed by local revenues has decreased at the expense of the state's own budget surplus. From a long-term point of view the GO bonds of the state should weaken in security as a result of this, since the state's budgetary reserves have already declined dramatically.

When looking at both the GO bonds of the local governments and those of the states, credit analysts must determine both the direct and the indirect implications of specific tax and budget restrictions. This is important in order to determine in a budgetary sense who benefits from the specific restrictions, who is not affected, and who is hurt. Obviously, to answer these questions analysts must study and make conclusions about the relationships and interdependencies between pressure groups, such as public employee unions, and political parties and leaders. Credit analysts invite criticism by speculating on the political implications of proposed tax restrictions, particularly if they later are proved to be incorrect. They must nonetheless offer investors their opinion of the direct and indirect political effects of the proposals.

Information Related to Revenues

The third general category of information covers data relating to the nature of the issuer's specific types and amounts of revenue.

Primary Revenues   The initial question is: What are the issuer's primary revenues? In general, states have the most diversified revenue sources, which can include personal income taxes, a variety of corporation and business taxes, real and personal property taxes, death and gift taxes, sales taxes, motor vehicle taxes, severance taxes, user fees, and federal grants-in-aid. The attractiveness of state credits over the credits of counties, municipalities, and school districts is largely a result of the diversity of a state's revenue sources and a state's ability, under its own laws, to make its revenue base even broader.

The local governments, in contrast, rely primarily on property taxes for their revenues. Some counties and municipalities have broadened their revenue bases through sales and income taxes. Such diversification is usually very difficult for a local governmental unit to initiate, since state legislative approvals are normally required. Nevertheless, many cities in recent years have convinced their respective state legislatures to grant them taxing powers beyond the property tax.

General Fund Revenue Trends Besides learning what the overall primary revenue sources are, the credit analyst should determine what the specific revenues have been in the issuer's general fund over a 4-year period. This is the governmental fund account in which all unrestricted revenues which can be used for debt service are placed. The reason for going back 4 years is to identify trends that may be developing in the issuer's revenue flows.

In the case of issuers who pay debt service on their GO bonds from a debt service fund (which, for example, may receive property taxes that do not pass through the general fund), this fund should also be included. The reason for separating general fund revenues from the restricted ones is that many revenues received by issuers, such as certain federal grants, are restricted as to purpose and cannot be used for debt service on GO bonds. Since many local governments, such as school districts and municipalities, include restricted monies in their general fund reporting, the credit analyst will have to separate the unrestricted portion from the restricted portion.

For urban counties, school districts, and municipalities, real property taxes, state grants, and federal aid monies are the major sources of revenue. In many cities, state and federal monies have displaced the property tax as the major revenue source. In most suburban and rural areas the property tax is the dominant source of revenue.

Economic Factors

The fourth major category of information required by the analyst concerns the overall economic health of the issuer. Indicators of economic activity and well-being include the trends of real estate valuation, population, unemployment, and total personal income.

While separately these economic indicators provide incomplete assessments of the economic vitality of the issuer, taken as a whole they provide clues as to the strengths and weaknesses of each community. Obtaining the data for the informational categories is easy, since data is available from either the local governments themselves or publications of the U.S. Bureau of the Census and the U.S. Department of Labor.

Real Estate Valuation Trend A major index of the growth of a community is the yearly change in its real estate value. Here, analysts are not as interested in the assessed real values, which are used for tax purposes, as they are in the full, or market, values of the real estate. This would only include the taxable real property. Tracking these values over a 4-year period provides a good indication of the health of the community and provides clear indications of a declining or stagnant community. It is also important to keep in mind that in an inflationary environment, growth in real estate values is not enough to indicate that a community is becoming wealthier; the annual growth must be higher than the annual inflation rate.

Ten Largest Taxable Properties In looking at counties, municipalities, and school districts, it is useful to identify the 10 largest taxable properties in terms of their full real values and business purposes. In so doing, the analyst can determine how much of the real estate base may be dependent on railroads, utilities, and private corporations. In the Northeast some of the largest real estate holdings belonged to the Penn Central Transportation Company, which for many years paid no real estate taxes on its properties. Additionally, certain communities may be dependent on one major shopping center or manufacturing plant for most of their property taxes. Therefore, the viability of that single property will determine the community's overall economic viability.

Properties: Taxable or Tax-exempt? When reviewing counties, municipalities, and school districts, it is necessary to learn what percentages of the total real estate wealth are exempt from local property taxes. Although a municipality can add new office buildings, hospitals, and governmental structures to its inner core, their contributions to the general real estate wealth of the community will be limited if they are tax-abated or -exempted. A corollary is to determine the distribution of the community's taxable property by purpose: What percentage is residential, commercial, industrial, held by a utility or railroad? From these figures the analyst can determine accurately which segment of the community's real estate is carrying the burden of the property taxes.

Building Permit Trend In looking at counties, municipalities, and school districts, another component of economic vitality is the building permit trend. Here the analyst is looking for at least a 3-year record of the annual total dollar value of all permits granted by the local governmental bodies for building and construction improvement. These figures are checked to make sure that building permits for tax-exempt properties are not included. One major value of this indicator is its ability to show the degree of business confidence in the future of the local economy.

Five Largest Employers It is important to learn who the five largest employers are in each county, municipality, or school district to be analyzed. The analyst should determine the number of workers as well as the nature of the business. In this way the analyst can determine how stable the community is and how dependent the local economy may be on one industry, such as the automobile industry (in Michigan), coal mining (in West Virginia), and textiles (in South Carolina).

Population Trend　Another useful index for investigating states and local governments is the population trend. An increasing population usually means a growing economy, while a declining or stagnant population usually indicates economic weakness. Besides having the raw population figures, it is worthwhile to break down the population by age group and by income level. A community that has a high percentage of senior citizens may have greater political demands for municipal services and reduced property taxes than one that does not. Also, communities with large numbers of unemployed or low-income residents usually require costly social services, and these services increase the budgets of the local schools, courts, welfare systems, and police departments.

Job Trend　Employment data are very necessary to the credit analyst. A 10-year comparison of the absolute number of employed people and their percentage of the population provides another clue as to the economic direction of the area. It is also helpful to determine the distribution of the nonfarm employment for at least the most recent year. The employment categories include manufacturing; retail/ wholesale trade; services; contract construction; and federal, state, and local government employment. This breakdown of employment according to type of job helps indicate, among other things, whether or not the economy is being supported by increased governmental jobs or by a vibrant private sector.

Unemployment Trend　It is helpful to compare local unemployment trends covering at least 3 years. It is useful to examine both the annual unemployment rate and the average number of workers unemployed during the year. For counties, municipalities, and school districts the comparisons should focus on the unemployment rates within the boundaries of the local area, the state, and the nation. If the unit of local government is within a metropolitan area, it is also useful to include the unemployment rates of the metropolitan area.

Economic Activity Indicators for States　When reviewing the economies of states, there are five categories of information which are particularly useful:

1. Statewide personal income trend for the past 3 years
2. Statewide retail sales trend for the past 3 years
3. Statewide motor vehicle registration trend for the past 3 years

4. Total number of people within a state who have received federal welfare for the past 3 years

5. Per capita personal income today, compared with the figure 5 years ago and with the national per capita income figures

The information gathered for these categories will quickly show whether a state is becoming wealthier in absolute terms and when compared with other regions of the country.

Economic Activity Indicators for Counties   When reviewing counties, municipalities, and school districts, the analyst will find that the following seven categories of information are useful:

1. Percentage of the population in the low-income bracket
2. Number of residents receiving federal welfare
3. Per capita income, compared with the national average
4. Median family income
5. Median home value
6. Percentage of owner-occupied housing
7. Age distribution of the population

Red Flags to Watch for

Perhaps the most critical short-term function of the credit analysis of GO bonds is to identify what might be termed the "red flags," or trends suggesting potential problems, in the fiscal stability of states and municipalities. There are four categories of red flags:

1. Revenue-based indicators
    a. Decreasing value of taxable property
    b. Increasing delinquent taxes
    c. Increasing tax rate
    d. Decreasing number and value of building permits issued
    e. Increasing incidence of actual revenues below budgeted amounts

2. Expenditure-based indicators
    a. Increasing excesses of current expenditures over current local revenues
    b. Increasing current expenditures in excess of total revenues
    c. Increasing expenditures in excess of the inflation rate
    d. Increasing incidence of actual expenditures in excess of the approved budget

     e. Continuing increases in the amount of the unfunded portions of the pension programs
3. Cash management indicators
     a. Reducing aggregate short-term investments
     b. Increasing amounts of unpaid current obligations
4. Debt indicators
     a. Increasing amounts of bonded indebtedness while the property values remain stagnant
     b. Increasing need to borrow in order to meet debt service requirements
     c. Use of long-term debt to fund operating expenditures
     d. Year-to-year increases in the amount of short-term borrowing remaining unpaid at the end of the fiscal year[5]

These are general signals to indicate the potential decline in the ability of a municipality to perform its functions within fiscally sound parameters.

Important Debt Ratios

In addition to looking for possible early warning signals, the analyst should develop debt-related ratios. The value of the ratios is twofold: (1) the ratios are among the analytical tools for evaluating the creditworthiness of the issuer's GO bonds, and (2) the per capita data allow the analyst to compare bonds of different communities.

Net GO Debt per Capita This figure represents the non-self-supporting GO bonds divided by the population. In theory, it represents the amount of debt per person that is supported by the general taxing powers of the issuer in the issuer's general fund. In general, the lower the number, the more attractive the issuer.

Net GO and Overlapping, or Underlying, Debt per Capita This ratio applies not to states but to the local units of government. It is a per capita debt figure which includes the issuer's own net GO debt as well as the GO debt of overlapping, or underlying, jurisdictions.

Net GO Debt as a Percentage of Full Real Estate Valuation This percentage indicates the debt as compared with the real estate wealth as represented in the most recent real estate evaluation. This statistic is perhaps one of the most important figures for the credit analyst, since it indicates the issuer's ability to pay.

Net GO and Overlapping, or Underlying, Debt as a Percentage of Full Real Estate Valuation For counties, municipalities, and school districts this figure is also used. It represents the relationship of the issuer's full real estate value to the sum of the issuer's own GO and overlapping GO debt.

Net GO Debt as a Percentage of Personal Income   For a state this figure is another major indicator of the ability of the taxpayer to support its debt. While this figure is desirable when reviewing all GO bond issuers, oftentimes such data are only available concerning states.

GO Debt Payout in 10 Years   This figure shows whether the issuer has a relatively rapid debt retirement schedule, which is desirable, or a debt service stretched out to, say, 30 or 40 years. In some cases payment of debt service on bonds may continue beyond the useful life of the capital projects financed by the original bond proceeds. While the debt payout schedule is not a debt ratio, it is necessary for evaluating the actual ratio figures. For example, high debt ratios may be less significant if most of the issuer's debt will be retired within 10 years. But above-average debt ratios combined with a slow debt retirement schedule certainly weakens a security substantially.

Each year, Moody's publishes its own debt ratio medians, which are derived from the hundreds of state, county, school district, and municipal GO bond issues that it annually reviews. The credit analyst looking at a new issue can quickly compare the issuer's debt ratios with the current Moody's medians to see how the new issuer compares with other issuers. Table 5-1 is based upon Moody's GO debt medians for 1978.

Conclusion

After having determined whether the GO bonds are double-barreled or not (and if so, what the quality of the specific revenue stream is); after having gathered the information about the issuer's debt structure, budget, revenue operations, and economic forces; after having checked for the red flags and trends; and after having compared the issuer's ratios of various debt burdens with Moody's most recently published medians, the credit analyst can make a generalization about the investment quality of the bond under review. While all these elements together are important indicators of bond quality, each provides, if taken separately, only a single isolated element not in itself sufficient for full-scale analysis. Therefore, the analyst must carefully review all these indicators so as to arrive at a judicious credit conclusion concerning the degree of risk involved in purchasing an issuer's GO bonds. As noted earlier in this chapter, this evaluation process is more an art than a science. Nonethe-

TABLE 5-1 Moody's GO Debt Ratio Medians for 1978

Group and population*	Net debt per capita				Ratio in relation to estimated full value				Ratio in relation to personal income
	Direct median	Overall			Direct median	Overall			Direct median
		Low	Median	High		Low	Median	High	
Cities over 1,000,000	$288.98	$360.04	$484.82	$ 849.32	3.0%	2.3%	5.8%	7.5%	—
Cities 500,000 to 1,000,000	312.54	273.20	471.81	976.71	2.5	1.8	4.2	11.8	—
Cities 300,000 to 500,000	265.54	174.81	500.01	1,091.04	2.3	1.1	4.4	14.3	—
Cities 200,000 to 300,000	287.10	301.37	451.42	1,251.23	3.0	2.0	4.4	13.4	—
Cities 100,000 to 200,000	277.05	205.02	468.10	1,602.99	2.6	1.8	4.4	12.1	—
Cities 50,000 to 100,000	279.90	177.00	460.06	1,439.08	2.6	1.6	4.4	12.9	—
Cities 25,000 to 50,000	322.60	106.84	612.45	2,440.05	2.5	0.9	4.6	15.0	—
Cities 10,000 to 25,000	305.40	181.14	536.62	3,529.61	2.7	1.2	4.6	16.9	—
Cities under 10,000	512.51	118.00	772.90	6,306.19	4.0	1.5	6.2	14.0	—
Counties over 1,000,000	87.67	332.37	567.87	979.28	1.2	2.2	4.4	10.2	—
Counties 250,000 to 1,000,000	82.05	126.76	492.47	1,194.00	0.8	1.1	4.1	8.6	—
Counties 100,000 to 250,000	128.33	94.58	473.91	793.13	1.1	1.0	3.5	9.7	—
Counties under 100,000	152.64	74.21	371.60	6,746.47	1.5	0.5	3.2	10.1	—
All states	196.90	—	—	—	1.7	—	—	—	3.2%

* School districts are included in the city categories.
SOURCE: Moody's Investors Service Annual Survey, 1978. Reprinted by permission.

less, we have attempted here to identify the basic background information that is required for making an overall credit assessment.

Notes to Chapter 5

[1] From an interview with Jackson Phillips on Sept. 12, 1978.

[2] Standard & Poor's Corporation, *Municipal and International Bond Ratings: An Overview*, p. 12.

[3] This is indicated in Moody's "Credit Report on Allegheny County," dated Aug. 11, 1978.

[4] This quotation is taken from an official statement for a $150,000,000 Urban Rental Project moral obligation bond sale held by the New York State HFA. The official statement was dated Sept. 17, 1979.

[5] This is based on a checklist by Hyman Grossman of Standard & Poor's, published in the *New Jersey Municipal Bond News*, vol. 2, no. 4, April 1976, pp. 1, 4. See also p. 263 of this text.

chapter 6

Regional Differences in State and Local Finance

One way to view the economic and financial variables discussed in the previous chapters, and one that has received wide coverage in the nation's press, is from the "regional" perspective. There has been much publicity given to broad-based statistics that seem to show that the Southern regions of the country are growing at faster economic rates than the nation's more mature regions. Such statements have implied that municipal credits in the South were stronger than those of other areas, and this fact has had a psychological spillover effect, thus impairing the marketability of many municipal issues in the Northeast region. Viewing state and local finance from a regional perspective does not really reveal much about the creditworthiness of a particular state, municipality, or revenue authority. Creditworthiness may be more easily shown through an analysis of fund balances, contingent liabilities like lease-rental payments, or hardcore economic data on a locality's economic base. However, a regional analysis provides a picture of America, its economic and financial trends, and its taxing and spending preferences. And, most important, such an analysis provides the comparative perspective on the economic and financial structures of America's states. It is this comparative perspective that is precisely what municipal credit analysis is all about.

For regional comparisons, however, the most significant finding from Table 6-1 is that the real income gap between the Mid-Atlantic region, the West, and the Great Lakes region appears to be widening. In these instances, contrary to popular belief, the Mid-Atlantic region is registering a relatively stable income growth that exceeds the growth of at least two other regions of the nation. For the last 30 years, New England's growth rate has hovered around the mean of the nation. So as a result, New England has held its own and has not shown a decline in real income relative to the nation's average.

TABLE 6-1   The Regional Real Personal Income Gap, 1929–1977*

Subregions	1929	1934	1944	1954	1964	1974	1977
Mid-Atlantic	133	149	123	113	113	115	117
West	115	117	125	118	110	108	105
New England	112	123	100	95	98	96	95
Great Lakes	105	101	107	110	105	103	102
Rocky Mountain	85	87	95	98	88	83	89
Plains	75	62	85	88	87	91	93
Southwest	64	64	80	83	83	86	87
Southeast	50	57	64	65	73	82	85

* 100 = U.S. mean. All numbers in Table 6-1 are percentages of the U.S. average of 100.

SOURCE: Adapted from *Empire State Report*, vol. 2, no. 9, p. 343. (Compiled from statistics from the U.S. Advisory Commission on Intergovernmental Relations. Figures are not controlled for cost-of-living differentials.)

As shown in Table 6-2, the Northeast still maintains a significant lead in per capita income over every other region in the country. Moreover, as percentages of the nation's average, the per capita incomes of the subregions of the Northeast are the only per capita incomes in the country above the national mean (using a mean of 100). New England is 4 percent above the national average, and the Mid-Atlantic area is 9 percent above it. What is also significant is the extent to which other

TABLE 6-2   Percentage Change in per Capita Income as a Percentage of the U.S. Average

	Per capita income, 1975	1964	1975	Percentage point change, 1964–1975
Northeast	$6305	113%	108%	−5
New England	6086	108	104	−4
Mid-Atlantic	6377	115	109	−6
Midwest	6011	103	103	0
Great Lakes	6131	107	105	−2
Great Plains	5714	92	98	+6
South	5120	81	88	+7
South Atlantic	5353	84	92	+8
South Central	4896	78	84	+6
West	6184	110	106	−4
Mountain	5374	90	92	+2
Pacific	6461	116	111	−5
United States	5834	100	100	0

SOURCE: Adapted from *National Journal*, June 26, 1976, p. 87. (Compiled from statistics from the U.S. Department of Commerce, Bureau of Labor Statistics.)

subregions are below the mean per capita income of the nation. Indeed, the Mountain and the South Atlantic states both are 8 percent below the mean per capita income. For the South Central region this gap rises to a whopping 16 percent.

To be sure, on a trend basis, the Northeast has, since 1964, dropped 5 percentage points from its former per capita income. However, the Midwest registered no increase above the mean over the same decade, and the West has registered a decline of 4 percentage points. Furthermore, no region or subregion showed what most observers would consider to be a dramatic increase in per capita income. Indeed, the region that registered the highest increase was the South Atlantic region, but even in this case the increase in per capita income was only 8 percent. In general, then, the prevailing myth that the states in the so-called sunbelt have shot ahead of the "old Northeast" does not appear to be born out by the facts.

Even if the income comparisons (of individuals or families) are restricted to large cities in the Northeast as opposed to those in the South, the Northeast still shows a per capita income substantially greater than that in the South. Robert Reishauer of the Brookings Institution recently wrote that "by and large, cities with the highest relative concentrations of low-income persons are located in the South, the poorest region of the country."[1]

Convergence of Regional Income: Importance of Growth

The U.S. government provides historical regional data as well as future projections of regional economic trends and income streams broken down into a vast variety of subcategories. It provides these statistics in its 10-year census reports and in *Area Economic Projections*, published periodically by the U.S. Commerce Department. They break down these statistics of historic and projected income growth by state, by region, and by standard metropolitan statistical unit (SMSU).

What emerges from these government studies is that the incomes and costs of living in each region of this country are becoming more homogenized and are tending to converge. For example, the Commerce Department's *Area Economic Projections 1990* concludes, "Historically, trends in relative income per capita (area per capita income expressed as a percent of national per capita income) in most areas have shown a pronounced tendency to converge slowly toward 100."[2]

All income streams appear to be growing (even if only slightly), but much of this growth in each region is pure inflation. As shown by various government reports and independent research studies that have used "shift share" analysis to analyze how each region and subregion is doing in comparison with other regions and subregions and with its own past figures over time, the one clear trend is this leveling off of all regions when total and individual incomes are considered.

Yet these figures indicate that the long dominance of the Northeast is becoming a thing of the past. The Northeast has for various reasons held its position relatively constant with regard to absolute income levels. But as far as growth is concerned, the South Atlantic, South Central, Pacific, and Midwest regions appear, according to certain measurements and scales, to be growing faster.

One reason why the Northeast has continued to maintain its apparent stability involves transfer payments from the federal government. Social security and welfare payments, while productive *on paper*, do not bolster a region's income. So long as these payments continue to grow and to be especially associated with a particular region, state, or municipality, they can continue to hurt that area's productivity—even when they, and thus the area's income, keep mounting.

Such increasing trends in transfer payments, or types of income not derived from the production of new goods and services, and especially in the percentage of the population who are unemployed are the statistics that usually lead to critical appraisals of New York and the Northeast as "a welfare sink" and of both as slower growth areas. The percentage of the population actually at work is, from this standpoint, a critical index of regional growth or stagnation. For example, if Houston and Dallas were contrasted with New York City, Philadelphia, and Cleveland on these scales, both the economic statistics and bond ratings would tend to reflect these differences.

However, such figures do not disprove the continued stability of the Northeast. Nor do these figures on growth indicate that Northeast credits are either of poor quality or more likely to default. Indeed, some of the worst economic areas, such as Newark, that have been losing tax-payers and industries have strong credits on some of their bonds because of federal and state backup.

The various regional studies suggest that while Northeast credits are not more likely to default than those of other regions, such as the South, the Midwest, or the Pacific states, Northeast bonds may be less likely to be upgraded or to improve in credit quality. Thus from the standpoint of an investor, the odds of buying an "improving credit" in the Northeast are poorer than in the South. (For those concerned with getting their principal back on time and each of their interest payments, there will be little risk if they hold the bonds until maturity. But if they sell before then, the picture becomes more cloudy, no matter what region of the country their bonds are from.) This improvement in credit quality means simply that if one bought an AA bond in the Northeast, it will probably stay an AA for the decade, but if one bought a BBB in certain parts of the South, it might well have a better chance of becoming an A.

Defense

Defense expenditures, like transfer payments, have had a strong impact on certain regions in the past 20 years. Ohio might still be exceedingly strong economically if war was still fought primarily with heavy steel-plated equipment, such as tanks. Because military procurement today is more concentrated on expenditures for missiles, electronic instruments, jets, and other sophisticated technological devices, California, Texas, Washington, and other states have been helped substantially.

Population and Unemployment

There is no question that the Northeast registered the lowest percentage gain in population since 1970, as shown in Table 6-3. While the South and West had almost 9 percent increases in population, the Northeast

TABLE 6-3   Population Shifts and Unemployment (In Thousands)

	1970	1975	Population percentage change	Percentage of unemployment
Northeast	49,061	49,461	0.8	9.5
New England	11,847	12,198	3.0	10.3
Mid-Atlantic	37,213	37,263	0.1	9.3
Midwest	56,593	57,669	1.9	8.1
Great Lakes	40,266	40,979	1.8	9.0
Great Plains	16,328	16,690	2.2	5.8
South	62,055	67,399	8.6	7.4
South Atlantic	29,922	67,399	10.2	7.9
South Central	32,133	34,399	6.6	6.9
West	34,838	37,878	8.7	9.2
Mountain	8,290	9,644	16.3	7.5
Pacific	26,549	28,234	6.3	9.8
United States	203,304	213,121	4.8	8.5

SOURCE: Adapted from *National Journal*, June 26, 1976, pp. 886–887. (Compiled from statistics from the Department of Commerce, Bureau of Labor Statistics, and the U.S. Advisory Commission on Intergovernmental Relations.)

did not even gain one full percent. However, it is interesting to note that the New England subregion of the Northeast gained 3 percent in population, indicating that New York and New Jersey lost population. New England's 3 percent increase outstripped the gain made by the Midwest and exceeded that of the Midwest's two subregions: the Great Lakes and the Great Plains.

There is an ongoing dispute concerning whether or not increases in population directly affect a region's, state's, or municipality's debt-paying capacity. There are clear arguments to be made on each side of this case. The influx of immigrants, illegal aliens, students, or prisoners would normally decrease the debt-paying capacity of a region or a municipality. The influx of high-income professionals would tend to strengthen the debt-paying capacity of a region. Therefore, without knowing in detail the makeup of the new groups entering a region, state, or municipality, there can be no direct causal link between sheer population increase and a region's debt-paying capacity.

The isolated fact that the Northeast did not gain in population does not indicate much about the Northeast's debt-paying capacity. Thus we must compare the employment and unemployment characteristics of this region with those of other areas to assess whether the Northeast has fallen behind. In Table 6-3 it is clear that when unemployment statistics for each area are considered, there are wide disparities when regions are broken down into subregions. While unemployment was about the same in both the Midwest and the South, there was no discernible difference in unemployment between the other two regions—the Northeast and the West. In other words, the idea that the Northeast has registered much higher unemployment rates than all other regions and subregions in the country is subject to contention.

Real unemployment is not rising faster in the Northeast than in other regions; in fact, it is rising more slowly. It is true that the highest percentage of unemployment of any subregion occurred in New England, one subregion of the Northeast, but this rise in unemployment was, we believe, related to an influx of immigrants. A recent study has shown that the Northeast and the Pacific states attract large numbers of immigrants.[3] The statistics indicate that New England had 5.8 percent of the nation's population but received almost 8 percent of the total immigrants that came to the United States. Furthermore, New England absorbed a disproportionate share of immigrants even while its unemployment level remained at about the national average. New England absorbed close to six times as many immigrants as a percentage of its population, which makes its strong per capita income figures and steady unemployment figures all the more significant when compared with those of other regions.

State and Local Finance: The Northeast in a Regional Perspective

State and Local per Capita Taxes

As shown in Table 6-4, the Northeast states, contrary to common perception, run almost from highest to lowest in a ranking of states according to levels of state and local per capita taxes. While New York and Massachusetts are high on the list and rank second and fifth, respectively, it is interesting to note the positions of the other states in the Northeast, especially considering the fact that per capita income is highest in the Northeast.

For instance, New Jersey and Connecticut fall significantly below Wyoming, Minnesota, and Nevada. Vermont falls below Illinois, Delaware, and Michigan. It is also worth noting that the three Northeast

TABLE 6-4   State and Local per Capita Taxes*

Alaska	$1,895	North Dakota	$667
New York	1,140	Nebraska	658
California	964	Kansas	651
Hawaii	935	Louisiana	610
Massachusetts	903	Virginia	609
Wyoming	847	New Mexico	598
Minnesota	823	South Dakota	596
Nevada	820	Utah	590
Maryland	814	Indiana	588
New Jersey	793	Ohio	586
Wisconsin	791	West Virginia	584
Connecticut	778	Texas	581
Illinois	769	*New Hampshire*	571
Delaware	768	Missouri	570
Michigan	749	Florida	566
Vermont	742	Georgia	549
Colorado	728	Kentucky	549
Washington	728	Oklahoma	530
Arizona	731	North Carolina	527
Rhode Island	711	Tennessee	493
Montana	709	South Carolina	489
Oregon	703	Mississippi	486
Iowa	701	Alabama	455
Pennsylvania	684	Arkansas	454
Maine	671		
U.S. mean	**705**		

* Northeast states are italicized.

source: Adapted from The Tax Foundation, Inc., cited in *The New York Times,* Mar. 8, 1978. (Figures are not adjusted for regional cost-of-living differentials. Data are for fiscal year 1976.)

states of Rhode Island, Pennsylvania, and Maine cluster around the mean in per capita taxes for the entire nation. These three Northeastern states have per capita taxes that are below those of Colorado, Washington, and Arizona. Moreover, Pennsylvania and Maine fall below Montana, Oregon, and Iowa. As previously noted, the relatively low rankings of these Northeastern states are particularly important considering their per capita incomes. New Hampshire, once again, falls rather low in state and local per capita tax rankings.

In addition, while the Northeast accounts for 18 percent of the nation's number of states, it has only 20 percent of the 10 states with the highest state and local per capita taxes. Even on this percentage basis, the idea that per capita taxes are heaviest in the Northeast is almost mythical. When the region's high per capita income is taken into account, the myth becomes even more pronounced. Finally, in all the public discussions about per capita taxes "no mention has been made of the fact that the generally wealthier residents of the Northeast and Midwest are able to write off a larger proportion of their heavier state and local taxes against their federal income tax liability than are the relatively poor taxpayers in the South and the West. This indirect federal subsidy reduces interstate differences in real tax burdens."[4]

Percentage Increase in State and Local Tax Burdens: 1953 to 1975

The increase in state and local tax burdens has traditionally been measured with reference to state and local tax revenues. Each of these trends has then been compared with the state's or municipality's rate of growth in personal income over time. Table 6-5 shows that five of the Northeastern states rank above the nation's mean, while four fall below the average. Aside from New Hampshire, which ranks near the bottom of all the states in the nation, the three Northeastern states below the mean are, nonetheless, close to it. It is also interesting to note that Connecticut and New Jersey rank below six and eight states, respectively, that are not within the Northeast. This finding is especially significant in light of the common perception that the increase in state and local tax burdens over recent years has been felt largely by the Northeast and felt most significantly by such states as Connecticut, New Jersey, and Massachusetts.

State Tax Effort

In this era of "the tax revolt" and the threat it poses for state and municipal bonds, it is important to conduct a region-by-region examina-

TABLE 6-5   Percentage Increase in State and Local Tax Burdens between 1953 and 1975*

(State and Local Tax Revenue in Relation to State Personal Income)†

Delaware	170%	*Massachusetts*	50
Alaska	120	Texas	50
Maryland	90	Minnesota	49
Illinois	88	Wyoming	42
Pennsylvania	86	Washington	42
New York	82	Oregon	40
West Virginia	75	Nebraska	36
Hawaii	72	Alabama	36
Connecticut	72	Georgia	30
California	71	Utah	30
Kentucky	70	Tennessee	30
New Jersey	69	Kansas	28
Virginia	68	Iowa	28
Rhode Island	67	Colorado	28
Indiana	65	Arkansas	23
Ohio	64	Mississippi	23
Montana	62	Idaho	22
Missouri	61	North Carolina	21
Nevada	60	*New Hampshire*	21
Arizona	59	South Carolina	18
Maine	55	Louisiana	17
Wisconsin	54	Oklahoma	12
New Mexico	52	South Dakota	10
Vermont	52	North Dakota	7
Michigan	51	Florida	3
U.S. mean	**60**		

* Northeast states are italicized.

† Average state and local tax burdens rose from 7.6% to 11.9% of personal income—an increase of 57%.

SOURCE: Adapted from U.S. Advisory Commission on Intergovernmental Relations, *Significant Features of Fiscal Federalism: 1976 Edition*, vol. 1: *Trends.* Report Series M-106, Washington, D.C., 1976, p. 44.

tion of the burden of state and local taxes as a percentage of the personal income of individuals and households. As noted in Table 6-6, there are significant differences between regions—and between states within the same regions—in state and local taxes as a percentage of personal income. However, while the South clearly ranks lowest in state taxes, there is no statistically significant difference between the Northeast and the West. Moreover, there appears to be no significant difference between the Mid-Atlantic and Pacific areas. Therefore, the strong reaction to California's Proposition 13 can well be expected to be echoed in the Northeast, though in a modified form because the state and municipal

TABLE 6-5 State Tax Effort
(State and Local Taxes as a Percentage of State Personal Income. U.S. Mean Is 12.3%.)

Northeast	*12.8*	Virginia	10.7
New England	*12.6*	West Virginia	12.3
Maine	12.6	North Carolina	10.6
New Hampshire	10.8	South Carolina	10.5
Vermont	15.5	Georgia	10.8
Massachusetts	14.2	Florida	9.9
Rhode Island	11.9	South Central	*11.0*
Connecticut	10.3	Kentucky	11.3
Mid-Atlantic	*13.3*	Tennessee	10.0
New York	16.7	Alabama	9.9
New Jersey	11.6	Mississippi	11.8
Pennsylvania	11.7	Arkansas	9.9
Midwest	*11.6*	Oklahoma	10.5
Great Lakes	*11.6*	Texas	10.6
Ohio	9.7	West	*12.6*
Indiana	11.1	Mountain	*12.2*
Illinois	11.7	Montana	12.6
Michigan	11.7	Idaho	11.0
Wisconsin	13.8	Wyoming	13.4
Great Plains	*11.6*	Colorado	11.6
Minnesota	13.9	Utah	11.6
Iowa	12.1	Nevada	13.2
Missouri	10.4	Arizona	13.3
Kansas	10.9	New Mexico	13.5
Nebraska	11.1	Pacific	*13.1*
South Dakota	11.6	California	14.6
North Dakota	11.0	Oregon	12.1
South	*11.05*	Washington	12.1
South Atlantic	*11.1*	Alaska	12.5
Delaware	11.7	Hawaii	14.4
Maryland	12.3		

SOURCE: Computed and adapted from U.S. Advisory Commission on Intergovernmental Relations, *Significant Features of Fiscal Federalism, 1976–77 Edition,* vol. II, *Revenue and Debt,* Report Series M-110, Washington, D.C., 1977, pp. 4–5. Data are for 1975.

jumps in tax rate did not take place in as short a timespan as in California.

It is important to realize that within the Northeastern states there are more and greater variations among state taxes than there are among state taxes within *any* other region in the country. These intraregional differences of the Northeast are particularly marked because of New York's and Vermont's high state taxes.

Federal Aid: A Regional Comparison

Federal Aid per Capita by Region

As shown in Table 6-7, the Northeast receives the largest amount of federal aid per capita of the four major regions in the nation. The region received $260.36 per capita in federal aid in 1975, while its nearest competitor, the West, received $245.72 in federal grants on a regional per capita basis. This finding is especially striking because the Northeast, in 1970, ranked third of the four regions in per capita federal aid. As a result, the Northeast registered a whopping 122 percent increase in federal aid per capita since 1970. This increase was the same as the Midwest's increase. However, the Midwest still ranked fourth in federal aid per capita in 1975, as it had in 1970. Interestingly, the South in 1975 ranked third in both federal aid per capita and percentage increase in federal aid per capita since 1970. These figures are aggregate ones, however, and thus belie the regional trends discussed below.

Federal Taxes and Federal Spending

A somewhat less significant measure of federal spending by region is shown in Table 6-8. Here, federal per capita taxes paid by each region are correlated with federal spending per capita by region. It is clear that the Midwest is the most disadvantaged region in terms of dollar flow, registering a net outflow of about $20 billion. The Northeast had a net outflow of almost $11 billion, while the South and the West received, on the average, $11 billion more than they paid in federal taxes. In some way, this circumstance will be corrected by the Fiscal Amendment Act of

TABLE 6-7 Federal Aid per Capita by Region

	1970	1975	Percent change
Northeast	$117.02	$260.36	122
Midwest	89.00	197.50	122
South	122.73	220.20	79
West	150.53	245.72	68
United States	119.52	233.31	95

SOURCE: Adapted from computations made by the Academy for Contemporary Problems with a research grant from the Office of Economic Research, Economic Development Administration, U.S. Department of Commerce. "Revitalizing the Northeastern Economy," 1977, p. 82, from data based on the 1970 and 1975 editions of the Department of the Treasury, *Federal Aid to the States,* and the 1970 and 1975 editions of the U.S. Department of Commerce, Bureau of the Census, *Governmental Finances.*

TABLE 6-8   Federal Taxes and Federal Spending per Capita by Region

	Spending per capita, $	Taxes per capita, $	Spending taxes ratio, $	Dollar flow, in millions
Northeast	1361	1579	.86	−10,776
New England	1470	1533	.96	−762
Mid-Atlantic	1325	1594	.83	−10,013
Midwest	1128	1177	.76	−20,074
Great Lakes	1064	1518	.70	−18,618
Great Plains	1287	1374	.94	−1,456
South	1387	1219	1.14	11,522
South Atlantic	1454	1303	1.12	4,986
South Central	1327	1137	1.17	6,536
West	1712	1431	1.20	10,000
Mountain	1615	1238	1.30	8,631
Pacific	1745	1497	1.17	7,008
United States	1412	1412	1.00	

SOURCE: Adapted from *The National Journal,* June 26, 1976, p. 881. (Compiled from U.S. Department of Commerce, Bureau of the Census, *Governmental Finances,* 1975.)

1976 to the State and Local Fiscal Assistance Act of 1972, commonly known as the Revenue Sharing Act.

Revenue Sharing

The major objective of the 1976 Fiscal Assistance Amendments to the Revenue Sharing Act of 1972 was to target additional federal funds to states and municipalities that have limited fiscal capacities to meet great demands for public services. The 1972 act, which provided $30.2 billion in federal aid for state and local governments from 1972 through 1976, was the largest domestic program ever enacted by Congress. The 1976 amendments extended that legislation and, as noted above, provided additional federal funds for the nation's areas of greatest need through a specially designed formula using the poverty-level population. Under the original 1972 act, federal monies were distributed to the states according to one of two formulas, depending on which yielded the highest return of federal funds to the state. Both formulas were based largely on population, per capita income, and tax effort. Federal assistance to local governments was computed on a similar basis.

Under the "Supplemental Fiscal Assistance" section of the 1976 amendments, it was projected that for the fiscal year ending June 30, 1976, states such as New York and Vermont would receive approximately $40 per resident in federal aid, as compared with per capita allocations of $24 per resident for Indiana, Ohio, and Florida. More-over, central cities and poor rural communities are to be the chief beneficiaries of the new 1976 amendments. The formula that is em-ployed to accomplish this goal uses the number of persons below the poverty level (or below 125 percent of the poverty level for central city aid) for per capita income as the basic measure of need.

Notes to Chapter 6

This chapter is largely the result of research which was completed at Thomson McKin-non Securites Inc. by Stephen P. Rappaport and which was covered in his report *Why Not the Northeast: An Economic Analysis of Regional Trends*.

[1] Robert D. Reishauer, "The Federal Government's Role in Relieving Cities of the Fiscal Burdens of Concentrations of Low-Income Persons," *National Tax Journal*, September 1976, p. 295.

[2] U.S. Department of Commerce, *Area Economic Projections 1990*, p. 193.

[3] Roger White cited in Dr. James M. Howell, "Economic Maturity—Choices and Costs," in New York State Senate, *Balance Growth for the Northeast*, Proceedings of a Conference of Legislative Leaders on the Future of the Northeast, Albany, N.Y., 1975, pp. 60–61.

[4] U.S. Advisory Commission on Intergovernmental Relations, *Measuring the Fiscal "Blood Pressure" of the States: 1964–1975*, Washington, D.C., 1977, p. 25.

part3

Revenue Bonds

chapter 7

Public Power Bonds

In total sales volume public power bonds represent by far the largest share of the revenue bond market, exceeding the sales volume of the next most popular type (water and sewer bonds) by nearly 50 percent. In fact, in only 4 years the sales volume of public power municipal bonds has almost quadrupled from $1.5 billion to over $6 billion in 1978. Public power municipal bonds now represent an impressive 13 percent of the entire long-term tax-exempt market, and public power authorities are today frequently the very largest issuers of any revenue bonds whatever, with several issuing $400 million to $500 million a year.

The investor and bond analyst who normally evaluate a public power bond by using the traditional methods of credit, yield, price, and long-term potential may encounter special problems because of the rapidly expanding field of public power bonds. First, and most obvious, is the difficulty in understanding the whole variety of new types of municipal credits in this field, such as the joint action bulk power supply agencies, rural electric cooperatives, international power supply contracts, and other joint venture projects that have developed or changed structure during the last decade. Next, investors must factor into their evaluation of each bond the effects of threats to its issuer's fuel supply over its life-span. Slowdowns or cutoffs in OPEC oil from Iran and other countries are one obvious uncertainty, but concerns over supplies of domestic oil, coal, nuclear power, and solar power are others.

Three other vitally important political factors must also be taken into account by bond analysts and investors in evaluating particular public power bonds. First, the impact of public outcries against nuclear power plants and the disposal of nuclear waste has been sufficiently strong in some areas to close down certain facilities and prevent new construction entirely. Second, the impacts of federal, state, and local regulatory requirements, especially the staggering expense involved in meeting antipollution (air, water, and solid waste) environmental protection laws, are key political pressures affecting the finances of many public power facilities. Third, sharp increases in the rates of public utilities could create revolts by customers against further increases and could cause some industries to leave municipalities. These and other credit risks will be examined in detail in the following pages on the range of public power bonds.

The Purpose of Public Power Bonds

The issuance of municipal bonds for the creation of public power facilities had its roots in the 1930s during the Great Depression and the New Deal eras. It began in quite concentrated form in the far Northwest, especially in the states of Washington, Oregon, and California, and also in Nebraska. The public power legislation, which was the crucial forerunner of all the public power authorities, grew out of a congressional desire to harness the gigantic power of the Columbia River and its tributaries in order to provide rural electrification for the entire Northwest.

The Public Power Act of 1930 had a public purpose clause (which in one form or another governed every single federal regional public power authority created afterward) that established the legal justification for creating a municipal public power authority to incur the vast initial expense of electrification. Until that act, there was a prevailing philosophy among all the private utilities that they would simply maximize their profits and ignore underdeveloped rural areas. In short, they would not take risks by going outside the high-profit urban regions. The first federal involvement in municipal public power was, therefore, actually a form of government subsidy that facilitated the electrification of vast areas of our country that would not have received power for years, perhaps decades.

Public power had another key purpose in the minds of its congressional backers: Their intention was to have public power provide stiff competition against the private utilities. Within 10 years public power did indeed offer a feasible basis on which municipal electric utilities could and did compete because the federal government had provided the base-load resources. At the beginning the cost differential between municipal public power and the privately owned utilities was quite small. However, the federal government had tremendous hydroelectric dams and, consequently, tremendous base-load resources; it sold at wholesale rates to the municipality, and public power became very cheap in comparison with private power.

Indeed, the federal government sold power even below actual cost.

This practice came about because at that time it was difficult, if not impossible, to measure the cost of a unit of public power. Even today this problem of measuring cost has not been solved. Because under the federal administration of dams water is allocated by government agencies (so much for flood control, so much to agriculture, and so much to public power), the cost is *not* controlled by supply and demand or by the ordinary price mechanisms that govern the economics of private power. Instead these allocations, made according to the federal policy guidelines, established the price. This pricing system prevails today, although it is changing.

Today's Market for Public Power Bonds

In 1978, as in the past, the market for electricity revenue bonds was dominated by a few historically large issuers. Indeed, the top five totaled $2.46 billion. However, for the first time the Municipal Electric Authority of Georgia, one of the newly created joint action agencies, entered the top five issues with $450 million; only Omaha Public Power District's $599 million and Washington Public Power Supply System's $595 million were greater. In 1976 the New York State Power Authority had the second largest municipal revenue issue of all time when it issued $610 million. The two other largest issuers were the South Carolina Public Service Authority with $421 million and the Salt River Project with $395 million. Both the New York Power Authority and the Nebraska Public Power District were above $200 million. In comparison with all these hefty $200 million to $600 million public power bond issues, the average issue of hospital bonds or water and sewer bonds is only $10 million to $30 million.

In 1979, although the top five public power authorities accounted for 43 percent of this market, the next five accounted for 21 percent, and the remaining 105 issuers accounted for 36 percent, or $2.11 billion. Many new districts were entering this market for the first time.

What is crucial for the investor and the analyst to realize is that the traditional domination by the historically large issuers of the market for public power electricity revenue bonds is decreasing as the newly created joint action agencies for bulk power supply commence their financing programs. In 1976 these agencies issued only $185 million, or 0.4 percent of the total market for public power electricity revenue bonds. In 1977 these agencies already accounted for over 19 percent of the total, with over $1.1 billion in issues. What is also critical to realize is that in 1976, when these agencies were created, there were only three such issuers: Platte River Power Authority, Massachusetts Municipal Wholesale Electric Company, and the Texas Muncipal Power Agency. Today there are dozens of issuers, and a bandwagon effect seems to have developed.

The entire municipal bond market for public power has changed drastically in the last 5 to 10 years. Whereas traditionally big issuers of municipal public power bonds came to market as well-known entities with a solid track record, good management, a strong equity position, and low rates, today there are countless issuers that simply did not exist a decade ago. In the past, the big issuers had low-cost bulk power or closed financings that guaranteed debt by a few well-known electric utilities. Today, the financial structure and the financial backing of the newly formed issuers are very complex and far harder for investors to follow.

Four Types of Public Power

There are basically four different types of utility systems. The first is a self-generation system in which a public utility has its own plant. The second is the distribution system in which power is purchased from a wholesaler, and the public utility needs only transmission lines. The third type is the large wholesale system which uses straight debt leverage to construct power generation units. The fourth type of system is the combination system which may use its own power for peak periods. Whether we are analyzing a retail operation or a wholesale operation, there are many factors that are common to each.

The vitally important contrasts between the debt, security, and character of these quite different types of financings must not be ignored by the investor or the bond analyst, for these key differences in structure dictate different characteristics for each type of bond. For example, massive wholesale power suppliers that generate bulk power tend to be more stable financially than distribution systems. This stability occurs because wholesalers have many customers, and their key financial support results from the many municipalities and various distribution systems that buy their power. Second, since the wholesaler's charges are an operating expense for the distribution system of each municipality, the wholesaler is paid before a distribution system pays its own debt service.[1] In contrast, municipal power distribution systems tend to be more volatile financially than bulk power wholesale generating systems because the former do not have the same breadth of customers.

The cyclical, regional, and operating characteristics of these quite different segments of the electric utility industry are critical for investors or analysts to consider when looking at each new bond. By comparing the performance of similar particular utilities the investor can judge creditworthiness. Each municipality's financial strength, debt burden, power output, unit sales, cyclical trends, and peak load requirements are key figures that are usually compared to give an indication of both the quality of management and the stability of operations.

Municipal Revenue Bonds and Bulk Power Supply

In the past large municipal utilities had quite distinct characteristics that distinguished them from small utilities. While a few of the large traditional utilities generated power, all the small ones acted exclusively as distributors. In the past small utilities offered small bond issues, and the proceeds could be used only within the particular localities.

Both of these traditional conditions are now changing. Many municipal power systems continue the recently instituted programs for bulk power (which guarantee long-term power contracts to their purchasers). However, the fact that some federal contracts to supply cheap power have ended means that certain power systems must immediately seek new supplies for bulk power. This requirement subjects them to the same demands with which small municipalities contend.

The new utilities that must now secure bulk power include three types of wholesale power purchasers: (1) those that own exclusive generating capacity and that finance for their own areas; (2) those that bought from large municipal electric systems and that were frozen out of the planning and acquisition of public power; and (3) those that had bought originally from low-cost federal hydroelectric facilities which no longer have excess capacity. Local utilities may also buy bulk power, but on an individual basis they are far smaller users.

Today is a particularly critical time for the entire municipal system of utilities, for the utilities are forced by obsolescent plants to invest vast sums in new facilities. They are also hit by new fuel costs, shortages of supply, environmental complaints, and fearsomely high rates of interest which affect any new municipal bonds they sell. The upshot of all these new capital costs and operating expenses is obviously that the cost of power has risen sharply in direct contrast to the steady historical decline in the cost of public power per kilowatt in the United States during the last 80 years. Most small public municipal utilities have been coping with these soaring costs by binding together toward direct or indirect participation in giant generating units in order to maintain an adequate supply of bulk power.

Because of the vast new uncertainties of the public power environment, most smaller systems have started considering joint action, "joint operating," or direct and indirect cooperation of some kind with a group of other public utilities. Traditionally, they have financed almost exclusively through rates. Many had neither experience with seeking external financing nor any power-generating capacity. The new pressures of inadequate supply and rising costs have forced small facilities to find an entirely new way of doing business. The same economic, financial, and supply pressures have also forced large systems to reassess future bulk supplies.

Method of Credit Evaluation

In general, an investor in public power municipal bonds is being asked to lend funds to a municipal electric utility which usually has a monopoly on providing electric power in a specifically defined geographic area. The bonds enable the utility to secure sufficient financial resources to meet its contractual obligations to provide certain minimum required services to customers.

There are four basic elements in the financing of an electric utility revenue bond. The first is the sole right of the utility to serve a limited geographic area. That monopoly ensures that the municipal utility is protected from competition by another utility offering a similar service at a cheaper price.

The second element for the investor or analyst to consider is the ability and the willingness of the electric power customers to pay for service. Both the political and the economic factors of the district should be weighed to determine the strength, level, and mix of that district and of that economy. Obviously, the greater the ability to pay, the likelier any debt problem may be overcome, but the political willingness of a district to make payments on its debt obligations must not be overlooked.

The next area the investor must consider is the ability of the municipal electric utility to deliver the power for which it has contracted at the price it has arranged. To evaluate this ability the investor should consider the existing power supply resources, plants now under construction, and plans to meet projected demand.

The fourth element, and the key factor according to many bond analysts and institutional investors, is the legal contractual protection provided for the bondholder. This factor is especially important today when so many joint municipal public power issuers are being created.

All four approaches, we believe, should be combined into one simplified technique.

The credit factors for most analysts examining the public power bonds of any municipality are the municipal power authority's financial operating statistics, dependability, customer rates, fuel(s) in use and alternative fuel(s), power sources, and projected debt over the next decade.

A municipality's financial operating record of performance—its past figures, or track record—is often the first aspect of its credit that analysts look at because these measures are the most readily available. The key trends the analysts look for are in power purchases, peak demand, and sales of power. They note (1) the dependability of sources of power supplies (whether they are via long-term or short-term contracts; the existence of power-swapping arrangements) and (2) the availability of interconnections with other power-generating facilities in other municipalities or public authorities in case of an unforeseen crisis.

Rates

Customer rates, both individual and corporate, are vital in any credit analysis because they must be judged sufficient to meet all operating expenses, fuel costs, fixed debt charges, short-term borrowing charges, and, obviously, taxes. Because a bond's term to maturity can extend 20 years or more, the track record of rate increases, needed to keep pace with inflation, is critical. The projected schedule of rate increases and evidence of customer willingness to accept future rate increases are of the first importance. Institutional investors are particularly wary of municipal power bonds which offer extensive "free service" to major power users.

A realistic schedule of rate increases is crucial where there appears the likelihood of failure to control or recoup costs. Because many municipalities set inadequate rates and then failed to revise them at frequent intervals, the costs per customer often increase soon after being set. Also, a problem that has frequently arisen in rate setting is across-the-board increases that fail to differentiate between levels of users. Unfortunately, both of these rate-setting problems tend to become habitual practices by management. With the recent escalation of all costs, these mistakes are becoming ever more expensive and difficult to rectify.

Most states allow municipally owned utilities to raise rates without requiring approval from a regulatory body, provided that the purpose of an increase is to permit the utility to continue to cover fully the costs of furnishing service. Nevertheless, some municipalities face state or local restrictions on charges. Yet, because this so-called self-regulation has prevailed in most states and for most public utilities, it has established a general assurance of revenue flow to pay any increased rates required for debt service charges.

The "independence" of such public utilities in setting and raising their own rates is now deeply in jeopardy. Because of the recent skyrocketing of fuel costs and the escalation in electricity rates, pressure for outside regulatory bodies to put a cap on rate increases has arisen. This pressure is now expected to undermine what for decades has been the strongest card of the public municipal utilities in going to the capital markets to issue bonds: namely, their independent ability to raise rates on their own initiative. The importance of this new political pressure on governing boards and on regulatory authorities is that it throws a severe cloud over the ability of the municipal utilities to pay cost increases in an inflationary period.

Fuel Mix

Traditionally, hydroelectric plants had the lowest costs, especially in the far Northwest and along the Tennessee River. They were, therefore, considered vastly superior to plants powered by oil, coal, gas, or nuclear fuel. Having continual river power, they had no fuel expense and no pollution or other environmental hazard. Today, however, there are almost no readily available river sites for constructing massive new plants. Our ever increasing demand for power is being met through the construction of plants which utilize scarcer or more expensive fuels, such as oil, gas, coal, and nuclear material. This trend is generally expected to increase sharply during the coming decade. Solar energy, the burning of solid wastes, and geothermal energy may, when fully developed, satisfy a small portion of American power needs, but they probably will not become major fuel sources for decades.

Ever since the OPEC oil crisis of 1973 and the more recent price increases of 1979, a crucial credit factor studied by institutional investors and bond analysts has been a municipality's particular types of fuel supply and fuel mixes. Most analysts feel that a municipality which has a *diversity*, or mix, of different fuel sources is far stronger than one which prefers a particular type of fuel such as hydroelectricity, nuclear material, coal, or oil. A mix provides flexibility; it enables management to cope with any eventual fuel cost changes or fuel shortages.

Power Supply Contracts

Power supply contracts that extend over the total life of the bonds are obviously preferred by investors to short-term or weaker supply contracts. In spite of such long-term contracts, recent experience has shown that utilities cannot be certain of every eventuality. Bond analysts are today especially interested in seeing interlocking arrangements between utilities, or "interties," in case of any emergency. These interties are expected to guarantee continuity of service and long-term reliability.

Major institutional investors virtually require evidence that the different participants (i.e., the power wholesalers, distributors, buyers, sellers, and producers) are all fully "locked into" any complicated financing arrangements. In other words, their prime focus is on the amount of emergency protection secured by contract. Thus the power sales contracts must appear strong and unquestionably enforceable, and the various covenants (i.e., additional bonds covenant, rate covenant, and various reserves funds) also must be both strong and enforceable. Otherwise, the major institutional investors may well either avoid the bonds or insist on a substantial adjustment in price to make the bonds worth their while, for investment.

Virtually all institutional investors prefer their power sales contracts to be "take or pay, come hell or high water," rather than ordinary take and pay contracts. The reason for this preference is that under a hell or high water contract a municipality which is buying power is obligated to pay the wholesaler even when it is not receiving power. This kind of contract provides far greater assurance of payment and ensures the complete performance of all the terms of the bond contract, since it requires a higher level for the reserve fund for debt service coverage to be put aside from the initial bond sale.

Engineering and Financial Projections

In the past bond analysts seriously considered only actual and certificate figures for historical growth trends in load supply, customer demand, revenues, costs, and overall experience. Indeed, Moody's refused even to consider rating many start-up situations because they had no track record. Today there has been an increasing willingness among bond analysts to accept engineers' "projections" and financial consultants' "expectations" for a new facility or an expansion of an old one. It appears that over the years bond analysts were forced by issuers, bond traders, and major investors to accept "experts' projections." Market participants together simply dictated that if there were going to be more and more start-up utilities, including new joint ownership and joint action municipal power projects, then expert projections simply had to be used to evaluate the creditworthiness of the new bonds. Otherwise, the bonds would not be sold successfully to the major institutional investors.

Today both historic and projected figures are carefully compared with the on-line resources of the enterprise presently under development to assess the adequacy of both sets of figures as standards of measurement. Obviously, any utilities that overbuild capacity that they cannot market must absorb heavy extra fixed costs; utilities with too small a power capacity are forced to buy during emergencies at prices that can necessitate a rate increase or throw financial accounting practices out of balance. For these reasons the reviews of past forecasts are compared with actual operating experience. The engineering consultants are pressed hard on all contingency assumptions and forecasts, especially those regarding the escalation of costs.

Perhaps the most common reasons for bond failures or for financial difficulties in the public utility area are cost and revenue miscalculations by engineers and financial advisers in their projections. Because of this fact institutional investors and bond analysts are particularly anxious that only nationally recognized engineers and financial consultants be chosen by the utilities issuing bonds. These engineers and consultants are thought to have the experience, skill, and track record necessary for making the most realistic assumptions.

Unrealistic projections of revenue (from power sales to customers, industries, and other municipalities) frequently emerge when bond issuers attempt to force projections of sales figures to satisfy artificial constraints instead of objectively estimating the natural level of sales. Obviously, there are a host of reasons for miscalculations that engineers and financial analysts could not be expected to foresee. Nonetheless, investors are anxious to ensure themselves protection in bond covenants against those unforeseen occurrences.

If a utility's management has been accurate in its past forecasts, kept its rate increases in line with budget requirements, appeared to cope over time with peak load requirements, and maintained a long-range plan, then its track record is considered a reliable measure of its future forecasts.

New Technology

What is not perhaps generally appreciated is that additional outlays for plant and equipment may in fact dilute the financial strength of a public power municipal issuer. This dilution can occur when vast new expansions of a utility's facilities weaken its operational characteristics by financially overburdening the enterprise. It is always critical to assess the degree to which a new capital improvement actually adds to the facility's earning potential without increasing its costs.

Those costs can substantially *increase* or *decrease* because of various technological changes used in power systems. Whether technological improvements are made in a single enormous capital expansion or on a piecemeal basis over one or two decades, in the long run they dictate the future flexibilities and constraints of the utility. Piecemeal changes generally lead to cost savings because of efficiencies. In contrast, the installation of a completely new technology for a brand-new system is frequently more likely to raise costs than lower them. The classic example of the steam-driven turbines that are unlikely to be further improved or result in future cost savings can be contrasted with solar power or geothermal equipment whose costs and revenue-producing potential are not yet fully known. For the investor or bond analyst, it is obviously somewhat hazardous to predict whether new technologies will, during the life of a new 30-year bond, fare as well as did a previous technology over the past 20 years. Therefore, any new technology, especially when undertaken not strictly for cost-saving reasons but because of federally mandated requirements and/or health or sanitation standards, may well pose severe long-term financial risks for a utility.

Joint Ownership

Any municipal power system or state power agency that purchases from a private or public power project is dependent on the owner/operator. While there may be no problems in this arrangement of dependency, occasionally, and increasingly during the 1970s, there have been problems of scarcities and allocation disputes. Because municipalities fully recognize the hazards of overdependency, a number of them have during the past decade started joining together to construct their own power-generating systems. To do so, they must go through exactly the same lengthy approval and construction process with all its attendant problems and risks. Many municipalities consider these difficulties to be preferable to their past dependence on external power supplies, since once new systems are built, the generation of power is under their own direct control.

Massachusetts, Georgia, Texas, and Colorado have witnessed the formation of state-created entities which purchase ownership shares of the output of power plants (whether nuclear, oil, or gas) under construction by private utilities and then work out a sharing of the power among the different distribution systems for municipal electricity. In these states such agencies are also using pooled or jointly-financed resources to construct their own power plants. The arrangements for new joint financing, joint ownership, joint power supply, and joint operating serve to provide economies of scale for the municipal power industries in forms which, unlike the case of hydroelectric dams, are not directly subsidized by the federal government. The agencies are also enabling municipalities to share among themselves the financial risks which are becoming ever more difficult for a single municipality to bear on its own.

Yet, the new power supply systems present new and far more difficult problems for the bond analyst and investor. First and foremost: Whose credit or security is being pledged for the new enterprise? The investor must ask: Are the participating municipalities "jointly and *severally* liable" for all costs and expenses in their dealings, or is each participant liable only to the degree to which it is a participant in a cooperative project?

If one of the partners in a joint ownership proves unable to continue paying its share, how certain are the other partners to pick up the expense of that extra burden or to find a replacement municipality in time to prevent default or delay on bond interest payments? Because of some of these uncertainties in initial joint financings, the security for the bonds has almost of necessity been contracts for long-term power sales. These contracts must last for the life of the bonds. Such contracts have frequently been between the state authority, the municipality, or the power supplier, regardless of whether the power ultimately comes from a private, municipal, state, or federal source. For that reason the power is only sold under hell or high water contracts that guarantee payment whether or not the power is used, whether or not the project is built, or whether or not the facility ever operates.

When a municipal power agency acts as an agent on behalf of several municipal distribution systems, the debt for the bulk power project frequently has a claim on the systems' revenues that is superior to that of each of the municipality's own bonds. Alternatively, municipal systems, themselves, sometimes act as issuers of the debt for the joint enterprise, in which case the investor or bond analyst must determine whether the new bonds are subordinate to or on a par with the presently outstanding bonds of the municipality.

New Issues

With bonds that are being issued for public power by a new agency or municipal entity that has not issued such bonds before, the credit analysis must be far more extensive than for most ongoing issuers. These new issuers have no track record, and they frequently have yet to construct a power-generating or power-distributing system.

In these situations, obviously, construction risks are paramount and involve failure to complete construction, delays that sometimes last years, and problems in engineering that can result in an improperly or inadequately functioning power system. In the case of a new issuer, the engineer's "feasibility study" is crucial, and the institutional investors, the rating agencies, and, of course, the issuer all rely on the engineer far more heavily than normal.

New start-up municipal power authorities that are issuing bonds for the first time raise extra legal questions about the automony of the issuer, its real right to issue such bonds, and its right to have a monopoly on offering power to residents within its geographic area. In addition, the caliber and past experience of the management itself must be weighed.

Because of new federal and state laws and regulations, not only the broad design but also the details of the specifications of start-up public power situations have to be *carefully* analyzed by any major investor. Frequently at each stage of financing and construction, permits, approvals, etc., must be obtained from each leavel of government for siting, environmental compatibility, construction strength and safety, and operational adequacy. The project has to be started on time; each stage must be fully completed by set deadlines and according to specific standards; and all fuels have to be purchased under long-term contracts. When completed, the whole facility must undergo rigid testing and operational checks. Obviously, there are many chances of delays and sources of cost overrun and financial as well as legal risks.

Because the governmental standards for safety, health, pensions, conservation, and environmental safety, as well as those for disclosure and liability, have all been upgraded recently, they have raised the costs of each new electric utility project and increased the lead time required to plan and construct a power plant or distribution system. Until an entire system is finally complete and its operations certified as acceptable, it does not earn money. Thus the longer the delays continue (sometimes for 2, 3, 4, 5, 6, and more years), the higher the fuel costs; and the higher the fuel costs, the higher the base rates that must be charged in order to recover the additional expenses.

Among the crucial concerns of investors and analysts are the possibilities of any failure to complete a new utility, any operating failure of the utility before construction is completed or before the utility is fully functioning, or any operating failure once the plant is operational. A large working capital is generally considered the best protection for a municipality in case of temporary failures, such as those resulting from weather conditions, fuel problems, or labor disputes. However, to guard against major failures, it is essential to look at the specific bond covenants and insurance provisions.

The additional bonds clause, or the municipality's ability to issue completion bonds, is really a double-edged sword: Its presence helps assure completion of the facility, but future bond issues have the potential to dilute the previous bond holders' credit by overpledging the same asset. Limitations on additional borrowing are needed, but in most cases they eventually serve to inhibit a utility's needed expansion.

The Legal Straitjacket

Because of the antiquated resolutions under which most large systems operate, they have been forbidden to issue additional bonds, to finance improvements or buy new supplies, or to enter into new contractual agreements with purchasers. The "additional bonds test" (which each municipal bond resolution included) was based on a decades old conception of the technology and cost structure for building and maintaining a public power system.

This legal straitjacket has forced many public power agencies to explore alternatives in order to continue to guarantee their requirements for bulk power supply. These have included (1) direct ownership of a generating facility by issuing new bonds, (2) long-term contracts for financing power supply from other utilities, and (3) long-term contracts for financing power supply for a joint municipal utility.

Because of the long heritage of legal constraints, direct ownership plans have been somewhat hampered with regard to financing vast new power expansions via the existing bond resolution. It has been felt that this would place an excessive burden on the existing ratepayers. Furthermore, because the lead time necessary to build a new power plant is frequently 10 years and the capitalization of interest payments is frequently prohibited by law, the current burden on ratepayers for financing a new facility is crippling. Although small capital additions in the past could be financed via rate increases, such financing is no longer possible because of the vast amounts of the capital expenditures that would be required.

Refunding bonds is a second way in which municipal utilities try to avoid the restrictions of their existing bond resolutions. However, today's far higher interest rates and the IRS's "arbitrage regulations" make this difficult.

Some municipalities attempt to close out the old bonds and issue new ones under a new bond resolution that they write which has far more flexibility than past bond resolutions. But the new bonds will then have a second lien on the revenues of the same utility system; therefore, they tend to be risky, for they guarantee no new revenues. These bonds thus will carry a lower rating and a higher relative interest cost than past bonds. Nevertheless, to get out of their legal straitjacket and to achieve flexibility, many municipalities have issued such second lien bonds. The higher risks should not be overlooked by the investor.

Another key alternative, one which municipal utilities have employed to avoid restrictive legal covenants, has involved the creation of *power supply systems* under a separate legal resolution and the issuance of new bonds secured by a power supply contract with the original system. These new bonds usually burden the facility with a new operating expense or debt service which usually has a lien on the revenues. This lien takes precedence over all currently outstanding debt. It weakens the rate covenants and constitutes an attempt to avoid the additional bonds test. Because of these tendencies, all these techniques have risks, and some bond resolutions explicitly prohibit their use.

Relying solely on an external municipal utility, or the *long-term contract for power supply*, is especially risky because the municipality lacks control. It has no right to review the costs, expenses, or availability of supply of the seller.

For all the above reasons, *joint action programs for bulk power supply* have spread rapidly.

Municipal utilities have joined together to form joint entities, to acquire power distribution, and to issue bonds backed by power supply contracts with each of the participating municipalities. These bonds of utilities have increased in *one* year from $185 million to $1100 million, and the joint action financings for bulk power supply are expected to become a major, if not *the* major, form of public power bond for the next decade. So far, Georgia, Massachusetts, Louisiana, Wyoming, Texas, Utah, Colorado, and a number of other states have them. Joint action financing takes two forms. *Closed-end financing* involves reliance on the power purchaser's credit over the life of the project, and *open-end* financing involves reliance on the power purchaser's credit only during the initial stage.

Each of these two types of financing permits additional bonds to be issued to complete the construction of power generators, to meet government requirements, and to meet joint ownership agreements. Both types avoid the legal straitjacket of severe restrictions in existing bond resolutions. Both also avoid the need for a long-term power supply contract and, therefore, the resulting excessive dependence on an outside municipality. Yet in each case the investor should make an effort to review the economic need, the financial creditworthiness, and the legal security arrangements for each of the different joint municipal partners that will repay the debt.

The fundamental security for any joint entity is the power supply contract. This kind of contract can take different forms: (1) guarantees of power supply by a hell or high water contract, (2) the take or pay contract in which the purchaser agrees to pay only for power actually made available, or (3) an agreement to pay only for the supply used.

Closed-end financing constitutes a guarantee to the municipal utility of a fixed percentage of debt service. Yet since the start-up joint entity has no finance track record, the investor or analyst should look only to the probability of payments by the municipal electric utilities.

Contracts for open-end financing entail the long-term supply of wholesale power and prohibitions that keep each participating municipality from building its own power generator or buying elsewhere. If additional power is later needed, the joint action entity will build a plant to generate such power. For the investor this raises a significant question for the future concerning costs, expenses, rate increases, and sources of supply. These questions can be particularly worrisome, since new, unknown partners can enter into the joint entity and additional bonds can continue to be issued under the quite flexible financing document.

Nevertheless, despite these concerns, joint action programs for bulk power supply and joint ownership of a facility by two or more agencies or municipalities are both obviously becoming common across the United States. Each of the various forms of joint ownership, such as participation, sharing, or cotenancy agreements, states the fixed percentage of ownership by each participant and thus the amount of power each can receive.

Joint ownership greatly increases the creditworthiness of the bonds. It greatly enhances the salability of the bonds because of the recognized names of the issuers and the direct security involved.

These strengths, however, do not provide absolute protection, and investors should be wary of financially weak participants who may default on their portion of the debt burden. The defaulter will have to be bailed out by the others and its power contract resold to a viable municipality or agency.

Cases

The Texas Municipal Power Agency

The Texas Municipal Power Agency (TMPA) is a municipal corporation composed of representatives from the Texas cities of Bryan, Denton,

Garland, and Greenville. The agency was formed to facilitate the construction and utilization of energy-producing facilities for the four cities. At the present time, each city owns and operates generation, transmission, and distribution systems for electric power for its population. The cities had previously relied on gas-produced energy; however, the cost of such energy was becoming burdensome, and the supply was dwindling. In addition, the needs of the service area were expected to increase greatly, well beyond the capacity of the present generating facilities. Its peak demand was projected to increase from 602 MW in 1973 to 1205 MW in 1978, reflecting an annual growth rate of 3.2 percent. Moreover, the total energy requirements of the system were expected to increase from 2466 MW in 1978 to 4956 MW in 1987, with an anticipated annual growth rate of energy requirements of slightly over 8.0 percent. Table 7-1 shows the projections of the total energy requirements and resources of the system for the period 1978–1987.

As a result of these projections, the TMPA embarked on a program of system expansion slated to cost approximately $1.2 billion. Included in this program was the construction of (1) Gibbons Creek, a steam electric station having a 400 MW capacity and powered by coal (lignite), and (2) two Comanche Peak Plants, consisting of steam turbine units having a total capacity of 1150 MW and powered by nuclear fuel, and projected to cost almost $110 million. These two plants were to be constructed by a subsidiary of the Texas Utilities Company, and TMPA was to have a 6.2 percent interest in the project. All projects were to be completed by 1983.

The bonds issued to pay for the projects were secured by an irrevocable first lien and a pledge of the net revenues of the agency. The cities had contracted with TMPA to purchase from the agency all the additional power that they did not generate from their own systems. The cities contracted to use the revenues of their own electric systems to fill the depleted reserves of TMPA, if this was necessary. Each city also covenanted that it would establish, maintain, and collect fees for the use of its electric system that would be at least sufficient, together with other revenues and available reserves of its electric system, to pay the agency

TABLE 7-1 Projections of Total Eneryg Requirements and Resources for the Texas Municipal Power Agency

Year	MW	City resources, MW	TMPA resources, MW	Total, MW
1978	692	932	—	932
1982	913	932	471	1303
1983	999	932	542	1474
1987	1406	932	542	1474

all the required amounts. The Texas Public Utility Regulatory Commission does not have any jurisdiction over TMPA, and the cities involved have original jurisdiction over their rates. The agency reviews its rates at least once each year so that they will continue to yield net revenues of at least 1.25 times debt service coverage. All four cities had an average coverage of approximately 2.20 times from 1973 through 1977, and projected debt service coverage of the cities from 1978 through 1987 was to be about 1.80 times. For TMPA, debt service coverage from 1981 through 1987 was to hover at 1.25 times, both coverage ratios attesting to what may be considered the security of the agency.

The Massachusetts Municipal Wholesale Electric Company: A Public Corporation of the Commonwealth of Massachusetts

The Massachusetts Municipal Wholesale Electric Company (MMWEC) was established to develop its own power resources through joint ownership of generating facilities, some of which were constructed by MMWEC and some of which were constructed by other utilities. The MMWEC is composed of 28 of the 30 municipal electric systems of Massachusetts, sometimes termed the "participants." These participants provide electric service for 35 of Massachusetts' 351 towns and cities, with a combined service-area population of 522,558, which is approximately 9.2 percent of the total population of Massachusetts. The combined system had a noncoincident peak demand of 619,666 kW in 1977, which represented 71.4 percent of the electric load served by all municipal electric systems in Massachusetts.

MMWEC's revenues are derived primarily from payments made by the participants under the power sale agreements for each project. These agreements require the purchase by the participants of 100 percent of the capability of the project. The power sale agreements, a form of "take or pay" contracts, require payment whether or not the power supply projects are operational. In the event of default by a municipal participant, the other participants must pay an additional levy that may be as high as 25 percent of their regular payment requirements. Such agreements for additional security payment may be termed "limited joint agreements."

The bonds of MMWEC are payable from and secured by a lien upon the revenues derived from MMWEC. Rate covenants exist, and so MMWEC is required to cover the debt service on the bonds by fixing sufficient charges. The participants must also set charges sufficient to

TABLE 7-2 Customers, Energy Sales, and Revenues of MMWEC

	1975	% of total	1976	% of total	1977	% of total
Customers						
Residential	166,485	88.90	167,349	88.37	169,463	88.52
Commercial and industrial	17,653	9.43	18,783	9.92	17,935	9.37
Other	3,131	1.67	3,235	1.71	4,039	2.11
Total customers	187,269	100.00	189,367	100.00	191,437	100.00
Energy sales (kWh) (000)						
Residential	1,061,111	41.70	1,101,525	40.64	1,111,299	39.80
Commercial and industrial	1,253,851	49.27	1,368,947	50.50	1,421,471	50.90
Municipal and other	213,724	8.39	219,639	8.10	220,371	7.89
Sales for resale*	16,249	0.64	20,629	0.76	39,280	.41
Total energy sales	2,544,935	100.00	2,710,740	100.00	2,792,421	100.00
Revenues from energy sales						
Residential	$ 44,594,807	43.14	$ 46,396,420	42.76	$ 50,811,783	40.93
Commercial and industrial	49,000,989	47.40	53,784,299	49.04	60,220,012	49.59
Municipal and other	9,267,654	8.96	8,379,585	7.64	10,669,367	7.51
Sales for resale*	517,675	0.50	618,248	0.56	2,429,694	1.96
Total revenues from energy sales	$103,381,125	100.00	$109,678,552	100.00	$124,130,856	100.00

* Includes sales of surplus energy between participants.

provide revenues to meet their obligations under the power sale agreement, and such rates are not subject to approval by the Department of Public Utilities of Massachusetts. As a result, the security of the bonds is actually dependent on the revenue-earning capacity of the participants' electric systems. This earning capacity is a function of the power sale agreement.

As shown in Table 7-2, MMWEC has a diversified customer base, one composed largely of residential customers. Since 1975, the total number of customers has increased 2.2 percent, total energy sales have increased 9.7 percent, and total revenues from energy sales have increased 20.8 percent. It was projected in 1979 that from 1980 through 1990 the total energy requirements of the system would increase 11.8 percent.

By mid-1979, it was projected that $1 billion in additional bonds would be issued through 1987 for new facilities and systemwide improvements to MMWEC's presently operating 12 projects. The projected goal of the total system capacity was 1088 MW, of which 53 percent would be generated by fossil fuel and 47 percent by nuclear energy. Under construction were Nuclear Projects No. 4 and No. 5 and the Sears Island Project. Nuclear Projects No. 4 and No. 5 consisted of MMWEC's proposed 4.33 percent and 1.097 ownership interests in Seabrook No. 1 and No. 2 generating units, which were being constructed by the Public Service Company of New Hampshire. The Sears Island Project consisted of MMWEC's 13.396 percent ownership interest in the Sears Island Coal Unit No. 1, which was planned for construction by the Central Maine Power Company. Projected revenues through system additions and improvements were anticipated to meet the power supply payments through 1988, as well as other financial obligations.

Note to Chapter 7

[1]Standard & Poor's Corporation, *Municipal and International Bond Rating: An Overview*, p. 33.

chapter 8

Housing Bonds

Americans spend more than 25 percent of their annual income on renting or purchasing homes or apartments. Each year spending for housing represents the largest segment of disposable income to be spent upon any one commodity; the purchase of a house or apartment is usually considered the largest investment a person will ever make.

Largely because of inflation during the past 20 years, rents and the costs of homes and apartments have sharply risen. Prices have increased to such an extent that many families fear they can no longer afford to purchase a house, or they are settling for smaller homes because of high costs. Likewise, ordinary rents in many cities have risen out of reach for many families.

For example, in the United States today there are 1.8 million new households created each year, yet simultaneously there has been a shrinkage in the number of rental units available since 1970 that has resulted in a net loss of 20,000 units annually. This loss has occurred primarily because of the declining production of new buildings, the abandonment and foreclosure of older apartments, and the conversion into cooperatives or condominiums of many sought-after units.

The key result of this shrinkage is that the government finds itself called upon to finance, and is financing, two-thirds of all rental units now being built (400,000 out of 600,000). In fact, in some cities the government has become practically the only financier of new rental buildings. For example, in New York City during the 1970s virtually no new rental buildings were built at all that were not backed by some form of federal government financing, federally insured mortgages, and/or tax abatement. New private production has virtually reached a standstill in some areas because of very high interest rates and the increasingly long pre-construction time required. Because very little building has taken place, rental units are scarce, and those available have escalated in price.

This difficulty of affording today's rents or house prices is one fundamental reason why federal, state, and local governments have continued to provide massive financial support through a whole variety of grants, subsidies, loans, and guarantees designed to ensure that American families can find adequate homes. This public policy of governmental support is multifaceted, and it encompasses special tax benefits for mortgage payments and special regulations for savings banks and lending institutions. It accounts in part for the whole collection of governmental housing agencies at all levels of government.

In 1978 Congress voted over $32 billion for housing (i.e., subsidies, grants, agencies loans, etc.). While this money will be spent over the next 40 years, it is important to realize that *each year* the government is continuing to appropriate sums of such size to support the housing market; the government is continually stretching out the length and increasing the size of its commitment.

It therefore should come as no surprise that all this government funding has had, and will certainly continue to have, a very substantial effect on the growth of the market for municipal housing revenue bonds, which in 1978 was approximately $5 billion. There are both direct and indirect relationships between this massive government funding of housing and the expansion in the market for housing revenue bonds. These relationships are both interdependent and complex.

It is largely because of the interdependence between the financing mechanisms for public and private housing that housing revenue bonds exist in such a wide variety of forms. The major divisions are between those for single-family homes and those for multifamily homes; those that have federal insurance and those that do not; and those that encompass a single housing project and those that involve a pool or whole portfolio of different projects in different areas.There are also some fundamental differences as to exactly which public entity is the issuer of the bonds: a city, a local housing agency, a state, or some other public agency. The owner of the housing project may be a profit-making corporation, a nonprofit enterprise, or a government housing agency.

In bond issues for multifamily homes there is a crucial distinction between issues that have federal insurance and those that do not. Those with federal insurance tend to be rated AA, and those without tend to be rated A (i.e., A−, A, or A+) or even BBB.

Traditionally, the single-family portfolios were also divided into those which contained FHA-insured or VA-guaranteed mortgages and those which did not. The FHA/VA issues received AA ratings because of the deep coverage afforded the bondholder, and the nonfederally insured or nonguaranteed issues were rated somewhere in the A category (unless they happened to carry a state moral obligation pledge). Recently, however, the use of various types of private mortgage insurance has become more pervasive, particularly as a result of the explosive growth and creative structuring of single-family mortgage bonds that are locally issued. The use in the local issues of private (nonfederal) insurance on the mortgage portfolio (generally in an amount equal to 10 percent of the principal amount of the mortgages in the pool), as well as on individual mortgages, resulted in AA ratings. This practice has now been adopted by state housing agencies.

In each case there are strengths and weaknesses in the quality of these bonds. A strength relates to the fact that despite the cyclical quality of economic history over the years, single-family mortgage bonds have been very secure as a category. However, a weakness of these bonds relates to the fact that the bonds are intended for low-income or middle-income people who often have a greater vulnerability to downturns in the economic cycle. (It should be noted, however, that certain newer housing issues have partly catered to income groups up to the $50,000 level. This is one of the criticisms by Congress.)

There is no question that inflation has brought remarkable increases in property values over this past decade and has thereby strengthened the fundamental real estate security behind the bonds for single-family homes. Nevertheless, inflation in housing prices is a double-edged sword because it has also raised the costs of debt, repairs, and taxes associated with homeownership. And even more important, were there now to be a severe recession or depression, the very high level of personal indebtedness among homeowners might well make the avalanche of defaults on mortgages very difficult to cope with. This is a possibility of particular concern to some of the newer local issuers (i.e., cities, towns, and counties) of mortgage purchase revenue bonds. Because of the payment delinquencies that would result, investors and bond analysts must keep in mind the possibility of recession- or depression-induced defaults with consequent property devaluation.

The credit strength of an uninsured portfolio of single-family or multifamily mortgages depends upon many factors, especially the following two: (1) whether there is any government support or private mortgage insurance and (2) whether the portfolio is being used to finance private-market housing or only subsidized housing.

Four Types of Bonds

There are essentially four major types of municipal housing revenue bonds, although there are many additional subclassifications which tend to make this market appear extraordinarily complex. We will give a brief summary of each of the four types and then discuss in detail their credit aspects.

Direct Loan Programs   These involve developers' receiving a direct mortgage loan from a state housing finance agency (or other public agency) to pay for building new multi-unit apartment buildings. The programs are designed to finance large portfolios of units for low- to moderate-income families or the elderly, who receive federal rent subsidies.

Mortgage Purchase Bonds   They provide single-family (or, sometimes multifamily) homes for low- and moderate-income families to be financed by mortgage money. The proceeds from the sale of these housing revenue bonds are used to buy mortgages from savings and lending institutions.

Local Housing Authority Bonds Issued under Section 8-11(b)   The U.S. Housing Act of 1937 provides low- or moderate-income tenants, whether families or elderly couples or individuals, with multiunit apartment buildings. Unlike direct loan programs, bonds under Section 8-11(b) are indirect financings. They receive no direct financing from the federal government (but instead only a comprehensive rent subsidy package). Their other distinction is that they are permitted to have an extraordinarily wide range of issuers.

Loans-to-Lenders Programs   These loans involve bonds generally issued by state housing or mortgage finance agencies and are quite similar to mortgage-backed bonds in the private housing market. In essence, loans-to-lenders programs use bond proceeds to make collateralized loans to lending institutions, which in turn make mortgage loans that are payable from loan repayments by the lending institution. Loans-to-lenders programs have been declining recently as states shifted to mortgage purchase programs.

Loans-to-lenders bonds can be collateralized by pools of mortgages, by government securities, or by both. They are fully collateralized issues. In such financings there is generally a provision that 150 percent of the loan value be held in escrow (in mortgages or securities), and if there ever is a default on that loan, the trustee need only take the portfolio and liquidate it to make good on the loan. As a result, loans-to-lenders bonds tend to be very secure bonds. They generally have been rated AA and could be rated even AAA if they were sufficiently overcollateralized. While there are a number of risks in the real estate, economics, and management of this type of program, these risks tend to be offset by the very strong collateral.

Direct Loan Program Bonds

Under direct loan programs, developers receive a direct mortgage loan from a state housing finance agency (or a public agency) or from some other issuer to pay for building the new housing. The programs are designed to finance portfolios of multiunit apartment buildings for the elderly or for low- to moderate-income families who receive federal rent subsidies.

The bonds are usually secured by, and interest and principal paid from, payments on mortgages, part or all of which is paid from federal subsidies. Occasionally, an additional backup credit is provided by the state government's moral obligation pledge of appropriations if and when the debt service reserve fund ever becomes deficient. Although some analysts stress that the primary security on the bonds is mortgage payments, and therefore the actual portfolio must be assessed, others insist that the state government's moral pledge is what is critical. The latter use an automatic formula based on the state's GO credit (when a moral obligation pledge is included) to determine the worth of these housing bonds. We will evaluate this dispute in more detail later on in this chapter in the section "Moral Obligation Bonds."

As mentioned earlier, the crucial distinction to be made concerning the direct loan programs is between those that are federally insured and those that are not. While the credit of federally insured housing programs is strong and the analysis of their bonds is often thought simple, they are not 100 percent guaranteed in all cases. For example, Section 221(d)(3) of the U.S. Housing Act of 1937 pays 99 percent of the principal of the mortgage. The same is true of Section 221(d)(4). Together, these two examples help to point up the problem for investors and bond analysts of where the missing funds are to come from. The direct loan programs that are not insured by the federal government are far more difficult to evaluate because the investor must carefully consider the nature of the federal rent subsidy; the worth of the state government's moral pledge; the underlying security of the real estate and housing units themselves; and, finally, the caliber of the management of the state housing agency. Each of these programs must be analyzed on a case-by-case basis.

In evaluating the mortgage portfolio in direct loan programs, it is not feasible for an analyst to examine each mortgage unless the portfolio is very small. Therefore, under these circumstances, particularly if additional mortgages can be added through the issuance of additional bonds, the credit evaluation focuses on the process used by the agency in underwriting the projects. The evaluation determines (1) if the systems and procedures are sound and are followed and (2) if the size and competence of the staff are adequate.

Another approach considers the balance and composition of the portfolio. Important factors include geographic diversity (inner city versus suburban or rural area), type of project (family versus the elderly), type of subsidy, and underlying state or local economic conditions. Some investors have developed a bias in favor of projects for the elderly and in favor of those which are subsidized according to Section 8-11(b). These investors are against issuers from the industrialized Northeastern states.

Mortgage Purchase Bonds

While state agency mortgage purchase bonds enable low- and moderate-income single-family (or, sometimes, multifamily) homes to be financed by mortgage money, the "Chicago-plan," or "city," issues have included higher-income participants. The proceeds from the sale of these housing revenue bonds are used to buy mortgages from savings and loan institutions or other institutions. Once again, the bonds' principal and interest payments come from mortgage payments. State housing agencies originally organized these mortgage purchase bonds, but now they have begun to be issued by cities, local agencies, and counties.

The distinctions between the different types of mortgage purchase bonds have to do primarily with whether they are used to finance new construction on a new site or to fund established housing developments and whether there are small, isolated, and concentrated groups of mortgages or large, highly diversified pools of mortgages. The small, geographically concentrated pool of mortgages calls for a more specific analysis, whereas the larger, more highly diversified pool of mortgages requires an actuarial, or statistical, approach to the portfolio risks.

In the simplest terms, four factors provide an analytical checklist for these bonds: cash flow, assets, legal protection, and management. These factors are not usually independent; instead they are interrelated, and therefore the investor or bond analyst should balance one against the other. For example, poorer assets, real estate, local economics, and demographics of the area where a housing project is to be built can be offset by greater insurance and/or more conservative cash flow assumptions. Since the housing assets have to be protected and the cash flow has to be balanced, there is usually not an either-or form of analysis but a weighing of different strengths and weaknesses.

Assets

One general approach is to consider asset protection as inherent in the composition of the mortgage portfolio. However, many of the pools of mortgages can include low- and middle-class houses in marginal areas or neighborhoods that are, or have been, on the decline. Thus much of the analysis of asset protection focuses on both the primary and secondary tiers of insurance, on supplemental insurance policies, and on mortgage reserve funds that are built up from cash. In a general recession, these two approaches are used to determine the kinds of storms the bonds can weather and the kind of protection they have either to prevent default or to fall back upon in case the prices of houses should deflate.

Federal insurance and guarantees are regarded as affording the strongest protection; with the different types of private insurance, the quality of the insurance company must be considered. The financial strength of the private insurance companies varies widely, and the company providing the insurance may have an impact on the bond rating.

Reserve funds are another source of protection. Unlike insurance which affords protection against loss of principal, such as from default, the reserves are designed to protect against temporary cash shortfalls, such as from delinquency in mortgage payments or delays in the payment of insurance claims.

The amounts and types of insurance and reserves are determined by the characteristics of the issue. The more marginal the neighborhood in which the housing is being built and the lower the median income of those who will own the houses, the greater the need for stronger and greater numbers of reserve funds and backup forms of insurance. It is necessary to consider the extent to which this pool of mortgages has a delinquency and foreclosure rate, whether it is higher or lower than the national average, and whether it is trending up or down. In established mortgage purchase programs for single-family homes, the track record of the portfolio is important. The larger the contribution of equity in the front end by the mortgagor, the better the performance. If the portfolio is restricted to 20 percent equity and 80 percent loan/value ratio, this is good protection for that pool of mortgages. In contrast, if the equity is only 5 percent and the loan/value ratio is 95 percent, this will be a decidedly negative factor.

Bond analysts and investors must weigh the different techniques of evaluating asset protection to see which is most appropriate for a given portfolio. While insurance, reserve funds, and real estate value can each be viewed separately, it may be helpful to consider their support of each other. It is not just the amount of insurance that is important but the type, range, and protection offered.

The types of insurance used for housing revenue bonds can be divided into three broad categories: (1) *credit* insurance against losses stemming from default by the mortgagor, such as FHA or private mortgage insurance; (2) *hazard* insurance, such as fire or storm coverage, which protects against various natural and people-made disasters; and (3) *performance* insurance against nonperformance, omission, or fraud on the part of an agent or contractor.

Since the various policies are quite specific as to what situations are covered and the amounts of protection afforded, and since payment may be contingent upon or interrelated with the payment of another policy, the result is a complex multidimensional web which must be closely examined.

For example, the following insurance coverage will be found in many single-family programs: each mortgagor's property is protected by a normal homeowner's policy; the individual mortgages are insured by a federal agency or private firm; and the mortgage portfolio is also insured against losses stemming from default. But payment on the portfolio insurance policy is made after payment on the individual insurance policy; and both the individual and portfolio insurance policies generally stipulate that if there has been a hazard loss, the property must be repaired with the hazard insurance proceeds before payment can be made on a default claim. Some hazards, such as earthquakes, are not covered by normal homeowners' policies. Therefore, if there were an earthquake which destroyed a property in the portfolio and the mortgagor defaulted on the payment of the mortgage, unless there is supplemental protection, there would be no insurance coverage. Therefore, the supplemental, or special hazard, policy was introduced to cover such situations.

Cash Flow

The most difficult and complicated part of the credit analysis for mortgage purchase bonds is estimating the cash flow over the life of the bonds. The cash flow for housing bonds is structured in a fundamentally distinct way. While public power bonds or water and sewer bonds have a relatively stable cash flow, the cash flow of housing bonds is excruciatingly difficult to predict. This difficulty stems from the uncertainty as to when, if, or in what numbers homeowners will decide to prepay their mortgages.

It is uncertain to what extent management will have to tap those prepayments for cash flows, or exactly when which funds will be available to pay all expenses. In contrast to simply running out trend lines, which is the practice for evaluating electric utility bonds and most other bonds, the analysis of housing bonds depends upon what are chosen as the basic assumptions. These assumptions include what the mortgage repayment schedule will be, what the bond repayment schedule should look like, and what the amortization on a monthly basis is going to be.

From each of these assumptions the analyst estimates what the spread between the mortgage repayments and bond repayments will be (and thus the income from interest and arbitrage) and what the expenses and servicing fees will total. Although all this figuring is now performed by bond analysts on calculators and computers, it is still a complex operation. It is made more complicated by the need to go through different models, or scenarios, of what would happen if a certain percentage of the mortgages were prepaid, or terminated, prior to the scheduled maturity date.

In general, the prepayments are tracked to the history of mortgages insured according to Section 203 of the Federal Housing Act. It has been found that mortgages are prepaid more often between the second and fifth years; the peak, for example, comes in the third year. From the FHA, which keeps detailed statistics on early terminations due to defaults or sales of houses as homeowners move, bond analysts develop their assumptions about how likely the prepayment of mortgages is.

The average life of mortgages has been decreasing substantially. Within the last two decades it has decreased from 12 years to approximately 8 years. This means that an ever increasing number of homeowners are prepaying very early, and thus a very large turnover in mortgage portfolios is taking place.

Usually, the prepayment estimate is stated as a fixed percentage of the FHA's experience: "75 percent of FHA" is a figure commonly used by many analysts. The FHA average tends to be a very conservative number, and so if the average goes below that 75 percent, the investor or analyst can be comfortable.

The simplest way to structure the analyses is to assume *no* prepayment of mortgages whatsoever. However, this approach fails to take into consideration the *actual life* of the mortgages. The actual life will, in all likelihood, be much shorter than the *nominal* life based on the scheduled amortization. The problem with this approach is that the market prices from the *average life* of the bonds outstanding are based upon the term and serial maturity, and it would result in a higher interest differential on these bonds. If only the printed schedule of bond maturities is used and if it is assumed that only a fixed amount of the principal payments will be coming in on the mortgages on the basis of the scheduled amortization, the average life will tend to look longer than it actually is.

The other approach is to assume that a certain number of mortgages will be prepaid and to further assume that this additional cash flow above scheduled amortization will be available to pay debt service. The serial (short-term) maturities can then be increased and the term (low-term) maturities decreased. This will shorten the average life of the bonds and therefore decrease the interest rate.

Either one of these two prepayment assumptions can result in very real problems. If principal repayments come in behind schedule, the housing agency may simply not have enough cash to pay up on the bonds when they mature. Such a shortfall can lead to default. Alternatively, the housing agency might dip into its reserves, miss an interest payment, or in various other ways find itself limited. For example, if an agency has to liquidate a debt service reserve fund, it may have its interest earnings reduced, and this leads to many other complications.

However, if the bond structure is based on an assumption of no prepayments, then another problem develops, for if the mortgage *is*, in fact, prepayed, the assumed earnings are lost and are not available to repay nonasset bonds which are used to pay the cost of bond issuance and other expenses. In the simplest terms, there is a double-edged sword. If very conservative prepayment assumptions are made, a problem might arise if prepayments come in too early. Also, if they come in too late, the necessary cash may not be available. One typical problem is that if prepayments come in too early during a period of low interest rates, the managers are not able to reinvest them at an interest rate high enough to cover the remaining expenses on the bonds.

Historically, this variation in prepayments and its sensitivity to a whole host of different factors usually lead to conservative assumptions by many analysts. For example, Standard & Poor's sometimes goes as high as 90 percent of FHA experience when the particular mortgage pool is well known, but it generally stays at 75 percent or below. Most bond analysts test all the cash flow assumptions which are worked out in detail by the independent financial advisers of the bond issuers. Any municipal issuer that moves very far from the 75 percent of FHA prepayment experience by assuming *heavy* prepayment is seriously questioned. As a result, wherever actual prepayments or projections run decidedly behind or far ahead of the schedule of the assumed levels, investors should be wary.

Finally, the demand for mortgage money at the moment can be a crucial factor in assessing the cash flow and asset value of a particular set of bonds backed by a particular pool of mortgages. Also, the level of "commitment fees" and "liquidated damages," which are used to assure timely delivery of new mortgages, is considered an extra check of cash flow.

Management

The requirements of management capability vary among all four types of housing finance programs. For example, loans to lenders can be run really by one person, for all that is necessary is to obtain a few certifications at the end of the year. The bonds are fully collateralized, and, therefore, if anything goes wrong, the trustee bank just turns to the portfolio and liquidates part or all of the collateral to satisfy whatever emergency financial claims are presented.

The management of a mortgage purchase program for single-family homes, in contrast, requires a more sophisticated approach. This requirement is especially valid today because of the greater difficulty in first projecting the cash flow and then managing it each period despite the uncertain conditions of early or late schedules of mortgage prepayment.

When the management of the housing agency is dealing with multifamily housing, whether under direct loan programs or under Section 8-11(b) programs, that management's capability becomes critical in importance to the real creditworthiness of the bonds. This is because the managers of multifamily agencies are really acting almost as bankers, making the loans, no longer just as distant financial intermediaries. The agency, itself, is to be managing the mortgage portfolios and overseeing the management of the projects for 40 years. The housing agency does not usually manage the properties directly. It only monitors. Only if the private management company is removed does the housing agency get directly involved in management.

In general, if the mortgage prepayment is at a rate less than anticipated for single-family issues, then an inexperienced management of a housing agency can find itself in difficulties in handling its cash flow. Therefore, month-to-month monitoring of its position is of crucial importance, and a very experienced and capable group of managers is required. In multifamily portfolios the management is directly in the real estate business. It must review plans, construction loans, rentals, etc. For multifamily direct loan programs, the housing agency managers must have sufficient management oversight and control over architectural design, construction engineering, legal problems, permits, and sophisticated financial staffs which are used to dealing with federal and state governmental bureaucracies.

Today the caliber of management varies greatly among the approximately 40 different state housing finance agencies. It ranges even more among the local housing agencies. Investors should, therefore, be well aware of whether the housing program that administers their bonds is run by a management tending to one of these extremes or the other. Origin of mortgages, their servicing, and period-by-period cash flow management vary enormously from one program to the next.

If, as in most cases, housing portfolios of single-family issues have several lending institutions acting as servicers of the mortgages, then bond analysts are particularly anxious about seeing that a clear mechanism exists for coordinating the different lenders, making sure that lenders meet their contractual obligations, and keeping the cash flows in order.

The Section 8 Subsidy Program

Since 1937 we have seen about 40 federal housing programs encompassing a dizzying array of names and numbers. Nevertheless, the U.S. Housing Act of 1937 remains America's basic piece of housing legislation. The Section 8 amendment to this act is currently our primary housing assistance program for low- and moderate-income families.

The Section 8 program evolved from and replaced many earlier programs: the Section 221(d) and Section 236 interest-subsidy programs, the rent supplement program, and the Section 23 leased housing program.

Section 8's most widely used predecessor program was Section 236, a program introduced in the late 1960s when interest rates were considered by the federal government to be too high and were thought to be discouraging housing production. Thus the government decided to introduce a program to subsidize interest rates to 1 percent. (Later this was increased to 3 percent.) This subsidy yielded a tremendous cash flow and gave the housing market an initial benefit. However, inflation and increasing operating costs hit the program very hard, and because it was a fixed subsidy program, its directors ultimately had to raise rents in order to cover these new expenses. The result was that the administrators of the program came to tread a very fine line between failing to cover increasing costs and raising rents so high that it would force out people or cause rent strikes. One reason Section 236 was a fixed subsidy was that its designers had assumed that tenants' incomes would rise roughly at the rate of inflation and thus cover all expenses. This assumption was incorrect, and many problems ensued because Section 236 was so inflexible.

Out of the experience of the difficulties of Section 236 was developed the new Section 8 program to ensure that if expenses increased faster than tenants' incomes, the federal rent subsidies would increase correspondingly. Yet it also provided that if the tenants' incomes increased more than the rate of inflation, the tenants would not automatically be thrown out of their apartments because they no longer qualified for residence on the grounds of narrowly limited income.

Section 8 is thus a very flexible subsidy that moves with the tenants' incomes and that increases with inflation. It is also a very comprehensive subsidy covering all the costs associated with projects' operating costs as well as debt service costs.

The Section 8 subsidy functions in the following manner: It is the difference between a government-approved contract rent (which cannot exceed a published fair-market rent for the area) and what a tenant can afford. For example, if the rent is $400 a month and the tenant can only pay $100 as 25 percent of his or her monthly salary, then the government pays the difference ($300) as part of a contract that is guaranteed for a 20- to 40-year period. If the tenant had no income, then the federal government would pay the full rent, i.e., $400 a month. Although the tenant is required to pay somewhere between 15 and 25 percent of family income, this amount is usually 25 percent, except under special circumstances. Indeed, the experience to date is that the federal government ends up paying about 70 percent of the contract rents in a given project.

Under Section 8 the lowest 40 percent of the U.S. population is always eligible for the program, and therefore it will not become inoperative if inflation pushes everyone into higher-income brackets.

While there are many undoubted advantages of Section 8 programs over their predecessors, there are some problems that they present to the investor and the bond analyst as far as credit evaluation is concerned.

First and most important, HUD, which administers Section 8, retains the right to withdraw the subsidy from a project under certain circumstances. If a project experiences extended vacancies or if the units, for whatever reason, do not meet HUD's standards for "safe and sanitary housing" (the guidelines are very specific), then HUD retains the right to determine whether it will continue the subsidy. Because HUD retains this right, investors and bond analysts must examine each new project on its own merits.

The second primary reason for the need to examine the credit of these projects is the great range of differences in the projects themselves: their caliber of managers, their reserves, forms of insurance and legal protections for the bondholder, the cost estimates, the strength of the trust indenture, the site of the project, and the demand of people to live in it.

Obviously, if a project is to be located next to a swamp, a slum, a dump, heavy industry, or an airport, there will be questions raised about the habitability of the units. However, the demand for housing today is so strong because of the scarcity of rentable units that it is easy to mistake the present circumstances for a permanent demand throughout the 20- to 40-year life of the bonds. Such long-term demand may well not occur, and so each project's individual characteristics must be assessed. Alternative housing must be taken into account, as should be the probability of a scarcity or an overabundance of future rentable units in an area. Vacancy of rental units is the major concern here, despite the partial government guarantees of backup support. This concern is great because, as mentioned earlier, HUD retains the right to terminate subsidies if the vacancies last longer than 1 year. However, HUD does guarantee 80 percent of the contract rent for the first 60 days of vacancy and also guarantees to pay debt service on that vacant rental unit for a whole year after that.

Therefore, in addition to its flexibility, the Section 8 program offers certain extra guarantees and special features to avoid the problems and inadequacies of Section 236 and earlier programs. The financial community has come to regard Section 8 as a strong program, especially because of this flexibility and collection of extra guarantees. It is concerned not with public housing in the old-fashioned way but mainly with privately owned property, usually with equity syndication. That is to say, although these projects are *issued* by state or local governmental authorities, they can be *owned* by private owners or nonprofit organizations.

For the Section 8 programs administered by state housing finance agencies, the fair-market rents are established by HUD, which sets rents for a whole variety of market areas throughout the country and which designates what rent is acceptable for each type of unit. During the life of the bond contract, the total of collected rent is kept in a reserve that HUD can use for adjustments in its subsidy allotments and for increasing operating expenses (should that become necessary). HUD, according to its regulations, is required to adjust annually the contract rents, and the state agencies can apply for hardship increases for taxes, fuel, etc., to hasten other rent adjustments.

Section 8-11(b)

Section 8-11(b) provides for 100 percent of the financing on Section 8 projects and thus can only be used for multifamily apartment buildings. Section 8-11(b) includes an especially broad range of issuers which come, in general, under the heading of public housing agencies but include cities, districts, and nonprofit corporations.

Section 8-11(b) financings essentially deal with an independent source of tax exemption from the IRS code's famous Section 103. The purpose of Section 8-11(b) is quite specific and should not be confused with other programs or tax exemptions. Under Section 8-11(b), bonds must be for permanent financing, while short-term notes can be for construction financing. The bond proceeds can be used to cover the development cost of a project, 1-year debt service, capitalized interest (which is usually the negative arbitrage of the issuing body during the construction period), and expenses of issuance.

Section 8-11(b) financings appear in many forms: (1) insured projects of the FHA; (2) projects guaranteed by some government, government agency, or authority; (3) uninsured financings; and (4) financings that are really tax-exempt mortgages and not tax-exempt bonds at all. There are many subdivisions within each of these categories relating to the different ways of structuring both the mortgages and the cash flow.

Once again, those issues with federal insurance are considered by far the strongest credits; those issues which have some other government guarantee are the next strongest; and so forth. These bonds are backed in a variety of other forms. Sometimes their security resembles a water and sewer deficiency financing agreement that guarantees to make up any deficiency. In both California and New Jersey there are also leaseback techniques, and in Pennsylvania there are even unconditional full faith and credit guarantees. And some states virtually issue a GO bond whose proceeds are deposited into an insurance fund which can issue mortgages.

Estimates differ as to exactly how many Section 8-11(b) financings have been undertaken since they originated in 1975, but approximately 200 to 300 is the range. The financings range in size from $0.3 million to $15 million, with perhaps the most typical Section 8-11(b) project being for the elderly, having 100 rental units, and costing $2 million to $4 million. According to one study, roughly 85 percent of the financings have been for housing for the elderly, 12 percent were for low- or middle-income families, and 3 percent were for combination projects in which families and the elderly both live. Seventy percent have been for 30-year terms, 16 percent for 40-year terms, and 14 percent for 20-year terms.

During 1978, approximately 100 Section 8-11(b) financings were marketed, and it appears that they are becoming a more popular issuing technique. This increasing popularity is underscored by the fact that the debt service coverage typically was over 120 percent but has now fallen steadily to below 110 percent. (Most analysts concur that there should be both a gross revenue pledge and a strong debt service reserve equal to or in excess of 1.00 times coverage after all expenses and all other reserves. Between 105 and 110 percent is often considered safest for the level of debt service coverage on these Section 8-11(b) bonds.)

HUD regulates these Section 8-11(b) bonds rather tightly and has successively stiffened its rules on fees, interest rates that will be paid, and arbitrage profits that will be permitted. The interest rate, in the case of a noncompetitive financing, for example, is required to be within so many basis points of The Bond Buyer's organization index and to fall somewhat below the Ginnie Mae rate. These restrictions and many others placed by HUD are argued by numerous critics to be far too restrictive: they make projects unnecessarily difficult, if not impossible, to undertake. Nevertheless, regardless of whether a private housing developer, a profit owner, or a public housing authority is involved, Section 8-11(b) financings are exempt from registration with the SEC.

Most uninsured financings of Section 8-11(b) were originally undertaken as private placements. These placements tended to have considerably higher yields and originally went unrated. Today, there has been a move to attempt to secure a rating for them and to sell them publicly.

Because these projects, whether publicly or privately owned and whether insured or uninsured, must be financed entirely within the budget of the contract rent, it is important to assess whether the financial feasibility study appears reasonable. Therefore, it is important that the local housing authority, which issued the bonds in the first place, be strong enough financially, sufficiently well managed, and permanent enough to carry the ultimate responsibility for the specific housing projects and for the payment on the bonds' principal and interest "in a timely fashion."

This problem amply points up the danger of having these bonds issued by a local housing authority which is really only a shell or has no real purpose beyond acting as a paper mechanism for financing these particular bonds. If the issuer is a shell, then there really is no backup credit on the bonds. (This lack of backup credit is one key danger pointed out by recent congressional critics of the various types of so-called Chicago plans. These plans are discussed in this chapter in the Section "Local Mortgage Bonds for Single-Family Housing: The Chicago Plan.")

A similar result can occur from an absence of a real backup credit behind the issuer if a local housing authority and a developer of a project engage in constant disputes. Where such fights occur, there are also severe questions about whether the ultimate credit security will be there for the bondholder in case of default. If an investor or bond analyst, therefore, knows of disputes between the local housing authority and the developer of a project or suspects that such disputes are occurring, it is wisest to avoid buying the bonds.

Legal Protections

Legal protections are in some ways more important for housing bonds than for many other types because of their complexity and sometimes profit-generating nature. Legal protections must include a debt service reserve fund equal to or greater than the maximum annual debt service. The underlying security should be a gross revenue pledge (not restricted), and before including interest income or other nonrental reve-

nue, the rents alone should be sufficient for paying debt service, maintenance, and operating expenses. All taxes, insurance premiums, and fuel
and electric bills should be paid out of escrow accounts to ensure that
funds are available on time to pay all such vitally important bills.

Although FHA insurance for Section 8-11(b) projects covers 99 percent of the principal amount outstanding on the mortgage, investors
must be alert to the following problem: Not only is the remaining 1
percent not federally insured, but other expenses, for costs of issuing the
bonds and for accrued interest on the bonds, may not be covered.
Therefore, the issuer should make it very clear that other insurance,
reserve funds, or backing (in the form of letters of credit, government
securities, or a separate issue of subordinate debentures) has been specifically set up and allocated to take care of what is commonly known as
"the shortfall." It is obviously important that such reserves should be
tapped *only* in the case of a mortgage default to pay off the bonds and to
prevent their being used up in advance of a mortgage default. For this
reason, both these reserves and the reserve for debt service should be
accompanied by a guarantee that the funds will always be maintained at
full value, in case of any sudden need at any time in the future.

Indentures: Closed-end versus Open-end

One of the most important provisions of the trust indenture, or resolution, in a housing revenue bond is whether or not additional mortgages
can be added to the portfolio, either through the issuance of an additional series of bonds or through the purchase of new mortgages (with
the proceeds of mortgages which have been prepaid). Those resolutions
which prohibit the issuance of additional bonds and which restrict the
use of prepayments to the early retirement of bonds are called "closed-
ended," and those resolutions which allow the addition of mortgages to
the portfolio are called "open-ended." Each type has its advantages and
disadvantages and is better suited to different applications.

The advantage of the open-ended approach is that the portfolio may
be strengthened. As new mortgages are added, the portfolio grows and
becomes more geographically diverse, and the impact of the default on
one mortgage is lessened. The disadvantage of the open-ended indenture, or resolution, is that instead of its being strengthened, the portfolio may be weakened or diluted at a later date by poor underwriting
decisions or management.

The advantage of the closed-ended approach, therefore, is that the
quality and composition of the portfolio is fixed: "What you see is what
you get." To many investors, this is comforting, and to the analysts, the

portfolio and cash flow are more susceptible to analysis. To some, another appealing characteristic of closed-ended programs is that they are less complex in structure. For example, in single-family issues, the cash flow of closed-ended indentures, or resolutions, is greatly simplified by the application of prepayments to the retirement of bonds and the prohibition on the issuance of new bonds. Open-ended programs, with their changing interest rates and maturities on mortgages purchased with prepayments or new bonds, have a complexity which calls for a sophisticated, computer-assisted, and ongoing management capability.

The choice between these two approaches, to an extent, is a subjective one. There are, however, certain considerations and caveats in approaching this choice. For example, the use of an open-ended approach is better suited to issuers with an ongoing program and a staff, such as state housing finance agencies. Issuers that envision a onetime or infrequent issuance or that have limited or nonexistent staffing capabilities and rely on outside administrators are better suited to closed-ended indentures, or resolutions. Some investment bankers, credit analysts, investors, and issuers also feel that closed-ended indentures, or resolutions, are better suited to multifamily programs where the *quality* of the mortgages in the portfolio is more important than the *quantity*. However, single-family programs may be better suited to the open-ended approach: These issues are approached more on a quantitative or "actuarial" basis, and the size of the portfolio itself is a factor to consider.

Because of the complexity in the open-ended indentures, single-family programs which typically allow reinvestment of prepayments on the mortgages require very sophisticated managers at the housing agency. Because the agency under an open-ened indenture can issue subsequent series of bonds, investors have to worry about the effect of the new bond issues upon the security of their prior bonds. Investors or bond analysts must consider whether an agency's management has the expertise to determine short- and long-range cash flow patterns.

In the case of an open-ended indenture, therefore, it is important that the housing agency's staff has a proven track record of cash flow management and has shown itself able to use a considerable degree of discretion in making decisions on the reinvestment of prepayments. Since many housing agency managers originate from savings and loan institutions or mortgage banking backgrounds, it is also important to gauge whether the housing agency's staff is large enough and sophisticated enough to test its different cash flow assumptions and projections on a computer—or whether the staff consists of political hacks.

The serious investor or bond analyst should try to secure the following: the official statement and bond resolution, or trust indenture. For Section 8-11(b) projects, a financial feasibility report and market analysis, a management plan, and an operating budget are important. It is also useful to have, for single-family mortgage issues, the mortgage sale and servicing agreement with the participating lending institutions.

Of all these documents, the first three are by far the most important. As is true for any municipal bond, the official statement and bond resolution are the easiest to obtain. An analysis of how to use these documents is in Chapter 13, "Legal Protection, Disclosure, and Liability."

The Section 8-11(b) issues have generally been structured with closed-ended indentures. Since these issues also generally involve only one housing project, which is the only source of revenue to pay off the bonds, the rating agencies and investors look to a feasibility study to provide information on the quality of this very limited "portfolio."

Once again, as we have mentioned in other chapters, the financial feasibility study for closed-ended financings of Section 8-11(b) issues should be prepared by a reputable and nationally known independent firm. In the case of real estate ventures, such as these, the financial feasibility study should forecast 2 years of operations of the project once it is built. The forecast should include all reserves and their funding, the working capital for covering debt service, specific projected balance sheets, income statements, and flow-of-funds statements. If available, the feasibility study should include a market study of future levels of occupancy, "rent up," and, in general, the forecasted demand and rate of delinquency. If no feasibility study has been made, or if the issuing public authority refuses to make a study available, such conduct should tell the investor something about the management and, in many cases, discourage investment in the bonds.

Moral Obligation Bonds

We have already mentioned moral obligation bonds in various parts of this book. We touch on them again because they are a particularly important factor in the housing bond market.

Moral obligation bonds are not backed by a state government's full faith and credit or its taxing power, as are that same state's GO bonds. Nevertheless, moral obligation bonds have a kind of pledge of support from the state government in case the bonds default. While there are, by now, a number of different specific types in different states, the general concept of moral obligation bonds remains the same as at their inception with the New York State Urban Development Corporation (UDC) in 1968. That is, moral obligation bonds were issued as a way to get around the tightening restrictions by taxpayers and legislators on issuing new credit requiring voter approval and full faith and credit and taxing power guarantees. In brief, they enabled many states to issue debt to finance projects; under traditional financing schemes they would have been prohibited by law. A dispute still continues concerning the merits of moral obligation bonds. Some claim that the bonds are a vitally important financing vehicle, that they enable states to expand their debt capacity for necessary programs and avoid the constraints of archaic laws and restrictions. Others, including Arthur Levitt, the former comptroller of New York State, argue against the continuance of the moral obligation bonds because they commit citizens to vast extra-debt obligations without allowing the citizens the right of voter approval.

The unfortunate notoriety of the financing of moral obligation bonds, which occurred when the UDC defaulted, brought this whole question under public scrutiny. (In fact, UDC's notes had not received the moral obligation pledge of support from the state; only the UDC bonds had.) New York State did make good on the defaulted notes, which suggested that the state was trying to protect the moral obligation bonds and, thereby, maintain its own access to the municipal bond market. The state's making good also indicated that the state recognized these bonds as having a public purpose, namely the building of housing and other projects. Meeting the bond payments further indicated that the Legislature had the authority to make state appropriations in that way and, indeed, that these bonds could be considered an integral part of state government finance. Not only have state governments in various instances backed up moral obligation issues when they were required to; they also did so well in advance of when they had to and at times when there was not even a moral obligation pledge.

Standard & Poor's has, after covering this issue for a number of years, reached a kind of standing policy with respect to rating moral obligation bonds. It declares that it will rate them one full category below that same state's GO bonds. This provides a floor, and, in a few cases, the underlying strength of a portfolio behind a bond has led Standard & Poor's even to rate moral obligation bonds a bit higher than the one full category below the GO bonds.

Local Mortgage Bonds for Single-Family Housing: The Chicago Plan

It is at present quite uncertain whether this type of financing will be allowed by the federal government to continue because the so-called Ullman Bill, now before Congress, is seeking to abolish it. Despite the very serious problems of public policy and questions of abuses associated with it, some form of the Chicago plan financing is expected to survive for certain specific cases, under very stringent restrictions. Upon that assumption we will proceed to outline the general character of this type of financing as it has emerged, but we are fully aware that the financing may be altered.

The Chicago plan issues were the attempt to take advantage of recent financing structures in the private sector, where pass-through securities and mortgage-backed bonds had become familiar. The pass-through securities, which are not bonds, were employed, for example, in the Bank of America's use of a portfolio of mortgages to back up a bond. In this case, there was a direct pass through of mortgage repayments and prepayments to the holder of the certificates. Thus it was a simple, clear payment by the mortgagor passed through to the certificate holder. Since these were, in general, high-equity mortgages for high-income individuals with single-family homes, this was considered a well-secured certificate.

Chicago plan financing was used to take this structure of the pass-through certificate and graft onto it the "mortgage purchase program" which had been used for many years in the municipal bond field of financing. By taking advantage of the tax-exempt feature, the interest rate was a considerable advantage and offered the opportunity to arbitrage the spread between the mortgage payments and the bond payments. It thus provided a greater flexibility in the issuers' cash flow and provided a larger market of investors to interest in these new types of bonds. By grafting these two types of securities together, the inventors had created a stronger security than is usually seen in the tax-exempt market. This strength was derived from the additional security provided by the structured insurance program (including the primary mortgage insurance, pool insurance, and hazard and loss types of insurance); from the specific restrictions on the portfolio used in the closed-ended indenture; from the prohibition against prepayments of the mortgage; and from mortgage reserve funds and debt service reserves. Finally, all this security was placed in back of a pass-through certificate type of financing with the very important advantages of an interest rate spread that offered clear opportunities for arbitrage and a strong cash flow. It was the familiar mortgage purchase program from the municipal housing revenue bonds market but dressed up with very strong and very attractive features.

It was little wonder that Chicago, Pueblo, and Denver, when they launched the Chicago plan financings, were thought to have created a new wave that would rapidly spread throughout the country. However, the key questions that began to emerge concerned whether such financings really served a public purpose by helping out developers and upper-middle-class or even upper-class home buyers. In short, should they be given the advantages of tax exemption for financing what otherwise were similar profit-making housing projects, such as cooperatives, condominiums, or rental units for the nonelderly and for non-lower-class families. Both Congress and the IRS seriously questioned whether funding such projects served a "legitimate public policy purpose" and whether that funding should be permitted to have the right to tax exemption.

Yet, although some sharp correction of the abuses of the tax-exempt privilege is called for, there is a good deal of sentiment that some form of single-city mortgage purchase pass-through bonds should be allowed to continue. The problems of such securities, aside from the public purpose question, involve the risk in municipal bonds issued by entities which are in fact "shells," or no more than paper organizations, set up exclusively to facilitate these financings and with no ongoing organizational life or broader public purpose. If these problems can be prevented by stringent regulations, then some form of this type of financing for local housing may well continue.

This continuation, if it occurs, will do so partly because there appears to be a more general move across the country toward decentralization of bond issuance. State housing agencies frequently have limited staffs and limited authorizations and thus have been able to develop only a certain number of projects. Therefore, as a result of extending to local housing agencies the participation in and origin and management of projects, there has been a widespread feeling that greater production of new housing would result. In the process, as already mentioned, there have been examples of local mismanagement and abuses, and so it is still not clear just how much further this move toward greater decentralization will continue.

Conclusion

To understand the exact security, investors and bond analysts above all should remember to study the documents for any issue of bonds. This is because the same portfolio of mortgages could carry an underlying credit ranging anywhere from AAA to a noninvestment grade; it depends entirely upon how the portfolio is structured and what security, insurance, reserves, and collateral stand behind it. Just looking at the cover sheet or noting where the project or portfolio of mortgages is located is likely to lead an investor into trouble.

There has recently been a problem of which investors should be keenly aware. It involves outright misrepresentation on some bonds that have been traded, particularly Section 8-11(b) issues. Some developers, issuers, or salespeople have represented to buyers that these are federally guaranteed and that they have the full faith and credit of the U.S. government. *This is not true.* The full faith and credit is behind the rent subsidy, not the government's pledge to build the projects. And even more important, HUD, because it reserves the right to terminate the subsidy if there are extended periods of vacancy or if the project does not meet HUD specifications, *does not guarantee the bonds by any means.*

Other crucial problems for investors involve developers; they may create an equity syndication and take advantage of the investment tax credit of the first years of the project and then walk away after the tax liabilities have been reduced. In such private syndications, if they begin to have operating losses that they cannot carry any longer, there may be a sudden need to refinance, perhaps at unfavorable rates. In this way sources of additional infusions of equity capital can be lost.

A number of recent innovations have been urged in the housing bond market involving backing by the Government National Mortgage Association, or Ginnie Mae. These innovations have taken the form of permanent loan certificates as a pledge for a bond; they are, in general, special backup credits for housing issues that might not be able to be financed because, for example, the housing was to be in a bad neighborhood or because of difficulties in raising funds in the public debt markets. Each of these arrangements is extremely complicated and somewhat unwieldy. Furthermore, given the recent federal decision to disallow the Ginnie Mae pass-through certificate that was being used for hospitals as a federal backup credit, it is very questionable whether a direct Ginnie Mae pass-through backup credit for housing bonds will be forthcoming.

Cases

The New York State Urban Development Corporation

On April 10, 1968, the assembly of the state of New York, in the wake of an intense lobbying effort by Governor Nelson A. Rockefeller, approved legislation creating the New York State UDC. It was the most powerful state urban renewal agency and building authority in the nation's history, with borrowing authorization which totaled $2 billion at its peak. Nine years later, almost to the day, the UDC defaulted on $130 million in short-term loans. It was one of the largest revenue authority defaults in American history and, certainly, the most publicized one. Interestingly, within 4 years after the default, New York State propped up the ailing UDC so that not only were its 113 projects completed and occupied, but the possibility of its going to market through lease/rentals for Chrysler and the American Stock Exchange facilities loomed large.

The importance of this series of events in American state and local finance cannot be understated. The bailout of the UDC shows how resilient municipal finance is under a default scenario; the bailout also serves as a model for other similar problematic situations in states and municipalities throughout the country.

Legislation authorized the UDC to issue bonds and notes and make mortgage loans to the builder/developer for low- and moderate-income housing projects that no housing agency, such as the New York State HFA, was willing to undertake because of the risks involved. Through its own borrowings and appropriations from the state, the UDC financed all the processes of construction, beginning with the feasibility studies, and eventually incurred all project development costs. Of the UDC's 113 residential projects, 100 of them received Section 236 interest reduction subsidies from HUD. The UDC's residential construction totaled 32,887 dwelling units, and the corporation has 41 industrial, commercial, and civic projects under way.

The UDC's obligations were backed secondarily by the state's "moral obligation," but not legal, responsibility to appropriate sufficient monies to the debt service reserve funds of the corporation to meet the UDC's debt service requirements if the funds were depleted.

The primary source of the UDC's revenues is HUD payments on residential projects. These monies come under Section 236(b) of the National Housing Act as amended by the Housing and Urban Development Act of 1968. The funds appropriated under this legislation provide the housing company mortgagors with a subsidy that reduces the interest rate of the housing agency for borrowing from 8½ percent to 1 percent plus amortization. These monies total approximately 65 percent of the scheduled mortgage debt service. Therefore, the housing company mortgagor must pay only the principal amortization and interest on a self-amortizing mortgage loan with an interest rate of 1%. (One hundred of the one hundred thirteen projects received such monies.)

The Scenario

On February 25, 1975, with $1.5 billion in bonds outstanding, the UDC found that it would be unable to repay $100 million in outstanding bond anticipation notes, as well as a $30 million loan secured on January 21, 1975, from 11 New York City clearing house commercial banks, that were scheduled to come due on February 28, 1975.

In response, New York State, on February 25, 1975, created the New York State Project Finance Agency (PFA), composed primarily of state officials from the HFA, to provide long-term financing for the UDC's operations and the completion of its projects (termed the "build-out program"). The New York State Division of Housing and Community Renewal (DHCR), an agency within the Executive Department of State that is authorized to administer housing programs under the state's Private Housing Finance Law, was given supervisory jurisdiction over all the UDC residential projects. Moreover, the UDC's borrowing was capped.

The PFA provided monies for the UDC by making loans to and purchasing mortgages owned by the UDC. The PFA also received appropriations from the state and additional funds through the issuance of bonds and notes. These latter were secured by a pledge of mortgages that were owned by the PFA through purchases from the UDC and/or by pledges of mortgages that were owned by the UDC but that were pledged to back cash loans made by the PFA to the UDC.

Loans Made by the PFA to the UDC   The PFA loaned a total of $184,620,000 to the UDC on February 6, 1976, and March 9, 1977. On December 15, 1977, the PFA loaned the UDC an additional $63,128,000.

Mortgage Purchases Made by the PFA from the UDC   As of October 31, 1976, the UDC had sold 48 mortgages to the PFA with outstanding balances of approximately $250 million. During March 1977 the PFA returned to the UDC six mortgages, worth about $45 million, that it had previously purchased. These mortgages were returned through a process called "rescission" which voided the original 1975 sales transaction. Repurchase was prohibited under the agreement between the UDC and the PFA. Consequently, the "rescission" was employed. During December 1977 the PFA purchased another 8 mortgages, and the UDC reacquired 16 mortgages from the PFA through another rescission of the original 1975 sales transaction.

During the spring of 1975, direct state appropriations to the PFA totaled $198,082,000. One year later, in 1976, the state made another direct cash grant to the UDC ($88 million) to pay the debt service on the UDC's general purpose bonds coming due during the state's fiscal year ending March 31, 1977.

In the spring of 1977, the state Legislature appropriated $18 million directly to the UDC, but the UDC did not draw down the funds.

With the monies appropriated to it, the PFA purchased mortgages and loaned funds to the UDC, thus enabling the UDC to use these assets to pay the principal and interest on the defaulted notes, to provide 1 year's debt service on the outstanding bonds, and to complete the UDC projects, of which approximately two-thirds were uncompleted.

On December 1, 1977, the PFA issued $243,765,000 in refunding revenue bonds secured by HUD Section 236 payments. The issue refunded the outstanding 1976 Series A bonds and the 1977 revenue bonds. The revenue bonds were secured by approximatley $438 million in 34 residential mortgages, of which 18 were owned by the PFA and 16 by the UDC. UDC-owned mortgages were pledged on the basis of an agreement between the PFA and the UDC. HUD payments for all the pledged mortgages were calculated to be at least 1.10 times the maximum annual debt service on the refunding bonds. The PFA also covenanted that (1) no future financing would result in a reduction of the 1.10 times coverage and (2) the agency would not issue other obligations secured by a lien on the 34 pledged mortgages if any of the bonds were outstanding.

As a result of the mortgage transfers between the UDC and the PFA since 1975, the UDC owned 87 of the 113 mortgages with an aggregate face value of approximately $935 million, and the PFA owned 25 mortgages with an aggregate face value of approximately $226 million. However, because 16 of the UDC's mortgages had been pledged to secure the PFA bonds of approximately $244 million (the UDC only received the residual monies after the debt service on these obligations and expenses were paid), the UDC in effect owned 71 mortgages which were called "owned, but unpledged."

As of January 1979, the UDC's bond anticipation notes had been paid in full, the corporation's debt service reserve funds had been fully funded, no further withdrawals from the debt service reserve funds covering UDC's general purpose bonds had been made, all UDC projects had been completed and occupied, and HUD Section 236 monies should be forthcoming. It is projected, however, that only 50 percent of the scheduled payments of mortgage debt service from the housing companies, which totals 35 percent of the mortgage debt service, will be received. Consequently, the UDC's projects are not, as yet, completely self-supporting. But even with this projection, the UDC anticipates that it will require only $170 million in total funds from the state through 1980.

After the $250 million in loans made by the PFA to the UDC, 2 major mortgage purchase transactions (the PFA buying UDC mortgages), and 2 major mortgage return transactions (the PFA returning UDC mortgages), the state, in the name of the PFA, has become inextricably involved in the financial operations and viability of the UDC. Such transactions symbolize the state's commitment to the UDC, its mandate to continue such support, and the ability to continue such transactions to keep the corporation afloat.

In brief, New York State appears to bear the ultimate responsibility for the financial viability of both agencies. This scenario is especially important in light of the state's "moral obligation" to pay the debt service on UDC and PFA bonds, if necessary.

City of Albuquerque, New Mexico: Residential Mortgage Revenue Bonds, 1979 Series A ($78,560,000)[1]

Establishment of the Program

The single-family mortgage purchase program of the issuer was initially established pursuant to a resolution adopted by the issuer on December 4, 1978. The primary objectives of the program are (1) to expand the supply of funds available to persons of low or middle income for new single-family residence mortgage loans on real property located within the city of Albuquerque and (2) to stimulate the provision of additional housing needed to remedy the shortage of decent, safe, and sanitary housing in the city, particularly in housing priority areas.

Specifically, the Series A bonds were issued to provide the city with money to acquire mortgage loans secured by first mortgage liens on single-family residences which were owner-occupied two- to four-family residences.

Program Eligibility, Mortgage Loan, and Income Limitations

The program makes the new mortgage loans for the acquisition or rehabilitation of single-family residences available to persons of low or middle income under two different types of mortgage purchase arrangements.

Under the first arrangement, a mortgage lender will originate new mortgage loans (forward commitment mortgage loans), commitments for which will have been made by the mortgage lender. The mortgage loans will be closed by the mortgage lender and then sold to the trustee acting on behalf of the issuer.

Under the second arrangement, a mortgage lender will sell mortgage loans from its existing mortgage portfolio (existing mortgage loans) to the trustee acting on behalf of the issuer. The mortgage lender must utilize the proceeds from such sales to make new mortgage loans (reinvestment mortgage loans) to persons of low or middle income for the acquisition or rehabilitation of single-family residences.

The program establishes income limitations on families to qualify them as persons of low or middle income thereby making them eligible to participate in the program. The limits are presently fixed at an adjusted gross income of $24,000 plus an allowance of $1000 for each dependent claimed on the prospective mortgagor's federal income tax return. Limits on the maximum principal amounts of forward commitment mortgage loans and reinvestment mortgage loans are presently fixed at $52,000 for one-family units and $20,000 per unit for two- to four-family units.

Housing Priority Areas

The program provides for the designation of certain areas in the city of Albuquerque as "housing priority areas." In these areas, there exists a special need for the rehabilitation, replacement, or construction of single-family residences. Housing priority areas include, but are not limited to, all areas designated by the issuer as community development and urban development areas. The regulations presently require that 10 percent of each mortgage loan obligation and reinvestment mortgage loan obligation be fulfilled through mortgage loans made within housing priority areas.

Insurance

If a mortgage loan to be purchased by the city is not insured by the FHA or guaranteed by the VA, and if the loan/value ratio exceeds 80 percent, private mortgage insurance (PMI) must be maintained by each mortgagor. PMI must have 25 percent coverage where the loan/value ratio exceeds 90 percent, and 20 percent coverage where the loan/value ratio exceeds 80 percent but does not exceed 90 percent.

Certain limitations are also imposed on the loan/value ratios of the mortgage loans. No more than 50 percent of the aggregate principal amount of mortgage loans, which are insured by a private mortgage insurer and are purchased from the net proceeds of any series of bonds, may have a loan/value ratio equal to or exceeding 90 percent; and no mortgage loan may have a loan/value ratio exceeding 95 percent. With respect to the Series A mortgage loans, no more than 50 percent of the aggregate principal amount of mortgage loans purchased from the net proceeds of the Series A bonds may have a loan/value ratio equal to or exceeding 90 percent; and no mortgage loan may have a loan/value ratio exceeding 95 percent.

A master policy of supplemental mortgage insurance must be maintained by the trustee. It covers certain losses in excess of the amount or type of coverage afforded by PMI, FHA insurance, or VA guarantees up to a policy limit of (with respect to Series A bonds) whichever is greater: $1,500,000 or 15 percent of the aggregate initial principal amount of all mortgage loans purchased by the city.

Normal hazard insurance and, if available, flood insurance must be maintained by each mortgagor to cover the mortgagor's single-family residences.

Special hazard insurance must be maintained by the trustee to cover losses resulting from coinsurance under the normal hazard insurance policies and certain risks not covered by such policies.

Security for the Series A Bonds

The Series A bonds are secured by and payable solely from the revenues, assets, and monies pledged under the indenture, including monies in the mortgage loan reserve fund and the bond reserve fund.

The mortgage loan reserve fund is to be maintained at 1 percent of the aggregate amount in the program fund; the bond reserve fund is to be maintained at 12 percent of the original principal amount of all outstanding series of bonds, subject to certain exceptions described herein. The 12 percent bond reserve fund requirement is equal to 147 percent of the maximum debt service on the Series A bonds.

The Virginia Housing Development Authority

During the fall of 1978, the Virginia Housing Development Authority came to market with a $100 million bond issue for home mortgage purchases. To be sure, this issue was only one of many programs in which the authority has engaged. At that time, the authority had provided mortgage financing for single-family and multifamily housing for persons and families of low and moderate income in Virginia. As of June 30, 1978, the authority had provided mortgage financing for 19,591 units of housing, and of these units, 12,076 were townhouses, garden apartments, and other multifamily dwellings and 7515 were for individual homes.

In addition, the authority provides temporary loans for housing sponsors for the construction and/or rehabilitation of single-family housing; makes loans for energy conservation and rehabilitation improvements to housing units; participates with private financial institutions in the construction financing of FHA-insured and multifamily housing; provides permanent financing for single-family housing under a separate bond resolution; and provides construction and permanent financing for multifamily units.

Home Mortgage Loan Program

The authority may make and may purchase mortgage loans for financing the ownership of single-family residential housing. Mortgage loans may be made in amounts not to exceed 98 percent of the sales price in excess of $25,000. *The maximum sales price currently permitted is $35,885, and the maximum adjusted family income that a mortgagor may earn is $16,000.* Mortgage loans are made directly by the authority and are originated and serviced by banks and savings and loan associations pursuant to agreements with the authority.

The General Bond Resolution requires that mortgage loans be insured or guaranteed by the Veteran's Administration, the Federal Housing Administration, or other institutions of the federal government, or have a loan/value ratio that does not exceed 90 percent, or, for the first 4 years, be subject to private mortgage insurance. However, all the mortgage loans of this issue were to be privately insured. This stipulation is important because, contrary to common perception, privately insured mortgages have lower rates of delinquency and foreclosure than do mortgages that are either insured by the FHA or guaranteed by the VA.

Financing of the Mortgage Loan Program to Date

With the home mortgage bonds, 1978 Series A, issued in August 1978, the authority began operations for permanent financing under the home mortgage loan program. A sum of $64,853,300 from this issue was deposited in the program account. With this sum and other funds, $43,700,000 was subject to forward commitment agreements with PDS agents for the making of mortgage loans before March 9, 1979, and $21,893,700 was subject to builder commitment agreements for the making of mortgage loans before June 7, 1979.

As of November 30, 1978, monies disbursed for mortgage loans under forward commitment agreements totaled $19,085,124, and monies disbursed for mortgage loans under builder commitment agreements totaled $2,352,300. The amount of $43,492,327 was left in the program account. *No mortgage loans were delinquent or in foreclosure under the program.*

The 1974 Resolution Program

Before August 1978 the authority made and purchased mortgage loans under this program. It had received $210,458,873 to finance mortgage loans from the proceeds of the 1974 resolution bonds outstanding. As of November 30, 1978, $9,327,347 of the original proceeds was undisbursed, and it is expected that by August 1979 this sum will be disbursed under forward commitment agreements and builder commitment agreements. As of the same date, $2,501,884 or 1.34 percent of the $187,229,181 in outstanding mortgage loans which were financed by the 1974 program were delinquent by one or two monthly payments or were in foreclosure.

As of the same November date, $16,201,457 had been received in prepayments under the 1974 program. Of this amount, $2,788,458 had been used to pay the principal on outstanding bonds; $7,730,626 will be applied to the payment of future principal installments on bonds; $521,571 had been utilized to pay the principal on outstanding bonds originally to have been paid from scheduled principal payments but not actually received as of November 30, 1978, because of delays in originating mortgage loans; and the remaining $5,160,802 had been utilized to purchase or make mortgage loans providing a weighted average yield, on such loans of approximately 8.27 percent.

Nonetheless, with the backing of the state of Virginia through its "moral obligation" pledge to pay the debt service on the bonds, if necessary, and the strong early record of the authority in a variety of other programs, the bonds of this issue should be rated about one notch below the state's GO bonds.

Note to Chapter 8

[1] Source: official statement, March 1, 1979.

chapter 9

Tax-Exempt Bonds for Hospitals

Hospital financing, until 1960, remained generally a small localized operation, a cottage industry. Most hospitals, until then, financed their capital improvements and expansion via local gifts and charity, income from operations, their own funded depreciation, and small federal grants. When such sources proved inadequate, hospitals turned to a bank mortgage or taxable mortgage bonds from either an insurance company or a bank.

However, in the last 15 years, health care has become, without question, one of America's fastest-growing industries. In fact, 9 percent of the GNP goes to health care in the United States today; it represents the second-largest industry in the country by number of employees and the third-largest in terms of revenues. Hospital construction costs alone have shot up from less than $1 billion in 1960 to close to $10 billion in 1979. New medical technology has introduced new procedures, medicare has caused a dramatic increase in the utilization of health services, and the higher standards of health care have necessitated upgrading. Changes in demographics, or the shifts of the population and concentrations of patients to suburban hospitals from inner-city hospitals, have also changed the character of medical finance. New medical technology has increased the rate of obsolescence for capital equipment and simultaneously forced the upgrading of all medical facilities.

These and other factors have caused tremendous financial pressures on the capital costs of building and new equipment for hospitals, on top of the severe inflation in all operating costs and capital costs. They have forced hospitals to seek capital outside the local community by entering the national public debt markets. These trends have completely changed the whole nature of hospital financing in this country.[1]

As a consequence, in the 5 years from 1969 to 1974 debt financing from all sources grew from only 32 percent to 58 percent of the total capital required for new hospital construction. By 1977, $5.5 billion, or nearly 90 percent of the total new capital required to finance hospital expansion, came via the issuance of some form of debt. And nearly 88 percent of this debt was financed through the issuance of tax-exempt bonds. Table 9-1 shows the amount of tax-exempt bonds for hospital financing from 1974 to 1978.

In 1979 the number of projects being financed was shrinking, as was the total level of financing. Yet the average size of an issue grew over 100 percent in the last 5 years, and even in 1978 when there occurred a substantial decrease from 1977, the tax-exempt bonds sold for new hospitals were still almost 7 percent of the entire municipal revenue bond market.

Hospital financing for ongoing operating costs was transformed during this same period because of the increasing reliance by hospitals upon *third-party reimbursement* for payments instead of on revenues from patient charges. The federal government's involvement in paying the nation's health care costs rose from $2 billion in 1960 to $60 billion in 1979.[2] In fact, it is projected to be over $100 billion by 1981. This dramatic increase was largely the result of medicare and medicaid patients whose benefits accounted for 74 percent of the 1976 expenditures, or $25 billion.

Up to 90 percent of all hospital revenues are derived from medicare, medicaid, and Blue Cross and other private health insurance plans. Hospitals now finance day-to-day operations and some of their capital needs out of anticipated reimbursements which they expect will come from insurance companies and from federal and state agencies.

The impact that changes in these reimbursements have on the creditworthiness of hospitals, therefore, depends upon exactly what the reimbursement plan in a particular area is. For example, a hospital has a choice under Blue Cross and medicaid of different reimbursement formulas, but there is no choice under medicare.

The variation between different states' formulas for Blue Cross or medicaid can be quite substantial. In fact, to take an extreme example, a particular hospital could be an extremely strong credit if it were in Massachusetts or in danger of default if it were in New York—entirely

TABLE 9-1 Hospital Tax-Exempt Bonds

Year	Amounts, in $ billions
1974	1291
1975	1959
1976	2726
1977	4731
1978	3122

because these two states had different Blue Cross (or other) reimbursement policies.

The majority of reimbursement is paid by commercial insurance. The rates vary, depending upon the coverage level and the quality of the insurance program. Reimbursement is paid by the various Blue Cross plans across the country, which vary from cost formulas to cost plus 6 percentage points to full charges. The plans can also vary from some modification of charges to prospective programs in risk situations. Federal government reimbursements to hospitals for medicare come through local intermediaries (frequently the Blue Cross plan is used, on the basis of the definition allowed for cost), and there are reimbursements in every state except Arizona.[3] In contrast, medicaid is a joint state and federal program that reimburses with federal funds on a matching basis up to a certain level whatever the state provides. Arizona, again, is the only state that does not have it.

Although the federal government has attempted through a whole range of measures to control the soaring health costs generated by many of its own programs, it has not succeeded in slowing the growth of these costs. For example, while "certificate of need" legislation was intended to slow the growth of hospital capital expenditures, it has not done so. What has happened is that this federal pressure has resulted in less financing going into new construction and more into modernization programs and the reconstruction of old facilities.

It is sometimes agreed that because medicare and medicaid allow for the reimbursement of interest payments and depreciation, this partially forms an indirect financial cushion for hospital bondholders. However, there are very complex arrangements for reimbursements under all the different formulas, and so this cushion cannot always be counted upon. For instance, if there are no patients in new hospital facilities, then there is no reimbursement cushion.

American Hospital Finance

There are basically four different types of hospitals in the United States: federal government hospitals, state and municipal hospitals, not-for-profit hospitals, and the private proprietary hospitals.[4] Of these four types the private, full-profit hospitals are only allowed to issue up to $10 million in tax-exempt bonds to finance capital additions. The federal hospitals, such as those run by the Veterans' Administration, do not need to issue tax-exempt securities, for they can simply finance new construction out of federal taxes. Therefore, it is the state and municipal hospitals, as well as the nonprofit hospitals, that enter the tax-exempt market in a sizable fashion to issue municipal revenue bonds. Nearly 50 percent of all the hospital beds in the United States are controlled by voluntary and nonprofit organizations or religious orders which can finance via tax-exempt bonds because of state-by-state legislation.

The growth in tax-exempt bonds issued by hospitals has accounted for most of the total growth in the long-term debt of hospitals. Between 1974 and 1977, the dollar volume of tax-exempt financing for hospitals more than tripled, and all other major forms of debt financing for health-care institutions grew by an estimated 60 percent. Of the total financings of all hospital capital expenditures in 1978, fully 75 percent were from issues of tax-exempt bonds.

Despite the enormous growth in health-care services, there are hardly any more hospitals today than there were in 1930 in the United States. The difference is that although fewer in number, the hospital units are larger. The average size is at least three times what it was 40 years ago. In a quite different but related development, small hospitals have been combining into large units, such as Intermountain Health Care in Salt Lake City, Utah. This facility is a highly visible example of a multihospital system, horizontally integrated and serving an entire intermountain region. There are numerous other facilities like Intermountain which constitute an increasingly significant portion of the financing work in which a number of underwriters engage. These financial institutions are by no means simply passive observers of the mergers of hospitals and conglomerations of health-care facilities. Instead, they are active initiators and key participants in this transformation of hospitals into larger units and systems.

Indeed, hospitals are changing the nature of their operations because of the discipline that is necessary in order to obtain capital from the private capital market.

Financing Hospital Tax-Exempt Bonds

One of the most important things in the preparation of a tax-exempt bond financing for a hospital is a "certificate of need" issued by the local health system agency or by a regional planning group (or by states or even by HEW). This certificate states that the hospital is hereby given the right to spend more than $100,000 to build an addition, or undertake a renovation or modernization, or add a number of beds. This certificate is essential because it is required by law[5] and by all third-party reimbursement payers. Increasing state regulation has made it more difficult to obtain certificates, especially in areas that are already oversaturated—

such as New York City, where there are over 5000 beds that the hospital authorities are trying to eliminate. Therefore, some municipal and voluntary hospitals in the city have closed down, and more may do so. (This pattern is not necessarily typical for all large cities.)

Assuming that this initial hurdle of the certificate is overcome, it is quite likely that the hospital will be financed via tax-exempt bonds because, as already mentioned, they account for over 75 percent of all debt financing of hospitals (in 1978). This percentage is expected to rise over the next decade.

The bond counsel for the issuing authority must first determine whether that particular state government has enabling legislation for the issuance of tax-exempt securities. As of February 1979, only four states did not have legislation permitting the tax-exempt financing of hospital projects: Alaska, California, Hawaii, and Nevada. (New pending legislation in California may allow tax-exempt financing on a limited basis.) In some states the hospital wishing to issue tax-exempt bonds must apply to the statewide authority; in others, to the local hospital authority.

Tax-exempt hospital bonds are issued by states, by municipal hospitals, by a county, or by a city. Alternatively, these bonds are issued by health-financing authorities that were originally instituted by the state, county, or city (or by a nonprofit corporation established under the tax guidelines of the IRS, if the beneficial interest in the new facility is given to the municipality at the end of the period covered by the debt issue).

Since it is the hospital's own financial strength that is the credit behind these bonds and not the municipality or the government issuing authority, a careful analysis of the creditworthiness of the hospital is crucial. It is important that bonds secure a BBB or better investment grade rating from Moody's and/or Standard & Poor's, for otherwise the potential purchasers of the bonds will reject the offering.

Although public offerings for hospital financings involve front-end costs that are higher than those of any other method of financing (front-end costs include printing fees, rating agency fees, legal fees, the fee for a financial feasibility study, and underwriting fees), they usually provide an interest rate 2 percentage points below the rate of any other method of financing. The front-end costs in a private placement of a hospital issue are lower, but a higher interest rate is incurred. Nevertheless, there are other financial advantages of public offerings of tax-exempt bonds. For example, the bonds usually can have a longer term to maturity (25 to 30, or even up to 40, years), and additional bonds can be sold during the life of the first series of bonds if the hospital maintains a good record of performance. But perhaps the other key advantage is that up to 100 percent of the total financing can be supplied by the public offering of tax-exempt bonds.

The extra time, however, that is necessarily involved in extra legal, financial, and rating analysis makes the financing of tax-exempt bonds take longer to complete than any other method of financing. (Significantly longer time periods are required for processing any federally guaranteed loan program.) Nevertheless, these extra steps cannot be omitted. The financial feasibility study, for example, is usually required by the issuing authority, by the rating agencies, and by the major purchasers of the bonds. The feasibility study makes projections to determine whether the project will, in fact, generate enough funds to pay off the debt and to cover timely payments of both interest and principal. To provide this information, the financial feasibility study, by surveying trends of costs and payments over the previous 5 years, sets out to project revenues and expenses over a 3- to 6-year period. Such studies also project the actual use of the new facilities being financed and evaluate the caliber of doctors and management, the socioeconomic background of patients and changing demographics of the area, and the likely competition from other hospitals. Because these estimates of the debt service coverage, the sources of future payments, and the future utilization rates of different hospital services are all so vital to the success of the facility, the financial feasibility study becomes the primary estimate of the credit quality of the bond issue. Obviously, the rating agencies make their own tests of these and other factors, and it is their ratings on which the investing public, as well as institutional buyers, rely. Nevertheless, the rating agencies rely heavily upon financial feasibility studies.

The security for a hospital bond issue may be a gross revenue pledge or a net revenue pledge. Second, the debt (from the standpoint of the issuing authority) may be a general or limited obligation. Third, although there will usually be a mortgage, in many cases there is not. Fourth, the hospital may pledge all its assets or, alternatively, only part of them. Fifth, the hospital may make monthly mortgage payments, monthly lease payments, or monthly debt service payments. (These are essentially quite similar in their cash-flow implications but involve different methods of repayment.)

Bascially there are two approaches to hospital financing: the lease method and the loan agreement method.

The Lease Method of Financing   Under one lease method of financing the issuing authority issues its bonds and with the proceeds buys the facilities from the hospital. It then leases the same facilities back to the hospital.

Under a second variation, the hospital is leased to the issuer of the bonds under a lease agreement. The issuing authority then subleases the facilities back to the hospital. The lease agreement is structured so that the lease payments are equal to the bond payments and secure the bonds.

This lease, sublease, or lease-back method of financing, instead of a mortage, uses an unconditional guarantee by the hospital to make payments on the lease. (This guarantee is something like a take or pay guarantee, used in other types of municipal financings and discussed in Chapter 7, "Public Power Bonds.")

The Loan Agreement Method of Financing   This second approach to hospital bond financing is being used more and more because it does not involve a change of title from the hospital to the authority. The hospital keeps title to the facility and simply receives a loan from the authority. Under this arrangement the mortgage to the new hospital facility is assigned to the trustee to secure payments on the bond.

The difference between these two methods (loan agreement versus lease) involves the rights of the trustee in the event of default.

Under the lease method, in the case of default the trustee has the right to reenter the project and take over. The trustee can also force payments through the unconditional guarantee provision. Under the loan agreement method of financing, the trustee can, in the case of default, obtain any revenues of the hospital and can also foreclose on the mortgage. The issuing authority usually assigns the loan or lease payments it receives from the hospital to the trustee as security for the payment of the revenue bonds. The authority will also assign the agreement and mortgage to the trustee in case the hospital defaults.

Most hospital bonds are secured by an agreement to pledge gross revenues, or gross receipts and a mortgage (or some other pledge as well as a mortgage). The mortgage is a general obligation of the hospital, under which it must make monthly or semiannual mortgage payments to a higher state issuing authority. These payments are equal to the debt service (i.e., principal and interest). The hospital must also make any other payments required by the agreement and mortgage. It is important, however, to realize that the mortgage on the hospital is really not of much value as a solid asset security for the bondholder. This is because there is some question as to what can be done with a hospital once it has gone bankrupt. Very little of solid asset value except equipment can normally be salvaged. Therefore, some hospital bond analysts hardly count the hospital's mortgage when analyzing the security on the bonds.

The mortgage on the hospital, however, is important in a different respect, aside from its asset value, because it prevents another creditor from securing a superior lien position, and it also provides a specific way for a creditor to remove the directors, in case of a default, and attempt to bring the hospital back on an even keel.

Credit Analysis of Hospital Bonds

Like industrial revenue "municipal" bonds, which are really backed not by a municipality but by a company, a hospital's municipal revenue bonds are really backed only by that hospital and its ability to generate revenues (unless there is a specific extra federal guarantee, which will be considered later).

Obviously the easiest hospital credit to analyze is the one which is not undertaking new construction but simply modernizing what it already has. In cases of bonds to finance modernization, the credit analysis simply tests whether the additional costs, given the same level of hospital services and revenues, will be sufficiently cost-effective to meet the higher debt service.

Most hospital financings, however, are far more complex, especially given today's strong tendency toward multihospital mergers. Hospital bond analysts, therefore, concentrate on a handful of key financial ratios for examining a particular hospital system and for comparing its competitive position with that of other hospitals. The comparison is in terms of historic and projected revenues and expenses, type and caliber of management, doctors, and the socioeconomic class of the patients.

First to be examined is the operating margin, which consists of gross revenues as a percentage of net income. Then for each 5-year period the forecast of future debt service coverage taken from the financial feasibility report gauges how much revenue will be available from hospital operations for covering the debt expense. The ratio of debt per bed, which used to be a standard, is now considered quite suspect, for the health-care emphasis of new hospitals may involve outpatients or ancillary facilities or be in other ways totally unrelated to numbers of beds.

The most important operational characteristics that serious investors or bond analysts should seek are number of beds, patient occupancy, gross revenues, and gross revenues per patient day. Of all the ratios, the operating margin and coverage of debt service are perhaps the most important. In general, it is also relevant to see if the hospital is staffed with enough younger doctors who have years of patient admissions ahead of them, and whether the staff includes a high percentage of board-certified or board-eligible doctors. Finally, in comparing hospitals over the last 15 years, it appears clear that the less dependent the hospital is upon medicare and medicaid, the higher its investment rating is likely to be.

Operating margins and debt ratios, although important, can frequently disguise long-term problems in a hospital's financial condition, and thus the investor or bond analyst is well advised not to judge solely according to the numerical ratios but to consider the quality of the area, the patients, the doctors, and the management. Some top analysts advise visiting the hospital to make sure it is clean and odorless.

As already mentioned, the reimbursement plans are a key test of a hospital's credit and are tied to a number of things. Because of the provision for reimbursement of capital costs for depreciation and interest payments, one of the fundamental considerations is the hospital's balance sheet strength, particularly the relationship between its net property plant and equipment and long-term debt. If the balance sheet is strong, extra cash flow, extra capacity to reinvest, and extra ability to pay debts result.

Bond analysts also check very carefully whether a hospital's charges for costs are above or below what is allowable under reimbursement programs. If the charges are above the ceilings, the hospital is going to have costs that are not even recognized.

Hospitals have loss leaders, such as obstetrics departments, which in themselves do not bring in much revenue but which are necessary to tie in gynecologists or other doctors who would leave to go to another hospital for their nonobstetric work if obstetrical facilities were unavailable. Hospital bond analysts therefore are wary of singling out especially unprofitable departments or unusually profitable divisions, such as x-rays and labs, because the key profit centers today may be dead fads tomorrow. Thus the analyst concentrates upon the total revenue of the whole hospital.

Despite their extraordinarily high running expenses, the soundest hospitals tend to be the major teaching hospitals. Some of them have hefty endowments, and many are in the forefront of all the new medical developments and changes in technology. Also, they are involved in all areas of medicine and so are never as dependent upon any one area as would be a specialty hospital. Finally, they tend to serve a geographic area that is far larger than the area served by any local hospital, although this advantage is not as strong as it used to be because specialists have saturated the suburbs. Even local hospitals have a range of specialists on call and need not refer as many cases to the great teaching hospitals as in earlier years. Finally, a teaching hospital's endowment alone translates directly onto the balance sheet, for the hospital can rely less on cash flow.

In the past the hospitals that got into trouble financially, were each in start-up situations where there was a projected population influx which simply did not materialize. However, in 1979 the General Accounting Office projected that many of the hospitals subsidized by federal programs such as FHA-242 and the Hill-Burton loan monies were candidates for default.

Bond analysts tend to favor strongly the newly merged chains of hospitals, such as Intermountain Health Care; Samaritan Health Services in Phoenix; Fairview Community Hospitals and Health Center in Minneapolis; and Sisters of Mercy Health Corporation in Farmington Hills, Michigan, which is the largest in the United States.

The Health Maintenance Organizations (HMOs), which are more like insurance companies than multiple hospital systems, also are emerging in many areas as large organizations providing the entire range of health-care services. These large organizations, like the large hospital systems, have a corporate structure and a staff to deal with reimbursement and drug purchasing, financial management, capitalization, the planning or long-term debt, and central control policy for administration; for delivery of care the large organizations employ decentralized institutions. In short, when all these resources are pooled and organized under a central corporate structure which is geared to serve a diversity of geographic service areas, the result is a spreading of the financial risk and a genuine pooling of the cash flow and other assets.

The Size of the Tax-Exempt Bond Issue

Before estimating the debt portion of the project's development costs it is necessary to differentiate the other funds from the reserve funds, government grants, endowments, gifts, and future cash flow. It is not simple to calculate the various available financing mechanisms that hospitals should use in this one particular case; nor is it easy to determine for certain a hospital's maximum debt capacity. The job of the bond underwriter or investment banker is to determine which financing method is best; normally, the best method will allow a hospital to use the cheapest method of raising the total debt. But the first step is to calculate how much is needed.

Nearly 90 percent of the capital funds of many hospitals are derived from tax-exempt bonds; nevertheless, financing is also obtained from hospital endowments, philanthropic gifts, and internal operations, which together account, even for tax-exempt projects, for over 10 percent of revenues.

As Table 9-2 suggests, although federal and state medicare and medicaid reimbursements are important for operating expenses and have

TABLE 9-2 Summary of Debt Financings for Hospitals, 1974 to 1978, in $ Millions

	1974		1975		1976		1977		1978	
	Dollar volume	Market share (%)	Dollar volume	Market share (%)	Dollar volume	Market share (%)	Dollar volume	Market share (%)	Dollar volume	Market share (%)
Tax-exempt public offerings	1291	58.3	1959	71.8	2726	69.2	4731	75.0	3122	73.9
Private placements	249	11.2	44	1.6	214	5.4	381	6.0	339	8.0
Taxable public offerings	250	11.3	275	10.1	300	7.6	350	5.5	275	6.5
Government-sponsored programs	275	12.4	350	12.8	500	12.7	600	9.5	290	6.9
Mortgages with commercial banks	150	6.8	100	3.7	200	5.1	250	4.0	200	4.7
Total	2215	100.0	2728	100.0	3940	100.0	6312	100.0	4226	100.0

SOURCES: For tax-exempt public offerings, *The Daily Bond Buyer*; for private placements, *Investment Dealer's Digest*; for government-sponsored programs, U.S. Department of Housing and Urban Development and *National Journal*.

become crucial to today's health market, direct, outright government grants for hospital financing have never been a truly significant source of capital for the health-care industry. As demonstrated in the University of Pittsburgh Capital Conference of November 1976, the federal government's Hill-Burton programs at their peak in 1960 supplied only 11 percent of the total capital required for hospital construction. Today those federal programs finance less than 1 percent of direct new capital construction.

As shown in Table 9-3, a significant amount of the capital used for hospital expansion and new construction *is* provided by the Farmers Home Administration, the Federal Housing Administration (FHA), the Government National Mortgage Association (GNMA), conventional mortgages, and taxable bonds.

There are now several different forms of federal government agency financing, insuring, or guaranteeing of hospital financing. The outright financing usually consists of an insured and guaranteed loan for up to 25 years. This approach has been an alternative to tax-exempt financing. The advantages, obviously, are that these mortgage-backed guaranteed bonds are backed by the insurance of the FHA and the guarantee of the GNMA. Disadvantages of this approach result because of the length of time it takes to process the application through the government bureaucracies of HEW, HUD, or other agencies and because of the very costly HEW standards that hospitals must meet. The disadvantages have caused this method of financing to be less popular than tax-exempt financing.

However, there has developed a new method of backing a hospital financing of a tax-exempt bond issue with an additional FHA/GNMA guarantee. This controversial program's key advantage was that hospitals which were less able to receive an investment grade rating, which were in disadvantaged economic communities, or which would normally be forced to pay a high rate of interest because they were barred from the tax-exempt bond market were given access to the tax-exempt market and provided with a federal backstop guarantee. Thus the federal

TABLE 9-3 Funding Sources

Source	Financed amount, in $ millions
Tax-exempt bonds	4904
Farmers home loans	142
FHA/GNMA	325
Conventional mortgages	750
Private placement and taxable bonds	500
Total	6621

government's guarantee supplied such bonds with the very strongest credit enabling them to be marketed at the lowest possible interest cost. The disadvantage of this combined tax-exempt, GNMA-backed financing system is once again the lengthy guarantee procedures which the federal government requires. This combination program was terminated in March 1979 by HUD. Its availability is currently being questioned in court (*Beth Israel Medical Center v. HUD*), and its tax-exempt status is being investigated by other government agencies.

The Risks of Tax-Exempt Hospital Bonds

The market for tax-exempt hospital bonds is really only a development of the last decade or two, but its extraordinary growth and the involvement by different participants during this period make it clear that the initial worries about its success were unfounded.

The typical investors today in tax-exempt hospital revenue bonds are municipal bond funds, some casualty companies, and individuals. While commercial banks tend to purchase the term maturities, individuals tend to purchase the serial maturities. The tax-exempt municipal bond funds are a relatively recent phenomenon. They account for an increasingly large percentage of the purchasers in this market because they buy in large block purchases. It has become very important for hospital bonds to secure an A rating or better because these municipal bond funds usually will not invest otherwise.

The bond rating was crucial in opening up this market for hospital tax-exempt bonds, for these were unknown securities until then. Once they were given an A rating and could seemingly be compared with other A-rated revenue bonds, they could easily be traded in the broader public markets.

There are almost no AAA hospitals because these are project financings. In 1978 the AA hospitals accounted for only 5½ percent of all ratings found in the AA category. These tend to be the major regional referral medical centers and have a larger-than-local market. The single A category (comprising A−, A, and A+) accounts for about 87 percent of hospital ratings by number of issues.[6]

Hospitals are a good example of why revenue bond A's are sold and traded differently from GO A's; the A of the hospital revenue bond will almost invariably sell at a higher interest rate and have a higher interest cost. Hospital bonds tend to be sold and traded differently from GO bonds and frequently differently from other types of revenue bonds as well. This is partly because a hospital cannot raise taxes as can a city with its GO bond, because the hospital market is often thinner due to fewer buyers, and because it is usually a project financing that will be paid for by the degree to which the hospital is actually utilized. Thus a hospital bond is generally more risky than, for example, a water and sewer revenue bond or a comparably rated GO bond. Whereas water and sewer users will almost never disconnect once hooked up, patients can, after all, simply shift to another nearby hospital.

The amount that the underwriter can normally make on a hospital deal is a typical spread of anywhere from 2.5 to 1.5 percent of the total issue size. To underwriters in the corporate bond market, such spreads are considered incredibly large, and the risks to them appear small.[7]

However, to municipal specialists the risks are viewed as substantial, especially for start-up situations, and fully justify their spread. We mention this comparative viewpoint on the perception of risk and reward in different securities markets because to those reading this book who come with experience exclusively in the fields of equities and corporate bonds, it should be noted that often the risks in municipal bonds are quite different from the risks in corporate ones, and thus the two are not directly comparable.

In brief, while corporate spreads tend to be thinner than the spreads for municipal bonds, it should be noted that the risks in municipal bonds often are quite different from the risks in corporate ones, and thus the risks and rewards of the two are not directly comparable. The spread for municipal bonds includes management fees, underwriting expenses, and take down or compensation to the salespeople. This last is the largest component of the spread, and frequently it is needed because it is harder to sell an unknown municipal bond than a well-known corporate name. The spread varies with the timing in the market, the rating, and the net interest cost. Also important are the taxing ability of the issuing entity, supply and demand and competition factors versus monopoly, the management capability of the issuer, and the essential need for the new facility to exist.

The primary risk of hospital financings centers upon actually getting patients into the beds. This is not to discount the risks of bad debts and insufficient reimbursement but to place those in perspective after the risk of totally inadequate occupancy. The risk to the bondholder of actual hospital defaults is quite small. There have been only 2 major defaults of all hospital bond issues.

Since up to 90 percent of the operating budget of a hospital has come from third-party reimbursees (meaning Blue Cross, Blue Shield, medicare, medicaid, private insurance companies), it is tempting to consider the risk of hospital financings as only the 10 percent remaining monies required for the operating budget.[8] This, however, is too simple, for such reimbursements are not, in fact, unconditionally guaranteed. Still, they do help provide the investor with a better degree of assurance than might be obtained on many other investments. For this reason, while hospital bonds are sometimes looked at as more risky than other types of municipal bonds, such as water and sewer bonds, their track record to date has been strong.

Partly because of this track record, according to a study projecting the health-care market to 1982 by Booz Allan and Hamilton for Standard & Poor's Corporation, debt financings are expected to be used in 100 percent of all projects and to account for 90 percent of all construction dollars.[9] Of that total, tax-exempt bonds are expected to account for nearly 90 percent of the debt issued.[10]

Hospital and health-care financing are so different from most of the rest of the municipal finance field that in certain firms a separate specialty or subsidiary has been formed. Specific firms are equipped to handle the financing of special types of hospital projects, but not others. Some firms specialize in financing simple hospital additions or single hospital units, whereas others focus upon large, extremely complex multihospital financings.

The Standard & Poor's Worksheet for Hospital Bonds

Figure 9-1 is a Standard & Poor's worksheet used in the firm's analysis of hospital revenue bonds, intended to give a clear outline of the most important determinants of a hospital credit rating.

Cases

Determinants of creditworthiness or fiscal stability may be ascertained by the information presented in the following three cases. The important factors are simply net income, debt service coverage, and cash flow rather than pages and pages of tables.

As a result, the major indicators are found in the feasibility studies of the major accounting firms and management consulting firms which assess the ability of the hospital to service the debt that it anticipates issuing. The point of the following cases, therefore, is to show the present methods of financing hospitals through public finance and the options for decreasing the costs of medical and hospital care in the United States.

STANDARD & POOR'S CORPORATION
HOSPITAL REVENUE BOND WORKSHEET

ISSUE: . . . .

FISCAL YEAR: . . . . COMPLETION: . . . .

FEASIBILITY CONSULTANT: . . . .

	HISTORICAL						FORECAST				
OPERATIONS											
BEDS											
ADMISSIONS											
PATIENT DAYS											
ALOS											
OCCUPANCY											
INCOME											
REVENUES											
EXPENSES											
NET AVAIL.											
EXCESS											
ANNL. D/S											
COVERAGE							x	x	x	x	x
MAX. D/S											
COVERAGE							x	x	x	x	x
MAX. D/S % REV.											
RATE INCREASE											
BALANCE SHEET											
CASH											
CURRENT ASSETS											
CURRENT LIAB.											
CURRENT RATIO											
NET PROP./PLANT											
LONG-TERM DEBT											
FUND BALANCE											

REVENUE COMPOSITION

BLUE CROSS: . . . .   FTE'S/OCC. BED: . . . .
MEDICARE: . . . .   BAD DEBTS: . . . .
MEDICAID: . . . .   ACCTS. REC.: . . . .
COMMERCIAL: . . . .
SELF PAY/OTHER: . . . .   ASSUMED INTEREST RATE: . . . . %

Figure 9-1 Sample of a rating work sheet for a hospital revenue bond. (SOURCE: Standard & Poor's Corporation, *Municipal and International Bond Ratings: An Overview*, p. 76.) Reprinted by permission.

Intermountain Health Care, Inc.

Skyrocketing increases in the costs of medical and hospital care have, as previously discussed, financially strapped many health-care institutions throughout the United States. The answer to trimming hospital and equipment costs may be found in the concept of "pooling" the resources of the medical facilities within a limited geographic area. There are few such systems operating today, but one that is sure to be a model for others to follow is the Intermountain Health Care (IHC) system of Utah, Idaho, and Wyoming.

In the late 1800s, the Mormon church (the Church of Jesus Christ of Latter-day Saints) established a hospital system in the area of Salt Lake City, Utah. Intermountain Health Care was formed in 1975 when the Mormon church decided that the hospitals that it owned and operated were not essential to its function as a religious institution. Accordingly, in that year it decided to divest itself of its hospital properties by spinning them off into a new nonprofit corporation that would not be controlled by the church.

Today, that system, one of the largest hospital systems in the United States, consists of 19 hospitals, 10 of which IHC owns and operates, 4 of which are leased from counties or municipalities and operated by IHC, and 5 of which are operated by IHC pursuant to management contracts. IHC also provides certain shared services for hospitals located in Idaho, Wyoming, and Nevada that are not included among the system's hospitals.

IHC has financed its expansion programs in part through the issuance of tax-exempt revenue bonds of the cities in which IHC hospitals are located. While different cities have issued bonds at different times, all such financings are essentially equally secured by all the revenues generated by IHC, regardless of sources. This has been accomplished through a master financing instrument called a Master Indenture. It was created for IHC and contains all the covenants and security provisions to which IHC has agreed. Each time IHC incurs any long-term debt, it issues its note to the lender, pursuant to the Master Indenture, for the principal amount of the debt. By this technique each lender, as a holder of an IHC note, is an equal beneficiary of the covenants, restrictions, and obligations of IHC as set forth in the Master Indenture. The notes are not secured by any of IHC's assets, but IHC has agreed not to pledge its assets for the benefit of any other lender.

In the case of the tax-exempt revenue bond financing which IHC has engaged in, the issuing city issues its bonds and lends the proceeds to IHC to build the project located in the city. In return IHC issues its note pursuant to the Master Indenture and delivers it to the city, so that the city is a lender to IHC on an equal standing with all other lenders (including other cities).

With this structure IHC has earned bond ratings of Aa by Moody's Investors Services and AA by Standard & Poor's Corporation, making it the highest-rated nonprofit hospital corporation which has issued its debt publicly.

The 19 hospitals of IHC have approximately 2500 beds. The 10 hospitals owned by IHC range in size from 20 beds to 570 beds and also accounted for 95 percent of the system's revenues in 1977. Occupancy rates, however, have varied considerably from hospital to hospital, ranging from 45 to 87 percent with a systemwide average of about 75 percent in 1977. In comparing the rates charged per admission by IHC with the rates of other comparable hospitals in the same general area, it is found that hospitals belonging to IHC charge considerably less than others, even when the size factor is held constant. The net income of the system in fiscal 1977 was approximately $14 million as against gross patient revenues of $135 million. Debt service coverage of the system's peak future debt service has been projected at 5.7 times in 1981, the year following the completion of the system's most current building project.

There are many ratios, as noted here, which may be used to compute what might be considered the relative creditworthiness of the system as compared with other systems or other hospitals. The point in this case, however, is not to simply make those broad-based comparisons. IHC's credit is uniquely established in the market, and many of its ratios are unique because of the size and the type of system involved. What is important is that IHC provides a centralized dispensing mechanism for costly hospital services, such as insurance processing, construction, purchasing, nursing, auditing, and personnel administration. Each hospital is charged to the extent that it avails itself of the centralized services, and thus this concept, not the hospitals themselves, is the contribution the system will make to medical care for the nation's future.

Delaware County Authority, Pennsylvania: The Crozier-Chester Medical Center

The more traditional type of hospital financing in American municipal finance today is exemplified by the Crozier-Chester Medical Center, which is the regional center for renal dialysis and burn care, and the teaching affiliate is the nationally known Hahnemann Medical College.

The authority issues bonds, and the medical center makes lease/rental payments to the authority, so that such payments cover the debt service. In this instance, and unlike IHC, the medical center pledged a security interest in the gross revenues of the hospital as well as its tangible personal property and intangible property. Occupancy rates have been historically high at this facility, averaging approximately 88 percent, and long-term debt per bed is about $60,000, which is close to the national mean. During the period 1976–1978, net patient revenues of the hospital averaged about $30 million, but moneys available for debt service were $2.2 million, attesting to the expense of operating a single hospital facility with the attendant high costs of sophisticated equipment.

When all factors analyzed appear in a reasonably comparable range, attention must be paid to the competing facilities in the hospital service area. In this case, the medical center's basic service area is Delaware County, which accounted for three-quarters of its total admissions. Area planning commissions and other studies forecasted continued growth, projecting a population increase from approximately 190,000 in 1976 to 201,000 in 1990, which included a large percentage of medicare patients. In addition, although there are seven other acute-care facilities in the service county, the medical center received almost 25 percent of all acute-care patients. All this pointed to the continued use and growth of the Crozier-Chester Medical Center, the traditional hospital in municipal America.

GNMA-Backed Tax-Exempt Hospital Financings

Although HUD has terminated this program, its availability is currently being questioned in court (*Beth Israel v. HUD*), and its tax-exempt status is being investigated by other government agencies, we include this case as an example of recent inventiveness by investment bankers anxious to create new types of securities.

In 1978 a new, inexpensive method of providing AAA-rated tax-exempt financing for New York State hospitals via a federal guarantee of sorts was devised. The program would allow for the inexpensive financing for inner-city hospitals across the country which might at best receive a BBB rating on their bond issues.

Summary of the Program

Under this program, an FHA-insured Section 242 mortgage loan closing and the issuance of tax-exempt bonds would occur simultaneously. An FHA-insured mortgage is a condition precedent to the issuance of GNMA securities, an integral part of this approach.

The proceeds of the bond issue are deposited with a trustee for the purpose of purchasing GNMA securities as they are issued during the construction period. The GNMA securities are deposited with the trustee as security for the bonds. During the construction period, bond proceeds are invested in qualified government obligations so that these investments will mature as needed to purchase the GNMA securities. Debt service on the GNMA securities, together with interest received on the qualified investments, is sufficient to meet debt service on the bonds. The bond issue is equal to the principal of the GNMA securities to be issued and the underlying FHA-insured mortgage.

The pledge of the GNMA securities as collateral provides enough security to allow the bonds to receive an AAA rating. Net earnings on the GNMAs and their maturing principal is sufficient to meet the debt service of the bonds. Since the collateralized bonds are of a quality comparable to that of the underlying GNMA securities and are of a tax-exempt nature, there is a substantial decrease in the debt service required in comparison with the debt service associated with other hospital capital financing alternatives.

Government Cost Controls on Hospital Bonds

The federal government has introduced many proposals over the last 3 years in an attempt to cut or control soaring U.S. medical expenses. Not only the President but also congress and various state legislatures have sought to institute such controls.

Today, because state officials must cope with the costs of federally mandated medicaid payments, with soaring increases in the cost of hospitals and health care, and with increasing citizen revolts against higher taxes, many states have instituted some form of medical cost-control measure. The following cost-control initiatives by states were taken through 1978:

- Minnesota established a program to review and approve all hospital rates and charges with the adoption of the Hospital Administration Act by the Legislature in 1976.

• New York established a separate office of Health Systems Management to control hospital costs.

• Maryland, through its Health Services Cost Review Commission, initiated a program of audits to verify compliance with the commission's cost-containment measures.

• Wisconsin implemented a rate-review structure in 1977–1978 in conjunction with the Wisconsin Blue Cross and the Wisconsin Hospital Association.

• The Health Facilities Commission of Tennessee imposed a partial moratorium on hospital capital expenditures for new facilities while allowing expenditures for replacement and renovation projects that were approved.

Not all state initiatives to control health costs have been successful, for these efforts have been thwarted by court cases and lobbying efforts. Nevertheless, most states have recognized the desperate need to cut health costs, and, as a first step, they are slicing out unnecessary duplications of effort and extra forms required for the numerous state bureaucracies.

Notes to Chapter 9

[1] The source of Table 9-1 is *The Bond Buyer*.

[2] The dramatic increase in health-care expenditures of the federal government and its agencies from $2 billion in 1960 to $60 billion in 1979 was largely a result of Title XVIII and XIX of the Social Security Act, known commonly as medicare and medicaid.

[3] Although there is no medicare in Arizona, there is an intermediary for the federal government.

[4] The American Hospital Association uses these four types and joins the nonprofit hospitals with the voluntary eleemosynary hospitals.

[5] The official title of the law is the National Health Planning and Resources Development Act of 1974 (PL 93-641).

[6] In 1978 Standard & Poor's "A" category of bond issues over $5 million included A− (21 percent), A (34 percent), and A+ (32 percent). Thus there was a total of 87 percent for the entire A category (A−, A, A+).

Municipal Bonds

7 Corporate underwriters argue that the municipal market is substantially less risky than municipal underwriters, traders, and salespeople suggest. They argue that the spread on a typical municipal revenue issue is very much greater than the spread on a typical corporate underwriting. As to whether such spreads are justified by the greater risk, labor, or time involved in the underwriting or by other reasons of expertise required is a matter of considerable dispute. Our second book will examine the arguments on each side of this question of comparative risks and returns in different securities markets.

8 A new philosophy has developed in hospital management that, instead of assuming a break-even operation, attempts to develop a "bottom line" or record of net income which will serve as a basis for future capital expansion. Despite this new philosophy, however most hospitals still remain extremely dependent upon reimbursements. Because these reimbursements are increasingly tied to a rigid set of costs for each service, they tend not to include any funds to help replace equipment or buildings, and in many cases they cover less than the total service on a fully costed basis. We now have a system that is called the pluralistic reimbursement system. According to this scheme some hospitals opt, for example, not to participate in the Blue Cross plan in certain states because they feel it did not supply enough money for them to operate. In fact all the hospitals in New York sued the Blue Cross in a kind of class action in an attempt to withdraw from the Blue Cross contracts in that state. However, the state court found that they could not withdraw.

9 Debt service, as a percentage of revenues in 1977, showed a decline. This was due primarily to the fact that a substantial portion of the 1977 new issues was for refunding and refinancing purposes. Of the 1977 estimated volume of $4.7 billion, approximately 36 percent, or $1.7 billion, was for refunding purposes, up substantially from the 1976 total of $506 million, or 19 percent. This increase was due primarily to lower interest rates in the tax-exempt marketplace. The result of these refundings was a reduction in the annual debt service to the hospital. This, coupled with a rising level of gross revenues, resulted in an overall decline in the hospital's debt service as a percentage of gross patient revenues. Another factor was that hospital revenues in 1977 grew at a rate faster than that of hospital construction costs. In 1978 and in 1979 refunding and refinancings shrank substantially from their 1977 height of 36 percent of the total hospital bond market.

10 While non-tax-exempt projects normally have a somewhat larger equity, the ratio between the amount financed through debt (the primary source of financing) and the amount available through other sources (endowment, internal operations, etc.) is nearly the same as for tax-exempt hospitals.

chapter 10

Water and Sewer Bonds

In 1978 the sales of water and sewer bonds led them to rank second only to public power bonds in dollar sales volume among all types of municipal revenue securities. A total of $5 billion were sold in 1978 alone, more than double and nearly triple the amount a decade ago, as Table 10-1 indicates.

It is of interest that while the volume has certainly grown in this type of revenue bond, the growth has been erratic in contrast with the generally steady growth in sales of some other municipal revenue bonds—for example, public power bonds and housing bonds.

Characteristics of Water and Sewer Revenue Bonds

Water and sewer revenue bonds are issued for the purpose of building or extending a water and sewer system to benefit residential and industrial landowners within a single municipal region. Depending upon state statutes, the municipality may issue its own GO bonds for this purpose, or it may issue municipal revenue bonds. Most communities, however, are reluctant to issue GO bonds to finance a purpose that has a clear revenue-earning potential from user charges. More important, a new GO bond issue would force the municipality to hold an election, and it could use up borrowing capacity unless the bonds were clearly self-supporting. As a result, today when communities need to borrow for so many other purposes, most municipal entities will devise a way in which they can issue revenue bonds whose debt service will be repaid via user charges or water and sewer rates.

Water and sewer revenue bonds tend, in general, to be thought of as among the safest municipal investments because people must have water and sewer services. However, ratings vary from the highest grade in

TABLE 10-1 Water and Sewer Bond Financing, 1968 to 1978

Year	Amount, in $1000s
1968	1,887,228
1969	1,357,049
1970	2,329,706
1971	3,617,497
1972	2,841,441
1973	2,296,073
1974	2,120,119
1975	2,461,694
1976	3,307,591
1977	4,459,140
1978	4,448,033

SOURCE: *The Daily Bond Buyer*, Annual Statistics, 1979.

long-established, stable service areas to lower grades in systems that are being newly constructed or rapidly extended. Credit analysis involves the economy of the area, engineering factors, and financial feasibility studies by engineers specializing in water systems and sanitary engineering. Key security covenants must also be examined, particularly as to rates, flow of funds, and additional bonds. Water bonds are more highly regarded than sewer bonds and sometimes command a higher rating than the GO bonds of the same municipality. Financings of a sewage treatment plant often involve several municipalities in a region, and the municipalities, through long-term contracts, agree to use their taxing power if necessary, as in New Jersey, for example. Often the revenues of both the water system and the sewer system are combined and pledged to the payment of debt service.

There are at least four types of bonds in the water and sewer category: (1) solely water revenue, (2) solely sewer revenue, (3) combined water and sewer revenues, and (4) sewage treatment plant authorities or districts where the taxing power is involved. The market for buyers of water and sewer bonds is the entire tax-exempt bond market. The higher-investment-grade issues are sold to a broad list of casualty insurance companies, banks, bond funds, and individuals. For those water and sewer bonds of lesser investment grade, the market is more limited, although the higher yield of such bonds attracts many sophisticated institutions and wealthy individuals.

Water and sewer revenue bonds tend to be traded slightly cheaper or sold for slightly lower prices in comparison with other municipal bonds because the issues are frequently smaller. They thus lack, to a slight degree, the marketability and liquidity of certain other revenue bonds, such as public power bonds which sell in issues of $200 million and $400 million.

Water and sewer systems, like public power utilities, are usually monopoly operations with absolute control over these essential services. Also important is control over rate making without regulation, which is usually the case. Where the facility is an established water and sewer system that has held this monopoly position for years or decades, the risks for the investor are usually thought to be small in buying such bonds issued to update, improve, or enlarge the system. However, the risk of start-up situations involving new land developers or new suburban construction can be quite substantial because of the acute uncertainty about whether customers will actually hook up rather than use their own wells and septic systems; whether new populations will actually move into the area at all; or whether the projected new industrial or commercial firms will be lured into the area to expand their business. Predicting with accuracy the number of customers, the time of their connection to the system, their amount of water use, and thus the actual operating cost of the newly constructed facility for water or sewer supply or treatment is problematical. On top of these uncertainties there are always the normal problems involved in any sizable construction project, for example, lengthy delays or expensive cost overruns.

Usually water and sewer systems financed by revenue bonds are built or financed separately from each other. However, they are often built and financed as a joint project. But whether or not they are jointly financed, they must be looked upon quite distinctly by the investor or bond analyst because their characteristics, economics, finances, and problems are quite different. After conducting a general appraisal of the community's economy, its growth or decline, its present debt per capita, and its level of debt, the investor should look at the water supply of the municipality to see if it is local or purchased from either a regional wholesaling authority or another municipality. The supply contract, the degree of external dependence, and the adequacy of the water available are important factors. The age, condition, and adequacy of reservoirs and storage, pumping, and treatment facilities are all critical to the amount of financing that is needed and especially as a clue to the amount of water that never reaches the customers due to leaks in the system. In general, it is essential that a feasibility report by a nationally recognized engineering firm be included in the official statement by which the bonds are being offered.

The federal and state governments which share the cost of construction of sewage treatment facilities with a municipality make their payments strictly contingent upon the project's meeting their high and ever increasing standards of quality. If grants are being relied on, all approvals should be in hand prior to financing. Moreover, because the type of sewage treatment permitted and the method of disposal are each now governed by federal and state environmental protection agencies (EPA antipollution laws), these new treatment facilities not only are mandated by the government but also must be improved often and updated continually to meet ever higher standards.

Perhaps most difficult for the investor or bond analyst to appraise is the caliber of management. Seeing whether financial and other reports from the municipality are available, up to date, consistent, and complete is a start.

Risk Factors in Water and Sewer Bonds

Two basic revenue streams are critical for analyzing water and sewer bonds: (1) user charges and (2) connection fees. Although user charges are usually quite uniform, whether by flat rate assessment or by meter reading of actual use, connection fees are unpredictable.[1] Where large amounts of revenue are projected from connection charges, the bond is more risky than when the revenue is anticipated from user fees. A far higher debt service coverage level is expected in these cases. Once customers are hooked up, rate increases tend not to affect usage to any great extent, and hence over the years bonds with large, economically strong service areas have rightly maintained and improved their credit value. However, today with the skyrocketing costs of meeting the government-mandated antipollution laws and sewage treatment levels, costs and expenses may well drive some industrial customers out of a district.

The first crucial risk for the investor to discern is whether the bonds are being issued for new facilities for any new residential development. Most water and sewer bond defaults have occurred in these start-up situations because the anticipated influx of population has failed to materialize.

The second major risk that investors should look for concerns the condition of the system. In some cases of older or badly designed systems, leakage has amounted to an incredibly high percentage of the water supplied. An antiquated system is obviously more prone to leaks and water loss, and so its rehabilitation can involve substantial expenditures beyond projections.

A third very substantial financial risk results from the new avalanche of federal, state, and local laws for pollution control which mandate higher and higher levels of sewage and water treatment. One outcome of very high standards has been that many municipalities have fought the government authorities in the courts to avoid, delay, or postpone such pollution control expenses. These legal delaying tactics have led to municipalities being less than 40 percent in compliance with the various laws, as compared with corporate industry, which is more than 85 percent in compliance. Because of continual inflation this ultimately means that the cost of the new pollution control installations will be that much more expensive than originally projected and that much more difficult to finance. From the standpoint of the investor, while the rate of return may be that much higher on bonds issued in the future to cover the water and sewer pollution control costs, there are substantial risks of voter and ratepayer resistance to unlimited rate increases. More important, there are clear signs of unwillingness among many key industries to blithely accept substantial rate increases when coupled with increases in the property tax rate and special tax burdens. Their threats of leaving districts have become wholesale.

Critical Interrelationships of Municipal Bonds for Water and Sewer Projects and Federal and State Government Grants

A water and sewer system upgrading to meet federally mandated standards can, for even a moderate-sized city, be extremely expensive, costing $100 million to $300 million. It also requires substantial amounts of lead time for construction and installation. Generally speaking, from first conception to final construction, a water and sewer system will take 10 years. The combination of these extraordinary costs and time delays is what makes the financial involvement of the federal and state governments in these projects so critical.

Under the Clean Water Act of 1972, the federal government is committed to providing capital grants to cover up to 75 percent of the total construction costs needed to build any municipality's water and sewer system. In addition, each state government also provides capital grants of up to 15 percent. This means that the municipality or authority that needs to build a new system or substantially upgrade an old one can acquire up to 90 percent of the construction costs from the federal and state governments, but only if it meets those governments' standards, deadlines, and inspection criteria.

The remaining 10 percent of the facility's cost must be financed by the municipality itself. The cost of the average water and sewer restoration or enlargement is between $100 million and $300 million. This means that 10 percent, or $10 million to $30 million, must be sought in a municipal bond issue. This is usually done by issuing revenue bonds but is something accomplished by issuing GO bonds.

The federal and state matching grants, covering $90 million to $270 million, are not handed over either easily or quickly. Instead, the federal government, and sometimes the state government, tends to become involved in the rate structure of the municipality's water and sewer system in an effort to ensure that local industries, which are the major users of water, do not get a free ride from the municipality as they did in the past. Thus both levels of governement are quite concerned with who pays and at what rate; in this way they influence the regulation of rates, for they supply their grants only if rates are considered adequate and industry pays its proportionate share.

The federal government, therefore, makes its payments on a staggered basis. All during construction, the government has certain requirements which must be met. First, a plan must be developed; then the water and sewer authority must set a rate structure and submit it to the government when construction is 50 percent complete. When the construction is 75 to 80 percent complete, the federal government insists upon approving the rate structure. Finally, the government requires that the municipality provide it, in advance of operation, with a complete engineer's guide to the operation of the whole water system.

Today, major users of a particular water and sewer system are quite important due to a recent amendment to the Clean Water Act of 1972. This amendment stipulates that industry is required to pay its "fair share." It also requires each corporation in the locality to repay its proportionate share of the federal grant over time. Municipal water and sewer rates are expected to fully reflect this repayment of the government grants by major industries' users, and the water and sewer district itself is to repay 50 percent of this amount to the government. The balance can go into the general fund of the system and be used for operations and for debt service.

For the investor or bond analyst the evaluation of the credit, price, or yield of any particular water and sewer revenue bond will involve an understanding of the following key factors, which are virtually identical to those that must be considered in evaluating any and all revenue bonds.

• A definition of the service area, i.e., the area in which the water and sewer system will provide its services

• The economic characteristics of the service area: its current and projected population, its growth of median income and wealth, its current property tax levy, and its overall tax burden per capita

• The economic trends of the community in the past and the projections as to its future growth

- Identification of the major users of the system, i.e., industrial versus commercial or institutional (such as a hospital, university, or prison)
- The flexibility the system is allowed in terms of its rate structure
- A conception of the demand for its service as it relates to raising the rates paid by its users
- A feel for the caliber of the existing or proposed management personnel of the system and the structure of management as it compares with other governmental units
- Bond resolution covenants, such as rates, flow of funds, and additional bonds
- Historical and projected debt service coverage
- The need for additional borrowing

Creating Water and Sewer Financing

First a municipality—or a water and sewer authority—on its own initiative or under federal or state government *direction* decides to build or expand its water and/or sewer system. The immediate task is to select a consulting engineer, a bond counsel, and an underwriter and then work with them as they structure the facility and bond offering.

The job of a consulting engineer is to design the proper system for that municipality's needs and to estimate its cost and time schedule of construction, including the scheduled breakdown of funds. The consulting engineer also makes a projection of revenues as well as operating and maintenance expenses in order to determine the net revenues available for debt service payments. The consulting engineer works closely with the underwriter or investment banker who is structuring the financing of the project and also consults with the rating agencies who assess the credit of this new bond offering.

Chapter 13, "Legal Protection, Disclosure, and Liability," has a very detailed account of the role of the bond attorney. Suffice it for the moment to say simply that the bond attorney is hired by the municipality (or by the underwriter for the municipality) and has the express task of representing the interests of the ultimate bond purchasers. In that capacity the bond attorney, first and foremost, will give his or her legal opinion on the tax exemption of the bond issue and will otherwise work with the issuer, the financial consultant, and the underwriter and their separate legal counsels as the bond issue is being prepared. Bond counsel and the investment banker insist upon a number of explicit protections for the ultimate bondholders, including a debt service reserve fund, a rate covenant, and a replacement and renewal, or maintenance reserve, fund.

To guarantee that the system will stay in proper working order throughout the life of the bonds, a maintenance reserve fund is required, especially if the municipality is heavily involved in the treatment of sewage. The IRS sets constraints on the size of maintenance reserve funds to be derived from bond proceeds, namely a 15 percent maximum. The IRS also fixes the income that can be derived from these reserve funds without incurring violations of the IRS arbitrage regulations.

If the engineer's report suggests a strong financial future for the water and sewer system, then the rate covenant will probably only require the municipality to set rates at a level just sufficient to cover operating and maintenance expenses as well as annual principal and interest payments. Even if the financial future is not projected to be extremely strong, in most cases the required rate coverage ratio will rarely exceed 1.25 times the yearly debt service requirement.

A debt service reserve fund will be created, usually equivalent to the maximum annual debt service for 1 year. This debt service reserve will be funded out of proceeds from the sale of the issue or accumulated during a given year. What the rate covenant and debt service reserve fund really mean is simply that the municipality "covenants," or guarantees, that if for any reason its net revenues fall below the required level or if it were to use any portion of the reserve fund, it will then raise rates to a level sufficient to meet the coverage requirement and restore the reserve fund to its preexisting maximum level.

In the case of a fully guaranteed municipal revenue bond (with its pledge of taxing power, if needed) for a new or expanded water and sewer system, the rate covenant may provide that rates produce sufficient amounts to ensure the payment of principal and interest after operating and maintenance costs; but it probably would not require the maintenance of a separate debt service reserve fund.

For many decades municipalities did not have the legal power to force property owners to connect to their system, for homeowners could insist on supplying their own water and their own septic system. However, recently a number of states have enacted new laws requiring that property owners in certain areas connect to the systems. This reinforced the municipality's legal right to charge annual fees for its services.

The first 5 years of the operation of a new water and sewer system are critical. If the debt service payments are made regularly without having to either dip into the various reserve funds or fall back on the municipality's guarantee, if any, the facility will probably continue to meet its obligations.

The soaring rate of inflation in capital construction costs has meant that the financing of water and sewer systems (even with the 90 percent support of state and federal grants) has become increasingly difficult because of customer resistance. To keep these debt charges down, many water and sewer authorities have decided to increase the initial assessment fee on each prospective user of the system. The municipalities or water and sewer authorities also have increased the charges for connecting each new customer to the system and for installing the water and sewer line connected to the house. Both assessment fees and connecting fees provide "up-front" operating capital to fund interest payments and to lower the amount of debt that the system must incur in a new bond issue.

Assessment fees can be paid by the property owner either immediately or at the end of the construction period when the new water sewer system is complete. The assessment charges must be paid, and to ensure this the municipality has a prior lien upon the homeowner's property in case of nonpayment.

In contrast, the connection fee usually cannot be made subject to a lien. Instead, a "notice to connect" is sent to the property owner. It states that in order to be connected to the water and sewer system, the property owner must acquire a "permit to connect." This permit requires prepayment of the connection charge. Both connection and assessment charges are one-shot fees, and, therefore, annual user charges usually represent the bulk of the new or rapidly growing revenue of the water and sewer authority.

During the last decade, the federal government adopted policies designed to encourage the joining together of separate municipal sewage systems in order to cut costs imposed by the new pollution control regulations. Although joint municipal systems have become more prevalent, especially the process of feeding collection systems into a major treatment facility, the hoped-for economies of scale have been generally found to become nonexistent as soon as the distance between the municipalities increases or the number of municipalities involved multiplies. This is because (1) sewage piping and transportation costs between districts are exorbitant and (2) the political wrangle between separate municipalities over the costs of installation and operation and the splitting of the revenues of a joint sewage-treatment system are time-consuming and expensive.

Cases

Buffalo Sewer Authority

Few observers of the municipal finance scene realize the critical importance of the Buffalo Sewer Authority to the history of municipal bonds in the United States. The authority was first created by Chapter 349 of the New York State Laws of 1935 and later consolidated with other public authorities under Chapter 870 of the Laws of 1939. Originally, the authority was designed to rid the Buffalo and Niagara Rivers and Lake Erie of pollution and sewage, thus transferring the sewage system of the city to the authority when the system was built.

In brief, the significance of the authority lies in court cases coming in the wake of its inception. For the first time in America, the courts of New York held that charges levied to finance a specific governmental function from which certain individuals within a limited geographic area received benefit were solely a revenue obligation; thus the charges were outside the responsibility of, as well as exempt from, the GO debt of the municipality in which the facility operated. Under the authority's bond resolution, adopted on June 1, 1936, the Buffalo Sewer Authority was to establish a system of charges sufficient to pay the debt service on its bonds and provide for funding certain reserves. The charges constituted a lien on the real property of the service area that was equivalent to the general taxes of the city of Buffalo. The city's Division of Water imposed a 32 percent surcharge on water bills, and the city's Tax Division levied a sewer rent of $4.36 per $1000.00 of assessed valuation of property.

Southwest Sewer District of Suffolk County: 1978 Refunding Issue

Shrouded in controversy and allegations of impropriety for the past 10 years, the Southwest Sewer District of Suffolk County, New York, still remains a landmark case in the credit analysis of sewer revenue bonds. The $60,835,000 refunding issue that came to market during the summer of 1978 was a prime example of the cross-fertilization that occurs among revenue bonds issued for different types of purposes and backed by a series of tiers of security.

The Southwest Sewer District consisted of a system for the collection and disposal of sewage. Construction on the project began in mid-1971, and the entire project was scheduled to be operational in late 1979. As of mid-1978, of a total of 830 miles of pipeline, approximately 530 miles were in the ground, 50 miles were under contract, and approximately 77 miles were bid on.

As a governmental pollution control facility, the Southwest Sewer District was eligible for and did receive substantial monies from the federal government. For the analyst, however, what is particularly important is the flow of funds from the various sources either at a given point in time or at the time of a specific bond's issue. It is then that the analyst can see how the construction and fund intake are progressing and thus judge the financial viability of the project for the immediate future.

As of July 31, 1978, the total construction cost of the project was estimated to be $614,908,000, which included an 8.61 percent annual inflation factor on all contracts that were to be bid. At that time, there were $50 million in bonds from two other unrelated and differently secured issues outstanding.

Disposal Facilities   For the disposal facilities, the grant commitments received for federal and state aid will fund 90 percent of the cost of construction, of which 75 percent is due from the federal government and 15 percent is to come from the state. The total amount of such aid is estimated to be approximately $224,615,000. Through July 31, 1978, the district received governmental aid totaling $106,501,820, of which $79,289,340 had been received from the federal government and $27,212,480 had come from the state. Also through July 31, 1978, the district had expended $125,640,000 for the construction of the disposal facilities.

Collection System   The county is eligible for grants from the federal government for the collection system to provide for 75 percent of the cost of the unit. Grant commitments presently in effect provide for federal aid of $102,726,000 to fund the collection system based on the estimated cost of $136,968,000. However, revised estimates for the cost of construction project that the aidable portions will cost $33,000,000 more than the original estimate, or approximately $170,000,000, so that the federal aid for the aidable collection system components should be $127,476,000. The county will apply for additional federal aid for the increased cost estimate, which will total $24,750,000 in additional federal monies.

This issue of the Southwest Sewer District of Suffolk County was actually a triple-barreled bond issue. In the first instance, the bonds were payable from income of the district, including charges to be levied on users and connection charges. In the second sense, the bonds were payable from a tax to be levied on the benefited real property of the district and also any federal and state grants-in-aid. It was revealed at the time of the underwriting that the county executive intended to recommend to the county legislature the following levies for imposition:

• An annual real property assessment to be levied on the district at the rate of 60 cents per $100 of full value. This levy, to be assessed on real property in the district beginning in 1980, is double the 30-cent-per-$100 assessment levied in 1978.

• An estimated charge for annual sewer use of $50 per single-family residence, with other property types to be charged proportionately.

• A preconnection charge of 12½ cents per $100 of full value to be assessed annually for a 3-year period.

If these revenues were insufficient, the bonds were payable from the levy of ad valorem tax on all taxable real property within Suffolk County without limitation as to rate or amount. As such, these bonds were both triple-barreled obligations and general obligations of Suffolk County. Consequently, an analysis of Suffolk County and its relation to the Southwest Sewer District is necessary.

Although the district includes only approximately 6 percent of the county's total area, it contains over 23 percent of the county's total population and approximately the same percentage of full-equalized valuation of property within the county. The district, therefore, provided substantial resources for its own tax levies, but the county also had the potential of providing much additional financial support if necessary.

Suffolk County itself had shown fund surpluses, a growing population (tripling since 1950), substantially increasing property values, and a relatively low percentage of uncollected property taxes. However, for counties of approximately the same population, Suffolk's ratio of overall debt to debt per capita was in the high range, and its ratio of overall debt to estimated full value was in the middle range.

At the time of the underwriting, Suffolk County was in the process of filing an application with the state comptroller so that the bonds for the Southwest Sewer District would be exempt from the county's statutory debt ceiling (excluded from computing the limit of the county's total debt). Under Article VIII of the New York State constitution and Title 9 of Article 2 of the Local Finance Law, the county's debt limit was determined by averaging the most recent 5 years' full value of all taxable realty in the county and then taking 7 percent of the average.

As of July 28, 1978, the county's full valuation of taxable realty had averaged since 1973 $16,177,979,721. Thus, the county's debt limit was

TABLE 10-2 Comparisons between Southwest Sewer District and Suffolk County

	Southwest Sewer District	Suffolk County
Population	300,000	1,333,000
Full-equalized valuation	$3,474,610,364	$19,409,931,933
Land area	57 sq miles	921 sq miles

7 percent of that sum, or $1,132,458,580. The net total present indebtedness of the county at that time was $261,949,255, or 23.1 percent of the amount of debt that the county could have issued under its statutes. Even with the additional debt issued by the Southwest Sewer District, the county's net indebtedness would not have increased substantially. However, any other debt issued in significant amounts would have also increased the county's debt ratios.

As noted earlier, this case is especially rich, involving both sewer and pollution control revenue bonds, backed by (1) user charges and property taxes on the benefited property and (2) substantial federal monies. Interestingly, in a third sense, the bonds of the Southwest Sewer District are backed by ad valorem taxes on real property within Suffolk County, thus making the issue in reality simply a GO bond of Suffolk. In this sense, the bonds of the Southwest Sewer District are certainly something more than simply contingent liabilities of the county, such as the lease/rental obligations and moral obligations of the state of New York. Even in the latter cases, New York State is responsible for at least its lease commitments, although they are not general obligations of the state. In the case of Suffolk County, there appears to be the potential for this kind of sewer debt, which is not considered within the debt limit of the county, to become enormous, burdensome, and, nonetheless, a legal responsibility that is on a par with voter-approved GO bonds issued by the county. These are the types of situations that require regular update analyses by salespeople, underwriters, and investors alike.

Note to Chapter 10

[1] There are three ways to calculate the annual charges that can be levied on users of a water and sewer system: (1) *a flat rate*, whereby each user of a similar nature is charged the same annual fee regardless of usage; (2) *fixture count rates* that are determined by the number of fixtures per unit; and (3) *user charges* that are determined by a meter which measures the intake of water or the exit of sewage. The flat rate is, by far, the simplest of these three methods to administer. Although they are more equitable than a flat rate, both user charges and fixture count methods of measuring charges are generally agreed to be inordinately expensive and complex.

chapter 11

Industrial Development Bonds and Pollution Control Bonds

Industrial development bonds and pollution control bonds are really corporate bonds disguised to look like municipal bonds. Although each is officially a type of municipal revenue bond, they differ from all the other types of bonds discussed in previous chapters, which have a direct backing of a municipality or public authority or an ultimate guarantee of the federal government. In contrast, pollution control bonds and industrial development bonds are backed solely by the corporation (not by any governmental unit at all) and as such are actually corporate credits.

They are nominally structured as municipal bonds in order to qualify for issuance under section 103 of the IRS code, which deals with tax exemption. However, aside from meeting certain government requirements, the joint intent of the issuer, the corporation, and the IRS is that these two types of municipal securities be, as much as possible, corporate bonds.

Both types of bonds offer substantial cost savings to the corporation, and this is, unquestionably, their central attraction. Indeed, because these bonds pay interest on a tax-free basis, they almost invariably carry a coupon of at least 2 percent (200 basis points) lower than the corporation's general indebtedness, and in 1979, carried a coupon of about 3.5 percent (350 basis points) lower than the corporation's regular bonds, whose interest would be fully taxable.

The proceeds from the sale of these bonds are used to construct industrial or commercial facilities, to purchase equipment, or to purchase pollution control devices (which are then usually leased to the corporation). Both industrial development revenue bonds and pollution control bonds can be structured as a municipal (1) lease, (2) installment sale, or (3) loan to the corporation. State law determines which way they must be structured, not the IRS code. It is crucial to note that these lease, loan, or installment sale payments from the corporation are specifically structured to cover all the costs of servicing the municipal bonds that have been issued, including all principal and interest payments.

The catalog of corporate projects financed to date with industrial development bonds includes ports and docks, sports facilities, manufacturing plants and distribution systems, warehouses, and even motels and convention centers.

Whereas the units of industrial development bonds are, like other municipal bonds, split between term bonds and serial bonds, the term bonds tend to be longer than other municipal bonds and range between 25 and 30 years. The serial bonds are the traditional, annual sequence of shorter maturities.

Genesis of Industrial Development Bonds

Industrial development bonds actually have their genesis 40 years ago in American state and local finance as offshoots of lease financings. Indeed, through a 1936 Mississippi industrial development program termed "Balance Agriculture with Industry," the state authorized the first American industrial development revenue bonds. They were issued by the city of Durant for the construction of a Realsilk Hosiery Mill factory. This effort was designed to draw industry into communities for employment and economic benefits through the use of tax-exempt financing. The financing is accomplished by a municipal entity that issues bonds to build and operate an industrial plant. The security of the plant is in the lease payments made by the corporation to the municipal issuer; the lease payments are equivalent to the debt service payments on the bonds. To be sure, this did not take a fast hold in American finance: only Kentucky and Mississippi sanctioned the use of such industrial leasing schemes. But by 1950 lease contracts between different government entities were becoming commonplace.

Industrial leasing, however, as might have been expected, engendered charges that such financings constituted an abuse of the tax-exempt privilege. The issue came center stage early in leasing history when in 1938 a Mississippi court held, in the case of *Abritton v. City of Winona*, that the construction of plants and the subsequent leasing to private industry served "public purpose" objectives and that the bond employed should therefore be "tax-exempt." The case was never appealed to the Supreme Court, presumably because of its earlier ruling in *Union Lime Co. v. Chicago–Northwestern Railway Co.* (1914) which made it a matter of future policy that the Supreme Court would not review decisions by a state court concerning what that government considered to be a promotion of "public purposes" as defined in its state legislation. Beginning in 1954, the IRS also formally supported the tax-exempt status of industrial development bonds.

From 1950 to 1968 industrial development financing finally began to catch on as leasing arrangements between corporations and governments gained state approval. By 1968 local governments had received authorizations for such financing in forty states. During this early period, the total dollar volume of industrial development revenue financing jumped dramatically from $1 million to $1500 million, annually, increasing from 0.1 percent of all municipal issues to almost 10 percent of the total volume. This dramatic increase outran the multiple increases registered by every other municipal security issued for any other purpose.

Nonetheless, as industrial lease financing became overwhelmingly popular, Congress reacted swiftly to what was perceived to be an abuse of the tax-exempt privilege. This was despite court decisions and IRS rulings, too numerous to detail here, which concluded that industrial-leasing arrangements provided "public purpose" objectives and that those bonds should be tax-exempt. As a consequence, Congress in 1969 limited the exemption to industrial-leasing issues under $1 million (or, for certain cases, up to $5 million), except for specified purposes such as pollution control, and the volume fell as shown in Table 11-1.

Table 11-1 clearly indicates the boom in industrial development bonds in 1968. This boom virtually disappeared in the period 1969–1970 as the federal government tightened its standards. Although erratic, the growth of industrial development bonds has resumed, but thus far the bonds have not returned to the striking level of 1968.

It should be stressed, however, that the total number of industrial

TABLE 11-1   Volume of Industrial Development Bonds

Year	Amount, in $1000s
1968	1,585,269
1969	24,020
1970	47,593
1971	219,510
1972	470,695
1973	269,762
1974	339,970
1975	517,801
1976	356,909
1977	463,816
1978	570,076

SOURCE: *The Daily Bond Buyer,* Annual Statistics, 1979.

development bonds is expected to increase sharply because of the new 1978 regulation which raises the limit of industrial development bonds from $5 million to $10 million for certain projects. Since a corporation can finance up to $10 million with such bonds for *each* plant it has in different municipalities by using different municipal issuers, it is able to greatly increase its financing from this source in a relatively short space of time. In today's period of high interest rates, corporations and commercial businesses are intensifying their search for ways to issue such bonds as one simple means to reduce their total cost of net interest.

One other vitally important new movement today is also expected to spur the growth of industrial development bonds. This new program would involve the possibility of vast extra tax-exempt financing for those industrial and commercial projects that are *specifically cited in "blighted areas."* The Urban Development Actions Grants (UDAG) for blighted or economically depressed areas will allow corporations to exceed the $10 million limit. Indeed, UDAG Grants at present have virtually no fixed limit. This new program, which was slated for October 1, 1979, was eagerly awaited, and there were already over $400 million in UDAG proposals by corporations being processed 9 months before they officially became legal.

Types of Industrial Development Bonds

Section 103 of the IRS code provides today for two types of industrial development bonds.

Unlimited Size Although unlimited in size, this type of bond is *restricted in the use of its proceeds* to the following: convention facilities; sports and trade shows; airports, wharfs, and docks; air and water pollution facilities; and sewage and solid waste disposal. Also, a few miscellaneous projects are allowed.

Limited Size Although limited in size, this type of industrial development bond has an *unrestricted use of proceeds*. Under this heading are included the two so-called small issue exemptions: (1) $1 million and (2) $10 million. A corporation can almost always get $1 million in bonds because there are virtually no restrictions on the corporation's finances. The category of up to $10 million in tax-exempt bonds keys directly off the level of capital expenditures that the corporation has made. The $1 million does not.

Under the $1 million restriction, the capital expenditures, which the bonds may finance, include the acquisition of land or the construction on or acquisition of depreciable property for use by a company.

Under the $10 million exemption, a municipality may borrow up to that total amount for the benefit of a corporation *if* that corporation has not exceeded and will not exceed that amount in capital expenditures over a 6-year period beginning 3 years prior to the issuance of the bonds.

If a corporation violates the restrictions on industrial revenue bonds, the IRS removes the tax exemption of interest received by bondholders. Those bondholders could always sue for damages "to make them whole" for this breaking of its covenants by the corporation. However, because the reliance on court suits for damages in such cases would be, inevitably, both costly and time-consuming, there occurred between 1975 and 1977 a general movement toward the adoption of a "special mandatory call" to avoid the need for such lawsuits. By 1979 this mandatory call had crept into most industrial development bond issues.

Although there are many variations on the form of a mandatory call, in general, if the bonds become taxable because the corporation violates a covenant in its lease, loan agreement, or installment sale agreement and such violation causes interest on the bonds to become taxable, then the corporation must immediately redeem the bonds at par.

Pollution Control Bonds

Coming in the wake of the Clean Air Act of 1970 and the 1972 Water Pollution Control legislation, the first recorded financing of a pollution control issue was underwritten in 1971–1972. As with the case of industrial leasing, the pollution control issues were accomplished not only by governments alone but also through leasing, loan, or installment sale arrangements between governments and corporations. The total dollar volume of pollution financing registered during the second year was a tremendous $2.1 billion, of which $1.8 billion was for industrial issues. By 1977 pollution control issues soared to $3.8 billion, and of that sum $2.9 billion went for industrial purposes, with such companies as Standard Oil, du Pont, Allied Chemical, and Atlantic Richfield coming to market.

The 1977 amendments to the Clean Air Act of 1970 postponed the deadline of the original legislation that required all areas of the nation to have attained ambient air standards by mid-1977. But those amendments tightened up on penalties for abuse, making noncompliance far more expensive than compliance. For the nation's governments, the deadline was extended to 1983, except for cities, such as New York, with severe carbon monoxide problems, which were allowed until 1988. State progress will be monitored through revised implementation plans for pollution control to be submitted in 1979 and 1982. Industries were given the option for 3-year delays in compliance, through permission from the state or the Environmental Protection Agency (EPA). These delays would allow them to operate from stationary sources to pollution even though emission standards were violated. Penalty assessments are calculated to be not less than the entire cost of constructing, operating, and maintaining the pollution control facility. For violations of the act, the new law authorizes the courts to impose civil penalties of up to $25,000 per day with the possibility of criminal sanctions for knowing violations of the delayed compliance penalty provisions.

The thrust of the 1977 amendments to the Water Pollution Control Act of 1972 closely resembles the "clean air" amendments: The deadline for swimmable and fishable waters was extended. In 1972 Congress set mid-1977 as the deadline for the installation by both governments and industries of the "best practical" treatment facilities for fluid wastes. It also shifted by 1 year (1983 to 1984) the time limit for the institution of the "best available technology" (BAT), with a 1985 goal of "zero discharge" of pollutants into the nation's waters. By the time the act's original deadline came, however, the compliance rate of municipalities had reached only 30 percent. Municipalities were outstripped markedly by industries, which registered an 85 percent rate of compliance. Interestingly, since 1972 municipalities have received over $28 billion in subsidies from the federal government in financing pollution control facilities.

Similarly, the cost to industries of pollution control has been anything but cheap. Businesses have spent about $3.8 billion each year on the construction of treatment facilities, an additional $4.0 billion on the operation and maintenance of those facilities, and almost $3.0 billion on the capital costs of interest and depreciation, all in an effort to meet the federal pollution standards.

Making matters worse for industries and government, the EPA, which was endowed with the prerogatives of enforcement of the new legislation, is instituting a crash program of compliance. On the business side, the EPA appears to be headed toward the steel, chemical, and paper industries. The agency is also considering two formulas for computing hefty fines for industry. These formulas are based largely on the economic advantages that noncompliers have over compliers: savings of capital that was not invested in the construction, operation, and maintenance of the pollution control facilities.

The Key Advantages of Tax-Exempt
Financing for Corporations

In addition to the obvious tax advantage for corporations using industrial development bonds, there are a number of other important advantages. Before noting them, however, it should be stressed that tax exemption is the main advantage. During the 25- to 30-year term to maturity of the bonds, the 2 to 3.5 percent interest cost savings over taxable corporate bonds makes tax-exempt bond financing the least expensive method of financing a project in most cases.

Another advantage is that tax-exempt bond financing allows for special arrangements for the corporation to depreciate the facility (of which it is the owner for tax purposes). Different methods of depreciation are allowed. One such method is covered by section 169 of the 1954 IRS code, as amended, and provides for a 60-month period over which to amortize the cost of the facility. If a corporation elects to depreciate by using section 169 and elects to use tax-exempt financing for the facility, then it is restricted to an investment tax credit of 5 percent.

If the corporation does not use tax-exempt financing, it may take an investment tax credit of 10 percent. Therefore, the corporation's method of financing will depend on what is more advantageous: a higher rate of depreciation or a higher investment tax credit. It should be noted that there are cases where the value of conventional accelerated depreciation is greater than that of depreciation allowed by section 169.

If the corporation decides to use section 167 rather than section 169, its investment tax credit will vary depending on the life of the facility. The range of investment tax credit under section 167 is generally between 5 and 10 percent.

There are three other major benefits for corporations from financing with tax-exempt municipal bonds. First, when the bonds have been fully paid for, the corporation usually is granted the right to purchase the facility for a nominal sum. Second, in contrast to most corporate securities offerings, which require extensive measures to satisfy the registration requirements of the Securities and Exchange Commission (SEC) under the 1933 Securities Act, the industrial revenue bonds, because they are "municipals," are exempt from such SEC registration. In many instances, they are also exempt from state registration requirements under specific state "blue sky" laws. Third, it should be noted that according to certain state laws, some states will allow the governmental unit issuing the industrial revenue bonds to be treated as the owner of the facility, and the new plant, facilities, equipment, or land may be partly or totally exempt from local property taxes or sales taxes.

The Status of the Lease

One of the most critical aspects of analyzing the credit of leasing schemes for industrial development and pollution control is the status of the lease in bankruptcy. In most rental agreements, the lease comes in the form of either a lease/purchase contract or an installment/purchase contract. Under the lease agreement, the rentals paid by the company to the municipality are designed to sufficiently service the debt or the principal and interest on the bonds. When the lease term has ended, the corporate lessee may purchase the facility. The defect in this contract, however, is that the receiver retains the option to terminate the lease in the event of bankruptcy. As a result, in reality, the lease constitutes a subordinate corporate credit and thus is rated one notch below the company's senior debt.

Corporate guarantees of payment under both types of leases, however, render the bonds general obligations of the company that are on a par with the company's senior debt. In the lease/purchase contract, the guarantee may come (1) through a corporate pledge of payment on the rental contract that a company subsidiary has entered into with the municipal entity or (2) through a corporate guarantee to the receiver. With the installment/purchase agreement, the company may assume title to the facility after construction is completed or when the bonds mature. Under this arrangement, the company's obligation to pay the purchase price of the facility, with sufficient interest to cover the debt service, yields a rating which is equivalent to that of the company's senior debt. How a company's lease and loan payments rank with its general indebtedness will be seen through the cases in this chapter. Discussions in the "Cases" section will also analyze the backing of the industrial development and pollution control bonds by more than one company.

State Governments and Industrial Development Bonds

In order to issue industrial development bonds, a municipality must, in addition to qualifying under the various federal laws discussed thus far, meet certain state government specifications. State laws, for example, often require proof that the proposed facilities will result in a net economic benefit to the community, whether they are for new industrial plants, land, or motels. Corporations are expected to demonstrate a public purpose that will be served by the tax-exempt financing of these new facilities. Increased employment for workers of the region, increased trade for local merchants, increased access of local economic interests to broader foreign or national markets, and the rescue of the industry base of a declining community are typical of the public purposes that corporations usually advance to support their applications for state government permission to use tax-exempt municipal financing.

State statutes, in addition to setting out this public purpose, are also important in specifying the exact form of authorization required for such a municipal issuance. The forms of authorization vary a good deal, and each one should be examined separately and carefully.

State statutes also will stipulate whether or not there will be an interest rate limit on the bonds, and they will specify the maximum maturity schedule permissible for these bonds and the exact manner of sale—whether a private offering or a public offering. Many states allow such private sales, but some do not. Furthermore, some states impose a ceiling on the total volume of industrial development revenue bonds or pollution control bonds that can be issued without the approval of the state legislature.

One of the key concerns for the bond analyst or investor is determining, in both state laws and federal laws, exactly which municipal entities within a state's borders are permitted to issue industrial development municipal bonds. Whether or not counties and municipalities can issue municipal bonds varies by state. Under federal law only "incorporated municipalities" may issue municipal bonds, but a number of quite embarrassing incidents have occurred in which "unincorporated towns and municipalities" issued municipal bonds. A row of question marks hung over their future until the government made a final determination in each case.

States also set up state commissions, state authorities, or other statewide bodies in some cases, and these must pass on the acceptability of each proposed project for industrial development bond financing. The entities vary from state to state, but generally, in effect, they establish other preconditions.

Cases

Potlatch Corporation (Solid Waste Disposal Bonds)

Over recent years, the Potlatch Corporation, like many other lumber and forest products companies, has been coming to market with solid waste disposal and pollution control municipal bond issues. These bonds have been issued through government entities—as were, for example, the solid waste disposal bonds issued recently for Potlatch by Nez Perce County, Idaho, in 1979. This particular issue of 1979 was for $70 million in solid waste disposal bonds and $1 million in "small-issue exemption bonds" for the purpose of environmental improvement at the company's plant in Lewiston, Idaho.

The first and most important aspect in analyzing the way this issue was put together is to note that the corporation had the choice of different methods of tax-exempt municipal financing, which, for example, included specifying this improvement as a pollution control bond or as a solid waste disposal facility. In many cases, the rules about whether a project strictly qualifies are determined by various government bodies, but it is the corporation that chooses the particular method of financing. It is crucial to examine the advantages and disadvantages of each. These two methods of financing (pollution control bonds versus solid waste disposal bonds) are each governed by a separate set of tax regulations. Had this been a pollution control issue for air and water, the corporation could not have financed the $70 million bond issue. The issue size would have had to have been much smaller.

Also, it should be noted that pollution control issues are subject to the "incremental cost rule." This states that the cost of a pollution control facility eligible for tax-exempt financing is reduced by the extent to which a company derives economic benefit from that facility by, for example, generating steam or using some other form of power.

In the case of Potlatch, the two types of bonds ($70 million solid waste disposal bonds versus $1 million "small-issue exemption bonds" for environmental improvement) were issued through separate agreements, and neither issue was entitled to the revenues pledged for the other. The county loaned the proceeds of the issue to the company by depositing them with the trustee bank in separate construction funds. The company then paid to the trustee sufficient monies to cover the debt service on the bonds, which corresponded to the notes payable to the trustee. The bonds of this issue were equivalent to the company's senior unsecured debt. (First-mortgage bonds are secured debt, having a lien on the facilities.) Most major companies have "negative pledge clauses" in their bond resolutions which prohibit them from issuing first-mortgage debt in any meaningful amount, which is usually 5 percent of the net tangible assets of the company. As a result, the bonds issued under such circumstances rank (in the event of bankruptcy claims) just about as high in relation to the company's other outstanding debt as is possible.

It should be noted that this issue of bonds was not a lease/rental in which the status of the lease in the event of bankruptcy is usually equivalent to a corporation's subordinate debt, unless there is a separate guarantee by the company for payment of the bonds themselves. In such a situation, the lease payments issued would be equivalent to the company's senior debt, as discussed earlier.

Frequently, an industry analysis is required to evaluate the ability of the company to make payments for the debt service on such industrial development bonds or pollution control bonds. In this case, Potlatch was, as noted, a forest products company and thus was tied closely to the lumber and housing industries. The housing industry has traditionally been an economic leader, and its growth paralleled changes in the GNP. Companies like Potlatch which are in related areas, such as lumber, have weathered changes in sales that correspond to changes in the number of housing starts.

Potlatch's 30 percent increase in net earnings during 1977 was largely a result of an increase in residential-housing construction. Although in the housing debacle of 1974 and 1975, housing starts dropped to one-half the 2.4 million annual rate of 1972 with the shutoff of mortgage money, only a moderate slowdown was expected for the housing industry in 1979. The number of housing starts was expected to decline by approximately 20 percent to an annual rate of about 1.6 million from the 2.0 million housing starts in both 1977 and 1978. If interest rates did not peak in the early part of 1979, the slowdown could have been deeper than was predicted.

However, it was anticipated that the building industry and companies in related fields, such as Potlatch, would not feel the impact as much as they had in the mid-1970s. By the end of 1974, the market had a 10.3-month supply of new one-family homes, which constituted an oversupply. As of late 1978, the home supply totaled only 5.3 months. Thus the ability of Potlatch to make debt service payments for its bonds seemed relatively certain, even in a housing industry downturn of the magnitude that was projected. Moreover, the corporation was a solid one, and its relatively secure pollution control bonds were on a par with its senior debt.

It is especially important to analyze the company because the debt service on the bonds depends on payments made by a single corporate entity. Potlatch, to be sure, is a major forest products company; it owns substantial timber resources and manufactures wood products. The company owns approximately 1.3 million acres of timberland, of which 540,000 acres are located in Arkansas, 514,000 acres in Idaho, and 246,000 acres in Minnesota. The company estimates that its lands have approximately 2.34 billion cubic feet of timber.

Net sales of the company increased approximately 10 percent in 1977 over 1976 sales. Net earnings, however, climbed dramatically—by approximately 30 percent in 1977 over 1976 net earnings—as a result of the company's wood products. A major factor for the increase in demand for lumber and lumber products was the relatively high level of residential-housing construction activity, particularly the construction of single-family houses. Table 11-2 provides some major data about the recent financial history of the company.

With the current issue, the long-term debt of the company totaled about $270 million, and stockholders' equity came to almost $417 million. The company has no first-mortgage debt and no public-rated debt outstanding.

The Louisiana Offshore Oil Port

In mid-August 1978, it was formally announced that one of the biggest financings of a project was coming to market in a week. The issue, for $450 million, was by the Louisiana Offshore Oil Port Authority (LOOP), a revenue authority of Louisiana authorized to develop and construct deepwater ports and offshore terminal facilities, licensed by the U.S. Secretary of Transportation under the Deepwater Port Act of 1974. To be sure, LOOP was actually an entity owned by five oil companies, as shown in Table 11-3.

In this case, LOOP was authorized to construct and operate a port complex to provide deepwater unloading accommodations for deep-draft oil tankers and onshore facilities for the storage of oil before it was transported to refineries located on the Gulf Coast and in the Midwest. The port complex was to include a marine terminal located 18 miles off the coast of Louisiana in the Gulf of Mexico, a pipeline to the onshore

TABLE 11-2 Recent Financial Data of Potlatch Corporation, in $1000s

	1977	1976	1975	1974	1973
Net sales	688,424	624,056	504,294	487,868	442,407
Net earnings	61,813	47,714	37,467	45,289	33,979
Net earnings per common share, in dollars	4.09	3.17	2.51	3.10	2.33
Ratio of earnings to fixed charges	6.51	6.65	6.11	7.71	6.79

TABLE 11-3 Ratings and Ownership Percentages of LOOP Owners*

	Moody's	S&P	Ownership %
Marathon Oil Company	A	A+	32.1
Texaco	Aaa	AA+	26.6
Shell Oil Company	Aaa	AAA	19.5
Ashland Oil	A	A	18.6
Murphy Oil Corporation	Unrated	Unrated	3.2

* The contracts provide for changes in the percentage for which each company is obligated.

facilities, and underground storage facilities located approximately 25 miles inland. The complex was to have a throughput capacity of 1.4 million barrels of oil per day. The entire project was to cost over $1 billion before completion in 1989.

The proceeds of the bond issue to finance the construction of a port complex were provided for LOOP, which would then provide the authority with a promissory note for repayment of the bond proceeds. To generate revenues for the repayment of the note, the five oil companies pledged to ship oil through the port complex; in this way the revenues derived from charges by LOOP would be sufficient to pay the principal and interest on the promissory note in accordance with each company's percentage of ownership of LOOP. These monies would then be used to pay the debt service on the bonds. If the revenues generated by LOOP were not sufficient to pay the monies for the promissory note, each oil company was obligated to pay the needed funds in the same percentage as before. Such an agreement was termed a "throughput and deficiency agreement" and was a several one, not a joint and several one, because each oil company was required to pay the needed monies only in the same percentage as it had ownership in LOOP. The agreement, therefore, is considered somewhat less secure than a joint and several one. An agreement that would be considered even less secure than a several one is one that requires the companies to pay the needed funds up to a limited percentage of what they were originally required to pay, such as up to 25 percent of their original payment requirements, if one or more companies found it difficult to pay their required sum. Such an agreement is introduced in this book as a "limited several agreement," a term which has not been used in traditional municipal credit analysis before.

While studying the agreement among the oil companies is an important part of analyzing the security behind the bonds, so is the effect of the agreement or the status of the lease in the event of bankruptcy of an oil company. In all five cases, the status of the lease was on a par with each company's subordinate debt, but with neither senior nor first-mortgage debt. Thus the lease payments, in this case and in the event of bankruptcy, were the least secure of three possibilities.

Of immediate and even primary importance in analyzing the credit of these bonds, however, was the ability of the companies to pay monies to LOOP if the revenues generated were insufficient to cover the debt service on the bonds. Here the analyst looks to the credit ratings of the companies and their percentage of ownership of LOOP. In the case of major oil companies, there is really no need to delve deeply into an industry analysis or study the market share of the companies involved. Suffice it to say that although Marathon Oil, which owns 32.1 percent of LOOP, is only A-rated, Texaco and Shell Oil, when taken together, own

46.1 percent of LOOP and are, in essence, AAA credits. Moreover, the unrated company, Murphy Oil, owns only 3.2 percent of LOOP. As a result, this municipal issue, while not bearing some of the important technical securities, such as joint and several obligations for debt service payments or payments on a par with the companies' senior debt, may be considered as a rather solid credit; two AAA-rated oil companies are virtually one-half of the project, and the debt service payments are small in comparison with the yearly net revenues and cash on hand of the companies.

Pollution Control: The Exxon Corporation

Although the following case did not really involve a credit question, the case analysis is interesting because Exxon, the world's largest industrial corporation, poured almost $1 billion into financing pollution control facilities in 1976. During that year, the Gulf Coast Waste Disposal Authority (GCWDA), a conservation and reclamation district designed to eliminate air and water pollution, issued $54.9 million in pollution control revenue term bonds, maturing in 2006, to be used for the construction of pollution abatement facilities for Exxon. GCWDA, located in Harris County, Texas, had for a long time been used for pollution control financing by such companies as Shell Oil and U.S. Steel. In this instance, however, the revenues from the bond issue were slated for the construction of both air and water treatment facilities for Exxon's petroleum and chemical manufacturing plants located in Texas. The new facilities were specifically designed to remove the "rotten egg" smell of hydrogen sulfide (a gas) from atmospheric discharges by the plants; they were also to treat wastewater and rainwater contaminated with sulfur compounds and hydrocarbons.

From the standpoint of credit, Exxon's 9 to 1 ratio of fixed-charge coverage posed few questions as to the company's high credit rating. Adding further to the security of the bonds was the leasing arrangement between Exxon and the GCWDA. In the form of an installment purchase contract, the payments constituted an "unconditional obligation" of the corporation. As a result, the bonds issued by the GCWDA were rated on a par with the company's debentures (senior debt permitted to be issued by only certain well-established companies). (The most important financial ratios for analysis purposes are the pretax fixed-charge coverage, cash flow to long-term debt, pretax return on total capital invested, and long-term debt to capitalization.)

Financial Summary*

Consolidated statement of income	1974	1975	1976	1977	1978
Sales and other operating revenue	(Millions of dollars)				
Petroleum and natural gas	$31,597	33,040	36,867	40,739	45,216
Petroleum products	8,488	9,548	8,474	9,628	10,340
Crude oil	903	1,262	1,509	1,791	2,123
Natural gas	1,099	1,114	1,260	1,406	1,623
Other	42,087	44,964	48,110	53,564	**59,302**
Total	2,787	2,594	3,238	3,578	4,034
Chemical products	147	238	278	387	560
Other	45,021	47,796	51,626	57,529	**63,896**
Total sales and other operating revenue	775	968	966	931	990
Dividends, interest and other revenue	45,796	48,764	52,592	58,460	**64,886**
Total revenue					
Costs and other deductions					
Crude oil and product purchases	18,607	21,702	26,776	29,274	31,408
Operating expenses	4,246	4,347	4,658	5,378	6,395
Selling, general and administrative					
expenses	2,439	2,628	2,719	2,955	3,640
Depreciation and depletion	1,231	1,471	1,392	1,494	1,678
Exploration expenses, including dry					
holes	431	485	527	642	775
Income, excise and other taxes					
Income	7,854	7,285	5,182	5,643	5,759
Excise, duties and other	7,419	8,047	8,318	9,948	11,757
Interest expense	366	385	396	399	425
Foreign exchange translation					
loss/(gain)	82	(165)	(105)	186	186
Income applicable to minority					
interests	126	123	114	98	100
Total deductions	42,801	46,308	49,977	56,017	**62,123**
Net income	$ 2,995	2,456	2,615	2,443	**2,763**
Net income per share	$ 6.69	5.49	5.84	5.45	6.20
Cash dividends per share	$ 2.50	2.50	2.725	3.00	3.30
Earnings to average shareholders'					
equity (*percent*)	20.6	15.4	15.1	13.1	14.0
Earnings to total revenue (*percent*)	6.5	5.0	5.0	4.2	4.3

* From Annual Report 1978.

part4

Future Issues in Municipal Finance

chapter 12

Municipal Accounting

Introduction

In 1975 New York City's books were balanced in accordance with the financial practices of the city. In actuality, the city had accumulated a deficit of close to $5 billion. Moreover, it was incurring an unfunded pension liability which it could not foresee paying and was negotiating contractual benefits with labor unions for which it was unable to carry the financial burden. Yet, the financial statements presented a picture of sound financial management. Everything balanced to "the penny," and the funds appeared in order. The "telephone book" financial statements provided a deluge of financial data, but the actual financial operation and position of the city was not apparent in its report to the public.

The financial emergency which struck New York City so severely in 1974–1975 shocked the financial community. How could such a crisis come about so precipitously and without warning? Why had not the reporting mechanisms revealed the deficiencies which had been building up for years? Moreover, did the problem which faced New York City indicate similar problems about the financial soundness of other municipalities across the nation?

Clearly, the accounting systems, the financial management, and the efficacy of that management in running the municipalities were in immediate question. A strict accounting of services and practices as well as accurate, timely, and fairly presented pictures of cities was required. The long-neglected areas of municipal accounting and accounting standards were coming into the limelight.

The purposes of this chapter are (1) to discuss the basic theories of municipal accounting, reporting, and budgetary practices and (2) to highlight problem areas which may be encountered when reviewing a municipality's financial reports.

The Municipal Budget

Investors and bond analysts, in order to obtain even the most basic idea of how a given municipality handles its debt, must look at that municipality's budget and financial statements.

The final budget is a more important document than the accounting statements because the budget sets out all the legally authorized expenditures for that municipality. In contrast, the accounts are intended to be merely a reflection of the expenditures and receipts that were previously authorized. Obviously, it is of key importance to the analyst to check if the budget and books of account do correspond to one another, or instead appear inconsistent.

Not only is the budget system more important than the accounting system, but the budget, in effect, sets the shape and scope of the whole accounting system and lays down the specific terms of the accounts—i.e., whether the accounting will be on a cash basis or on an accrual basis is determined by the municipality's budgetary expectations.[1]

The Budget and Budgetary Accounting

The exposure of the abuse of public monies by public officials and the consequent outcry from the public for more conservative financial practices resulted in the adoption of budgets by governmental units. As early as the 1900s, muckrakers were revealing the misuse of public funds and calling for reform. By the 1920s most of the major municipalities had, in the light of financial reforms, adopted some type of budgetary practice. Legislation was enacted on the state and local levels requiring budgets for at least the general fund of each municipality. Formal comparisons were required to be made between budgeted expenditures and actual amounts utilized. If a formal audit is not required by law, the general fund is usually accounted for by presenting a comparison of it with its adopted budget.

The budget provides a standard of measurement by which the performance of the municipality in achieving predesignated goals can be seen. With increasing controls and evolving reforms, the municipality's incorporation and use of budgets are being encouraged for most funds.

> In government, a budget is the financial plan embodied in the law, introduced and enacted in the same manner as any other ordinance or statute. Thus the budget is included in the financial report in order that governments can meet the first objective of governmental accounting, namely to demonstrate compliance with the law. . . . The budget is the goal; it is management's plan for securing and allocating resources. Comparing the actual results with the budget is another way of demonstrating accountabil-

ity and managerial performance. It discloses the extent to which the financial plan was achieved.[2]

The development of the budget is essentially a "political" process, which is the governmental unit's means of delineating fiscal and social policy. The timing as well as the content and format of the budget will vary from municipality to municipality. Some statutes will define the information and structure of the budget, whereas others are vague in their specifications. The National Committee on Government Accounting recommends that the annual budget be prepared using the modified accrual basis of accounting; the accounting system becomes the control mechanism ensuring that revenues and expenditures are used as defined in the budget.

The Budgetary Process

The budgetary process can be looked at as a cycle. The first step is the initial preparation of the budget itself: Department heads submit programs, projects, and operating costs according to their estimated needs. Financial information is correlated, and projected program requirements based on historical data are developed. Financial officers of the municipality compile the estimated revenues and expenditures. They review the programs and departmental needs and prepare a "balanced budget" document.

The next step in the cycle is the submission of the proposed budget to the legislature; while the legislature reviews the document, public hearings are held. If necessary, in order to raise additional funds, appropriations and tax levy ordinances, such as a property tax, are drafted and adopted. Expenditures are established through an appropriation act, and an act is legislated which stipulates maximum spending authorizations. Expenditures cannot exceed the spending limit unless the act is amended. Depending on the terms of the law, appropriations which are not spent by the end of the fiscal year may lapse or be continued in the next year. Thus the legislature will either approve, reject, or modify the budget.

Once the budget is adopted, the next step is its implementation. The terms of the budget must be complied with, and monies are spent according to specified allocations. Interim reports may be prepared on a monthly or quarterly basis to detail the progress of the services and programs provided. Administration of the budget entails the accounting for, as well as the implementation of, revenues and personnel.[3]

At the end of the fiscal year, financial reports are generated. This is the final step in the budgetary cycle. The financial statements are frequently audited to determine their accuracy and compliance with gener-

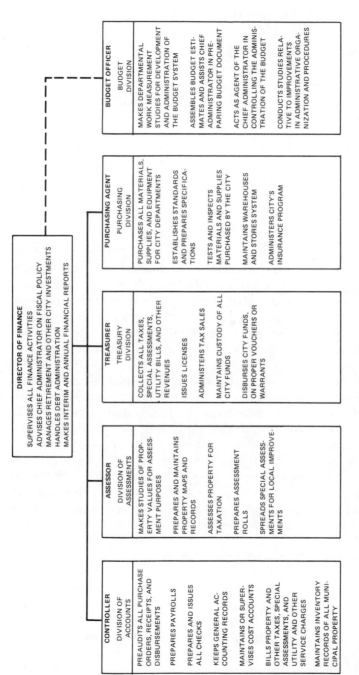

Figure 12-1 A typical organizational plan for a municipality's finance department, including descriptions of the responsibilities of the different divisions. Divisional names may vary, but essentially the functions and duties will follow those outlined. (*Note:* The dotted line between the director of finance and the budget officer indicates that the latter is often primarily responsibly to the chief administrator, being physically located in the finance department to prevent duplication of records. In many cities, the finance director handles the budget.) SOURCE: AICPA, *Introduction to Local Government Accounting*, New York, 1977, p. 11.)

ally accepted accounting principles (GAAP); moreover, their compliance with legal and budgetary requirements is reviewed. Financial and statistical data are compiled for the fiscal year and summarized in many of these reports.

The budgetary cycle is an integral part of the management of a municipality. With the increasing complexity of the financial management of a governmental unit, there is a greater need for planning, and the budget is an essential tool for adequate planning and management. It is also used to evaluate the performance of the municipality.

Methods of Budgeting

Budgets can be distinguished in terms of purpose, being either operating budgets or capital budgets. The operating budget, or annual budget, applies to the general and special revenue funds and may be used for the debt service fund where it is specifically adopted. The capital budget is adopted for long-term financial planning. It is an outline of ongoing "capital improvement programs" (CIP). Annual preparations for such plans will specify the necessary appropriations for the forthcoming fiscal year and will show estimates for 5 years thereafter. This budget is necessary for the analysis of proposed plans as well as the estimated means of financing such projects. Rating agencies review this document: It is considered an essential component for a well-managed municipality.

There are three types of budgets that are commonly used: traditional budgets, performance budgets, and program budgets. The traditional budget is determined by the objectives of the expenditures. The objective of this type of budget is to define accounting and administrative responsibilities and delegate them to department heads. The revenues are determined by the needed expenditures. In its basic form, the traditional budget does not provide a measure for total expenditures for specific services, duties, or activities. Prior years' expenditures are used as the basis for determining the needs in future years.

The second type of budget is the performance budget. It attempts to present a clearer relationship between the use of resources and the resultant services. The purpose of this type of budget is to present quantitative data concerning the "units of work" performed or services provided, identified by organizational areas. This data can then be used as a means of measuring the work output of the departments. Moreover, it is used to determine the funding requirements.

The program budget is based primarily on the program of work and secondarily on the nature and purpose of the program. It is viewed as a compromise between the traditional budget and the performance budget. The program budget attempts to measure the overall cost of a program, and it tries to establish a criterion under which one program can be evaluated against another in terms of importance. One major flaw is that it may not clearly show certain information which may be necessary in order to evaluate specific operations within a program, especially when increased expenditures are involved.

In the 1960s a new approach to budgeting—the Planning, Programming Budget System (PPBS)—was developed. Through a definition of the objectives and goals of the programs offered, this method attempts to coordinate the program, planning, and budgeting processes. The objective of PPBS is to identify the long-term consequences of current decisions in compliance with the stated objectives. Selections are made from alternative means of attaining stated objectives on the basis of a full analysis of the cost/benefit findings of each alternative. PPBS provides a "multiyear" perspective; i.e., it covers a specified number of years into the future.

PPBS is but one means in a trend toward developing a set of criteria for measuring the success of a program by quantifying the actual benefit derived from it. Another approach being developed follows the method used by the General Accounting Office (GAO) in its audits of federal agencies. Basically, the GAO sets forth three standards for evaluating performance, each being dependent on the preceding step. The guidelines used are review of financial compliance, which includes the basic evaluation of compliance with budgetary and regulatory requirements; evaluation of economy and efficiency, which will determine those areas where revenues can be enhanced and costs reduced; and evaluation of program results, whereby the program's actual results are compared with the original objectives.

In responding partially to the needs of the taxpayer as well as to those of the investor, municipalities are beginning to issue the "budget in brief," a summary of the major areas of the budget for both the operating and capital budgets. It is, in essence, a readable breakdown of the budget and provides enough data to evaluate the governmental unit.[4]

Budgetary Accounting

The budget not only is a "legal financial plan" for the municipality but also serves as an essential element in the financial planning, control, and evaluation of the operations of the governmental unit. *Governmental Accounting, Auditing & Financial Reporting Standards* (GAAFR) recommends that annual budgets be adopted by all municipalities. The annual budget would cover the fiscal year, and its basis of accounting should follow that used for the differing funds. Budgets are recommended for governmental funds because of the need to incorporate a control mechanism over these funds. Requirements for the use of budgets vary from state to state as well as from municipality to municipality. For financial reporting purposes, the statement of revenues and expenditures of the general fund and certain special revenue funds should have a comparison with a "formal budget."

A distinction should be made between fixed budgets and flexible budgets. A fixed budget has a set dollar amount, and a flexible budget, on the other hand, has a changeable dollar amount—an amount that depends on the demand for goods and/or services.

The annual budget provides control over the use of resources for the municipality. The accounting system must provide the information to show that legal requirements are being met. Budgetary accounts may be integrated into the fund accounts, but these accounts will not have an effect on either the financial position or the fund balance as shown on the financial statements.

Proprietary funds usually do not require budgets. Those that are recommended are flexible budgets, which are more like approved plans than formalized budgets. The rationale behind this type of budgeting is that since proprietary funds provide goods and services, the demand for these functions will determine the level of necessary revenues and expenses. In addition, these funds resemble private enterprises inasmuch as differing levels of expenditures are budgeted according to expected demand. Fixed budgets are usually not used for these funds, unless stipulated by law.

The types of budgets used for fiduciary funds vary according to the nature of the fund, whether it is expendable or nonexpendable. Trust funds are similar to special revenue funds and may require budgets, whereas agency funds do not require the use of budgets, since they are of a custodial nature.

Variations in the Budget

A final approved budget legally authorizes a municipality's financial managers to spend and to collect specific amounts of money during the budget period. However, although the budget is quite rigid legally, it does have some flexibility which arises from its administrators' desire for at least a degree of discretionary control and from the administrators' desire to include reserve accounts (e.g., in case of uncollectible taxes or other revenues or unexpected expenses).

Uncertainties about the accuracy of the budget may occur because grants or monies from federal or state governments which municipalities anticipate receiving may or may not materialize. Likewise, revenue-producing municipal enterprises that are expected to provide specific amounts of money may fail to do so. Despite these inevitable uncertainties, the proposed budget, to the extent that it can feasibly do so, should attempt to anticipate the actual expenditures and revenues.

Often the budget is changed during the fiscal year to which it applies, and so the projected budget and the final budget can differ substantially. (However, budgetary discrepancies even of major emergency proportions are not necessarily, by themselves, indicative of bad management.)

Incrementalism

Although zero-based budgeting has been discussed, practiced, and studied a good deal in Washington and elsewhere over the past decade, most state and municipal budgets are still prepared on an "incremental basis." This means that the municipality's financial managers start by assessing their last fiscal year's budget and then forecast from that the budget for 1 or 2 years ahead. The estimates from all the municipal departments and subdepartments which are requested in order to make up the budget also tend to be based upon an assessment of the previous year's budget.

Despite this incremental growth in municipal budgets, many observers of the municipal budgetary processes have noted that financial managers repeatedly demonstrate a tendency to avoid asking for a tax increase to cover the growth in appropriations, even when they think it is needed. and justified. Instead, they will attempt to get by on inadequate appropriations by resorting to emergency expenditures, or by making use of deficiency reappropriations. Obviously, if over 5 or 10 years this appears to be a pattern for a particular municipality, a bond investor should become wary.

Municipal Accounting Standards

In the past the subject of municipal accounting was the primary concern of the Municipal Finance Officers Association (MFOA), formed in 1906. In 1934 the MFOA created the National Committee on Government Accounting (NCGA), whose purpose was to develop a standardized set of accounting principles for governmental units. The product of the NCGA was the "bible," or blue book, *Governmental Accounting, Auditing & Financial Reporting Standards* (GAAFR), which was published in 1968 and contains the generally accepted accounting principles for governmental accounting. In a recent major restatement of GAAFR, the underlying principles for governmental accounting were organized into seven major categories: (1) generally accepted accounting principles and legal compliance, (2) fund accounting, (3) fixed assets and long-term liabilities, (4) basis of accounting, (5) the budget and budgetary accounting, (6) classification and terminology, and (7) financial reporting.[5] The purposes of the redefinition were to refine existent GAAFR principles and to provide a clearer definition of these principles and their application. The categories will be discussed throughout the chapter.

Generally Accepted Accounting Principles

The entrance of the American Institute of Certified Public Accountants (AICPA) into the field of governmental accounting has been recent. In 1974 AICPA published an industry audit guide: *Audits of State and Local Governmental Units* (ASLGU).[6] The guide incorporates GAAFR with generally accepted accounting principles (GAAP), and a certified public accountant must follow it when performing an audit of the financial statements of a municipality and in providing an opinion on them. Differences may arise between the accounting methods and reporting systems of a municipality and GAAP due to statutory requirements. In such instances the auditor will determine the nature and effect of the departure and comment on it.

GAAP is considered to provide a "minimum" standard for accounting and reporting mechanisms. However, in following GAAP, municipalities do not assure the creation of financial statements of a comparable nature. There are numerous variations permitted under GAAP, and so the accounts of 10 cities can differ drastically even though all of them were prepared in accordance with GAAP. The issue of comparability of statements in governmental accounting has been troublesome.

For the reader of financial statements it is necessary to implement a standardized method of accounting and reporting in order to better analyze the financial reports on an equal level. Nevertheless, investors or bond analysts must keep in mind that standardized methods of accounting do not assure the accuracy of the reporting within those statements.

New York City dramatized several of these points. With the fiscal crisis of 1974–1975, the Securities and Exchange Commission (SEC) investigated the accounting practices of the city. Questions arose as to the adequacy of the accounting system, the consistency in recording transactions, and the quality of the overall reporting system. It was shown that the methods used by the city concerning the consistency, accuracy, and timely reporting of financial events were not major considerations for its actual financial practices in use.

The faults that were brought to the surface in the city's accounting system had a direct bearing on the confidence of the investor in the city's municipal securities. The financial picture presented during that time was not complete. Thus a true analysis of the city in relation to its ability to carry the burden of outstanding debt and issue new debt was seriously threatened. The concept of this security as a "safe investment" was jeopardized, and the SEC hearings on the crisis of New York City emphasized this fact.

In sum, the purpose of an accounting system is

> . . . (a) to present fairly and with full disclosure the financial position and results of financial operations of the funds and account groups of the governmental unit in conformity with generally accepted accounting principles; and (b) to determine and demonstrate compliance with finance-related legal and contractual provisions.[7]

Fund Accounting

A municipality, or governmental unit, is a nonprofit organization. Its purpose is to provide services which are determined by the needs of the community, within legislative and political constraints on the local, state, and federal levels. Unlike a private business enterprise the municipality does not derive revenue from the goods produced and/or the services provided. Revenues are received from tax levies, grants, appropriations, and revenue-sharing programs. There are exceptions to this, such as a water and sewer facility, which receives revenues from rates charged to its users. Such rates are intended to be at least commensurate with its costs and expenditures.

There are many restrictions imposed on a governmental unit in its spending practices. Some of these restrictions are internal to the municipality and may involve political, legal, or statutory constraints. Other restrictions are imposed upon the municipality from outside by the state or federal government, or by legal agreements with some other governmental authority. Because of these internal and external restrictions a municipality is not able to invest its revenues in each and every project that its financial administrators deem appropriate. The governmental unit must comply with predetermined plans and can only use those funds for the stipulated purposes. Compliance with these requirements is stipulated in the budget, ordinances, and appropriations. Thus the municipality must show legal compliance in its accounting system.

While there is no guarantee that the fund concept will force a municipality to avoid the misuse of funds, it does provide an additional control mechanism because the monies are segregated, as are related expenditures, according to designated purpose.

A fund is defined as an independent fiscal and accounting entity, a self-balancing set of accounts recording cash and/or other resources together with all related liabilities, obligations, reserves, and equities which are segregated for the purpose of carrying on specific activities or attaining certain objectives in accordance with special regulations, restrictions or limitations.[8]

Funds may be established for a variety of reasons. They may arise because of constitutional requirements or statutes legislated by the state, or they may be established by local charters or ordinances or by the local council. In addition, they are organized to facilitate financial management by the municipality. To determine the extent to which a fund can be utilized, it must be distinguished according to the purpose for which it was created. Funds are also classified according to the sources of revenues and the uses of those monies. The reader must remember that each fund is a separate accounting entity and that there are practical and real differences between accounting entities and legal entities. Transactions that occur between funds frequently do so on a creditor/debtor relationship. Thus, interfund accounts receivable/payable are usually set up so as to segregate these transactions into the familiar accounting categories of debits and credits in separate columns for each account. (For examples of transactions between funds that are *not* based on a creditor/debtor relationship, see pages 10 and 11 of the AICPA audit guide.)

Funds are classified into three basic groups:

Governmental, or "Source and Disposition," Funds   These are expendable funds; the revenues allocated are to be spent within a specified period of time and are considered to be current accounts. The difference between the assets and liabilities of the funds in this group is the fund equity, or the "fund balance." Measurement for these funds is based on changes which occur in the financial position (i.e., sources, uses, and balances of financial resources) rather than on net income.

Proprietary, or Nonexpendable, Funds   This type of fund is similar to a commercial enterprise in that the purpose of the fund is to build on the initial resources allocated to it while meeting current expenses out of current revenues. Thus proprietary funds will last beyond a specified period. The purpose of this group, in that these are "income determination" funds, is to determine the net income, financial position, and changes in financial position.

Fiduciary Funds   With these funds, the municipality acts in a custodial capacity over the assets or resources held in its trust. The governmental unit will act as a fiduciary for a group of individuals, an organization, or another government agency. It is its responsibility to watch over and control the distribution of these funds.

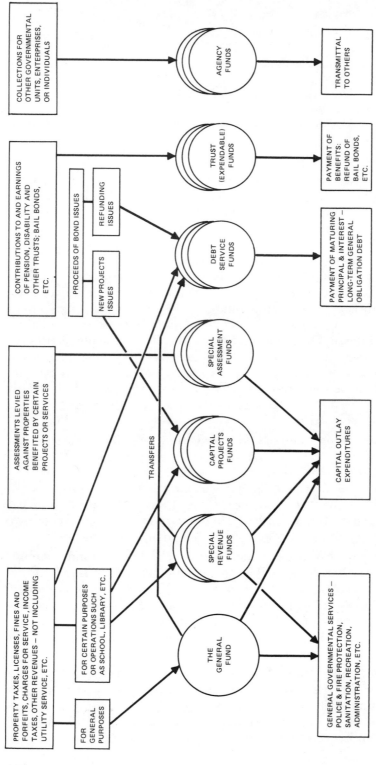

Figure 12-2 Fund resource flows, excluding flows to and from self-sustaining funds. Funds not included are those which are similar to commercial enterprises, such as enterprise, intragovernmental service, and certain trust funds. (SOURCE: AICPA, *Introduction to Local Government Accounting,* New York, 1977, p. 40.)

GAAFR recommends eight types of funds to be used within the three classifications of account groups:

Governmental funds

1. *General fund.* Accounts for ordinary operations of a governmental unit which are financed from the taxes and other general revenues. All transactions (and unrestricted resources) which are not accounted for in other funds are accounted for in this fund.

2. *Special revenue fund.* Accounts for revenues from specific taxes or other earmarked sources which, by law or administrative action, are designated to finance a particular activity or project. An example would be funds received from a federal grant for a research or training program.

3. *Capital projects fund.* Accounts for resources used for the acquisition of major, long-lived assets other than those financed by special assessment and enterprise funds. This fund includes the collection and disbursement of revenues from a variety of sources, such as bond issues, loans, or grants. A separate capital project fund is usually created for each capital project.

4. *Special assessment fund.* Accounts for the construction of improvements or the provision of services which are financed, totally or in part, by special assessments levied against benefited private property. Examples include sewer, sidewalk, construction, or street improvement.

5. *Debt service fund.* Accounts for the payment of interest and principal on all general obligation debt other than that serviced by enterprise funds or special assessment funds. Primarily, long-term debt is serviced by this fund.

Proprietary funds

6. *Enterprise fund.* Accounts for funds which resemble a private business in that they are primarily self-supporting from revenues received from "user charges" for services performed. These include water supply and sewage disposal, public hospitals, public transportation, recreation facilities, and airports.

7. *Intragovernmental service fund.* Accounts for goods and services provided by designated departments on a fee basis for other departments and agencies within a single governmental unit. Examples are a central garage which provides maintenance and repair for all vehicles of the municipality and a centralized purchasing agency for office supplies.

Fiduciary funds

8. *Trust and agency funds.* Accounts for assets held by a governmental unit in a custodial position or as an agent for individuals, private organi-

zations, or other governmental units and funds. Examples are expendable trust funds, nonexpendable trust funds, and agency funds.

These funds are usually reviewed and funded on an annual basis, and in order to assure budgetary compliance, the fiscal period is used as an accounting period. Yet, certain funds are not based on a periodic basis but rather on a project basis. These funds are capital projects and special assessment funds whose projects will continue beyond the fiscal year. Therefore, the accounting for the eight funds will be for a current period and an ongoing review of those funds which contain projects of an extended nature. Resources and the use of those funds must be accounted for in order to arrive at the transactions of the fiscal year and to arrive at the financial position of the funds at the end of this period.

The number of funds used should be based on a municipality's size and the complexity of its operations. An inordinate number of funds will prove unwieldy and dysfunctional, whereas maintaining the minimum number of accounts will facilitate financial and administrative management. Each of the eight funds mentioned will be used only if necessary.

Fixed Assets and Long-term Liabilities

One main objective of governmental accounting is to show the funds available and how those funds are being expended. Assets which belong to the governmental unit as a whole and are not used in services provided should be recorded in a separate group of accounts called "general fixed assets"; otherwise, their inclusion in the financial statements could be misleading. The general fixed assets are disclosed in the summary of accounting policies, and they should be recorded either at cost (the price of the asset) or at estimated cost, if determinable.

The investor or bond analyst should take note that a municipality's treatment of fixed assets sometimes can be potentially misleading in the balance sheet, but it must be disclosed in the accounting policies note to the financial statements. It is also important for investors to remember that the fixed assets of a municipality are often different in certain crucial respects from corporate assets. This is because, for example, a city's roads or bridges usually cannot simply be sold to improve the city's cash position at any time the city chooses. Likewise, the accounting treatment of fixed assets belonging to municipalities is also somewhat different from the treatment of fixed assets in the private sector, especially with regard to depreciation.

Municipalities usually do not report depreciation for separate government activities, such as the police department, the fire department, or the parks department. However, municipalities have the option of recording the depreciation for all fixed assets of all government activities together, and they are encouraged to exercise this option.

In contrast, each enterprise activity of the municipality *is* expected to record depreciation and is expected to record its fixed assets separately. In the treatment of both fixed assets and depreciation, an enterprise activity of a municipality is quite close to conventional accounting practice in a private enterprise.

It should be noted by investors and bond analysts that since depreciation is a reimbursable item for monies from state and federal governments, municipalities—when they receive external government funding for a specific project—keep records of both the fixed assets and the depreciation for the project.

Depreciation of fixed assets should be included in the fund balance for proprietary and trust funds. Depreciation is the allocation, in a consistent and rational manner, of the cost of the asset over the asset's useful life, and it is a major factor in determining income. In governmental accounting, *expenditures*—not expenses—are measured; thus depreciation should be shown in the funds mentioned, but for the general fixed assets it is optional. To show depreciation expense would be an incorrect mixture of expenses with expenditures. The general fixed assets which require the use of governmental funds are shown as expenditures. The sale of these fixed assets provides resources for other uses. Thus depreciation expense is neither a source nor a use of governmental funds.

As with fixed assets, a distinction must be made for long-term liabilities between those liabilities which are to be accounted for through fund accounts and those which are shown in account groups. Those bonds, notes, and other long-term liabilities (such as for pensions or capital leases) which are directly associated with and will be paid from proprietary funds, special assessment funds, and trust funds should be shown in the fund accounts. Basically, these are liabilities of a specific fund, despite the fact that the full faith and credit of the governmental unit may be backing them.

On the other hand, all other unmatured long-term debt of the municipality is considered long-term debt, and this should be shown in the general long-term debt account group. This includes the unmatured principal of bonds, warrants, or other types of noncurrent long-term indebtedness. Long-term debt is backed by a municipality's authority to raise general credit and revenue rather than related to specific assets or funds. This type of debt does not require resources available for current appropriation or expenditure of financial resources. As with general fixed assets, it would be misleading to include long-term debt in the current fund balances. Such types of debt would be shown as term bonds, serial bonds, and other general long-term liabilities. The balancing accounts show the funds available in the debt service funds to pay the principal on the debt and that amount which will be necessary for future payments of principal.

Basis of Accounting

The basis of an entity's accounting should reflect the nature of its transactions to provide an accurate and timely matching of revenues with expenditures.

In terms of time period, a municipality's accounts are split according to whether the primary impact or major transactions of the accounts occur in the past, the present, or the future. Prior years' accounts, current accounts, and future years' or deferred accounts thus specifically indicate which period the accounts are meant to cover.

There are three bases of accounting: (1) cash, (2) accrual, and (3) modified accrual. The cash basis of accounting recognizes only the cash transactions. Revenues are recognized and recorded when cash is actually received, and disbursements or expenditures are recorded when paid. This method is most susceptible to fraudulent manipulation; moreover, the cash basis is not in compliance with GAAP. Some state or local statutes may require that certain funds be maintained on a cash basis. When this occurs, an auditor cannot give an unqualified opinion on cash-basis financial statements, for GAAP must prevail.

The accrual basis is the system whereby revenues and gains are recorded when earned and all expenditures and losses are recorded when incurred. Enterprise funds, intragovernmental service funds, and capital project funds tend toward the accrual method. Revenues for trust and agency funds and for special assessment funds, however, are not adaptable to the accrual basis; thus revenues for these funds are recorded as received by using the modified accrual basis.

The modified accrual basis is a hybrid method of accounting, incorporating characteristics of both the cash method and the accrual method. Revenues are recorded when received or when they are both measurable and available, thereby being susceptible to accrual. Expenditures are recorded when the service is performed, when items, such as prepaid expenses, are incurred, or when interest on long-term debt is due. The general fund, special revenue funds, and debt service funds are required to use the modified accrual basis.

Some municipalities use a combination of the cash and modified accrual bases of accounting in order to avoid deficits at the end of their fiscal years. New York City, for example, was criticized by the SEC, during its investigations of the city's financial and accounting practices in 1976, for its misuse of accounting methodology. The city was recording its revenues on an accrual basis, whereas the cash method was being used to record expenditures; it was halting certain payments, which in actuality were legal obligations, in order to balance the budget; it was recognizing uncertain receivables in order to show that higher revenues were anticipated than were being collected; and it was committing other transgressions.

The cash basis of accounting, although simplistic, is discouraged by AICPA and GAAFR. The accrual basis presents a more realistic and accurate overview of the municipality's ability to maintain accounting records, but using the accrual method alone could cause problems with budgetary and financial accounting requirements.

Another danger of accrual accounting concerns anticipating revenues before they are actually in hand. The municipality can find itself in financial difficulties if, for whatever reason, monies do not arrive on schedule. Thus, the convenient rule of thumb used in accrual accounting is to say that amounts should only be counted as having accrued when the sum is definite, its source is definite, and the date is definite. The best examples of accounts which can be accrued are those for property taxes. Property taxes are of a known specified amount, due on a particular date from specific taxpayers. Some enterprise revenues or license fees may also be accrued in this same manner. However, because of the uncertainty about whether, or when, all these sums will come in, each municipality sets aside reserves for losses. And because many funds that are listed as having accrued surpluses can, in fact, have cash deficits, the investor or bond analyst should look not simply at the totals for each fund's assets and liabilities but more particularly at each fund's cash and current liabilities.

Recognition of gain and loss under cash, accrual, and modified accrual systems can be quite different. Take the example of vacation pay. Under the cash basis it would not be recognized as an expenditure until it was paid. Under the accrual system it would be recognized when earned, so that if municipal employees had worked half the year, then half the vacation pay would be recognized on the accounts as earned, regardless of when it was paid later on. However, under the modified accrual system a municipality's financial managers might not recognize the expenditure of vacation pay until the money was spent, but they might well add a note at the end of the financial statements mentioning that vacation pay would become due at some stage.

Municipal Dependence upon External Governmental Funds

The investor or bond analyst should determine what portion of local revenue is provided by property tax and what portion comes from other internal and external funding sources. In recent years the property tax in many communities has made up a smaller fraction of local revenues, and increasing reliance has been placed upon other types of internal revenues such as city income taxes, sales taxes, local business taxes, gross receipt taxes, service fees or charges, and license and franchise fees. Increasing reliance has also been placed by many municipalities on external government grants, aid, or revenue sharing.

Since the municipality itself does not have control over transfer payments and revenue sharing from other governments, its main areas of control over its own budget come from setting or raising property taxes, fees, or service charges. Legally, the property tax is a very powerful municipal tool, for if the tax is not paid, the municipality has the legal right to seize and appropriate the property, and later to sell it.

Investors and bond analysts should consider for each bond the specific effect of various intergovernmental funding programs because these funds have become extremely important sources of revenue for some municipalities. Whether such intergovernmental payments to a particular municipality are in the form of revenue sharing, inducements, or equalization grants can make a good deal of difference in evaluating the credit strength of the municipal bonds. This is because, as we explained in Chapter 10, external government grants can tend to support or weaken a municipality. Where the federal or state government is in effect forcing a program onto a municipality, it can actually be very expensive and financially disruptive for the municipality to accept a matching grant. Whether the external funding takes the usual form of a matching grant, as for urban renewal or public transit, or is a federal reimbursement for monies the municipality has already spent; either way the municipality will be called upon to put up its own cash. Where the intergovernmental program is optional and not forced upon the municipality, the local finance officer can carefully determine whether the grant would tend to strengthen the local community or instead make it overly dependent upon continued outside funding. As we mentioned in Chapter 1 and Chapter 5, on balance the effect of most intergovernmental grants has not been to strengthen a local municipal financial administration but to make it more dependent upon external funding than upon its own devices. Investors or bond analysts should thus be wary of interpreting a municipality's budget or books of accounts as necessarily stronger because there are hefty external government funds contributed. The timing of these external grants is of special concern because the grants can be delayed or cut off, and there is little, if anything, that the municipality can do about it. In short, these external funds are outside the local municipality's control, and therefore counting upon them may lead to disappointments.

Equalization grants tend to be more supportive of local municipal finance than most other forms of external grants or funding. These grants have become quite important in local public school finance because of recent state supreme court decisions, as, for example, in New Jersey. These new court rulings have ordered that a state's funding for education per student be far more equitable than in the past when the bulk of school funding came from the local property tax, which varied greatly between rich and poor communities. The local property tax has long been argued to be inherently unequal. For example, it produced within the state of Texas a disparity regarding the support of school systems: $20 spent per child in one community versus $1 spent per child in another community.

Common Terminology and Classification of Accounts

To provide a viable, comparable accounting system and reporting mechanism, it is essential that common terminology and classification be used in the budget, accounts, and financial reports of each fund. This is essential in maintaining a functioning and standardized accounting system. Uniform classification of all the account groups and funds will improve the planning, control, and reporting ability of the municipality.

Financial Reporting

The documents of a municipality which provide information as to the events of the prior fiscal year are the financial statements and reports. The nature of these reports and the informational content are determined by the reporting requirements of the municipality and the laws with which it must comply. The overall purpose of financial statements is to provide an accurate, timely, and fair presentation of the financial operations and position of the municipality.

The needs of the users of these statements, whether taxpayers, investors, municipal bond analysts, or financial administrators, must be considered. Consideration of their needs in the light of the financial data, analyses, and adequate disclosure practices will have an effect on the content of the statements. Prior to 1978, when the first independent audit of New York City's statements was performed, the annual report presented myriads of financial, budgetary, and statistical data in a "telephone book" format. The reader had to sift through tons of these statements to reach the essential, relevant material. Many times it is only a question of presenting the *relevant* material in a logical and organized format.

Financial statements serve two primary sets of users; there are statements for internal managerial use and statements for external readers. Interim financial statements may be generated in addition to annual reports for purposes of financial and operational planning and control. Separate from the detailed internal annual report are the external general-purpose financial statements, which can range from informational reports to comprehensive financial statements. Audited financial statements are becoming more widespread among both state and local levels. Yet some major municipalities, such as New York City, escaped this requirement for a long time. When audited, financial statements can provide an independent opinion of the financial position of the governmental unit as well as adequate disclosure of its financial and accounting policies and practices.

In addition to audited financial statements, the Municipal Finance Officers Association (MFOA) has for many years awarded a "certificate of conformance," which recognizes a municipality's "sufficient financial control" in financial reporting and conformance with GAAFR. This certificate should be included in the financial statements of a municipality because it not only indicates compliance with GAAFR but also shows that the governmental unit maintains sufficient control over its financial operations.

Financial Statements

In its revision of GAAFR, the National Council on Governmental Accounting (NCGA) has developed the "financial reporting pyramid" (see Figure 12-3), which shows the required as well as the optional reports that make up the annual reports of a municipality. The NCGA recommends that every governmental unit should publish a comprehensive annual financial report (CAFR) which covers all funds and account groups. The general purpose financial statements (GPFS) by fund type and account group should be included in a CAFR. The GPFS can be issued separately from the CAFR and can be used in official statements for municipal bond issues and for users who require less detailed data than are shown in the CAFR. The GPFS includes only data by fund type and account group, with notes to the financial statements and disclosures

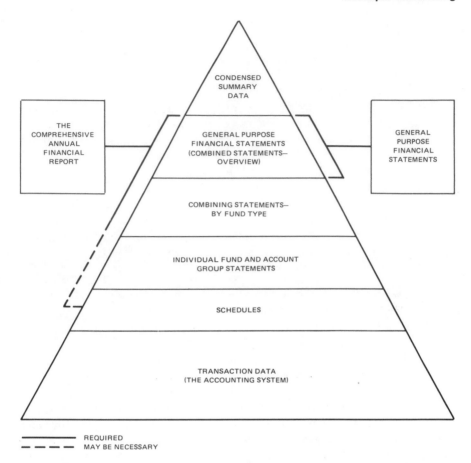

CONDENSED
SUMMARY
DATA

THE
COMPREHENSIVE
ANNUAL
FINANCIAL
REPORT

GENERAL PURPOSE
FINANCIAL STATEMENTS
(COMBINED STATEMENTS—
OVERVIEW)

GENERAL
PURPOSE
FINANCIAL
STATEMENTS

COMBINING STATEMENTS—
BY FUND TYPE

INDIVIDUAL FUND AND ACCOUNT
GROUP STATEMENTS

SCHEDULES

TRANSACTION DATA
(THE ACCOUNTING SYSTEM)

———————— REQUIRED
— — — — MAY BE NECESSARY

Figure 12-3 The financial reporting pyramid. (SOURCE: National Council on Governmental Accounting, *Statement 1: Governmental Accounting and Financial Reporting Principles,* Municipal Finance Officers Association, Chicago, 1979, p. 52.)

of material departures from legal and contractual provisions as well as other necessary material information.

Comprehensive Annual Financial Report

The CAFR should be generated and distributed as soon as possible either after the end of the fiscal year or when mandated by law. Outlined below is the minimum information which should be included, as recommended by the NCGA:

I. Introductory section

Table of contents, letter(s) of transmittal, and other material deemed appropriate by management

II. Financial section

   A. Auditor's report

   B. General purpose financial statements (combined statements—overview)

      1. Combined balance sheet—all fund types and account groups

      2. Combined statement of revenues, expenditures, and changes in fund balances—all governmental fund types

      3. Combined statement of revenues, expenditures, and changes in fund balances—budget and actual—general and special revenue fund types (and similar governmental fund types for which annual budgets have been legally adopted)

      4. Combined statement of revenues, expenses, and changes in retained earnings (or equity)—all proprietary fund types

      5. Combined statement of changes in financial position—all proprietary fund types

      6. Notes to the financial statements

      (Trust fund operations may be reported in 2, 4, and 5 above, as appropriate, or separately.)

   C. Combining and individual fund and account group statements and schedules

      1. Combining statements—by fund type—where a governmental unit has more than one fund of a given fund type

      2. Individual fund and account group statements—where a governmental unit has only one fund of a given type and for account groups and/or where necessary to present prior year and budgetary comparisons

      3. Schedules

         a. Schedules necessary to demonstrate compliance with finance-related legal and contractual provisions

         b. Schedules to present information spread throughout the statements that can be brought together and shown in greater detail (e.g., taxes receivable, including delinquent taxes; long-term debt; investments; and cash receipts, disbursements, and balances)

         c. Schedules to present greater detail for information reported in the statements (e.g., additional revenue sources detail and object of expenditure data by departments)

III. Statistical tables

(These tables are separated from financial statements due to the fact that they contain data for more than 2 fiscal years and may show nonaccounting information.)

A. General governmental expenditures by function—last 10 fiscal years

B. General revenues by source—las 10 fiscal years

C. Property tax levies and collection—last 10 years

D. Assessed and estimated actual value of taxable property—last 10 fiscal years

E. Property tax rates—all overlapping governments—last 10 fiscal years

F. Special assessment collections—last 10 fiscal years

G. Ratio of net general bonded debt to assessed value and net bonded debt per capita—last 10 fiscal years

H. Computation of legal debt margin (if not presented in the GPFS)

I. Computation of overlapping debt (if not presented in the GPFS)

J. Ratio of annual debt service for general bonded debt to total general expenditures—last 10 fiscal years

K. Revenue bond coverage—last 10 fiscal years

L. Demographic statistics

M. Property value, construction, and bank deposits—last 10 fiscal years

N. Principal taxpayers

O. Miscellaneous statistics[9]

This statistical data is invaluable in a trend analysis of the track record of the governmental unit. Moreover, it indicates the economic and population changes as well as the taxing power of the populace available to the municipality.

General Purpose Financial Statements

In addition to the comprehensive annual financial report, a general purpose financial statements (GPFS) can be published by the municipality and focus on aggregate information as to the fund type and account group information. They are considered to be adequate in presenting an abbreviated picture of the financial operations and position of the municipality. The GPFS is included in the CAFR and is an essential component of it. Those statements which should be included in the GPFS, thereby assuring that it is in conformance with GAAP, are listed below:

- Combined balance sheet—all fund types and account groups

- Combined statement of revenues, expenditures, and changes in fund balances—all governmental fund types

- Combined statement of revenues, expenditures, and changes in fund balances—budget and actual—general and special revenue fund types (and similar governmental fund types for which annual budgets have been legally adopted)
- Combined statement of revenues, expenses, and changes in retained earnings (or equity)—all proprietary fund types
- Combined statement of changes in financial position—all proprietary fund types
- Notes to the financial statements[10]

Notes to the Financial Statements

Integral parts of both financial statements are the notes to these statements. Included in these notes are a summary of the significant accounting policies and a summary of major disclosure items. These items are of a material nature; examples are significant contingent liabilities, pension plan obligations, accumulated unpaid employee benefits, any material violations of finance-related legal and contractual provisions, debt service requirements to maturity, and commitments under noncapitalized leases. These notes and summaries should be read carefully to detect any material events or potential liabilities which could have a major effect on the financial position of the municipality. In addition, such notes indicate the financial and accounting policies utilized by the municipality.

The financial reports presented by municipalities vary, depending on the needs of the users. The types of reports which should be issued, as suggested by the NCGA and the AICPA, are not issued by every governmental unit. Attainment of a standardized governmental accounting system and reporting mechanism for all municipalities is still to be realized. Many times, the problem is that the municipality must comply with the accounting standards as set by the legal and regulatory requirements and environment, which differ from GAAFR and GAAP. Other times, the obstacle is the insufficient resources allocated toward the implementation of an accounting system; other factors are the lack of proper monitoring and the lack of necessary controls which must accompany the accounting and information system.

The first part of the chapter dealt with governmental accounting theory. The remainder will now discuss the issues of both a financial nature and an accounting nature which are essential in understanding the controversial nature of municipal accounting. The reader must be aware of these topics in order to understand and analyze the reports as well as the municipality.

Warning Signals

In reviewing the overall financial statements of a governmental unit, certain warning signals, or "red flags," can be incorporated into the analysis and are listed below. (See Chapter 5 for source material.)

1. Revenue-based indicators
   a. Decreasing value of taxable property
   b. Increasing ratios of delinquent taxes to total tax levy
   c. Increasing ratios of current tax rate to maximum legal tax rate
   d. Decreasing number and value of building permits issued
   e. Increasing incidence of actual revenues below budgets
2. Expenditure-based indicators
   a. Increasing excesses of current expenditures over current local revenues
   b. Increasing expenditures per capita in excess of the inflationary rate
   c. Increasing excesses of current expenditures over total revenues
   d. Increasing incidence of actual expenditures in excess of budgets
   e. Continuing increases in amount of unfunded portions of pension programs
3. Cash management indicators
   a. Reducing amounts of aggregate short-term investments
   b. Increasing amounts of unpaid current obligations
   c. Reducing income from short-term investments (that are a result of falling interest rates)
4. Debt indicators
   a. Reduced ratings on bonds
   b. Increasing amounts of bonded indebtedness per capita
   c. Increasing ratio of bonded indebtedness to total property value
   d. Increasing need to borrow in order to meet debt service or liquidation requirements
   e. Increasing use of long-term debt to fund current expenditures (This is a dangerous sign if the municipality must resort to using the marketplace to constantly finance current needs.)
   f. Increasing amounts of short-term borrowing remaining unpaid at the end of the fiscal year

These indicators will point to the problem areas which should be further investigated. Some contend that these indicators are "traditional ratios" and that more dynamic analytic methods should be employed, such as regression analysis.[11] Yet, for a trend analysis, these indicators will prove invaluable in a variance analysis of the financial performance and prior track record of a governmental unit.

There are other areas in which adequate disclosure should be investigated. These items are of a "high-dollar" magnitude and could have a major impact on the future financial position of the municipality, but studies have shown that these high-dollar items (which include pension plans, overlapping debt, inventories and receivables, leases, and accrued vacations and sick leave) are not always fully disclosed. Current revisions of accounting practices and reporting methods will effectively deal with this problem. In the meanwhile, the "red flags" referred to above will point out the trouble spots. Some of the major areas are discussed below.

Pension Plans

A Coopers & Lybrand study of the disclosure practices of 46 cities in the United States indicated that the unfunded pension obligations of 33 cities total more than $13 billion.[12] This figure does not include unfunded pension liabilities of "overlapping jurisdictions," such as school districts. Close to 80 percent of the cities surveyed do not disclose the actuarially computed value of their unfunded vested pension liabilities in their annual financial statements. The study concluded that "given the basic uncertainty underlying much of the issue it is likely that if the facts were known the amounts would be considerably higher than currently reported."[13] Although the actual funding of the plan is not an accounting question, it is important to be aware of the municipality's financial policy regarding its pension plan and its associated liability. This liability could have major repercussions on the future ability of the municipality to pay its pension plan obligations. Thus disclosure of the nature and degree of obligation of the pension plan provisions to determine their magnitude should be sought.

Overlapping Jurisdictions and Debt

The tax base of a municipal unit is an important determinant of the ability of the municipality to finance its obligations, especially in terms of debt incurred. GAAFR has defined overlapping debt as "the proportionate share of debts of local governmental units located wholly or in part within the limits of the reporting government which must be borne by property within each governmental unit."[14] Governmental units, since World War II, have "overlapped" in services and shared the burden of providing the services; school districts, for example, may be supported by two separate governmental entities. Thus, the assessable tax base available to both entities must be determined.

The total "bonded indebtedness" of a municipality also includes "special assessment" debt, which is issued to pay for all or a portion of a specific service or improvement provided by the municipality. (For example, the municipality may issue water and sewer bonds or pollution control bonds.) This type of debt circumvents the legal debt limitation placed on the governmental entity. It is necessary to distinguish the share of debt of another governmental entity which is being carried by the tax base of the governmental unit being reviewed.

Special assessment debt, although not a part of the legal debt limitation, is, in reality, a portion of debt which is charged against the property tax base, which is the main source of revenue for overlapping units of local government. "Piling up" of debt in layers has evolved from the complex structure between state, local, and special districts. Adequate disclosure showing overlapping debt, as well as direct debt, should be reviewed by the analyst or investor. This is essential so that the debt burden taken on by a governmental unit is not understated.

Two other crucial measures are a municipality's success in increasing its tax rates and its history of tax collections. Although these are not strictly accounting issues, they are essential components in the financial analysis of the performance and the revenue base of a municipality. Two tax rates may be indicated: (1) the rate of the governmental unit and (2) the total rate for all the municipalities combined. It is important to separate the tax rates for debt service from the tax rates for operations. If the tax limit has been used up, the means by which the municipality will meet the debt service on additional outstanding debt should be sought. Tax rate information for a 10-year period is useful in the trend analysis of the financial and operational performance of the governmental unit.

The collection history of a municipality indicates its management and financial security. The collection of current and delinquent taxes is a means of measuring the ability to secure revenues for payment of debt service. New York City—in its issuance of short-term financing notes, such as Revenue Anticipation Notes (RANs) and Tax Anticipation Notes (TANs)—depended on the timely payment of taxes due on real estate assessments.[15] Default on payments increased during 1974, caused a substantial loss in revenue, and proved to be a critical problem in raising necessary funds to pay debt obligations. Information as to delinquency rates, penalties, rate structure, interest charged, and the tax collection calendar may be found in the annual report and, depending on the nature of the security being issued, in the official statement.

Inventories and Receivables

In governmental accounting, inventories represent the expenditures, and the receivables represent the revenues which will be spent when and if collected.[16] The question arises as to whether these are legitimate accounts. A municipal finance officer's foreknowledge regarding the collectibility of taxes and other receivables is essential in planning short-term financing. This planning is based on the estimated, collectible incoming tax revenues. The decline in collectibility of such taxes will severely affect the ability of the municipality to pay off RANs or TANs in the next fiscal year.

In reviewing the accounts and the long-term obligations of a municipality, the overriding concern is whether the municipality is able to carry its debt burden; the information presented must be analyzed to determine this.

Leases

Leasing is used by a municipality to secure the long-term use of facilities without incurring debt service requirements. It is also a means of circumventing the municipality's legal debt limitations and avoiding having to ask the electorate for a vote of approval for a new debt issue.

The theory behind leasing is that instead of purchasing a facility (by issuing notes or bonds), a municipality will rent it. The cost, or indebtedness, of the governmental unit will increase only by the amount of the annual rent and not by the full cost of the facility, regardless of the fact that the governmental unit may take title to the facility when the cumulative rents are equal to the full capital costs of constructing it. An alternative method is to create a separate authority which will issue revenue bonds to pay for the construction of the project—which, when completed, will be leased directly to the municipality. The outstanding debt is not the responsibility of the governmental unit, although the lease payments are.

In order to adequately analyze the future cash needs of a municipality, such arrangements should be reviewed; however, their disclosure is not always present in annual reports. The study by Coopers & Lybrand indicated that 93 percent of the cities did not disclose information on these alternative means of financing (leasing arrangements in particular) even though the current requirement is that

> Information on noncapitalized lease commitments should be disclosed, including rental expense for the accounting period, minimum rental commitments, and other information necessary to assess the effects of lease commitments on financial position, operations and changes in financial position of the lessee.[17]

Analysts must be aware of these arrangements and include the effects of the arrangements in their financial analysis.

Accrued Vacations and Sick Leave

Another major expense area with a potential liability to the governmental unit is accrued vacations and sick leave. Despite the fact that municipal employees will not use their vacations and sick leave all at once, adequate disclosure is necessary in planning the cash needs of the governmental unit. But, once again, most cities neither disclose this financial obligation nor set aside separate funds to handle this expense. It has been estimated that for seven cities alone, this expense was $130 million. Severe financial repercussions can occur because of the lack of recognition and provision for these liabilities.

The areas mentioned are financially oriented. Issues within the accounting domain for governmental units have questioned the very nature of fund accounting and the method of financial reporting as well as issues such as depreciation and encumbrances. Moreover, the issue of implementing a standardized set of governmental accounting principles which transcends the local and state legal requirements has been under consideration. Pending legislation would require the creation of a government commission to set accounting standards for municipalities, but the fate of this legislation is uncertain.

Issues and Controversies

The most important issues facing governmental accounting are (1) searching for a new municipal accounting model, (2) determining exactly what is the government entity on which to report, (3) deciding what we need information for, (4) deciding which information is needed and useful, and, finally, (5) determining what should be done with the financial audit.

If these issues appear elementary, they are nonetheless vital. To take but one example, let us look at the issue of what is the municipal entity that should be reported on. If we look at accounts of the City of New York, we see key department totals missing. The Education Department, the Health and Hospitals Department, and the Transit Department, not to mention the Port Authority or Off Track Betting, do not list their general financial figures with the New York City financial figures because they are entities officially chartered by New York State. Only those specific subsidy payments from the city to these departments or authorities are included in New York City's books of account.

Also important as an issue facing municipal accounting is this question: Do financial accounting statements really convey meaning? An auditor's report on a municipality only assures the reader of the accounts that the financial statements are in conformity with GAAP as of that moment, but it does not by any means say that those accounts are truly informative. In fact, the financial statements of a complex governmental entity, according to Robert S. Anthony in the *Harvard Business Review*, may be virtually impossible to understand despite the fact that they conform to GAAP.

Independent Auditors

If a particular municipality prepares its own accounting statements, there may be reason for investors and bond analysts to be wary. The accountant, if he or she is part of the state or municipality's government structure, should still in various ways be separate from the municipality's managers. The accountant should, for example, have a separate office, a separate salary appropriation, and separate powers totally independent of whichever mayor or other governmental officeholders are in power. Because such independence is rare, and because of the danger of lack of objectivity on the part of an internal auditor, many municipalities feel required to obtain an external audit from a well-regarded CPA firm.

An investor or bond analyst who does not see an external accountant's opinion should note whether state or local municipal law stipulates that the books of account must be prepared by the state's accountant or by the municipality itself. Legally binding statutory requirements may prevent external accountants from preparing the accounts. However, if no external audit is performed and there is no legal reason why one was not performed, then there may be reason for the investor or bond analyst to be wary of that municipality's bonds.

The investor should also be aware that even when the financial statements have been audited by an external auditor, there may be significant improprieties that go unreported. Other significant problems may be only vaguely alluded to in a note and not spelled out.

Combined versus Consolidated Statements

An important development in municipal accounting is the move toward consolidated financial statements. The NCGA's *Statement 1*, concerning consolidated financial statements, *encourages* municipalities to aggregate all funds statements into one column of account groups, but *requires* presentation of the grouping of all eight columns of funds of a homogeneous nature (e.g., fixed asset group, long-term debt group of accounts). Thus even if a municipality has 100 funds, it is expected to group them into eight groups of funds.

Many authorities have differed as to whether municipal accounting should introduce one single consolidated statement instead of listing only separate funds or groups of funds. In terms of municipal accounting, combined statements are recommended over consolidated statements, whereas the reverse is true for a commercial enterprise. Consolidation in terms of a municipality would encompass the merging of all eight funds and two account groups into one overall economic unit. The problem encountered with this is the necessary segregation of funds for reporting purposes. Each fund is a distinct entity, and to consolidate all of them into one unit would, again, obscure the legal and other requirements which, by nature, must be separated.

Second, consolidation for a corporation is based on ownership: A corporation which owns 50 percent or more of a subsidiary represents that subsidiary as part of itself in its financial statements. Ownership considerations for a municipality differ: There are no "equity" interests as with a corporation. Legal requirements also distinguish certain authorities or agencies within the jurisdiction of a governmental unit as not being part of it. Thus ownership must be determined, and this is, indeed, a difficult task—one which would hinder the realistic reporting of the financial operation and position of a municipality.

The Basis of Accounting

The question has arisen as to whether the use of funds as the basis for accounting for municipalities is valid. Some contend that municipalities should be accounted for just as private commercial enterprises are. Yet there are reasons for the use of the fund as the basis for municipal accounting: Governmental units receive funds through grants; through local, state, and federal allocations; and by other means. They are not profit-motivated. The monies received must be spent as specified. Thus the accounting system must fulfill two objectives: (1) to show compliance with legal requirements and (2) to show compliance with GAAP. Furthermore, the segregation of funds is necessary to show that the municipality has been properly using its allocated resources. The fund basis of accounting accomplishes these objectives. To treat municipalities as commercial enterprises would obscure the characteristics that distinguish the two types of entities. Moreover, the necessary accounting information and controls of a private enterprise would not be instituted over a governmental unit.

Fixed Assets and Depreciation

The general fixed assets of a municipality are not recorded in the funds but are segregated. Depreciation of these fixed assets is optional, at the discretion of the governmental unit. The decision not to record fixed assets is made by the municipality which, basically, does not feel the need to expend resources to maintain such information. Yet, with the increasing costs of maintenance as well as inflation, this attitude is changing.

While municipalities tend not to record depreciation, commercial enterprises do record such expenses. Depreciation is a means of allocating the cost of the asset over its useful life. It is not an actual expense but is maintained for tax purposes. For a municipality, once resources have been expended for a fixed asset, it is considered to be a sunk cost. The fact that no depreciation is taken on an asset in no way affects its cost to the municipality.

Encumbrances

Encumbrances are defined as obligations in the form of a purchase order, contract, or salary commitment. These obligations are chargeable to an appropriation item for which a part of the appropriation is reserved. Once the actual liability is established or the encumbrance is paid, it ceases to exist. The problem with encumbrances is that they are not actual liabilities of the municipality. Those who favor their use believe it is in line with the "flow of funds" which underlies the basis of measurement of resources for a governmental unit. In essence, encumbrances are part of the allocation process and segregate those resources which are no longer available for expenditure. An encumbrance represents a contractual liability; therefore, although it is not an actual liability, it must be represented as one. Confusion does arise as to the differences between an actual liability and an encumbrance, and care is needed when distinguishing them on financial statements.

Conclusion

Municipal accounting theory is complex. It is undergoing changes and refinements to provide a sound framework which municipalities can implement in their accounting practices. Many obstacles are blocking the path for the incorporation of a standardized set of accounting principles. Legal and statutory requirements of the individual states and localities do not accommodate the institution of a standardized municipal accounting practice; however, the need to concentrate on the development and refinement of their accounting systems and reporting practices must be satisfied.

Since reporting practices are not standardized, major organizations, such as the NCGA and the AICPA, are working jointly to promote the use of suggested reporting formats. Yet, due to the various needs of the different users of these reports, the design and content are not uniformly presented from municipality to municipality. The trend is toward presenting meaningful statements which conform to a general standard and toward increased disclosure of not only financial information but also economic, demographic, and statistical data.

The overall objective is to develop a reporting system which will provide relevant information for managers and enhance financial decisions by internal and external readers. A reader of the reports must be aware of the underlying accounting theory and the practical limitations involved. Since complete disclosure of every major area is not evidenced by recent studies, a reader must be careful in assessing the reports.

Federal regulation of municipalities has been limited, but with the advent of the fiscal crisis of New York City in 1974–1975, federal scrutiny has increased. Improved disclosure practices are being encouraged by all participants (see Chapter 13, "Legal Protection, Disclosure, and Liability"). Many times it is not the amount of information furnished that matters but, rather, the quality of the data presented. The municipal analyst or investor must recognize this fact and be able to not only pinpoint the potential trouble spots but also have a basic understanding of both the reports and the accounting theory behind the reports.

Notes to Chapter 12

[1] Most municipalities have budgetary and accounting systems that parallel each other. However, there are some communities that continue to have budgets and accounts on different fiscal year time schedules or otherwise in discrepancy with each other.

[2] Harold I. Steinberg, *Local Government Accounting: Explanations and Recommendations*, Peat, Marwick, Mitchell & Company, New York, 1978, p. 1.

[3] Felix Pomeranz et al., *Auditing in the Public Sector*, Warren, Gorham & Lamont, New York, 1976, pp. 107–110.

[4] Ibid., pp. 9–14.

[5] National Council on Governmental Accounting, *Statement 1: Governmental Accounting and Financial Reporting Principles*, Municipal Finance Officers Association, Chicago, 1979.

[6] American Institute of Certified Public Accountants, *Audits of State and Local Governmental Units*, New York, 1974. This industry guide was prepared by the Committee on Governmental Accounting and Auditing (CGAA), which is a major organization in governmental accounting and also a part of AICPA.

[7] National Council on Governmental Accounting, op. cit., p. 2.

[8] Harold I. Steinberg, op. cit., p. 10.

[9] National Council on Governmental Accounting, op. cit., pp. 50–59.

[10] Ibid., pp. 59–60.

[11] Interview with Felix Pomeranz, a partner with Coopers & Lybrand, in October 1978.

[12] Coopers & Lybrand, *Financial Disclosure Practices of the American Cities: A Public Report*, University of Michigan Press, Ann Arbor, p. 27.

[13] Ibid., p. 27.

[14] National Committee on Governmental Accounting, *Governmental Accounting, Auditing, and Financial Reporting*, Municipal Finance Officers Association, Chicago, 1968, app. A, p. 165.

[15] Real estate tax delinquencies in New York City increased by 22 percent, or $26,603,210 in 1974 over 1973. The city, although stating that the delinquencies can be collected in later years, is dependent on the current cash flow to meet operations. Thus, at that time it increased its short-term borrowing, and one major component was via the issuance of TANs.

[16] It is important to make the distinction between expenditures and expenses in governmental accounting. An expenditure is an allocation of monies to be spent for a specific purpose. The authorization to use the monies may be through state law or an administrative ordinance. Whatever the dictate, the expenditure may be for one purpose only.

[17] Coopers & Lybrand, op. cit., p. 32.

NOTE: This chapter was written with the assistance of Lynn Togut.

chapter 13

Legal Protection, Disclosure, and Liability

Introduction

Why is the question of full disclosure so crucial today in the area of municipal bonds? Municipal securities have been considered second to federal securities in terms of safety in timely payment of interest and principal; and the dollar figures for defaulting municipal issues are minimal in comparison with the actual dollar volume of municipal debt outstanding. During the Great Depression approximately 7.2 percent of outstanding municipal debt defaulted. From 1954 to 1975, only 18 new municipal bankruptcy cases were filed, and little or no "permanent loss" to the creditors resulted. Then, why is the topic of disclosure to controversial?

The New York City and New York State crises occurred during a national economic recession in 1974–1975, with a combined outstanding debt of close to $30 billion. In the midst of this crisis, the financial statements for New York City showed that all funds "balanced" and that technically everything was in "order." The financial emergency of New York City highlighted the enormous potential of both state and local governments to go into default across the country. Moreover, it brought to the surface the need for a reexamination of disclosure procedures used by the participants in a municipal debt offering. Both the procedures and the reporting mechanisms, such as the annual report, the budget, and the official statement, needed to be refined in the informational content.

As stated, the concept of a municipal security being a financial risk to the investor was viewed as unlikely, regardless of the disparity in the types of securities issued, such as a GO bond versus a revenue bond. Today, the economic and financial disclosure pictures on the national, state, and local levels are changing. There has been a lack of adequate disclosure as to the solvency of many municipal issuers. This has raised the consciousness of the public, thereby raising questions as to the overall solvency of the municipal issues on the market. Investors want reassurance beyond the traditionally appealing tax-exempt nature of the security, including more detail as to the history and nature of the issuer, the economic and political environment under which the issuer must operate, and the interrelationship between the issuer and state and federal agencies.

In light of the consumer-oriented environment, changes are occurring in disclosure practices. In order to understand these modifications, it is necessary to review the history of the regulatory environment and the nature of the responsibilities of the participants in the municipal marketplace. The ultimate beneficiary of these changes in disclosure practices will be the investor. The investment decision will be enhanced with increased disclosure and refinement of the reporting mechanisms.

History

The question of municipal default was not uppermost in the investor's mind because the securities were considered safe investments, yet there have been periods in the past when municipal securities have gone into default. In the 1840s, a number of canal and internal improvement bonds defaulted. After the Civil War and during subsequent periods of financial panics, railroad aid bonds defaulted. During that time, railroads were seeking to expand their lines and sought the support of the municipalities. The payments of interest and principal on the resultant bonds were made by the railroads to the municipalities. When severe economic and financial troubles plagued the railroads, they defaulted on their payments. Municipalities, then, claimed no responsibility to the bondholders; moreover, it appeared that certain bonds were not legally issued and thus were not binding obligations of the municipalities. The investors were left without recourse or protection regarding their investment, and, as a result, investor confidence in the municipal bond marketplace waned severely. Municipalities, other than large cities, found it difficult to market their securities.

In order to regain investor trust and to reassure the investor that the municipal securities were valid obligations, the municipality retained an outside, independent legal counsel. It was the function of this expert counsel to opine as to the unqualified, legal validity of the issue. Thus in the event of default, the investor would have a binding obligation on which it would be able to recover its legal rights.

With the advent of federal income tax, certain interest on municipal securities was exempted. The independent bond counsel then undertook another duty and opined on the tax-exempt status of the interest on the municipal security. The investor was reassured as to both the legal, valid obligation of the issue and its tax-exempt qualifications. The tax-exempt characteristic of municipal securities further enhanced their appeal to the investor, in addition to their perceived degree of safety.

The exemption from federal taxation also appealed to individual investors who were in higher income tax brackets. Yet with the increase in the effective rate of income taxes, middle-income investors have entered the municipal bond marketplace. The number of municipal offerings and their dollar volume have increased substantially in the past 20 years. Although the percentage of individual investors has declined, their investment has increased from $30 billion in 1960 to $89.4 billion in 1978.

Yet the federal involvement in the municipal securities market till 1975 was minimal: The ability of a municipality to cover its principal and interest on outstanding debt was not questioned. During and after the Great Depression, especially, it was in the arena of corporate securities that the federal government enacted and enforced strict securities legislation and regulation. The investor in the municipal securities market was thought to be sophisticated enough to analyze the risk involved, but the composition of that market has changed:

> Despite the fact that holdings of nonhousehold investors comprise almost seventy-five percent of total municipal bond holdings, the large absolute amount of household holdings and the trend toward investment by nonaffluent, relatively unsophisticated investors increases the potential for fraud and abuse in the municipal securities market far above the level existing when Congress originally created the municipal bond exemptions of the 1933 and 1934 Acts.[1]

Thus the issue of full disclosure is being reconsidered; it is complex, and the solutions are not easily found. How does one define disclosure? The courts; federal, state, and local governments; and organizations within the industry are attempting that task.

Regulation of Municipal Securities

Regulation of the municipal securities industry has come from federal legislation, state constitutional and statutory requirements, local municipal charters and laws, and the municipal securities industry itself. The municipal sector is unique. The municipal security encompasses a "variety" of debt instruments such as GO bonds, revenue bonds, and industrial development bonds; each has its own characteristics, intricacies, and numerous subgroups and distinctions.

Control over the sale of these securities comes from various sectors. Conflicts arise regarding the overall nature of the responsibilities of not only federal and state powers but also those who participate within the industry. The individual issue determines the nature and degree of involvement by each participant. The definition of full legal disclosure results from the collective judgment of those involved parties, such as bond counsel, issuer, and underwriter. When the need arises to interpret legislation in order to establish guidelines, the court system becomes involved. Thus the issue of regulation and the attempt to establish and enforce disclosure guidelines are complex.

Federal Legislation

Municipal securities were considered relatively sound investments in the 1930s when federal legislation for them was being enacted. Apparently, it was the legislator's attitude at the time that "misrepresentation" by municipal issuers was unlikely. In addition, the municipal securities marketplace was not a primary source of revenue for governmental units. Moreover, in light of the stock market crash of 1929, private corporate securities were in dire need of regulation. Thus the Securities Act of 1933 (1933 Act) and the Securities Exchange Act of 1934 (1934 Act) exempted municipal securities from the stringent regulatory and registration requirements and from the general purview of the newly formed Securities and Exchange Commission (SEC) which was imposed on private corporate securities. These securities were perceived as posing a greater risk to the investor because of the greater probability of fraud.

In the 1933 Act, municipal securities were categorized as one type of security and enumerated as "exempt" from the regulations contained in the act. "Exempt" according to the 1933 and 1934 Acts did not mean exempt from federal income taxation (that is determined by section 103 of the IRS code) but, rather, exempt from the provisions of the acts unless otherwise stated. This exemption, in the 1933 Act, excluded municipal securities from registering prospectuses and disclosures. In addition, the exemption excluded these securities from the "extensive civil liabilities" of sections 11 and 12, which relate to the sales of securities which are made prior to the registration of prospectuses. Section 17 [and section 17(a) in particular], which covers general antifraud regulation, does apply to municipal securities. This section deals with the omission of facts and/or the material misstatement of facts in an official document given to a potential investor. The liability associated with this act is very broad in nature, and it needs definitions through the courts as to the degree of negligence attached with the participants in the offering. This section is the only restraint on municipal bonds in the 1933 Act.

The 1934 Act does not contain a broad definition of exempted securities, and each section must be reviewed to determine if municipal securities are exempted from it. The "comprehensive" reporting rules contained in section 12 of the act do not apply to municipal securities. Section 10 prohibits the "use of any manipulative or deceptive device in connection with the purchase or sale of any security."[2] Rule 10(b)(5) of this section, in particular, covers antifraud but does not specifically state that municipal securities are included in its stipulations.

The two antifraud provisions—section 17(a) and section 10(b)—in the 1933 Act are relied upon for recourse in cases of alleged fraud, and power is given to the SEC to investigate such cases (although it is rarely used). The distinction between fraudulent intent and error of omission is not clearly defined in these acts. The definitions must be provided by the courts in their interpretations of the laws as cases are adjudicated. In court cases, section 17(a) is usually referred to, whereas rule 10(b)(5) of section 10(b) is the major law ruled upon in the decisions set forth.

Court cases have arisen over the topic of reasonable care in performing "due diligence" investigations of issuers of municipal securities and their actual financial positions, and in defining the responsibilities of the participants who bring municipal securities to market. These cases, generally on the level of the federal circuit courts, defined the actual legal responsibility under rule 10(b)(5). Initially, the issuer is responsible for all the facts it presents in the official statement. Yet the circuit courts have had little difficuly in widening the scope of responsibility, and thus the scope allowed for negligence in cases of alleged fraud. With the decision from *Ernst & Ernst v. Hochfelder* (1976), the Supreme Court narrowed the definition of liability of the parties and allowed for a good faith defense on their part, thereby reducing the scope of negligence liability.

Prior to this case, *Sanders v. John Nuveen & Co.* of 1970 resulted in the most comprehensive definition of the functions of the underwriter in a municipal issue. The crux of the case was that the Seventh Circuit Court held the underwriter, Nuveen, liable for fraudulent conduct despite the fact that the underwriter had performed an investigation of the securities during the initial sales period. *Hochfelder* caused the *Nuveen* case to be remanded for reconsideration. Here is what the Supreme Court expressed in *Hochfelder*:

> The failure to investigate another's action or statements in the transaction, without more, is neutral conduct. The decision not to investigate becomes

significant only when the putative investigator knows of fraudulent activity or of a misstatement or omission of a necessary material fact. In such a case the decision not to investigate but to conceal can itself become a direct violation of rule 10b-5.[3]

In the case of bond counsel's duties, there have been few cases adjudicated. The *Hochfelder* decision would apply if there was knowledge of misstatement or omission of material facts in the official statement by bond counsel. The courts are the avenue for recourse for interpreting the scope and applicability of the federal securities laws. In this role, the courts have tried to narrow the definition of the responsibilities and functions of the involved parties.

The two provisions—section 17 and section 10—were the only federal limitations relating to the issuance of municipal securities until amendments to the 1934 Act were legislated in 1975. Further federal regulation of the municipal marketplace was felt unnecessary, as the risks of default and potential fraud were considered minimal. Extensive disclosure requirements which were applied to private corporate securities were not applicable to municipal bonds. Disclosure requirements are evolving as standards and guidelines are set by the security industry, establishing the degree of acceptable practice. But there do not exist disclosure guidelines that are uniform, legal, and federally required, which should be used in every municipal offering.

The 1934 Act empowered the SEC to regulate broker/dealer activities through the antifraud provisions. In addition to section 10b and rule 10(b)(5), rules 15(c)(1) and 15(c)(2) also relate to any fraudulent means of purchasing or selling any security (these sections do not relate to issuers). It should be noted that the substance of the two security acts is basically the same. The main concern of the 1933 Act was the issuance and sale of securities by underwriters, whereas the 1934 Act was directed toward the stock exchanges and broker/dealers in terms of purchasing, selling, and trading. In the 1934 Act, the SEC was also granted the power to regulate and supervise any registered broker. Self-regulatory bodies primarily regulate the securities markets, and all national securities exchanges must register with the SEC. The over-the-counter market is accounted for in section 15(a), which requires national securities associations to register with the SEC, although membership in these associations is not required.

The National Association of Securities Dealers (NASD) is the only association registered under this provision, and its membership includes virtually all broker-dealers conducting an active business in the over-the-counter markets.[4]

Essentially, NASD has established a set of comprehensive rules which are designed to protect the investor and govern its members' practices. The SEC supervises NASD, and if any action is taken against a member, both NASD and the SEC will do it. Yet before this can be initiated, the rules require a very high burden of proof for enforcement.

Even before the 1974–1975 fiscal crisis in New York, the indifference of the federal government to the self-regulatory ability of the municipal securities market was shaken. Scandals in broker/dealer practices occurred in the late 1960s and early 1970s in Florida and Tennessee, for instance. One reaction was the amendments in 1975 to the 1934 Act. The purposes of these amendments were

> . . . to prevent fraudulent and manipulative acts and practices, to promote just and equitable principles of trade, to foster cooperation and coordination with persons engaged in regulating . . . and facilitating transactions in municipal securities, to remove impediments to and perfect the mechanism of a free and open market in municipal securities, and in general, to protect investors and the public interest. . . .[5]

In essence, the exemption of brokers and dealers who were trading municipal securities from registering with the SEC was removed. Any one involved in this activity is required by law to register with the SEC. Applications must be filed with the SEC, and the SEC may deny an applicant acceptance according to its guidelines. Thus any "nonbank" dealer who is not a member of NASD will be regulated directly by the SEC.

The amendments also created the Municipal Securities Rulemaking Board (MSRB), which requires every broker or dealer of municipal securities to comply with its rules. The MSRB is a product of a joint effort of Congress, the SEC, and the security industry. The purpose of the MSRB is to oversee practices within the municipal securities industry. It was established as an independent, self-regulatory organization that would be the primary rule-making authority for the industry. The MSRB is composed of 15 members coming from three groups: securities firm representatives, bank dealer representatives, and public members. Each group has equal representation on the board. The MSRB is mainly concerned with the standards of professional practice, including qualifications of broker/dealers, rules of fair practice, record keeping, and so forth.

The MSRB does not deal directly with the problem of disclosure, for it is in a precarious legal position. Due to the fact that municipal securities are authorized and issued by states and their political subdivisions, federal regulation of that activity may be contested on the age-old battlefield of states' rights. Thus the MSRB does not directly regulate the disclosure practices of municipal issuers; more important, these issuers are still exempt from federal securities laws. The "Tower Amendments" were two sections tacked onto the 1975 amendments which codified the exemption of municipal issuers. This only resulted in greater confusion among underwriters, issuers, and dealers as to who is responsible for adequate disclosure.

The MSRB requires dealers to provide certain information which must be obtained from the issuers who are not subject to MSRB rulings. This, then, further complicates the issue of disclosure and adequate investigation of the issuer by the underwriter. The end result is still the lack of clearly defined disclosure requirements for the municipal securities marketplace.

A major participant who does not fall within the 1934 Act's definition of broker/dealer is the commercial bank. In order to limit commercial bank involvement in the securities marketplace, Congress passed the Glass-Stegall Banking Reform Act of 1933, which was a product of the Great Depression environment. This arguably limits the underwriting capabilities of national commercial banks to only GO bonds and prohibits their involvement with most revenue bonds. The congressional intent was to limit the risks of bank-financing activities and further regulate the commercial banks and assure their solvency, in the aftermath of the bank collapses of the late 1920s and early 1930s. Regulatory authority was granted to the traditional bodies, such as the Comptroller of the Currency and the Federal Reserve. A consequence of this limitation is that commercial banks underwrite over 50 percent of the new GO bonds; however, they have become involved with revenue issues, particularly those for housing, universities, and dormitories. When questions arise as to whether a commercial bank is allowed to underwrite certain types of municipal issues, the Comptroller of the Currency determines the solution.

On the whole, since 1938, federal legislation and regulation in the municipal securities arena has remained comparatively minimal. The IRS code does provide restrictions which must be complied with in determining a tax-exempt security; for example, tax-exempt industrial development bonds are described in section 103 of the code (1954). The rules and regulations of the IRS interpreting this section are being revised, rewritten, and ruled on in the courts. It is the responsibility of bond counsel in drafting the bond opinion to carefully review the tax laws as they apply to the specific issue. If there is any uncertainty as to the tax-exempt nature of the offering, a ruling may be requested from the IRS. If a ruling is necessary, counsel's opinion will not be released absent a favorable ruling, but the underwriter will not begin to sell the issue until the bond counsel has rendered its opinion.

Other federal regulations have been enacted over the years. Arbitrage regulations came into being in 1969, when Congress amended section 103 of the code. The intent of the amendment was to assure that the issuer of tax-exempt bonds did not take an "improper" advantage of the difference in the interest rates of tax-exempt issuances as opposed to the rate available to taxable securities. The statute was initially fairly simple in purpose, yet with subsequent temporary and proposed regulations of sinking funds and refundings, the area has become extremely complex. Bond counsels must deal specifically with the tax consequences of differing financing methods and must render advice on structuring financings and drafting arbitrage certificates. Regulations in other areas, such as pollution control, must be complied with. Parties to the financing must be aware of the impact of the regulations and how they might affect the issue in the future. Special consultants may be retained for the purpose of analyzing the regulations and trends in these areas.

With the advent of the crises of New York City and New York State as well as the attempted modification of the bond contracts of the Port Authority of New York and New Jersey by both states, there emerged the specter of widespread municipal insecurity. Compounding this was the $135 million default by the New York State UDC, the largest public housing developer. Uncertainty was manifested in the municipal market, and the question of adequate disclosure and regulation of the market came into the forefront. The federal government came onto the scene with the infusion of "seasonal" short-term loans of up to $2.3 billion in December of 1975 to forestall bankruptcy by New York City.

Federal action at that time was not limited to Congress. The SEC held hearings in 1975 into the events leading up to the financial emergency faced by New York City. The result of these investigations was that the SEC took a strong stand against the participants and the practices within the municipal securities industry. It commented on the abuse of the accounting system and the inadequate financial management and control of the city's operations. Moreover, legal counsels as well as underwriters came under its scrutiny. Disbelief was expressed by the SEC as to what it felt was the lack of due diligence by the outside parties in investigating the actual financial practices of the city.

The SEC contended that the participants did not delve deeply enough into these areas and that they placed too great a reliance on the certificates of the financial officers which attested to the validity and accuracy of the figures presented. Their lack of awareness hindered the complete disclosure of the true financial situation of the city as an issuer.

The traditional roles and practices of bond counsels, underwriters, and their counsels were under attack. The question of what is reasonable care in investigating and presenting the nature of the issuer within the confines of cost and time considerations was argued.

After the financial emergency of 1974–1975, action was taken to remedy the fiscal situation facing New York City by federal, state, and local levels which dealt with the accounting system and disclosure practices of the city's financial operations and issuance of securities. In early 1979, New York City issued and successfully marketed $125 million in short-term notes, the first public issuance in almost 5 years. The 200-page official statement which accompanied the notes was described by local officials as the "most comprehensive disclosure statement ever carried out by a local government."[6] In February 1979 the SEC reconfirmed its stand on the need to enact federal legislation which would "improve and standardize financial accounting rules and stiffen disclosure requirements for marketing of municipal securities."[7]

Legislation was proposed in 1975 by Senator Eagleton to bring municipal securities within the regulation of the SEC by amending the 1933 Act. It proposed to require municipal issuers to file registration statements with the SEC prior to the sale of the securities, as is the case with corporate securities. A political problem with this bill was that the costs which would be incurred would be borne by the taxpayer; these costs could prove to be exorbitant due to the need for registration statements and other SEC requirements.

Additional legislation was proposed by Senator Harrison Williams in February 1976 to implement only one "regulatory scheme" for all securities but to regulate the disclosure practices of municipal issuers over a certain dollar size. The SEC would review the information included in distribution statements presented to the investor. The intent was not to include antifraud provisions, for Senator Williams felt the investor was afforded this protection by the state's approval of the issue.

On December 1, 1977, a similar bill was introduced by Senator Williams which proposed to require a "uniform basis" of annual report preparation. It also tried to define more clearly the responsibilities of those who participate in the municipal securities marketplace. It proposed to amend the 1934 Act and create a new section 13(a). Municipal issuers with issues of $50 million or more of outstanding debt would be required to issue annual reports under dictated SEC guidelines.

The municipal securities industry responded to the proposals of these bills (which were not enacted) by stating that the requirements proposed were overburdensome in light of the minimal risk involved. Moreover, such proposed regulation was seen as hindersome to the municipal bond marketplace.

In 1976 an attempt to protect the continuing functioning of local governments was implemented by the amendment of the Bankruptcy Act of 1938. The amendment was due to the fact that the original act was not designated to provide a plan of relief for creditors and securities investors of major municipalities, such as New York City. The purpose of the amendment was to relieve the burden the municipality had in obtaining approvals from difficult-to-identify creditors. Under the original act an identification was essential. Basically, the act, as now amended, provides the municipality with easier access to judicial relief in case of default and subsequent bankruptcy.

Existing federal regulation of the municipal securities industry and of municipalities is based primarily on the limited powers granted in the 1933 and 1934 Acts. The SEC is taking "administrative" actions against participants within this industry to assure that the ultimate investor is protected from fraudulent behavior. Yet, it does not have the staff capabilities to regulate the industry. Moreover, it has not been empowered with the same regulatory and supervisory authority it has over the corporate securities marketplace. It must be remembered that the corporate and municipal securities markets differ greatly. Congressional action within this area has diminished as the crisis which New York City underwent in 1974–1975 has appeared to improve and as the confidence in this market has been restored. However, if the expansion in revenue bonds and industrial development bonds continues, federal regulation may be sought.

Self-Regulation by the Municipal Securities Industry

Regulation of municipal securities has also come from within the industry on a voluntary basis; it has responded to the evident need for improved reporting mechanisms and disclosure practices. State constitutional limitations and statutory requirements, such as "blue sky" laws (which vary from state to state), evolved as a result of exposed abuses of outstanding municipal debt and mismanagement of funds by municipalities. The state regulations and sometimes even the constitutional limitations are amended from time to time, in the process of implementing changing public policies and redefining "public purpose." This redefinition allows for a wider range of municipal financings. Debt limitations by state constitution or statute are often placed on municipalities as to the amount of general obligation and, sometimes, revenue debt they may issue. Few states, however, set disclosure requirements for the types of debt instruments used, and the guidelines have usually emanated from the industry itself.

The active response has come from major organizations within the industry, such as the MFOA and the NCGA, as well as from those outside the industry, such as the AICPA. These changes are a result of the desire of the participants to determine their legal exposure and liability by delineating their responsibilities and to enhance the degree of professionalism practiced throughout the industry.

In general, there has been greater disclosure in official statements and offering circulars for revenue issues and industrial development bonds than for GO bonds. A major reason for this is that investment bank managers of negotiated revenue bond issues have for many years voluntarily and customarily retained underwriters counsel with securities act experience to assist them in the preparation of official statements that met high full-disclosure standards. This practice, which began in the 1940s and 1950s with the large toll road issues, continues unabated in all types of revenue bonds. In 1976 the MFOA published *Disclosure Guidelines for Offerings of Securities by State and Local Governments*.[8] These guidelines resulted from a concerted effort by the industry to provide an outline for the format and information of GO issues which should be contained in the official statement.

The MFOA guidelines are fast becoming the "bible." They are followed by participants in providing timely and sufficient material information for the ultimate investor. Underwriters, bond counsels, and issuers have become increasingly aware of their potential legal liabilities in their roles in drafting the official statements. Therefore these parties are attempting to include material data which will help the investor have an overall picture of the issuer as well as the issue. The guidelines are not legally binding, and compliance is on a voluntary basis, but since their inception, there has been a positive response to them. This is but one effort by the industry to standardize within flexible constraints the structure of official statements.

The MFOA guidelines suggest that the issuer divide information into the following four categories and their subcategories:

Financial Report Information

1. Current and detailed operating statement
2. Operating statement for prior years
3. Basis of accounting used
4. Financial statement audited
5. Current "pro forma" or budget statement
6. Detailed balance sheet
7. Balance sheet for prior years
8. Contingent liabilities (or lack thereof)

Revenue Information

1. Current-year assessed property value
2. Assessed value for prior years
3. Current market value of property
4. Market value for prior years
5. Composition of assessed property
6. Method of assessment discussed
7. Current real property tax rate
8. Tax rates for prior years
9. Tax collection (or delinquency) rate
10. Tax collection rate for prior years
11. Policy toward tax collections
12. List of "top 10" taxpayers
13. Discussion of intergovernmental programs
14. Property tax limits (or lack thereof)

Debt Information

1. Current direct bonded debt
2. Direct debt for prior years
3. Authorized but unissued debt
4. Future debt service requirements
5. Current overlapping debt
6. Discussion of debt limitations
7. Calculation of unused debt capacity
8. Nature of short-term debt (or lack thereof)
9. Legal rights of bondholders
10. Description of employee pension plan

*Demographic, Economic, and
Governmental Information*

1. Population of issuer
2. Population trends
3. Per capita or other income
4. Unemployment rate
5. Description of economic base and activity
6. List of principal firms or employers
7. Information on building permits
8. Discussion of governing body and key officials
9. Discussion of governmental services[9]

In conforming to these guidelines, official statements for municipal bonds have become more comprehensive than in the past. Each issue is unique in type of issuer, structure of the issue, and financing agreements

**TABLE 13-1   Amount of Increase in Disclosure from
Fall/1975 to Spring/1976**

Description of information	% Increase
Revenue information in general	10
List of top 10 taxpayers	11
Population of issuer	12
Demographic, economic, and governmental information in general	30
Discussion of governmental services	30
Discussion of governing bodies and key officials	42
Future debt service requirements	43
Debt information in general	58
Current and detailed operating statement	43
Operating statement for prior years	96
Current pro forma budget statement	193
Contingent liabilities (or lack thereof)	455
Legal rights of bondholders	482
Basis of accounting used	498
Description of employee pension plan	1140

SOURCE: R. K. Desmond and D. J. Robinson (cochairpersons), *Municipal Bonds 1978*,
Practising Law Institute, New York, 1978, p. 426.

securing the issue. Thus compliance with the guidelines is based on their applicability to the offering. Table 13-1 shows the definite increase in disclosure which occurred within a 6-month period. Prior to that time this information could only be obtained by reviewing the underlying documents and agreements supporting the summarization within the official statement.

An ongoing review is made of the MFOA guidelines by representatives of bond counsels, underwriters, and other participants. The MFOA has issued further exposure drafts which refine the guidelines and are commented on by the industry. It also issues position statements which recommend changes in disclosure practices, such as that releases should be made by an "issuer or enterprise" which brings the investor up to date as to current, material changes which may affect the issue.

The accounting profession has also responded to the need for standardized accounting methodology and reporting disclosure for governmental units. The NCGA and the AICPA are working together in revising GAAFR so as to refine the financial statements that independent auditors generate and standardize the accounting practices used by municipalities (see Chapter 12, "Municipal Accounting"). Auditors, in refining these accounting techniques, are lessening their exposure as reporting systems are improved. Timely and accurate information will thus be presented to investors, taxpayers, public officials, underwriters, bond analysts, and other users of the statements.

Although self-regulation of the municipal securities market has appeared successful in increasing disclosure so far, there has been an adverse reaction to federal regulation and SEC supervision of the industry. This type of potential regulation is generally felt to be restrictive in terms of cost/benefit, in view of the associated investment risk. Burdensome registration requirements will increase the costs to the issuer and also the price to the investor. And it is possible that they could hinder the timing in bringing the municipal issues to market.

With increasing evidence of voluntary compliance with disclosure guidelines, reporting mechanisms will be improved and material information provided. Information, as outlined by the guidelines, consists of not only financial detail but also data as to the environment and the constraints under which the issuer must function. The overall picture presented is extensive and informative. In the past the rating agencies were relied upon for evaluating the financial solvency of the issuer, but with the advent of more comprehensive disclosure practices, the external users of these documents will be given more information on which to base their investment decisions. In sum, with the success evidenced by the industry in controlling, updating, revising, and concertedly moving toward establishing its own regulation, the need for or threat of federal intervention will lessen. The end result will be beneficial for internal participants as well as for investors (who will be afforded greater protection), analysts, and taxpayers.

Documents Found in a Municipal Offering

Before continuing with the discussion of disclosure and the roles of the participants in a municipal offering, it is important to become familiar with some of the major documents found in a municipal offering. Following is a description of those major documents and agreements.

The Official Statement

Similar to a corporate security prospectus, the "official statement" is the major tool used to market municipal securities. Basically, the official statement is a legal document which summarizes all the salient features of the underlying documents and agreements which support the offering. It is considered the disclosure document which presents information that is "material" to the offering. Unlike a corporate prospectus, the municipality's official statement is neither registered nor reviewed by the SEC. The content and format of the official statement depend on the type of security (GO bond versus revenue bond versus industrial development bond) and the complexity of the issuance itself.

Changes in the format and size of the official statement have occurred within the past few years. In the past the official statement concentrated on providing information on the "attractive" characteristics of the issue. Certain traditional documents appeared in all statements, such as bond counsel's opinion. Yet, some statements were mere short-form summary circulars of the issuance. With increasing demands for more detailed financial and economic information about the issuer as well as the issue, official statements have provided more comprehensive detail. Some offerings have become so complex that in the beginning of the official statement the introduction summarizes what is contained within and may provide an outline to assist the reader.

Today most issuers of municipal bonds feel that it is necessary to provide a better description of their relationships with various local, state, and federal agencies and more in-depth data for the investor. Guidelines for disclosure have been developed by the industry, and voluntary compliance by participants in the municipal securities market is being evidenced. The financial crisis of New York City helped to cause this shift in content. The municipal bond industry has recognized that in order to protect its own liability, greater disclosure of material information is essential.

Initially, a preliminary statement is drafted which is known as the "red herring," due to the words in red ink on the front which state that it is preliminary in nature and subject to change. The red herring is used to market the proposed issue prior to the date of sale. The official statement is then circulated, and the exact terms of the sale, such as the redemption provisions and interest rates, are summarized. In competitive bid financing agreements, the red herring is used to premarket the issue and arouse interest among various underwriters and institutional investors. The recipients will analyze the proposed offering and decide whether or not to submit a bid. If submitted, the bid will contain the interest rate at which the bond will be sold. Once a bid is accepted by the issuer, the terms outlined in it will be incorporated into the final, official statement. It should be noted that the final statement usually varies slightly from the preliminary statement.

In a negotiated sale, the red herring is used to solicit interest in the marketplace. The underwriter will, during an initial sales period, determine the price at which the issue will be sold in the secondary marketplace.

The official statement should contain what a reasonable investor would need to know in making a decision about the issue. Thus this document will usually include a description of the issuer, a description of the purpose of the project being financed, a description of the security of the bond, a summary of the principal financing documents, any feasibility studies which relate to the security, and any other "key information" (such as major contracts or obligations of the municipality in general which are specifically related to the issue and/or which might affect the issue). Contained in the description of the security of the bond is the lien, which describes the protection of the bondholder by outlining what is pledged and what is not in terms of remedies in the event of default. Types of funds provided are discussed, such as the debt service fund—if it exists and how it is to be funded. Other security protection afforded is described, e.g., redemption of funds; the flow of funds in the trust indenture; the existence of a building, equipment, and a reserve fund; and so on. In essence, this description contains any facts relevant to the security of the bonds, the nature of the issuer, and any problems the issuer may be having or did have in the past with other bonds issued. Full disclosure about the security provisions is essential.

The Bond Opinion

In the front of the official statement, there is usually a reference to the bond counsel; the opinion of the bond counsel is rendered within the statement. The role of the bond counsel is *not to opine as to the creditworthiness of the issue or the issuer* but to state categorically that the interest on the issue is tax-exempt according to federal income tax laws, state laws, and local laws. In addition, the opinion verifies that the issue is a legal, valid, and binding obligation of the issuer. The bond opinion is often a requisite component in any official statement. This opinion may be the only legal opinion contained in the official statement.

The specific topics that the bond opinion refers to are as follows:

• Organization and existence of the issuer; and its power and authority to issue and sell bonds

• Ordinance duly adopted (the issue is thus legal) and valid, binding, and enforceable

• Bonds duly authorized, executed, and delivered and valid, binding, and enforceable

• Lien on revenues being valid, and perfected first lien and security interest

• Tax exemption under state and federal laws

No underwriter will release an offering till the bond counsel has provided a "clean" opinion. This opinion may be quite complex since the financing agreements have to comply with the IRS code and other regulations. The official statement may say that the counsels of the underwriter and the issuer may opine on certain outstanding items, but their opinions will not appear in the official statement. They may have relevance to the issue but are not of a material nature to be mentioned in the official statement, whereas the bond opinion is generally an essential component.

Bond Resolution and Indenture of Trust

One of the fundamental documents included in the official statement is the indenture of trust, or the contract, which is made between the borrower (the issuer) and the lender (the trustee representing the interests of the bondholder). The trust indenture establishes the exact nature of the security of the bonds and the trust provisions. It is frequently a two-party agreement. Different names are used for it, such as bond resolution, but essentially its purpose is to satisfy the legal formality of a "trust" type of relationship whereby the issuer enters into a trust with the trustee.

The nature of the document varies, depending on the type and financial complexity of an issue. For a *general obligation issue*, a bond ordinance is adopted. A state statute usually provides for the provisions of the issue, such as the revenue and security terms.[10] In a general obligation issue, a trust indenture is not normally necessary. In a *revenue bond issue*, the trust indenture is the primary document. It defines the terms of the security and financing structure of the issue, outlines the type of revenue utilized to pay the principal and interest, includes the flow of funds, and sets forth the security terms. A summary of these terms is provided in the official statement.

With the move toward fuller disclosure, the full text of the trust indenture is often appended to the official statement. Provisions in a revenue bond indenture define the degree of protection for the bondholder in use of the pledged revenues and detail the management of the project. Sections commonly included in a revenue bond trust indenture are as follows:

- Definition of terms
- Description of the project to be built
- Definition of pledged revenue and its segregation, if necessary
- Definition of the way in which revenue is to be applied in meeting various claims against it
- Provision for advance retirement of bonds by either refunding call or sinking fund, if any

- Permitted investment for idle funds
- Conditions under which additional bonds may be issued
- A commitment as to the maintenance of rates so that income covers debt service
- Remedies on default
- Conditions under which an amendment to the contract will be permitted
- Covenants concerning faithful observance of agreements and general good management of the project in the bondholder's interest

The sections concerning revenues, their definitions and rate coverage, and the bondholder's claim on them are of major concern to the investor.

It is to this contract that the bondholder will look for satisfaction in case of default. For this reason, the terms of the financing agreements must be carefully and completely outlined and defined.

The Rate Covenant

The rate covenant, in most issues, is the promise by the issuer that the rate structure of the facility (e.g., water rates or electricity rates) will be increased in line with rising costs and expenses each year to provide the necessary revenues for the maintenance of the facility or project and the debt service.

In the early 1970s, there was 125 percent rate coverage of net revenues. Today, 125 to 150 percent rate coverage is considered more than necessary and allows room for error by the management of the facility. Usually, rate coverage is 100 to 110 percent, which gives the management greater leeway. Contained in the rate covenant, the rate coverage is unique to each issue and is dependent on various factors, such as the type of facility, its ability to change its rate structure, the jurisdiction or area it serves, and the financing structure. Essentially, the underwriter negotiating these terms must have a feeling for the marketplace, the authority, and the facility's ability to generate sufficient revenues to cover expenses and satisfy fund requirements.

Additional Bond Clause

In order to be able to finance future expansions to serve the needs of the community, the issuers of revenue bonds need the alternative of issuing additional bonds. The "additional bond clause," created for the purpose of financing future needs, is contained in a lien which, in general, determines the position and status of the bondholder, especially in the case of default. The additional bond clause, provides terms for the issuance of further "parity bonds," which protect the original investors against the dilution of the debt service coverage. One of its major terms, which protects the original bondholders, is the "earnings test." This test sets a minimum level of coverage of debt service, interest, and principal for all outstanding bonds and for future debt. Included in the terms is the allowance for an increase in the debt service fund to handle new debt. The most conservative method of determining the earnings test is to use current financial performance, such as net revenues of the last 1 or 2 fiscal years, against "estimated future maximum annual debt service."[11]

Financial Statements and the Annual Report

The official statement contains the financial statements of the issuer. Accompanying these statements, if they are audited, is the "cold comfort letter" written by the independent accounting firm that audits the statements. The cold comfort letter attests to the financial performance of the issuer over the past fiscal year and reassures the bondholder of the accuracy of the financial figures presented. Yet, this letter does not attest to the eventual solvency of the issue at the maturity date of the bond.[12] This opinion does verify the accuracy and full presentation of material information in the financial statements. Depending on the scope of the audit, the accountant will specify those funds it did not review and thus cannot provide an opinion on.

The number of municipalities issuing annual reports is increasing. In the past, revenue bond issuers who came to market frequently (such as dormitory authorities) would usually issue annual reports, whereas fewer GO issuers did so. As monies available to municipalities are shrinking and costs are increasing, there is a need to see evidence of financial control and management of the available resources. The federal government is becoming more stringent in its requirements for federal revenue-sharing programs and is requiring audited financial statements by both state and local governments. President Carter approved $25.6 billion for general revenue sharing to last from January 1, 1977, to September 30, 1980. The law requires that those revenue-sharing funds in excess of $25,000 must have audits in accordance with GAAP.

In addition to the disclosure of the annual budget, many states require certified financial statements. Major metropolitan issuers escaped this requirement for years, but after the fiscal crisis of New York City in 1974–1975, they were required to have audited annual reports. It should be noted that a number of states still do not require audited local financial statements.

The annual report is used by the issuer as a summary of its operations for the prior fiscal year, but its information content varies from issuer to issuer. Major organizations involved in municipal accounting are working together to provide a more comprehensive and meaningful annual report format. Alternative reporting methods are being suggested by the AICPA, the NCGA, and other accounting organizations. In Chapter 12 the section "Financial Reporting" discusses these different methods in detail.

As is evidenced with all of these documents and agreements, the municipal securities industry is moving toward providing the investor and the taxpayer with increasing disclosure of material information. The documents are structured so as to protect not only the bondholder but also the participants within the municipal industry who bring these issues to the marketplace.

Participants in a Municipal Security Offering

Introduction

The expansion of the municipal securities market can be largely attributed to the creative energies of the investment banking community. By designing innovative financing mechanisms and structuring new forms of offerings, the investment community has greatly assisted the municipal sector in the ever expanding concepts of and projects for "public purpose" programs. Concomitant with this market growth, the participants in municipal bond offerings have assumed greater responsibilities and have also increased their legal exposure and liability. The traditional roles of the bond counsel, underwriter and its counsel, issuer, financial advisers, and other participants have changed over the years. In light of the "consumer beware" environment, the participants in this industry are under greater scrutiny by the SEC and the courts in their practices and disclosure of material information.

The role each assumes is not clearly defined because it depends on the complexity of the issue and the sophistication of the participants. Each issue is unique and has its own history. Smaller offerings are generally simple in structure, and the roles of the participants are relatively clear. As an issue grows in complexity due to factors such as financing agreements, structure, and underlying security, the distinction between individual functions becomes less clear, and as the functions become more interwoven, the delineation of legal responsibility becomes more difficult. The investor or analyst should, therefore, be familiar with the general duties performed by the usual participants in a municipal offering as well as their expanded roles.

Depending on the nature, size, and type of issuance, the number of legal counsels involved varies. Usually, the number of participants, including legal counsels, is three to five sets: There is the bond counsel, the issuer, the underwriter, the issuing authority, and, in the case of an industrial development bond, the corporation (and its counsels—both internal and external). The issuer may not have its own legal counsel and thus may depend on bond counsel for guidance. The underwriter may also be without legal counsel and will utilize the experience of bond counsel.

With a revenue bond, for instance, the nonactive market issuers usually remain in the background during the drafting of the official statement. This process is left to the underwriter and bond counsel. The more active issuer has gained experience in bringing the security to market and is invaluable in this process. Yet even this becomes qualified, for it depends on whether the issue is a negotiated sale or a competitive bid situation.

In a negotiated sale, the underwriter is involved in the early stages of the development of the issue. Usually, if the issuer has come to market frequently, the underwriter has an ongoing relationship with it. On the other hand, if it is a competitive bid situation, the underwriter's involvement is limited to the final stages of bringing the bonds to market. The issuer and, at times, its financial adviser will take a more active role. In this instance, the issue is open to public bids. The underwriter submits a bid based on a preliminary official statement. If its bid is accepted, the underwriter is awarded the bonds and sells them on the market. The underwriter has little involvement, if any, in drafting the official statement, other than finalizing the statement according to terms agreed upon in the bid.

It should be noted that in most states an issuer is required to sell GO bonds through competitive bidding. On the other hand, revenue bonds are often free from this requirement, and depending on the price the issuer can receive, revenue bonds are sold through a financing arrangement that is negotiated. After a bid is accepted in a competitive bid situation, the liabilities of the underwriting syndicate are determined by contract. The issuer and underwriter enter into the bond purchase agreement, whereby the underwriter protects its liabilities and sets forth certain stipulations. The underwriter also includes in the bid a "good faith check" (usually 1 to 5 percent), which is lost if the bidder breaches the contract by failing to pay for bonds upon delivery.

Since there are no clear-cut definitions of the functions of the participants, the issue of responsibility for disclosing types of information is further complicated. At the same time that the participants are developing their own definitions of what constitutes necessary disclosure practices in conjunction with various legislation, they are also attempting to more clearly define their individual duties. Standardization of these definitions within the industry has not yet been achieved, but the overall direction is toward greater disclosure and increased protection of the ultimate investor.

The Role of Bond Counsel

The traditional role of bond counsel is to act as an independent "legal auditor" serving two purposes. The first is to render an opinion as to the unqualified, legal validity of the bond issue as a binding obligation of the issuer in accordance with state and local laws. Second, it serves to opine as to the unqualified tax-exempt nature of the interest on the issue in compliance with federal, state, and local tax laws. The analysis of bond counsel's duties follows this traditional definition that bond opinion is narrow in both "scope and reach," which delineates the bond counsel's function and the reliance on the opinion by the investor.

According to the traditional definition of responsibility, counsel will jeopardize its independent status if it becomes involved in the drafting of the official statement. By complying with the defined duties, bond counsel limits its legal liability to only the investor's reliance on the bond opinion. Although it is retained by the issuer and is paid from the proceeds of the bond issue, it does not usually act as a regular counsel to any of the participants in the issuance. Bond counsel may suggest financial alternatives that are open to the issuer, but such advice should originate from the legal requirements that bond counsel must fulfill when drafting its opinion. The course of action undertaken by the issuer will be determined by the final advice provided by its own counsel and financial advisers.

In drafting the bond opinion, bond counsel determines and requests the material information it needs from the issuer. The "documentation" requested from the issuer is similar for most issues, but there are some exceptions, particularly in the case of revenue issues, where it is more complex. Listed below are the types of documents bond counsel requested from New York City, for example, prior to writing its opinion.

- A copy of the charter of the municipality
- A certified copy of delegation of authority by the mayor to the comptroller to issue the securities
- The certificates authorizing the issuance of the securities
- A confirmation of sale

- A certificate of the chief of the Division of Municipal Securities concerning compliance with certain notice requirements
- A copy of the bids by managing syndicates received by the city
- A certificate of award to the winning syndicates
- Certificates as to the genuineness of signatures on various documents and as to the absence of litigation
- A certificate of delivery and payment
- A specimen of a security
- An arbitrage certificate

Once the documents are received, bond counsel relies on the certificates for the validity and accuracy of the facts presented. Counsel then opines on the issuance. It performs a "formal review" of the facts presented but usually does not delve into the material in an investigative capacity. The opinion states that bond counsel has examined the certified copy of the transcript of the bond proceedings of the authorized bonds as well as one of the executed bonds.

On the basis of these representations, bond counsel states whether the securities are actually legal and binding obligations of the issuer. In addition, counsel specifies any specific funds pledged and obligations of the issuer which are exempt from federal income tax. In the case of an industrial development bond, the legal opinion varies from the norm. The security's underlying credit is that of a private corporation, and so the bond opinion is more extensive due to the risk associated with the issue. Bond counsel may attest to the incorporation of the company, the accuracy of the portions of the offering circular which describe the bonds, and the primary documents which are directly related to securing the bond.

In general, the scope of the bond opinion does *not* include the *creditworthiness* of the issuer or the associated interest and market risks of the security. Reliance on the documents presented by the issuer is made by bond counsel. Investor reliance on the bond opinion has brought the expanded role of bond counsel and its responsibilities into the limelight; therefore, bond counsel may extend its duties beyond those traditionally defined. It may provide a negative assurance as to the fact that neither material omissions nor a misstatement of material facts exists in the official statement. The negative assurance is based on the documents presented to bond counsel by the issuer, and counsel may perform a limited review of this information. A traditional bond counsel may be retained by the underwriter, and if so, it is not paid from the proceeds of the bond issue; it will act as the underwriter's counsel and provide legal advice as to the issue and its structure.

Bond counsel may play a crucial role in implementing an innovative financing concept. Furthermore, it may act in a lobbyist capacity or be retained by state legislative or executive branches to draft the legislation and try test cases. Such a trial is done to see if the concept withstands statutory and constitutional limitations. The state in implementing public policy and social programs may need revenues to finance these projects. Bond counsel may be retained to provide the legislative ability to seek this financing. Counsel may also opine whether such legislation will meet a constitutional test, if it satisfies the definition of public purpose, whether state monies could be appropriated for the project, and so forth. This legislation will either create an agency or authority to issue the securities to finance the program or empower a jurisdiction to do so.

Once this is accomplished, bond counsel may work closely with the in-house counsel of the authority or municipality and with other special counsels to establish guidelines which will comply with statutory and constitutional requirements. The development of "moral obligation" securities is an example. These securities are essentially backed by the expectation that the state legislature will appropriate funds for the issue of an authority if other funds of the authority are not available to meet its debt service requirements.

Moral obligation bonds should be distinguished from GO bonds, which have the full faith and credit and taxing power of the municipality. In the case of a "moral obligation," this support is not legally enforceable. The only assurance is the moral promise by the state legislature to appropriate funds if necessary, but this promise is subject to legal opposition and public policy changes. Yet, it is generally expected within the municipal market that in case of default the state will provide the necessary funds.

With the increasing complexity of financing structures, more sophisticated legal advice is required. Bond counsel is able, with its expertise, to provide this advice; consequently, its direct involvement with the various parties to the transaction has increased. Yet, the nature and degree of the involvement of bond counsel depends on the history of the issue, its complexity, and the "interests" of the parties involved. The following list summarizes some of the duties of bond counsel:

- Preparation of the ordinance under which the bonds are issued

- Preparation of the bonds

- Representation of the issuer in connection with the negotiation of the bond purchase agreement with the underwriters

- Direct involvement with those parts of the official statement relating to the ordinance and the bonds. (Since many new issuers lack sufficient staff to develop an official statement, bond counsel frequently drafts the entire statement.)

• In financings that involve power sales contracts, installment purchase agreements, leases, mortgages, or back-to-back loans, the preparation of those documents[13]

Bond counsel has departed from the traditional role of the "legal auditor" to become an active participant in the drafting and developing of legal standards which are applied to municipal financings. Underwriters seek "supplemental" opinions in the areas listed below:

• Power and authority of the issues to operate as described in the official statement, frequently including the extent of rate regulation.

• Due authorization, execution, and delivery of the bond purchase agreement by the issuer.

• Ordinance and bonds accurately summarized in the official statement. Adoption of same does not result in any defaults or violation of the law or require approval of governmental authorities.

• Exemption of bonds under the Securities Act of 1933 and of the ordinance under the Trust Indenture Act of 1939.

• Confirmation of specified legal matters described in the official statement.

• No knowledge of any material litigation.

• Negative assurance as to the entire official statement concerning misrepresentations and omission.[14]

Although the duties and responsibilities of bond counsel have become complex, there is no straightforward answer to the issue of to whom counsel is responsible: the investor or the issuer? Opinions as to the ultimate nature of bond counsel's responsibility vary from counsel to counsel. A definite fact is that the legal liability and exposure of bond counsel have increased as bond counsel's duties have expanded. The independence as defined in traditional terms is not always the case today. Its role can be both "broad and narrow." Yet, bond counsel is trying to help a municipality achieve a social purpose, while at the same time attempting to present a security worthwhile for investment. In fulfilling its responsibility, bond counsel also tries to protect the investor as well as the issuer within the confines of its duties.

Role of the Underwriter and Underwriter's Counsel

The underwriter is in a tenuous position in that it must represent the interests of both its clients: the issuer and the investor. The underwriter's relationship with the issuer is determined by whether the financing agreement of the issue is to be a competitive bid or a negotiated sale. Like bond counsel, the underwriter may be involved in promoting an innovative financing structure for a municipal security issue and may act as a lobbyist in state legislatures and executive branches. Its relationship with the issuer may be a historical one, and it may also recommend to the issuer which bond counsel it should retain.

In its responsibility toward the investor, the underwriter negotiates contractual agreements with the issuer and reviews the financing and security agreements set forth in the underlying documents supporting the offering. By doing so, it attempts to give the investor as much security as possible in terms of payment of interest and principal and adequate debt service provisions.

An underwriter should not release an offering unless adequate disclosure and legal verification are provided. The rating agencies may perform a review of the issue, but a thorough analysis of the issue, the issuer, and the financing supporting the issue should also be performed by the underwriter. Depending on the degree of involvement with the municipal issuance, the underwriter's duties can range from those of a lobbyist (which sees the implementation of the financing concept, the creation of an agency, or the empowering of a jurisdiction to issue the security) to those of a participant in the drafting of the official statement. During this process, the underwriter works closely with bond counsel and the issuer.

There is a concerted effort in the municipal industry to improve disclosure requirements, and underwriters have been involved with this movement. With the increasing complexity of the issues, underwriters may retain separate counsel in negotiated sale offerings. The need for this counsel is due to the underwriter's awareness of potential liability under federal and state securities laws and the need to lessen its legal exposure. Second, underwriters are regulated in the secondary market by the Municipal Securities Rulemaking Board (MSRB). To assure compliance with MSRB regulations, the underwriter's counsel will provide advice. (This counsel is paid from the discount the underwriter receives on the bonds.) The underwriter will take on those roles which bond counsel does not. This does depend, though, on the issue and the relationships between the parties. By retaining a separate counsel, the underwriter provides the investor with an added assurance that its interests are being protected.

The underwriter's counsel reviews the exempt status of the security. Relying on the opinion of the issuer's counsel, this counsel determines whether the bond purchase agreement between the issuer and underwriter is "legal, valid, and binding"; it provides a negative assurance as to information contained in the official statement, other than the financial statements and consultant's reports, that there is neither omission nor misstatement of material facts. In addition, counsel drafts the memorandum on the "blue sky" laws applicable in the state where the issuer is located.

Listed below are four duties which the underwriter's counsel performs, including the drafting of its opinion:

> 1. Underwriter's counsel participates in the preparation of the ordinance and the other financing agreements on behalf of the underwriters, in an attempt to insure that the documents adequately reflect the terms set by underwriters for the proposed offering. . . . These often complex documents are typically prepared by bond counsel. Underwriter's counsel reviews them from the standpoint of determining their conformity to the terms and standards which underwriters set.
>
> 2. . . . prepare and represent the underwriters in connection with the negotiation of the bond purchase agreement. There are frequently meaningful negotiations over various aspects of bond purchase agreements, including (i) the scope of the bond opinion, the supplemental opinion of bond counsel, and the opinion of general counsel for the issuer; and (ii) the auditors' cold comfort letter.
>
> 3. It is not unusual for underwriters' counsel to assist in the preparation of the financing documents in cases where bond counsel does not take on this role, and to assist in the preparation of the official statement in cases where issuer's counsel is not experienced in public offerings of municipal securities and the related disclosure burden. Such assistance can vary from helping to organize the preparation of the official statement to direct involvement in drafting the financing documents, including the official statement.
>
> 4. Reviews the overall legal environment of the transaction with a view to insuring that the due diligence obligation of the underwriters is discharged. This role involves such matters as a review of provisions of local law concerning the authority of the issuer to conduct its operations and to issue the bond; the tax aspects of the transaction; environmental matters; material contracts; litigation; pending legislation and compliance with laws.[15]

The underwriter's counsel must be aware of the above functions so that it can advise the underwriter on any of the potential legal liabilities associated with the issue.

The Issuer and Issuer's Counsel

The issuer of a municipal security may be a municipality, an agency, an authority, or a combination of a municipality and a corporation (as in the case of an industrial development bond). The interrelationships the issuer has with federal, state, and local governments should be clarified and understood. In a revenue bond issue, for example, the issuer may be a public authority which was created for a distinct purpose. Such authorities were sometimes created to circumvent the bureaucracy encountered within a jurisdiction or by a constitutional restriction. In essence, the powers granted to this agency are specific in nature, and the authority cannot assume powers beyond those stated in either state legislation or the state constitutional amendment which created the authority. Issuers such as municipal hospitals may have special relationships with federal agencies. In the example of the pass-through financing arrangement of the Government National Mortgage Association (GNMA, commonly referred to as Ginnie Mae), there is a special relationship between the federal agency and the state or local authority whereby the bonds issued by the latter are guaranteed by the federal agency. There is one condition: The issuer must be in compliance with the regulations stipulated by the agency.

The issuer may be inexperienced in the municipal marketplace and lack the staff and/or financial sophistication to draft the necessary financing agreements. During the negotiation of the bond purchase agreement and the drafting of financial agreements, the issuer will rely on bond counsel's advice so that the provisions of the covenants in the bond resolution—in a revenue issue, for instance—will not prove too restrictive. It will also rely on the expertise of the underwriter and its counsel.

Counsel separate from bond counsel may be retained by the issuer. In other cases, in-house counsel may be present. The issuer's counsel will take on the role played by bond counsel in drafting the underlying financing documents and official statement if it has the necessary expertise. The nature of the issuer, the size and complexity of the issue, and the expertise of this counsel will determine the degree of involvement that the issuer and its counsel will have in the offering.

The Trustee

The trustee is purportedly the representative of the bondholder in a third-party beneficiary relationship with the issuer. The trustee enters into an agreement with the issuer with the intent of protecting the interests of the bondholder. Selection of the trustee in a revenue bond issue, for example, can occur in one of two ways. The trustee can be recommended by the underwriter and would be one who is willing to purchase a substantial amount of the first issue of the security. Once chosen, the trustee will also assist in the marketing and placing of the bonds.

The second method of selection occurs if the deal is particularly complex, but its security agreements and financing documents are close to completion. At that time, a bank will be chosen as the trustee; it can provide its expertise in finalizing the documents. The trustee will then have directly participated in the last stages of the financial structure of the securities. Many times, a trustee is selected in advance due to a prior satisfactory working relationship with the issuer or underlying credit (a corporation in an industrial development bond issue).

A trustee, such as a local bank, can be in a locality other than a major money market center. In this case, and if the bonds are expected to be widely held, a cotrustee, or paying agent, is chosen which is located in a major financial center to assure that the funds will be available for payment of interest and principal on the bonds. This results in the trustee acting also as the paying agent on the bonds.

Responsibilities of the trustee include a surveillance function: It assures that the covenants are adhered to, thus protecting the bondholders' interests. To further protect these interests, the trustee generally takes a conservative interpretation of the provisions in the trust indenture. If problems arise with the issue, the trustee must follow certain courses of action set forth in the bond covenants. If the issuer desires to alter certain provisions in the indenture agreement (for a refunding plan, for example), the trustee must be consulted. Before any changes can be made, the trustee must approve the proposed alterations—to safeguard the legal standing and interests of the original bondholders. For example, Standard & Poor's believes that an acceptable trustee bank is one that has at least $300 million in deposits.

The participants in a municipal security offering have overlapping functions; nevertheless, they work closely together in bringing the municipal issue to the marketplace. On the other hand, the complexity of the relationships and the intricacy of the roles these participants undertake further complicate the issue of disclosure and the responsibility as well as the exposure of the individual participants.

Conclusion

The issue of disclosure in municipal securities offerings comes full circle. In order to define what disclosure is and what adequate disclosure practices should be, it is necessary to understand the nature of the municipal securities market and its history, the types of securities issued, the forms of underlying agreements and documents, the participants in the municipal marketplace, and the needs of the investors in the securities. The amount of information disclosed is not always the question.

The underlying issue is often the nature and materiality of the data being furnished.

It has been contended that investors were provided with sufficient information in the annual report of New York City prior to the city's financial crisis in 1974–1975. Yet, the report was likened to a "telephone book" in the amount of data included. Studies on the disclosure practices of municipalities, on a voluntary basis, are discouraging as to the degree of information lacking in the annual reports. Official statements have shown a noticeable increase in disclosures made, which has been evidenced in a voluntary response by the industry to following the disclosure guidelines as set forth by the MFOA. Compliance by issuers has also been evidenced; they are becoming aware of their increasing legal exposure and liability. The industry has made a concerted effort toward self-regulation because of the underlying feeling against potential federal regulation of the municipal marketplace. The degree of risk associated with municipal securities is still relatively minimal regardless of the fiscal emergency of New York City. The SEC, it has been felt, did not state that investors lost relatively much during that time, and the emergency was remedied in light of the circumstances. The positive outcome of that crisis has been the recognition of the need to change disclosure practices, to improve these practices, and to refine the reporting documents which support the issues. The needs of the users of the statements, such as legislators, municipal administrators, bondholders, and taxpayers, are coming into view.

The industry has responded to a threat of federal intervention. Constitutional issues could arise if the federal government intervened in a traditionally sovereign territory of a state (in that states usually approve a municipal issue). The practical aspect of this is the exorbitant costs which would be incurred in order to comply with proposed registration requirements and other regulatory stipulations; it would make municipal financing too costly for both the investor and the issuer.

Another problem would be the fact that the federal method of achieving uniformity in disclosure practices would not be flexible enough to accommodate the needs of the different types of debt instruments used as well as the needs of the various types of issuers of municipal securities. Compounding this problem further is the fear aroused among underwriters and dealers that, in light of the risk involved, their legal exposure and liability would be too great. Thus, the industry's response toward its own definitions of the behavior of individual participants in this arena has forestalled federal regulation. Yet, the municipal securities market is expanding, and potential federal regulation does loom in the background.

Self-regulation and self-definition of the responsibilities of the participants are not simple tasks. The issue of disclosure and disclosure practices is complex and multifaceted.

An approach proposed by Robert Doty when testifying before the Senate in February 1976 seems to be a plausible alternative to federal regulation. It was his contention that a single federal agency, such as the SEC, would be unable to regulate the municipal securities market. More important, such regulation by the SEC could have detrimental consequences for the marketplace. His proposal was as follows:

> An alternative [to SEC regulation] would be to provide a Federal statutory framework—hence the national jurisdiction—to the States themselves to establish uniform standards. I appreciate this would be a rather innovative approach to federalism, but it would seem to me to be worth trying. . . . The statute would provide for a national council appointed by the President composed solely of state and local government officials, and possibly a chairman who is a former such official, to implement the general municipal disclosure and accounting standards called for in the statute. The President could be required to consult with appropriate State and local government organizations in making his appointments. The Council could be assisted by advisory committees and the SEC in performing its functions. Thus, the sovereign states could be said to be jointly establishing their own uniform disclosure standards with the benefit of Federal jurisdiction.[16]

The compromise appears reasonable and applicable to the problem of establishing practices for standardized disclosure from state to state.

No simple solution can be arrived at. Major organizations within the industry, such as the MFOA (and its subpart, the NCGA) and the AICPA, are establishing and refining disclosure and accounting practices for participants such as municipalities, underwriters, and bond counsels. The traditional relationships and definitions of concomitant responsibilities for participants, such as bond counsel, are not always applicable. The expansion of the marketplace and the creation of new financing mechanisms have contributed to the complexity of the municipal securities marketplace, thereby complicating the issue of disclosure. It is evident that the general trend within the industry is toward increasing the disclosure of material information and quality information and refining the reporting documents containing this data. Those who shall ultimately profit from this movement are the investors in the securities.

Notes to Chapter 13

[1] Bruce N. Hawthorne, "Municipal Bonds and the Federal Securities Laws: The Results of Forty Years of Indirect Regulation," *Vanderbilt Law Review*, vol. 28, 1975, p. 565.

[2] Ibid., pp. 576–578.

[3] C. R. Johnson and R. H. Wheeler, "Securities Law Duties of Bond Counsel," *Duke Law Journal*, vol. 1976, no. 6, 1977, p. 1231.

[4] Hawthorne, op. cit., p. 579.

[5] Michael Jones, "Federal Regulation of Municipal Securities," *Duke Law Journal*, vol. 1976, no. 6, 1977, p. 1271.

[6] Steven Weisman, "SEC Says City Should Improve Its Bookkeeping," *The New York Times*, Feb. 6, 1979.

[7] Judith Miller, "SEC Ends Inquiry on City's Finances: Safeguards Sought," *The New York Times*, Feb. 6, 1979.

[8] Municipal Finance Officers Association, *Disclosure Guidelines for Offerings of Securities by State and Local Governments*, 1976.

[9] J. Petersen et al., "Searching for Standards: Disclosure in the Municipal Securities Market," *Duke Law Journal*, vol. 1976, no. 6, 1977, p. 1185.

[10] States usually have more control than municipalities over the funding and expenditure levels of GO bonds. Levels of funding are determined statutorily, not constitutionally, and there is a certain realistic set level of funding. Yet the state, due to its "sovereign powers," can change tax due dates and major disbursement dates; thus it has the power to affect cash flows. Municipalities do not possess this power and must comply with the terms stipulated in the appropriations.

[11] Standard & Poor's Corporation, *Municipal and International Bond Ratings: An Overview*, p. 30.

[12] The underwriter, in order to protect itself, may incorporate the requirement for the cold comfort letter in the terms of the bond purchase agreement.

[13] Austin V. Koenan, *1978 Municipal Bond Buyers Conference*, Key Largo, Florida, Jan. 30, 1978, p. 31.

[14] Ibid., p. 32.

[15] Ibid., pp. 33–34.

[16] R. K. Desmond and D. J. Robinson (cochairpersons), *Municipal Bonds 1978*, Practising Law Institute, New York, 1978, p. 870.

NOTE: This chapter was written with the assistance of Lynn Togut.

chapter 14

Municipal Credit Analysis
for the Future

In the last 20 years the number of municipal long-term bonds and short-term municipal notes sold each year has soared. Yields on these debt securities have also soared. This tremendous volume of debt, at ever higher costs to municipalities, has not reduced the overall rate of municipal borrowing. And despite occasional months of poor municipal bond markets, this 20-year growth has apparently whetted the appetite of the investing public and institutional investors for still more tax-exempt municipal bonds.

It is in light of this spiraling expansion of municipal debt that the fiscal crises of New York City and the New York State UDC as well as the financial threat of Proposition 13 movements must be viewed. The tax revolts of voters were directly fueled by their growing concern over federal, state, and municipal waste of public funds and high taxes.

Today important questions are being raised at all levels about the future of the municipal bond market and its relation to the federal, state, and local methods of financing expenditures. Such questioning is quite understandable because over these past 20 years fundamental changes have taken place in federal-state-local fiscal relationships. Many of the specific responsibilities of local governments are now partially or wholly accepted by the federal government, including not only welfare, poverty, education, and mass transit but also problems of pollution and urban decay. Although still in its formative stages, federal revenue sharing has enabled municipalities to slow their increases in taxes and spread their various local expenses. However, revenue sharing has not yet adequately derived a system of dividing clear responsibilities and allocating them to the different branches of government. Thus the federal government, which really has only itself to blame, continues to be regarded as the lender, or financer, of last resort.

Today's "crisis in municipal credit analysis," therefore, springs to life partly from these extraordinarily complex interdependencies of different layers of government financing that involve massive amounts never dreamt of in the days when our federal Constitution or state constitutions were first written.

Simultaneously, this period of double-digit inflation has caused the costs of all government services and all capital expenditures to mount at every level, wrecking havoc with many budgets. Just as taxpayers' views on the inevitability of escalating tax burdens have been affected by the two decades of rampant inflation, so have investors' expectations of long- and short-term interest rates for municipal and all other securities markets been affected.

Although the federal government has repeatedly attempted to halt the rising inflation rate of the nation and has tried to stop being viewed as the lender of last resort to ailing municipalities, it has not succeeded on either count. Therefore, future federal involvement in municipal bond financing is almost universally expected by authorities on the local, state, and national level. While, obviously, a sizable portion of that involvement will be in direct payments to states and municipalities in one form of revenue sharing or another, the equally significant type of federal involvement takes the form of a guarantee, or backstop credit, to all sorts of new types of municipal financing.

The entering wedge into the state and local debt markets of such federal guarantees of GO bonds is already somewhat apparent. The federal and New York State backing of New York City enabled the city to sell notes in 1979 before its rating had been reinstated and while investors were still unclear as to exactly what the city's finances were. If those notes had not had the state pledge and if the federal loan guarantees had not been available to the city, then New York, on its own credit standing, could not possibly have come to market and sold its municipal securities.

Another even clearer federal backstop guarantee (in the form of a Ginnie Mae pledge) for certain municipal housing and hospital bonds was discontinued in 1979 when it became obvious that this federal financing support was being abused by unscrupulous developers. The guarantees by Ginnie Mae had been intended to benefit inner-city hospitals and housing projects for lower-income people because if they wanted to obtain funds in the public market, they would be forced to pay exorbitant rates of interest. Although the federal guarantees for needy municipal issuers have been halted for the moment, they are generally expected to be reinstated.

If the already crippling high rates of interest continue, these federal guarantees for local municipal housing and hospital financings can be expected to be pushed forward once again. This is especially likely today because many new municipal bond counsels and investment bankers are continually thinking of new ways to expand the double- and triple-barreled types of debt financings.

Regional and Local Developments

The various recent regional efforts to band states and localities together to create new bond-issuing entities are also quite likely to continue to increase over the next decade. This can be seen especially in the area of public power. In the Northwestern states, where public power began, there are efforts to initiate new regional developments of contracts for public power supply. States of the Northeast are today negotiating to issue bonds in order to buy their power from Quebec. And various states of the Tennessee Valley Authority are joining together to be able to issue bonds for public power.

In the area of hospital bonds, it is widely expected by many authorities that Intermountain Health Care, which pools hospital resources and bond-financing capacities over an extended geographic area, will become the wave of the future. In the future far larger financings of $200- to $400-million hospital bonds will come to market under one regional umbrella instead of as $20-million individual bonds of separate municipalities.

Other forms of joint efforts of two or more cities or communities are clear in the new financing forms of water and sewer bonds. Sharing or splitting the cost of horrifyingly expensive new facilities for pollution control is enabling more and more communities to find ways to finance federally mandated projects. Likewise, port and airport revenue bond issues, such as those sold for the Dallas–Fort Worth Airport, are typical of a whole range of efforts by cities, counties, and districts to find practical ways to obtain needed facilities while not suffering under impossible financial debt burdens.

Because issuers of joint municipal bonds can come to market in far larger issues than a single municipality, they have a far broader market on a national scale; they are also charged a lower interest rate because of more competition among underwriters to secure the deal. Third, these joint entities tend to become far more efficient because they are less likely to duplicate services in adjoining areas; they share the new expensive facilities together.

Finally, there are a number of efforts made by state governments today to pool the municipal debt of their constituent entities into conglomerate bond issues; this helps cities, counties, or districts to meet their financial strains by reaching the national sales market. One such established effort is the state "bond bank"; it attempts to pool the municipal bond issues of a number of communities coming to market at the same time in one state and give them a better credit rating and more national market exposure by supplying a backup credit.

Next, there are the more recent efforts by the state of California, in the wake of Proposition 13, to establish a state backup fund for any defaulting municipality. Other states are also initiating these measures.

The Advisory Commission on Intergovernmental Relations has found that for several years Massachusetts, New York, New Jersey, Michigan, and California have been aggressively assisting local governments rather than leaving all the financial assistance up to the national government. Clearly, in the way of various tax reform movements in over 20 states, these initiatives in state capitals have now been faced with a new set of dimensions to deal with, but such state efforts are expected to continue.

Most of these state initiatives have involved establishing financial incentives for economic development, especially in economically depressed urban and rural communities. Arkansas and Indiana have established housing agencies, and Colorado and Kentucky are establishing a state fund for school finance. Texas and New Mexico have set up funds for school finance as well as for water and sewage treatment and other capital improvements. Strong regional patterns to this state aid have been emerging; it appears that in the Northeast and North Central states virtually all the financing is going to urban projects, whereas in the Southeastern and South Central states the financing has gone to rural projects.

Finally, there are a number of local developments that are quite startling in their originality and that are also significant for the changes in the municipal bond market during this next decade. The first is the so-called Chicago plan. Under this plan a local housing development is backed by mortgages and the financial shell of a local housing authority issuer. That "issuer" is neither a statewide authority nor a permanent authority; it does not have a substantial pool of assets beyond the project. The Chicago plans are considered somewhat suspect by many government officials and bond analysts because they, like other types of mortgage-backed securities, have been found, in some instances, to have abused the public purpose doctrine behind the tax-exempt privilege granted to municipal bonds. They have done this by issuing municipal housing bonds to build expensive units for condominiums as well as other projects for wealthy or upper-middle-class people instead of restricting their tax-exempt projects to the housing developments for lower-income people that would need tax-exempt support.

Proposition 13

The impact of California's Proposition 13 on state and local financing is crucial to the future of the municipal bond market.

Out of the taxpayers' revolt in California on June 6, 1978, came Proposition 13: a crucial amendment to the California constitution. Its main provision is that tax increases in real property may not be enacted. Other taxes must be approved by two-thirds of all the members of both houses of the state Legislature (a virtual impossibility), and special taxes may be imposed by local governments but require a two-thirds approval of the local electorate. More important, taxes on real property, which presently in California average 3.2 percent, are to be rolled back and limited to 1 percent of the market value of the property based on the past 1975–1976 tax bill.

Because Proposition 13 passed by a 2 to 1 majority, it was clear from the outset that this storm against the entire direction of local, state, and federal taxes would spark a wave of similar propositions on the ballots in other states. It was no surprise, therefore, that in the 1978 elections 20 states had such initiatives introduced on the ballot; at least 4 of the 16 which passed were very similar to Proposition 13. While 12 of the other states imposed weaker government spending restrictions, it was, nevertheless, clear that the voters across the nation regarded their tax burdens as being excessive. They put local town managers and state legislatures on notice that they were prepared to fight them to prevent a continuance of wasteful spending and exorbitant taxes.

A devastating impact for all the GO issues was anticipated by many experts, yet the initial consequences were masked in California and elsewhere by huge fiscal surpluses for 1978 and 1979; this has prevented the harsh reality of these new measures from being clearly evaluated until 1981 or even later.

Economists predict that the Proposition 13 type of tax revolt will have significant short- and long-term impacts, including the following: a weakening of local government and the shifting of much financial responsibility, first up to the state legislatures and then ultimately to the federal government. This may appear to be a curious outcome of a tax revolt designed to break government control, but, in fact, there appears almost no question that local municipalities, which are blocked by new statutory provisions from seeking funds via their traditional bond resolutions and traditional taxing power, will be forced either to create new types of non-tax-based bonds (such as user charges) or to obtain some sort of state or national backing for their financing.

There will inevitably be an ever increasing reliance upon various sorts of revenue bonds, special enterprise bonds, and industrial development bonds—all as ways to circumvent the traditional GO bonds, which voters may not continue to support.

One recent example of such a financing by user charges involved the Los Angeles Fire District. It bought fire equipment (without resorting to the restricted GO bonds) by setting a fee on each user of its services. Other traditional municipal services, such as garbage disposal and road maintenance, may soon also be paid for by a system of user charges. Moreover, what is crucial is whether this trend away from GO bonds and toward financing by user charges will be used to cover not only operating expenses but also new capital expansion.

During the next decade the striking increase in revenue bonds, which now represent two-thirds of all new municipal issues, is expected by most analysts to continue because many municipal officers find themselves tied in knots and/or prohibited from further expansion in GO bonds.

This entire question of fears about what voters will agree to will probably force local governments to pay more to issue their debt; thus they will be required to offer more attractive yields to investors. Many other municipalities may be forced to buy municipal bond insurance to guarantee their debt issues against taxpayers' changes of mood, and this will also increase costs.

Another result of Proposition 13 may be an increased trend for municipalities to hire private firms to provide municipal services. This would not only cut down an operating budget but also eliminate a very large chunk of capital outlay. Thus communities that are unable to use their taxing powers to pay for new capital equipment or services may devise a whole schedule of municipal services to be contracted out to local corporations. In this way they will not have to buy expensive capital equipment or incur a long-term debt.

One of the unintended but, nevertheless, inescapable consequences of the Proposition 13 type of law is that businesses will gain enormously at the expense of homeowners. This will occur because the tax-limiting schemes in California and four other states freeze tax assessment until the property is sold, after which the assessment is immediately raised to the market price. Property owned by most businesses is infrequently sold, but homes are turned over far more rapidly; therefore, the incremental tax burden will benefit businesses rather than individual homeowners. This occurrence may well lead to an attack on business by taxpayers in the not too distant future. Perhaps anticipating just such a taxpayer backlash, the California corporations universally opposed Proposition 13.

States' Efforts

States and local authorities have a variety of approaches to cutting their taxing and spending in order to comply with Proposition 13. Forty-seven states holding sessions specifically to consider tax and spending cuts have led to an avalanche of bills, recommendations, and amendments calling for rebates, rollbacks, and credits. In some states—Missouri, for example—the most drastic slashes in taxes on property, inheritance, utility sales, and even farm machinery have been enacted, whereas most of the more moderate states, such as Georgia and Ohio, restrict their initiatives to spending cuts and to preventing tax increases.

One key result of all these efforts is that the National Conference of Governors believes that the general fund balances of the states are expected to decline from $8.9 billion (1978) to $4.3 billion (1979). Since states generally have tried for balances of 5 to 7 percent, this new move will leave them with only 3.6 percent.

Some state legislatures, believing that even these spending cuts are not sufficient, are likely to force tax cuts and limits to property taxes this year. These are the legislatures of Arkansas, Colorado, Connecticut, Florida, and other states.

One of the primary reasons why these movements for tax and spending reductions have started and gained such momentum in the Far West is that the states in that region accumulated the largest tax surpluses. Moreover, state surpluses have mounted each year over the last decade, and state governments have literally been unable to spend the money. Economists believe that if municipalities are forced to tighten their belts and cut their spending, then the regional advantages to their states will be dramatic. Also they will further hasten the explosive expansion in business and private incomes in these states that has occurred in the West and South. This continued Western and Southern growth will perhaps make the Northeast and Great Lakes regions (which have consistently lost capital, population, and employment compared with these other regions) appear stagnant.

In the two years since Proposition 13, the movement for a constitutional amendment that would require a balanced budget has gathered great momentum. The amendment would prohibit the federal government from engaging in deficit spending. (In late 1979, Iowa became the twenty-eighth state to vote for this amendment.) After state and local governments passed restrictions on spending and taxes, the federal government was the lender of last resort that bailed out communities in trouble. But this new initiative for a balanced federal budget could have severe municipal repercussions.

Underwriting of Municipal Bonds by Commercial Banks

The entire market for municipal bonds has changed so dramatically in the last decade that it is risky to even hazard a few predictions about changes in the 1980s. Nevertheless, the range of key issues should be examined to assess some of the likely problems because municipal bond dealers, salespeople, specialists, and, especially, investors must be aware of these potential quicksands.

Perhaps the most exciting issue is the perennial question of whether commercial banks will be allowed to underwrite municipal revenue bonds: *If so*—what effect will this have on the entire municipal market? *The authors will not state any personal bias in this heated dispute; however, we feel it is necessary for readers to be well aware of the current state of this continual argument.*

The famous Glass-Steagal Banking Reform Act of 1933, prohibiting commercial banks from underwriting most types of revenue bonds, was a result of the painful experience of the stock market crash of 1929 and the hundreds of bank failures during the Great Depression. At the time of the act, the federal government was extremely anxious to restore public confidence in the financial institutions of the nation, and it sought to ensure the prevention of any future financial catastrophe. Specifically, the government legislation sought to ensure that commercial banks would not take on excessive financial burdens and risks, attempt to deal on their own behalf in municipal and other securities, or monopolize the municipal bond market.

For nearly 40 years a dispute has continued over the removal of the legal barrier prohibiting commercial banks from underwriting most revenue bonds. The issues in this dispute involve billions of dollars, and the power and personal prestige at stake make this fight a kind of heavyweight championship of the American financial markets.

A variety of studies have been done by government agencies, university academics, and banking industry associations on both sides of this question. Understandably, those most prominent in presenting the issues in this dispute have been the Dealer Bank Association (DBA), consisting of 160 commercial banks, and the Securities Industry Association (SIA), consisting of over 450 securities firms that underwrite revenue bonds and that each employ full-time lobbyists in Washington, D.C.

Today Congress, the Department of the Treasury, and the Comptroller of the Currency are reexamining the traditional public policy which prohibits commercial banks from engaging in a whole range of financial practices (including the underwriting of most revenue bonds). The outcome of this extraordinary and most extensive review is eagerly awaited by the financial community.

Both commercial banks and investment banks have played a very active role in providing arguments and evidence relating to this ongoing debate. The argument made by commercial banks was that by their mere presence as competitors to underwrite each new revenue issue, they would lower the profit margin of investment banks because of the bidding competition between banks. For example, the profit, or spread, on revenue bonds was traditionally and still is far higher than for GO bonds, for which commercial banks are allowed to compete as underwriters. Commercial banks argued that the costs to municipal issuers would decrease if they would be permitted to enter these new underwritings and that market sales would grow.

Investment banks countered with arguments and studies to show that the market for municipal bonds would not necessarily grow and that profit spreads would not necessarily be reduced because so much more work was involved in financing revenue bonds (especially for issuers that have never come to market before) than for most GO issues.

According to the Senate Judiciary Committee, which in 1972 investigated this prickly question of bank underwriting of revenue bonds, commercial banks were themselves the primary customers of bank underwriters for GO bonds. Also, the committee indicated that substantial amounts of the GO underwritings of commercial banks were sold to the trust departments and special accounts of the same commercial banks as well as to their own correspondent banks. Yet the argument of commercial banks for allowing increased competition for the business of municipal underwriting was considered a significant one, especially because revenue bonds were becoming two-thirds of the municipal business.

Therefore, if the market for revenue bonds were opened, who would benefit, the public or the municipal bond market? And to what degree? Commercial banks produced evidence that the public would benefit, but the investment banks disputed their evidence and presented new studies of their own.

In part, what this whole dispute really amounts to is that enormous sources of revenue for investment banks from the underwriting of revenue bonds are at stake. To a securities industry already severely shaken by the dramatic reduction of the number of firms during the last decade, this latest move by commercial banks to press an all-out campaign to capture a very profitable line of business is a very real threat.

The Future of the Municipal Bond Market

Basically, the future of the market for municipal bonds depends upon crucial questions about the volume of issues and sales of each type, their future quality and credit, the management structure of the municipalities, and the mood of the American taxpayers after Proposition 13.

In the future, as in the past, the prices and yields of municipal bonds will be primarily affected by the level and term of interest rates, something which most experts say cannot be predicted. The price of municipal bonds will also continue, as in the past, to be affected by the rating or credit of the issuer; the relative supply and demand for similar securities; the money supply at that moment; the value of the U.S. dollar both at home and abroad; and, finally, the monetary policy of the U.S. Federal Reserve.

Two-thirds of the tax-exempt bonds are purchased by the institutional market today, and that percentage is generally expected to increase. No doubt many individual investors who find themselves driven by inflation into ever higher tax brackets will seek out municipal bonds as one of the few tax shelters left. The individual investor is expected to enter this market via municipal bond funds, trust departments, or bank investment accounts; thus while individual holdings will increase, they will be managed primarily by institutions. The bond funds are expected to grow proportionally far more rapidly because the individual who buys shares in them can do so in denominations as small as $100 in some cases and invariably less than the $5000 price for most single municipal bonds. All this has substantial implications for the future of the market for municipal bonds. For example, this will tend to enlarge the bond issues and joint municipal offerings because institutions are less capable of handling or unable to handle small issues.

Second, while it is generally agreed that interest rates cannot be predicted, the investing public's expectations of inflation over the past decade have indicated to many economists and bond analysts that it would be difficult if not impossible to return to pre–World War II or even pre-1960 debt interest rates of 3 and 4 percent. Thus there may well be a built-in market tendency toward high yields rather than stable or low ones.

This conclusion is reinforced by the fact that over the past 20 years the municipal markets for local bonds of all kinds have been steadily drawn out of the regional backwaters, where bonds were previously sold with a great degree of national, regional, and even statewide ignorance. As issuers with billions of dollars of local municipal bonds began to seek buyers in the national marketplace, they had to conform their bonds, in terms of prices, yields, and other dimensions, as well as their disclosure documents and ratings, to the nationally traded bonds. Thus in the trading of municipal bonds, regional and local idiosyncratic differences are being eliminated. Likewise, municipal bonds are corresponding somewhat more closely to other nationally traded securities. This trend is expected to continue.

Municipal Bond Insurance

Municipal bond insurance is a recent phenomenon that is likely to become an especially significant factor if credit crises, such as those of New York City and Cleveland, or taxpayer revolts, such as Proposition 13, continue. This insurance, purchased by the issuer or underwriter in advance, guarantees the payment of all principal and interest on the issue. So far there are only two primary firms in this field. The number of issuers insured is small (750), and the insurance totals just $4 billion. Nevertheless, should any hard times or full-scale national depression or general financial crisis occur, the institutional mechanism of insurance is now in place, ready to backstop most of the credit worries of certain investors.

The two firms in this field so far are Municipal Bond Insurance Association (MBIA) and American Municipal Bond Assurance Corporation (AMBAC). MBIA, which was created in 1974, is jointly sponsored by four very large insurance companies which act as members of MBIA and cosharers of the insurance risk on all municipal bond issues they back. These four companies and their percentage of participation are the Aetna Casualty & Surety Company (40 percent), a division of Aetna Life & Casualty Company; Fireman's Fund Insurance Company (30 percent), a division of American Express Company; Aetna Insurance Company (15 percent), a division of Connecticut General Insurance Corporation; and, finally, United States Fire Insurance Company (15 percent), a division of Crum & Forster Insurance Companies.

Municipal bond insurance guarantees the payment of principal and interest only on qualified new issues of municipal bonds. These issues do not need insurance in order to gain their rating or be sold; however, the intent is to enable good and solid issuers of small to medium municipal bonds to find a wider, more national market and to help reduce their interest cost. The MBIA insurance policies on such issues are irrevocable and unconditional, with not only a full guarantee by MBIA's member companies but also an automatic AAA rating by Standard & Poor's. Moody's does not give this rating guarantee, probably because it does not rate insurance companies.

The participation of each insurance company is backed by that company's full resources; therefore, each company shares the risk quite substantially. In contrast to the 4771 municipal defaults in the 1930s and the 2000 defaults since, the four MBIA insurance companies have never defaulted. Some argue that this type of insurance is totally unnecessary, especially for larger issues, and the large institutional buyers tend to be slightly reluctant to pay more for insured bonds than noninsured ones.

In the event of default of any insured municipality, the principal and interest payments due on the bonds will be made as originally scheduled. There are no deductibles or cancellation provisions. The insurance premiums are paid in full in advance of the date of issue. The insurance is usually attached to or printed on the front of the bond and the documents for issuing the bond; it becomes an integral part of the security.

In general, the key principle that makes this system work is the high standards that municipalities must meet to qualify for such insurance; these standards stem from exhaustive research on all previous municipal defaults. In effect, no bond issue which could not be readily sold on its own merits without insurance would be approved for insurance at all.

Standard & Poor's grants AMBAC- and MBIA-insured municipal bonds an AAA. Yet it must again be stressed that this a very high rating for bonds which must meet a test of being at least BBB in Standard & Poor's ratings. Initially Standard & Poor's had a special arrangement with both AMBAC and MBIA when they were created to evaluate the municipal issues submitted for insurance. While MBIA now does this credit analysis on its own, AMBAC continues to have Standard & Poor's perform this function.

A key difference between AMBAC and MBIA is that AMBAC is willing to insure hospital bonds and other types of revenue bonds, whereas MBIA limits its insurance largely to GO bonds and to those types of revenue bonds, such as water and sewer bonds, or electric issues, which entail service fees that completely cover operations, maintenance, and debt service.

Other Future Issues Confronting the Municipal Bond Market

While the key legal issues will obviously be in the areas of new disclosure requirements and increased liability of issuers, underwriters, financial advisers, and bond counsels, there are other legal imponderables facing the municipal market.

Inflation is one key uncertainty that will, in part, determine whether municipalities will be able to pay principal and interest on a timely basis.

A continuation of double-digit rates of national inflation might appear to make it easier for municipalities to pay off their debt obligations with cheaper dollars in the future. Nevertheless, the key impact of inflation will be upon the operating expenses and the inevitable cost overruns on the capital expenditures of municipalities. This may well bring issuers, investors, and analysts into that gray area of long-term financial guesswork to anticipate inflation rates in terms of capital goods, services, operating expenses, and overhead.

Future energy costs are a second imponderable facing municipalities. Westinghouse found, to its agonizing embarrassment, that the cost of energy which it contracted to supply over a 20-year period can simply go out of sight. And so the long-term supply contracts of many utilities and municipalities for energy can prove to be next to worthless.

Because of the continuing energy crisis, it appears quite likely that fuel shortages will impact heavily on the municipal market for public power bonds and to varying degrees upon each type of GO or revenue bond. The severity of the effect will depend upon the exact reliance of each public facility on sources of energy obtained from beyond the community's borders.

The accident at the Three Mile Island nuclear plant in Harrisburg, Pennsylvania, has pointed out the potential dangers of municipal nuclear power, nuclear fuel, and nuclear installations; it has raised legal, political, ethical, economic, and financial questions that will also touch the municipal bond market. The scare of the full-scale disaster of a "meltdown" must now be considered as another potential factor in the list of worries of municipal issuers and bondholders.

On other fronts, water and sewage treatment facilities and pollution control installations for water, air, and solid waste are likely to be subject to even stiffer laws in the future, despite the various delays toward mandatory compliance. Those communities that preferred to wait or delay to see if the standards would be dropped or reduced will probably be forced to far greater expense to meet these requirements on a crash basis.

Finally, the future of the two major rating agencies appears to be very bright, indeed. A few members of Congress and officials of the SEC are considering instituting a requirement that municipal and corporate issuers have national ratings. The grounds for this requirement would be that ratings are a significant factor for market comparisons of investors and should, therefore, be available as part of the public information about each issuing entity.

As mentioned in Chapter 3, "The Rating Agencies: Their Role in the Municipal Marketplace," the rating agencies, have been expanding extraordinarily rapidly in the municipal field during the past decade. They anticipate expanding still further to try to keep pace with the proliferation of new and more complex types of municipal bonds, notes, and issuers which will continue to keep the municipal bond market growing and vibrant in the years to come.

part5

Appendixes

Any book this long which covers the broad spectrum of municipal finance and credit analysis, going into areas that have not been dealt with in any other volume, is bound to turn up a number of significant and even important topics which, for one reason or another, do not really fit into any topical chapter. Taking this argument one step further, many of these topics or issues could even be chapters or books in themselves.

As a result, there are a number of appendixes which we have decided warrant significant attention. They range from what one accounting firm uses as a guideline to help municipalities write financial statements to a discussion of the Municipal Assistance Corporation for the City of New York (MAC)—the agency which rescued New York City from near bankruptcy. In addition, included here is a description of the nation's first public authority (still one of the largest public authorities): The Port Authority of New York and New Jersey. Also covered here is a study of the nation's largest locally supported system of higher education: the City University of New York. This study shows how municipal bonds may be backed by additional "layers" of security, a fact which is alien to the corporate finance world.

It is hoped that this section of appendixes, however lengthy, provides an in-depth look at some of the important topics not covered elsewhere in this volume and spurs additional research in these areas.

appendix A

Municipal Financial Statements

The following are examples of the types of documents which would be found in a municipality's annual report, primarily the financial statements. The first item is the public accountant's opinion, which will be included in certified financial statements. Second are two examples of financial statements. The first set of detailed financial statements is more for internal managerial use. The second set of financial statements consists of summary statements which are oriented toward the general public, which does not need to have the extent of detail reported in the first set of statements. In essence the second set of statements summarizes the operations of the municipality in a logical and more meaningful manner for the general public. Accompanying the summary statements is an example of the notes to the financial statements. As mentioned in Chapter 12, "Municipal Accounting," the reader should review these notes to become aware of any significant disclosures which may have an effect on the financial position of the municipality.

NOTE: These statements have been excerpted from a bulletin on state and local governmental accounting by Peat, Marwick, Mitchell & Co.

SOURCE: *State & Local Government Bulletin,* Peat, Marwick, Mitchell & Co., Feb. 28, 1978. Np. 1978-2. Reprinted by permission.

The Honorable Members of the City Council
City of Example, Any State:

We have examined the financial statements of the various funds
and account groups of the City of Example, Any State, as of and for
the year ended December 31, 1977, and issued our report thereon
dated_____. Our examination was made in accordance
with generally accepted auditing standards, and accordingly
included such tests of the accounting records and such other
auditing procedures as we considered necessary in the
circumstances.

The examination referred to above was directed primarily toward
formulating opinions on the individual financial statements of the
various funds and account groups of the City of Example, Any
State. The accompanying summary financial report, which is
presented for supplementary information purposes only,
aggregates the amounts of various funds and account groups
which in most instances cannot be commingled. The summary
financial report has been subjected to the auditing procedures
applied in the examination of the basic financial statements of the
individual funds and account groups and, in our opinion,
summarizes fairly in all material respects the individual funds and
account groups when considered in conjunction with such
individual financial statements.

> Signed by the public accounting firm performing
> the audit

(Date)

If an unqualified opinion is not rendered on the financial statements, the nature of the
qualifications should be set forth, and the effect on the summary financial report should be
considered in rendering an opinion thereon.

City of Example, Any State

Balance Sheet

December 31, 19X2, with comparative total figures for December 31, 19X1

	Governmental funds				
	General fund	Special revenue funds	Debt service funds	Capital projects funds	Special assess-ment funds
Assets and Other Debits					
Cash	$258,500	$101,385	$145,834	$ 431,600	$232,185
Investments, at cost or amortized cost	65,000	37,200	160,990	—	—
Receivables (net, where applicable, of allowances for estimated uncollectible amounts):					
Notes	—	—	—	—	—
Loans	—	—	—	—	—
Accounts	8,300	3,300	—	100	—
Taxes, including interest, penalties, and liens	58,300	2,500	3,829	—	—
Special assessments, including liens	—	—	—	—	646,035
Accrued interest	50	25	1,557	—	350
Due from other funds	2,000	—	—	—	—
Due from other governments	30,000	75,260	—	640,000	—
Inventories, at cost	7,200	5,190	—	—	—
Prepaid expenses	—	—	—	—	—
Advances to other funds	65,000	—	—	—	—
Property, plant, and equipment (net of accumulated depreciation)	—	—	—	—	—
Amount available for retirement of bonds	—	—	—	—	—
Amount to be provided for retirement of bonds	—	—	—	—	—
	$494,350	$224,860	$312,210	$1,071,700	$878,570
Liabilities					
Vouchers payable	$118,261	$ 33,850	—	$ 29,000	$ 20,600
Contracts payable	57,600	18,300	—	69,000	50,000
Judgments payable	—	2,000	—	22,600	11,200
Accrued liabilities	—	—	—	—	10,700
Due to:					
Fiscal agent	—	—	—	—	—
Other taxing units	—	—	—	—	—
Other funds	24,189	2,000	—	1,000	—
Taxes collected in advance	15,000	—	—	—	—
Deposits	—	—	—	—	—
Advance from general fund	—	—	—	—	—
Advance from municipality —general obligation bonds	—	—	—	—	—
Matured bonds payable	—	—	$100,000	—	—
Matured interest payable	—	—	2,000	—	—
General obligation bonds payable	—	—	—	—	—
Revenue bonds payable	—	—	—	—	—

	Proprietary funds		Fiduciary funds	Account groups		Totals (memorandum only)	
	Enterprise fund	Intragovernmental service fund	Trust and agency funds	General fixed assets	General long-term debt	19X2	19X1
Assets and Other Debits							
Cash	$ 370,595	$ 29,700	$ 216,701	$ —	$ —	$ 1,786,500	XXX
Investments, at cost or amortized cost	176,800	—	1,239,260	—	—	1,679,250	XXX
Receivables (net, where applicable, of allowances for estimated uncollectible amounts):							
Notes	2,350	—	—	—	—	2,350	XXX
Loans	—	—	35,000	—	—	35,000	XXX
Accounts	29,130	—	—	—	—	40,830	XXX
Taxes, including interest, penalties, and liens	—	—	580,000	—	—	644,629	XXX
Special assessments, including liens	—	—	—	—	—	646,035	XXX
Accrued interest	650	—	2,666	—	—	5,298	XXX
Due from other funds	2,000	12,000	11,189	—	—	27,189	XXX
Due from other governments	—	—	—	—	—	745,260	XXX
Inventories, at cost	23,030	40,000	—	—	—	75,420	XXX
Prepaid expenses	1,200	—	—	—	—	1,200	XXX
Advances to other funds	—	—	—	—	—	65,000	XXX
Property, plant, and equipment (net of accumulated depreciation)	5,769,759	103,100	—	7,326,500	—	13,199,359	XXX
Amount available for retirement of bonds	—	—	—	—	210,210	210,210	XXX
Amount to be provided for retirement of bonds	—	—	—	—	1,889,790	1,889,790	XXX
	$6,375,514	$184,800	$2,084,816	$7,326,500	$2,100,000	$21,053,320	XXX
Liabilities							
Vouchers payable	$131,071	$ 15,000	—	—	—	$ 347,782	XXX
Contracts payable	26,107	—	—	—	—	221,007	XXX
Judgments payable	—	—	—	—	—	35,800	XXX
Accrued liabilities	49,175	—	$ 3,700	—	—	63,575	XXX
Due to:							
Fiscal agent	139	—	—	—	—	139	XXX
Other taxing units	—	—	1,000	—	—	1,000	XXX
Other funds	—	—	—	—	—	27,189	XXX
Taxes collected in advance	—	—	—	—	—	15,000	XXX
Deposits	63,000	—	—	—	—	63,000	XXX
Advance from general fund	—	65,000	—	—	—	65,000	XXX
Advance from municipality —general obligation bonds	700,000	—	—	—	—	700,000	XXX
Matured bonds payable	—	—	—	—	—	100,000	XXX
Matured interest payable	—	—	—	—	—	2,000	XXX
General obligation bonds payable	—	—	—	—	$2,100,000	2,100,000	XXX
Revenue bonds payable	1,846,000	—	—	—	—	1,846,000	XXX,

City of Example, Any State *(continued)*

	Governmental funds				
	General fund	Special revenue funds	Debt service funds	Capital projects funds	Special assessment funds
Special assessment bonds payable	—	—	—	—	555,000
Total liabilities	$215,050	$ 56,150	$102,000	$ 121,600	$647,500
Encumbrances outstanding	38,000	46,500	—	941,500	185,000
Fund Equity					
Contributed capital	—	—	—	—	—
Investment in general fixed assets	—	—	—	—	—
Retained earnings:					
Reserved for revenue bond retirement	—	—	—	—	—
Unreserved	—	—	—	—	—
Fund balance:					
Reserved for inventory of supplies	7,200	5,190	—	—	—
Reserved for advance to intragovernmental service fund	65,000	—	—	—	—
Reserved for employees retirement system	—	—	—	—	—
Unreserved	169,100	117,020	210,210	8,600	46,070
	$494,350	$224,860	$312,210	$1,071,700	$878,570

See accompanying notes to financial statements.

	Proprietary funds		Fiduciary funds	Account groups		Totals (memorandum only)	
	Enterprise fund	Intragovernmental service fund	Trust and agency funds	General fixed assets	General long-term debt	19X2	19X1
Special assessment bonds payable	—	—	—	—	—	555,000	XXX
Total liabilities	$2,815,492	$ 80,000	$ 4,700	—	$1,100,000	$ 6,142,492	XXX
Encumbrances outstanding	—	—	—	—	—	1,211,000	XXX
Fund Equity							
Contributed capital	1,392,666	95,000	—	—	—	1,487,666	XXX
Investment in general fixed assets	—	—	—	7,326,500	—	7,326,500	XXX
Retained earnings:							
Reserved for revenue bond retirement	129,155	—	—	—	—	129,155	XXX
Unreserved	2,038,201	9,800	—	—	—	2,048,001	XXX
Fund balance:							
Reserved for inventory of supplies	—	—	—	—	—	12,390	XXX
Reserved for advance to intragovernmental service fund	—	—	—	—	—	65,000	XXX
Reserved for employees retirement system	—	—	1,426,201	—	—	1,426,201	XXX
Unreserved	—	—	653,915	—	—	1,204,915	XXX
	$6,375,514	$184,800	$2,084,816	$7,326,500	$2,100,000	$21,053,320	XXX

City of Example, Any State

Statement of Revenues, Expenditures, Encumbrances, Transfers, and Changes in Fund Balances

Year ended December 31, 19X2, with comparative total figures for year ended December 31, 19X1

	Governmental funds				
	General fund	Special revenue funds	Debt service funds	Capital projects funds	Special assessment funds
Revenues and other sources:					
Revenues:					
Taxes and special assessments	$ 881,300	$ 189,300	$ 79,177	—	$240,000
Licenses and permits	103,000	—	—	—	—
Intergovernmental revenues	186,500	831,100	41,500	$1,250,000	—
Charges for services	91,000	79,100	—	—	—
Fines and forfeits	33,200	—	—	—	—
Miscellaneous	20,800	71,625	7,140	68,250	27,495
Total revenues	$1,315,800	$1,171,125	$127,817	$1,318,250	$267,495
Other sources:					
Bond proceeds	—	—	—	900,000	—
Fixed asset additions	—	—	—	—	—
Transfers from other funds	—	—	—	—	—
Total revenues and other sources	$1,315,800	$1,171,125	$127,817	$2,218,250	$267,495
Expenditures, encumbrances, and other uses:					
Expenditures and encumbrances:					
General government	$ 124,505	$ 24,700	—	—	—
Public safety	259,345	465,800	—	—	—
Highways and streets	91,500	431,500	—	—	—
Sanitation	49,900	—	—	—	—
Water and sewer	—	—	—	—	—
Central garage	—	—	—	—	—
Health	45,450	—	—	—	—
Social services	48,100	—	—	—	—
Culture-recreation	57,250	265,400	—	—	—
Education	563,450	—	—	—	—
Debt service	—	—	$100,420	—	—
Capital projects	—	—	—	$2,357,000	$348,100
Miscellaneous	—	—	—	—	16,400
	$1,239,500	$1,187,400	$100,420	$2,357,000	$364,500
Other uses:					
Fixed asset disposals	—	—	—	—	—
Transfers to other funds	—	—	—	—	—
Total expenditures, encumbrances, and other uses	$1,239,500	$1,187,400	$100,420	$2,357,000	$364,500
Excess (deficiency) of revenues and other sources over expenditures, encumbrances, and other uses	$ 76,300	$ (16,275)	$ 27,397	$ (138,750)	$ (97,005)
Equity balances at beginning of year	84,300	133,295	182,813	147,350	143,075
Return of advance to intragovernmental service fund	10,000	—	—	—	—
Increase in reserves	(1,500)	—	—	—	—
Equity balances at end of year	$ 169,100	$ 117,020	$210,210	$ 8,600	$ 46,070

See accompanying notes to financial statements.

	Proprietary funds		Fiduciary funds	Account group	Totals (memorandum only)	
	Enterprise fund	Intragov-ernmental service fund	Trust and agency funds	General fixed assets	19X2	19X1
Revenues and other sources:						
Revenues:						
Taxes and special assessments	—	—	$1,205,800	—	$ 2,595,577	XXX
Licenses and permits	—	—	—	—	103,000	XXX
Intergovernmental revenues	—	—	—	—	2,309,100	XXX
Charges for services	$ 727,150	$88,000	—	—	985,250	XXX
Fines and forfeits	—	—	—	—	33,200	XXX
Miscellaneous	8,830	—	95,580	—	299,720	XXX
Total revenues	$ 735,980	$88,000	$1,301,380	—	$ 6,325,847	XXX
Other sources:						
Bond proceeds	—	—	—	—	900,000	XXX
Fixed asset additions	—	—	—	$2,211,000	2,211,000	XXX
Transfers from other funds	—	—	2,530	—	2,530	XXX
Total revenues and other sources	$ 735,980	$88,000	$1,303,910	$2,211,000	$ 9,439,377	XXX
Expenditures, encumbrances, and other uses:						
Expenditures and encumbrances:						
General government	—	—	—	—	$ 149,205	XXX
Public safety	—	—	—	—	725,145	XXX
Highways and streets	—	—	—	—	523,000	XXX
Sanitation	—	—	—	—	49,900	XXX
Water and sewer	$ 564,180	—	—	—	564,180	XXX
Central garage	—	$84,750	—	—	84,750	XXX
Health	—	—	—	—	45,450	XXX
Social services	—	—	—	—	48,100	XXX
Culture-recreation	—	—	—	—	322,650	XXX
Education	—	—	—	—	563,450	XXX
Debt service	—	—	—	—	100,420	XXX
Capital projects	—	—	—	—	2,705,100	XXX
Miscellaneous	92,988	—	$ 785,370	—	894,758	XXX
	$ 657,168	$84,750	$ 785,370	—	$ 6,776,108	XXX
Other uses:						
Fixed asset disposals	—	—	—	$ 184,100	184,100	XXX
Transfers to other funds	—	—	2,530	—	2,530	XXX
Total expenditures, encumbrances, and other uses	$ 657,168	$84,750	$ 787,900	$ 184,100	$ 6,962,738	XXX
Excess (deficiency) of revenues and other sources over expenditures, encumbrances, and other uses	$ 78,812	$ 3,250	$ 516,010	$2,026,900	$ 2,476,639	XXX
Equity balances at beginning of year	1,991,569	6,550	137,905	5,299,600	8,126,457	XXX
Return of advance to intra-governmental service fund	—	—	—	—	10,000	XXX
Increase in reserves	(32,180)	—	—	—	(33,680)	XXX
Equity balances at end of year	$2,038,201	$ 9,800	$ 653,915	$7,326,500	$10,579,416	XXX

City of Example, Any State

Summary of Assets and Liabilities

December 31, 19X2, with comparative figures for December 31, 19X1

Assets	19X2	19X1
Current assets:		
Unrestricted:		
Cash	$ 258,500	$ 184,600
Marketable securities, at cost which approximates market	65,000	—
Receivables, net of allowances for estimated uncollectible amounts	96,650	75,300
Inventories, at cost	7,200	5,700
	$ 427,350	$ 265,600
Restricted:		
Cash	$ 1,451,829	$ 1,206,781
Marketable securities, at cost which approximates market	383,740	127,500
Receivables, net of allowances for estimated uncollectible amounts	1,384,371	1,728,633
Inventories, at cost	68,220	65,200
Prepaid expenses	1,200	900
	$ 3,289,360	$ 3,129,014
Total current assets	$ 3,716,710	$ 3,394,614
Other assets:		
Deferred assessments	$ 622,200	$ 339,000
Long-term investments, at amortized cost (market value $154,790)	131,150	131,150
Taxes to be billed in future years for payment of long-term liabilities (including $210,210 and $182,813 already available in debt service funds)	2,100,000	1,410,000
Total other assets	$ 3,853,350	$ 1,880,150
Property, plant, and equipment:		
General fixed assets	$ 7,326,500	$ 5,299,600
Water and sewer works (net of accumulated depreciation of $657,700)	5,769,759	5,589,406
Central garage (net of accumulated depreciation of $16,900)	103,100	100,550
Total property, plant, and equipment	$13,199,359	$10,989,556
Total assets	$19,769,419	$16,264,320

See accompanying notes to financial statements.

Liabilities, encumbrances, and equity	19X2	19X1
Current liabilities:		
To be paid from unrestricted assets:		
Vouchers and other payables	$ 175,861	$ 103,100
To be paid from restricted assets:		
Vouchers and other payables	1,137,241	476,438
Accrued expenses	60,875	7,200
Current maturities on long-term debt (note 3)	523,000	254,000
Total current liabilities	$ 1,896,977	$ 840,738
Long-term debt payable, less current maturities (note 3):		
General obligation bonds:		
To be redeemed from taxes and general revenues	$ 1,825,000	$ 1,885,000
To be redeemed from water and sewer revenues	650,000	700,000
Revenue bonds	1,798,000	1,842,000
Special assessment bonds	505,000	545,000
Total long-term debt	$ 4,778,000	$ 4,972,000
Other liabilities:		
Taxes collected in advance	$ 15,000	$ 3,000
Deposits	63,000	55,000
Total other liabilities	$ 78,000	$ 58,000
Encumbrances outstanding	$ 1,211,000	$ 1,266,545
Equity balances (Exhibit B)—(note 2):		
General government activities:		
Operating funds	$ 575,400	$ 487,818
Capital funds (notes 5, 7, and 8)	7,565,220	5,729,125
Enterprise activity funds	3,664,822	2,910,094
Total equity balances	$11,805,442	$ 9,127,037
Total liabilities, encumbrances, and equity	$19,769,419	$16,264,320

City of Example, Any State

Summary of Revenues, Expenditures, and Other Changes in Equity

Year ended December 31, 19X2, with comparative figures for the year ended December 31, 19X1

	Operating funds—budget	General government activities		Enterprise activities funds	Total	Total prior year
		Operating funds	Capital funds			
Revenues and other additions:						
Revenues:						
Taxes and assessments	$1,151,177	$1,149,777	$ 240,000	—	$1,389,777	$1,200,000
Licenses and permits	125,500	103,000	—	—	103,000	100,000
Intergovernmental revenues	1,078,750	1,059,100	1,250,000	—	2,309,100	2,100,000
Charges for services	168,000	170,000	—	815,150	985,250	950,000
Fines and forfeits	32,500	33,200	—	—	33,200	30,000
Miscellaneous revenues	108,115	98,265	52,425	8,830	159,520	140,000
Total revenues	$2,664,042	$2,613,442	$1,542,425	$ 823,980	$4,979,847	$4,520,000
Other additions:						
Transfers from other funds	2,530	2,530	74,500	—	77,030	60,000
Capital contributions	—	—	—	672,666	672,666	100,000
Bond proceeds	—	—	900,000	—	900,000	200,000
Fixed asset acquisitions	—	—	2,211,000	—	2,211,000	1,700,000
Total revenues and other additions	$2,666,572	$2,615,972	$4,727,925	$1,496,646	$8,840,543	$6,580,000
Expenditures, encumbrances, and other deductions:						
Expenditures and encumbrances:						
Current services (note 6)	$2,530,790	$2,453,890	—	$ 741,918	$3,195,808	$2,740,000
Capital outlay	—	—	$2,705,200	—	2,705,200	1,600,000
Total expenditures and encumbrances	$2,530,790	$2,453,890	$2,705,200	$ 741,918	$5,901,008	$4,340,000

Other deductions:						
Transfers to other funds	74,500	74,500	2,530	—	77,030	60,000
Fixed asset disposals	—	—	184,100	—	184,100	200,000
Total expenditures, encumbrances, and other deductions	$2,605,290	$2,528,390	$2,891,830	$741,918	$6,162,138	$4,600,000
Excess of revenues and other additions over expenditures, encumbrances, and other deductions	$ 61,282	$ 87,582	$1,836,095	$ 754,728	$2,678,405	$1,980,000
Equity balances at beginning of year		487,818	5,729,125	2,910,094		
Equity balances at end of year		$ 575,400	$7,565,220	$3,664,822		

See accompanying notes to financial statements.

City of Example, Any State

Statement of Costs of Current Services (1) (2)

Year ended December 31, 19X2, with comparative amounts for the year ended December 31, 19X1

	Net costs	Related revenues			Total costs	Total costs—prior year
		Special taxes	User and other charges	Inter-governmental revenues*		
General government:						
Legislative	$ 19,500	—	—	—	$ 19,500	$ 18,000
Judicial	16,650	—	$ 24,300	—	40,950	36,000
Executive	37,945	—	47,530	—	85,475	90,000
Total general government	$ 74,095	—	$ 71,830	—	$ 145,925	$ 144,000
Public safety:						
General	$247,395	—	$ 11,000	—	258,395	$ 254,000
Police	(1,100)	—	55,400	$201,000	255,300	263,000
Corrections	(8,225)	—	325	207,600	199,700	188,000
Total public safety	$238,070	—	$ 66,725	$408,600	$ 713,395	$ 705,000
Public works:						
Highways and streets	$ 6,900	—	$ 8,500	$422,500	$ 437,900	$ 427,600
Sanitation	45,250	—	11,000	—	56,250	45,000
Water and sewer	(78,812)	—	735,980	—	657,168	523,000
Total public works	$ (26,662)	—	$755,480	$422,500	$1,151,318	$ 995,600

Health and welfare:					
Health	$ 44,500	—	—	—	$ 44,500	$ 47,750
Welfare	46,800	—	—	—	46,800	25,000
Total health and welfare	$ 91,300	—	—	—	$ 91,300	$ 72,750
Culture and recreation:					
Culture/recreation	$ 39,900	—	$ 15,500	—	$ 55,400	$ 58,100
Parks	(3,550)	$189,300	70,700	—	256,450	240,000
Total culture and recreation	$ 36,350	$189,300	$ 86,200	—	$ 311,850	$ 298,100
Education	$559,150	—	—	—	$ 559,150	$ 513,700
Debt service (on general obligation debt)	$ (27,397)	$ 79,177	$ 7,140	$ 41,500	$ 100,420	$ 100,000
Total costs of current services (note 6)	$944,906	$268,477	$987,375	$872,600	$3,073,358	$2,829,150

* Excludes federal revenue sharing, as it is not related to a specific service.

NOTE: (1) The format of this report assumes the government can identify expenditures separate from encumbrances. If it cannot, this statement should reflect expenditures *and* encumbrances and notes 1(d) and 6 should be modified.

(2) While recording depreciation as an expenditure of the operating funds is not in conformity with generally accepted accounting principles, the amount of depreciation, if known, can be included in this statement in total or by function. Other items which would be considered a cost of providing services even though a budgetary appropriation was not made and the item was not recorded as an expenditure, e.g., unused vacation, can be included provided the practice is disclosed in the summary of significant accounting policies and the amount is included in the reconciliation of costs of current services to resources utilized.

See accompanying notes to financial statements.

City of Example, Any State

Statement of Sources of Support for the Net Cost of Current services

Year ended December 31, 19X2, with comparative figures for
year ended December 31, 19X1

	19X2	19X1
Taxes:		
General property taxes—current	$ 878,500	$ 798,500
Penalties and interest on delinquent		
general property taxes	2,800	1,500
Total taxes	$ 881,300	$ 800,000
Other revenues:		
Licenses and permits	103,000	89,400
Intergovernmental grants	186,500	178,300
Fines and forfeitures	33,200	30,000
Miscellaneous revenues	19,500	17,000
Total revenues	$1,223,500	$1,114,700
Other available funds:		
Parks fund	5,400	2,700
State gasoline tax fund	9,000	6,200
Motor vehicle license fund	6,500	—
Parking meter fund	500	1,000
Amount set aside for unliquidated encumbrances	—	2,000
Total available	$1,244,900	$1,126,600
Other applications:		
Transfers to capital projects and special		
assessment funds	(74,500)	18,000)
Increase in general fund equity	(76,300)	(43,000)
Increases in other fund equities	(114,744)	(111,000)
Increase in amounts set aside for unliquidated		
encumbrances	(34,450)	—
Available to support the net cost of		
current services	$ 944,906	$ 954,600

See accompanying notes to financial statements.

City of Example, Any State

Notes to Financial Statements

December 31, 19X2

(1) **Summary of Significant Accounting Policies**

The accompanying financial statements are a summarization if the complete financial report prepared by the City. The significant accounting policies used for the preparation of the summary are as follows:

(a) Basis of Presentation

The City maintains its accounts in accordance with the principles of fund accounting in order to comply with the limitations and restrictions placed on the resources made available to the City. While this requires classification of transactions into several individual funds, for this presentation the transactions have been classified into three basic categories:

1. *General government activities—operating funds,* to reflect activities the City considers to be general services, and which are therefore to be supported out of available revenues, regardless of whether a "profit" or "loss" can be attributed to that service or group of services;

2. *General government activities—capital funds,* to reflect the capital resources that have been made available to the City in order that it can provide the general services; and

3. *Enterprise activities,* to reflect the financial results of the services provided by the City for which the determination of a profit or loss is relevant and appropriate.

(b) Basis of Accounting

The objective of the City is to provide services, expending no more than the resources made available to it while operating within the parameters of the law, and not, as with commercial entities, to earn a profit. The objective of the financial statements (in respect of the basis of accounting) is to disclose whether the City has been able to operate within the available resources. Accordingly, the City utilizes the modified accrual basis of accounting, in which revenues are recorded when susceptible to accrual, i.e., measurable and available to finance the City's operations, and expenditures are recorded when the liability is incurred, for the general government activities—operating funds; and the accrual basis of accounting, in which revenues are recorded when earned and expenditures are recorded when the cost is incurred, for the general government activities—capital funds and the enterprise activities.

(c) Restrictions on Certain Assets

Certain assets of the City of Example are restricted as to use by City charter, statutes, higher levels of government, contract or for other reasons. The summary of assets and liabilities segregates those assets which are restricted as to use from those which are unrestricted and therefore available for general purposes.

(d) Encumbrances (1)

Encumbrances, e.g., purchase orders, contracts, and other commitments for the expenditure of funds, are recorded and reported in the summary of revenues, expenditures and other changes in equity in order to reflect the resources that have been applied and are therefore no longer available. Encumbrances are not included in the statement of costs of current services as the purpose of that statement is to reflect the amounts expended during the year to provide the desired level of services. A reconciliation of the amount expended for services to the amount of resources utilized is provided in note 6.

(e) Inventories

Inventories are stated at cost. Inventory acquisitions are recorded as expenditures at the time the purchases are made. An accountability for the inventory is maintained by reporting the amounts on the summary of assets and liabilities and by reporting equivalent amounts as not available for appropriation.

(f) Interfund Receivables and Payables

Amounts owing from one fund to another have been eliminated from the summary of assets and liabilities.

(g) Taxes to Be Billed in Future Years for Payment of Long-term Liabilities

The City, like most cities, borrows money in order to acquire land and construct improvements, buildings and equipment. This policy enables the cost of these capital assets to be borne by the present and future taxpayers receiving the benefit of the capital assets. The taxes to be billed in future years for payment of long-term liabilities represent the amounts authorized by the City Council to be collected in future years from taxpayers and others for liquidation of the long-term liability.

(h) Property, Plant and Equipment

Fixed assets acquired or constructed for general governmental services are recorded as expenditures, and then reported at cost in the general fixed assets category. In the case of gifts or contributions, such assets are reported at the fair market value at the date received. Depreciation is not recorded for these fixed assets as the purpose of the financial statements for the general governmental services is to report the expenditure of resources, not costs.

Fixed assets acquired or constructed for the services for which a profit or loss needs to be determined are also stated at cost, but depreciation is recognized over the estimated useful life using the straight-line method. The estimated useful lives are as follows:

Improvements to land	16⅔ years
Structures	40 years
Interceptors and regulators	100 years
Equipment	10 years

(i) Equity Balances

There are limitations and restrictions on all of the City's funds except the general fund. This means that only the general fund equity balance is available to the City for any purpose whatsoever. Furthermore, portions of certain fund equity balances, including the general fund, have been appropriated for special purposes. The restrictions associated with each of the remaining equities are as follows:

- special revenue fund—limited by law to the financing of certain governmental functions;
- debt service fund—limited to the payments of principal and interest on long-term debt other than revenue and special assessment debt;
- expendable trust fund—limited to purposes designated in the trust or similar agreements;
- capital projects fund—limited to the acquisition or construction of designated fixed assets;
- special assessments fund—limited to payments related to improvements

which are to be paid for by assessments levied against the benefitted property;

- nonexpendable trust fund—principal must be preserved intact, and the expenditure of the income is limited to purposes designated in a trust agreement;
- general fixed assets—already expended for property, plant and equipment utilized by the City in its general operations;
- enterprise fund—limited to operation of the water and sewer activity;
- intragovernmental service fund—limited to the operation of the central garage activity.

The amounts of each fund balance and the amounts appropriated are presented in note 2.

(2) Equity Balances

The City's equity balances at December 31, 19X2, are as follows:

	Appro-priated	Unappro-priated	Total
General government activities:			
Operating funds:			
General	$ 7,200* 65,000†	$ 169,100	$ 241,300
Special revenue	5,190*	117,020	122,210
Debt service	—	210,210	210,210
Expendable trust	—	1,680	1,680
	$ 77,390	$ 498,010	$ 575,400
Capital funds:			
Capital projects	—	$ 8,600	$ 8,600
Nonexpendable trust	—	184,050	184,050
Special assessments	—	46,070	46,070
General fixed assets	—	7,326,500	7,326,500
	—	$ 7,565,220	$ 7,565,220
Enterprise activities:			
Enterprise funds	$129,155‡	$ 3,430,867	$ 3,560,022
Intragovernmental service funds	—	104,800	104,800
	$129,155	$ 3,535,667	$ 3,664,822
Total equity balances	$206,545	$11,598,897	$11,805,442

NOTES: * Appropriated for inventory reserve.

† Appropriated for advance to an enterprise activity.

‡ Appropriated for revenue bond requirements.

Agency fund balances, which amounted to $711,185 at December 31, 19X2, have been reclassified as vouchers and other payables as these are considered liabilities of the City.

(3) Long-term Debt

The annual requirements to amortize all debt outstanding as of December 31, 19X2, including interest payments of $1,723,000 on bonds carrying interest rates of 1¼% to

4%, are as follows. The amounts reflect both principal and interest in thousands of dollars.

Annual Requirements to Amortize Long-Term Debt
January 1, 19X3

(in thousands of dollars)

Year ending December 31	General obligation bonds	Revenue bonds	Special assessment bonds	Total
1977	$ 504	$ 113	$ 72	$ 689
1978	245	115	70	430
1979	240	117	68	425
1980	235	129	66	430
1981	230	137	64	431
1982 through 1999	2,088	1,978	453	4,519
Total	$3,542	$2,589	$793	$6,924

The change during the year ended December 31, 19X2, in amounts required in future years for the retirement of general obligation bonds is as follows:

Balance at January 1, 19X2	$1,410
New debt issued:	
19X2 Civic Center bonds	700
19X2 Barton Heights	
Recreation Center bonds	200
Debt retired:	
Serial bonds	(110)
Term bonds	(100)
Balance at December 31, 19X2	$2,100

The City is subject to the Municipal Finance Law of Any State which limits the amount of bonded debt (exclusive of revenue bonds) the City may have outstanding to 10 percent of the average assessed valuation of the past five years. At December 31, 19X2, the statutory limit for the City was $2,934,290, providing a debt margin of $344,500. The authorized unissued debt at December 31, 19X2, was $200,000.

There are also certain limitations contained in the revenue bond indentures, of which the most significant is a restriction against improving or extending the water system unless sufficient monies are available for servicing the revenue bonds. Sufficient monies were available at December 31, 19X2.

There were no anticipation or other notes issued during the year ended December 31, 19X2, to finance operating needs.

(4) Employees' Retirement System

The City maintains the Employees' Retirement System covering all of its employees except the public school teachers, who are eligible for the Any State Teachers Retirement System. The total pension expense for the year was $89,243, which includes amortization of prior service cost over a 17-year-period. The City's policy is to fund pension cost accrued. The actuarially computed value of vested benefits for the plan as of December 31, 19X2, exceeded the total of the pension fund assets and balance sheet accruals by $243,000. The City accounts for the activities of the Employees' Retirement System in a separate expendable trust fund and the amounts for that fund are not included in the accompanying financial statements. The fund deficit of $243,000 represents an increase in actuarial deficiency from the prior year of $7,650.

(5) **Property Tax**

The City's property tax is levied each May 15 on the assessed value listed on the prior September 1 for all real property located in the City. Assessed values are established by the County Assessment Board at 66⅔% of assumed market value, and a revaluation of all property is required to be completed no less than every ten years. The last revaluation was completed for the list of September 1, 19X9; the assessed value for the list of September 1, 19X0, upon which the 19X1–X2 levy was based, was $28,482,600. Taxes are due in two equal installments on the January 1 and July 1 following the levy date, although a 30-day grace period is provided for. Current tax collections for the year ended December 31, 19X2, were 97.9% of the tax levy.

The City is permitted by the Municipal Finance Law of Any State to levy taxes up to $5.00 per $100 of assessed valuation for general governmental services other than the payment of principal and interest on long-term debt and in unlimited amounts for the payment of principal and interest on long-term debt. The combined tax rate to finance general governmental services other than the payment of principal and interest on long-term debt for the year ended December 31, 19X2, was $3.74 per $100 and which means that the City has a tax margin of $1.26 per $100 and could raise up to $358,881 additional a year from the present assessed valuation of $28,482,600 before the limit is reached.

(6) **Reconciliation of Costs of Current Services to Resources Utilized (2)(3)**

The costs of current services includes all costs for services provided including costs that do not require the expenditure of funds and which were therefore not budgeted. The costs of current services can be reconciled to the expenditures and encumbrances charged against the current year's budget authorization as follows:

Costs of current services	$3,073,358
Less:	
Amounts charged to prior year's budget	(46,250)
Unneeded encumbrance reserve	(3,800)
Plus:	
Amounts encumbered but not yet expended	84,500
Amounts expended and profits charged by intragovernmental service funds	88,000
Expenditures and encumbrances charged against the current year's budget authorization	$3,195,808

(7) **Special Assessment Fund Deficit**

A $2,000 unanticipated deficit arose this year in Street Paving Project #77 due to an unexpected and substantial increase in the cost of concrete. As this project is being financed by assessments of property owners bordering on the paved streets, and the

City Charter permits an adjustment of assessments up to 2 percent of the originally authorized amount, the City plans to eliminate the deficit over the next three years by increasing each property owner's assessment.

(8) Capital Projects and Fixed Assets

The City has the following capital projects in process:

	Municipal auditorium	Storm sewer system	City-County Civic Center	Congress Avenue bridge
Initial authorization	$300,000	$50,000	$2,000,000	$250,000
Remaining financing	None required	None required	Sale of bonds ($700,000); state grant ($1,250,000); general fund revenues ($50,000)	Sale of bond anticipation notes and bonds ($50,000)

All of these projects have been authorized by the City Council. The City-County Civic Center has also been authorized by a public referendum. There are no material balances remaining from completed projects; the City does not have or anticipate any cost overruns on projects in process.

(9) Leases and Other Commitments

Commitments under lease agreements for facilities and equipment provide for annual rental payments approximating $450,000 and $250,000, respectively. Lease agreements typically provide for automatic termination on July 1 of any year in which the City fails to appropriate funds to meet rental payments.

(10) Contingent Liabilities

A number of claims against the City are presently pending for injuries received as a result of alleged defective sidewalks and roadways, ice and snow, etc., and alleged extras in the construction of the new Recreation Center. Also, litigation is pending with respect to tax appeals, planning and zoning appeals, and other miscellaneous cases. It is expected that the final settlement of these matters will not materially effect the financial statements of the City.

NOTES:
(1) This footnote assumes the government can identify expenditures separate from encumbrances. If it cannot, the format of the statement of costs of current services should be modified to include encumbrances and this footnote should be appropriately modified.
(2) This footnote would not be necessary if the government cannot identify expenditures separate from encumbrances and therefore includes the latter in the statement of costs of current services.
(3) This reconciliation should also include amounts for the depreciation of general fixed assets, the costs of unused sick leave or vacation, unfunded pension costs and other costs not requiring the use of current resources to the extent they are reported in the statement of costs of current services.

Items Included in the Official Statement*

Introduction
  Background
  The Financing
  Intervening Litigation and Settlement
  Power Sales Contract

The Agency
  Governmental Structure and Governing Board
  Powers under the Act
  Management
  Financial Statements
  Security for the Bonds
  Pledge
  Rate Covenants
  Contract Obligations of Cities and Agency
  Application of Bond Proceeds

The Projects
  Cost Summary and Financing Requirements
  Projected Financing Schedule
  Load and Energy Requirements and Resources

Projected Cost of Power
  Unit Cost to Cities
  Retail Cost of Power to Customers

Cities Electric Systems
  Historical Operating Statistics
  Operating Results

Description of the Bonds
  General
  Optional Redemption
  Mandatory Redemption of Term Bonds

Debt Service Requirements

Description of Certain Provisions of the Power Sales Contract
  Sale of Power and Energy
  Purposes for which Bonds may be Issued; Approvals Required
  Rates and Charges
  Payments by Cities
  Rate Covenant of Cities
  Sale of Electric Distribution System by Cities; Assignment of Rights
  Amendments

Auditor's Report
  Financial Statements of Cities Involved

Municipal Bonds

Description of Certain Provisions of the Resolution
  Pledge of Revenues and Funds; Application of Revenues
  Revenue Fund
  Bond Fund
  Reserve Fund
  Contingency Fund
  Construction Fund
  Investment of Monies in Funds
  Additional Bonds
  Refunding Bonds
  Subordinated Indebtedness
  Incurrence of Other Indebtedness
  Covenant as to Rates and Charges
  Certain Other Covenants
  Amendment of Resolution
  Discharge of Indebtedness
  Notice of Redemption of Bonds
  Events of Default and Remedies of Holders

Factors Affecting the Electric Utility Industry

Regulatory Bodies
  Public Utility Commission
  Interstate Transmission

Litigation
  Pending Litigation
  Settled Litigation
  Settlement

Tax Exemption

Certain Legal Matters

Legal Investment

Underwriting

Letters of Various Consulting Engineers
  Financing
  Status of Project
  Zoning Study and Cost Estimates
  Permits and Approvals

Agency Financial Statement

Form of Opinion of Bond Counsel

Copy of Bond Resolution

* SOURCE: James L. Lentz, president, M. G. Lewis & Co., from "The Financial Advisor."

appendix B

Transportation Bonds

Transportation bonds led America into the municipal bond market through toll road financing and bonds issued for port facilities. The revenue authority that was one of the first in America has become one of the largest issuers of transportation bonds, with almost $3 billion presently outstanding. This authority is, of course, the Port Authority of New York and New Jersey. At the present time, it has virtually every transportation-type facility under its wing, including such entities as Kennedy and LaGuardia Airports, the bridges and tunnels connecting Manhattan to the surrounding land masses, and even the World Trade Center towers. Bonds issued for port facilities, highways, and airports are discussed here also.

The Port Authority of New York and New Jersey*

The Port Authority is a municipal corporate instrumentality of the States of New York and New Jersey, created in 1921 by Compact between the two States, with the consent of the Congress of the United States. In the Compact, the two States recited their confident belief that a better coordination of the terminal, transportation and other facilities of commerce in the Port of New York would result in great economies benefiting the nation as well as the States and that the future development of such facilities would require the cordial cooperation of the States in the encouragement of the investment of capital and in the formulation and execution of necessary plans. They recited that such result could best be accomplished through the cooperation of the two States by and through a joint or common agency, and to that end, after pledging, each to the other, faithful cooperation in the future planning and developing of the Port of New York, they created the Port of New York District and The Port of New York Authority.

* Adapted from various official statements.

Effective July 1, 1972, the name of the Port Authority was changed from "The Port of New York Authority" to "The Port Authority of New York and New Jersey."

In general, the purpose of the States in establishing the Authority was to provide transportation terminal and other facilities of commerce within the Port of New York District and for such purposes they have from time to time authorized specific facilities and have given the Authority power to borrow money upon its bonds or other obligations and to make charges for the use of such facilities. The Port District comprises an area of about 1,500 square miles in both States, centering about New York Harbor, the boundaries of which are shown on the map appearing as the frontispiece of this Official Statement. The Port District includes the Cities of New York and Yonkers in New York State, Newark and Jersey City in New Jersey and over 200 other municipalities, including all or part of seventeen counties, in the two States.

An important function of the Port Authority is the effectuation of the Comprehensive Plan for the development of the Port District which was adopted by the two States in 1922 and supplemented from time to time thereafter.

By legislation adopted in 1931, the two States declared that the vehicular traffic moving across interstate waters within the Port District constitutes a general movement of traffic which follows the most accessible and practicable routes, and that the users of each such vehicular bridge or tunnel across these waters benefit by the existence of every vehicular bridge or tunnel, since all the bridges or tunnels relieve congestion and facilitate the movement of traffic. Accordingly, the two States provided that the construction and operation of such bridges and tunnels authorized by State law should be unified under the Port Authority. The legislation referred to leaves the Congress of the United States free to exercise its powers with respect to interstate crossings. Litigation challenging the decision of the Federal Highway Administrator of the U.S. Department of Transportation which upheld the Authority's 1975 toll increase is presently pending.

In 1947 the two States adopted legislation authorizing municipalities in the Port District to cooperate with the Port Authority in the development of marine terminals and empowered them to consent to the use by the Port Authority of any municipally owned marine terminal development, including the right to convey, lease or otherwise transfer such marine terminal development to the Port Authority. The Port Authority may also acquire privately owned marine terminal properties under the original Compact.

The two States also adopted legislation in 1947 declaring that the problem of furnishing proper and adequate air terminal facilities within the Port District is a regional and interstate problem and that it should be the policy of the two States to encourage the integration of air terminals so far as practicable in a unified system. In furtherance of said policy and in partial effectuation of the Comprehensive Plan, the Port Authority was authorized to proceed with air terminal development within the Port District. These statutes were amended during 1971–1973 to authorize the Authority to provide mass transportation facilities connecting with John F. Kennedy and Newark International Airports.

In 1951 the two States adopted legislation consenting to a waiver of the Port Authority's immunities from suit and from liability, subject to, among other requirements in specific cases, the filing of a valid and timely notice of claim in an action for money damages and commencement of suit in all actions within one year from the date the cause of action accrues.

In 1962 the two States authorized the Port Authority to proceed with the acquisition, rehabilitation and operation of the Hudson Tubes, consisting of the properties formerly operated by the Hudson & Manhattan Railroad Company, and certain extensions to the Hudson Tubes; also the States authorized a new facility of commerce known as the World Trade Center. These statutes were amended during 1972–1974 to authorize the Authority to effectuate an extension of the Hudson Tubes from the City of Newark to the vicinity of the City of Plainfield in New Jersey and to undertake a series of New Jersey rail improvements with respect to direct Erie-Lackawanna railroad service into Pennsylvania Station in New York City. The amendments also provided for the repeal of the provisions of the statutory covenant contained in the 1962 legislation which limited the Port Authority's financial participation in additional deficit passenger railroad facilities. The Supreme Court of the United States has determined that the retroactive application of the repeal to affected bonds issued prior to May 10, 1973 was invalid as a violation of the United States Constitution.

On September 28, 1977, the Committee on Finance of the Port Authority approved a priority study of a refinancing concept designed to lead to the replacement of the 1962 statutory covenant to permit the Authority to proceed with plans for capital investment in mass transit including authorized passenger rail transit projects. The refinancing concept envisions the advance refunding of those bonds affected by the 1962 covenant through the issuance of new bonds, so that the provisions of the 1962 covenant would no longer be effective. However, the concept does not include further Port Authority responsibility for passenger rail transit operating deficits. The proceeds of the new bonds would be utilized to purchase special U.S. Treasury obligations, the interest and principal of which would secure and be used to pay the advance refunded bonds as they become due and payable. The study was nearing completion, in December, 1977, when a proposed regulation of the U.S. Treasury Department with respect to refunding of certain industrial development bonds on a tax exempt basis technically impeded the progress of the proposed refunding.

The Authority raises the necessary funds for the construction or acquisition of its facilities upon the basis of its own credit, its reserve funds and its future revenue. In the past such funds have been supplemented in certain cases by state and federal contributions. The Authority has no power to levy taxes or assessments. Its bonds and other obligations are not obligations of the two States or of either of them, and (except for New York State Guaranteed Commuter Car Bonds) they are not guaranteed by the States or either of them. The revenues of the Authority are derived principally from the tolls, fares, landing, dockage, rental and other charges for the use of and privileges at its various facilities hereinafter described. Gross revenues of the Authority totaled approximately $575 million in 1979. The Authority had approximately $3 billion in bonds outstanding as of that year.

Sources of Bond Payments

The surplus revenues of all facilities of the Authority now in operation (not including cars acquired under the aforesaid New York State Commuter Railroad Car Program) are payable into the General Reserve Fund to the extent required by the statutes. These facilities are:

Holland Tunnel
Lincoln Tunnel
George Washington Bridge
Bayonne Bridge
Goethals Bridge
Outerbridge Crossing
Port Authority Bus Terminal
Hudson Tubes
New York Union Motor Truck Terminal
Newark Union Motor Truck Terminal
LaGuardia Airport
John F. Kennedy International Airport
Newark International Airport
Teterboro Airport
Port Authority–West 30th Street Heliport
Port Authority–Downtown Manhattan Heliport
Columbia Street Marine Terminal
Port Newark
Hoboken–Port Authority Marine Terminal
Brooklyn–Port Authority Marine Terminal
Erie Basin–Port Authority Marine Terminal
Elizabeth–Port Authority Marine Terminal
New York City Passenger Ship Terminal
World Trade Center

Rate Powers and Covenants

As a result of legislation contained in Chapter 47 of the Laws of New York of 1931 and Chapter 4 of the Laws of New Jersey of 1931; in Chapter 802 of the Laws of New York of 1947 and Chapter 43 of the Laws of New Jersey of 1947; and in Chapter 209 of the Laws of New York of 1962 and Chapter 8 of the Laws of New Jersey of 1962, the two States convenanted with each other and with the holders of any bonds of the Authority secured by its General Reserve Fund (including Consolidated Bonds), that the two States will not diminish or impair the power of the Authority to establish, levy, and collect tolls, rents, fares, fees, or other charges, in connection with any facility owned or operated by the Port Authority the revenues of which shall have been pledged in whole or in part as security for such bonds. All present Port Authority facilities (not including cars acquired under the aforesaid New York State Commuter Railroad Car Program) and the charges therefore are covered by these statutory covenants, so long as such bonds or other obligations remain outstanding.

Under the 1962 statutes the States also have covenanted that they will not diminish or impair the Port Authority's power to determine the quantity, quality, frequency or nature of the service provided in connection with each such facility.

The Authority has convenanted with the holders of Consolidated Bonds (which include Consolidated Notes) to establish charges in connection with facilities whose net revenues are pledged as security for such bonds (all present Authority facilities not including cars acquired under the aforesaid New York State Commuter Railroad Car Program) to the end that at least sufficient net revenues may be produced therefrom to provide for the debt service on all Consolidated Bonds, but in the event that such net revenues are insufficient to provide for the debt service on Consolidated Bonds, to make good any deficiency out of the General Reserve Fund or other available revenues, moneys or funds and for that purpose to establish charges in connection with facilities the surplus revenues of which are payable into the General Reserve Fund (including all its existing bridges and tunnels, air, marine, bus and truck terminals, the Hudson Tubes, and the World Trade Center) to the end that combined surplus revenues may be produced therefrom at least sufficient to cover debt service on Consolidated Bonds.

Repeal of Statutory Covenant

In 1974, the States of New York and New Jersey acted to repeal absolutely the statutory covenants adopted in 1962 (Section 6, Chapter 209, Laws of New York, 1962, Section 6, Chapter 8, Laws of New Jersey, 1962), limiting the Port Authority's ability to apply pledged revenues and reserves to additional deficit passenger railroad facilities. Effective May 10, 1973, the two States had enacted legislation to preclude application of the covenants prospectively to bonds issued after such date (Chapter 1003, Laws of New York, 1972; Chapter 208, Laws of New Jersey, 1973), and effective June 15, 1974, the States acted to repeal the covenants without qualification (Chapter 993, Laws of New York, 1974; Chapter 25, Laws of New Jersey, 1974). On April 27, 1977, the Supreme Court of the United States held that the 1974 retroactive repeal was invalid as a violation of the United States Constitution.

On April 30, 1974, the United States Trust Company of New York commenced an action in New Jersey Superior Court, Bergen County, on its own behalf, as trustee for the Fortieth and Forty-first Series of Port Authority Consolidated Bonds, and on behalf of the holders of all Port Authority Consolidated Bonds, against the State of New Jersey and the Governor and the Attorney General of the State of New Jersey seeking a declaratory judgment that the action taken in 1974 to repeal retroactively the 1962 statutory covenant described above violates both the United States Constitution and the New Jersey Constitution. In its complaint, the Trust Company alleged that as a result of the repeal of the covenant, the secondary market for Consolidated Bonds of the Authority was adversely affected to the detriment of the Trust Company and all holders of Consolidated Bonds. The defendants' answer denied this allegation. On May 14, 1975, the validity of the 1974 action repealing the 1962 statutory covenant was upheld by the Superior Court. This decision was affirmed on

February 25, 1976 by the New Jersey Supreme Court. On April 27, 1977, the United States Supreme Court reversed the judgment of the New Jersey Supreme Court, and determined that the 1974 retroactive repeal was invalid as a violation of the United States Constitution.

Bonds for Port Facilities

Evaluating the security behind port bonds involves a study of such factors as: financial stability of the shipping companies which use the port, the competitive environment of the port, the ability to raise rates and charges, and the general trends in the amount of cargo and other such items handled by the facility.

Highway and Toll Road Bonds

Among the major factors considered in analyzing toll road and highway bonds are the ability to raise rates and tolls and the extent of competition for the road. Roads financed by tax-exempt bonds include the New Jersey Turnpike, the Indiana Toll Road, and the Kansas Turnpike.

Airport Revenue Bonds

Generally speaking, bonds issued for airports can be divided into two broad categories: those supported by net revenues of the facilities at the airport and those backed by payments made by specific airlines. Because of the financial viability of certain major air carriers, analysts and investors have come to regard the former type of airport revenue bond as having stronger security than the latter, although this may not always be so. Among the more general factors considered are the competitive environment of the airport, the ability to raise fees and charges, the diversity of the revenue stream supporting the bonds, and the ability of the support facilities at the airport to handle the present and projected increase in passengers. In this regard, emphasis is placed on the feasibility study for future demand projections, including the number of enplanements originating at that airport, the number of airlines flying that airport, and whether or not the airport serves as the "home" of an airline. Major airports financed through municipal bonds include: Dallas–Ft. Worth Airport, the airport of Los Angeles, and the Atlanta Airport.

Education Bonds: The City University of New York[1]

Although unrelated, municipal bonds issued for education and municipal bonds issued for transportation purposes are the only two areas of the municipal bond market that have not increased in volume significantly over recent years. These two types of bonds actually make up a relatively small proportion of the total municipal bonds issued each year, and one category, namely transportation, has even declined in total volume over recent years as well as in terms of a percentage of total municipal underwritings.

Nonetheless, the case presented here is especially rich in material for studying municipal credit analysis. The first major case for education is the financing of the nation's largest locally supported system of higher education, the City University of New York (CUNY). CUNY's outstanding municipal obligations total almost $1 billion, and its revenue stream is tied not only to tuition and fee income, but also, and interestingly, to financial support by both New York State and New York City. Without discussing this issue in too much detail at first, it is sufficient to state that a close look at the underlying security of CUNY's bonds reveals both how interesting the backing is and how resilient the financing mechanism behind certain municipal bonds may be. In addition, and perhaps most important, the analysis of the security backing CUNY's bonds strikes at the heart of the "weakest link" theory traditionally employed by certain analysts and investors.

The Financing Arrangement for CUNY Facilities[2]

Dormitory Authority of the State of New York: The Dormitory Authority is authorized to acquire property for educational and medical use and to construct such facilities through the issuance of bonds and to lease such facilities to qualifying institutions. When leased by the City University of New York, the University is responsible for the operation and maintenance of the facilities. At the time when the indebtedness period is terminated, title to the facilities reverts to the City of New York, and the leaseholds appear as assets in the financial records of CUNY.

City University Construction Fund (CUCF): The Fund is authorized to provide for the construction of facilities for all the institutions of the University. It is presently administered by a board of nine trustees chosen as follows: two are designated by the Governor of New York State; four are designated by the Mayor of New York City; and the Chairman of the Board of Higher Education, the Chancellor of the City University, and the Chairman of the Planning Commission of the City of New York are all ex-officio trustees of the Fund. All trustees, except those who serve ex-officio, have terms expiring at the end of the term of the elected official who appointed them.

After the trustees approve plans for the construction of a facility, the sale of tax-exempt bonds through the Dormitory Authority is arranged. The Dormitory Authority owns the facility during the period of time that the bonds are outstanding, and during this same period leases the facility to the Fund for use by the City University. As a result, the Fund pays to the Dormitory Authority an annual rental which is designed to cover the debt service on the bonds issued for the construction of the facility as well as to cover the Authority's administrative expenses and debt service reserve requirements.

Indebtedness: Presently, the outstanding indebtedness related to the City University is approximately $680,000,000, of which $440 million is for the University's Senior Colleges and $240 million for the Community Colleges. The Community Colleges are presently limited to the issuance of no more than $650,000,000, of which there is a $470 million ceiling on the total outstanding principal amount of Community College bonds that are secured by a debt service reserve fund to which State funds are apportionable. Bonds may be issued above that amount that are not so secured and may not be on a parity with the bonds issued under the ceiling.

The Bond resolution limits the maximum annual debt service on the bonds outstanding to an amount not to exceed the aggregate amount of Instructional and Non-Instructional fees received during the preceding fiscal year from both the Senior and Community Colleges. Fees totaled approximately $150 million for the fiscal year ended June 30, 1977, and debt service for that year totaled approximately $50 million.

The 6 Tiers of Bond Security: The "Layered Effect"

1. and **2.** The debt service on the outstanding bonds of CUNY is paid through annual lease rentals provided to the City University Construction Fund. The State and the City each are required to pay 50 percent of the annual rentals payable by the Fund.

3. If the City fails to appropriate its 50 percent share to the Fund, the State is required to pay the City's portion, which is to be taken from the next State aid payment apportioned to the City as per capita State aid for the support of local governments under Section 54 of the State Finance Law. Such monies provided to the Fund from per capita State aid slated for the City are not to exceed $65 million in any one given year relating to leases of both the Senior and Community Colleges combined. (However, the $65 million limit may not be effective if the outstanding bonds of the New York State Dormitory Authority that were issued to finance facilities through the Fund are accelerated as a result of a default under the Dormitory Authority bond resolutions. All such outstanding bonds of the Dormitory Authority could then be due and payable, and could have a prior claim on per capita aid to the extent of 50 percent of such principal amount.)

The payment of per capita State aid to the Fund must come before such aid that is paid, if necessary, to the:

1. New York City Housing Development Corporation
2. New York City Transit Authority
3. New York City Police and Pension Fund
4. Municipal Assistance Corporation (under the Second General Bond Resolution)

4. If the funds above are not sufficient, the Fund is obligated to pay annual rentals from all Instructional and Non-Instructional fees received from the Senior and Community Colleges for their respective debt service obligations. (Such fees from the Senior Colleges are subject to a prior pledge of the first $50 of tuition received from each graduate student as a result of a prior agreement between the Board of Higher Education and the Dormitory Authority executed on January 10, 1966, for the financing of CUNY's graduate center. The maximum annual debt service on these bonds is $521,063.) If this is the case, such funds will not be available for operating expenses.

5. As additional security for the bonds of CUNY's Senior and Community Colleges, debt service reserve funds are established equal to the maximum annual debt service on each system's outstanding obligations. If such monies are used, the Fund is required to include such an amount needed to replenish the debt service reserve fund in its estimate of the amount of monies that will be required from the State and the City in the next fiscal year.

6. Finally, in the case of the Community Colleges, the State of New York has pledged its "moral obligation" to appropriate monies necessary to restore the debt service reserve fund to its required level, under the standard deficiency make-up arrangement.

(The bonds of the Senior and Community Colleges are issued under separate resolutions, and the sources of payment for each are not transferable.)

The "Layered Effect" in Theory: A Conceptual Model

One of the more intriguing aspects of the security of municipal bonds today, which is alien to corporate obligations, is introduced here as the "layered effect," a mechanism providing increased security to certain municipal obligations. The concept is based on the increasing practice of tieing the security of municipal bonds to a series of "layers" or tiers of fund sources from which payments of the debt service on bonds can be made, above and beyond the traditional funds such as the debt service reserve and capital reserve funds.

The idea behind the "layered effect" is that if one tier of funds is not sufficient to pay the entire debt service on the bonds, the amount of monies left to be paid after payment is made by the first tier is provided by the second tier of funds, and so forth through the other tiers of revenue sources. The use of each fund reduces the amount of debt service that must be paid by the following fund, and the series of funds, when taken together, increases the debt service coverage in the aggregate.

The argument in favor of advancing the "layered effect" theory is clear: each tier of security is not dependent on any other; if one tier of fund sources is slim or weak, the other tiers make up the difference, and the debt service may still be paid over a period of years; and when the monies from each tier are combined, the debt service coverage is increased by the size and number of tiers of security.

The "layered effect" theory thus strikes at the heart of the "weakest link" argument traditionally employed in municipal analysis. The latter theory suggests that the security of the bonds is generally only as strong as the weakest link of the security and can really never be stronger than the strongest source of payment for the bonds. In the "weakest link" argument, the effect of the combination of funds from the many tiers is not taken into account. Under the "layered effect," the additional tiers of security in fact provide additional security.

The "layered effect" also provides additional security under default conditions in American state and local finance because as funds from each tier are used to pay debt service over a period of years, additional time is provided for municipalities and public authorities to work out their financial problems. During this "refinancing period," state monies may be appropriated, new agencies may be created to assume the default debt, monies from funds may be transferred where needed, and various other intergovernmental rescue programs may be implemented, and even statutorily enacted. Much of the impetus behind such rescue operations is directed at preventing the impairment of the credit standing of surrounding governmental entities or similar ones nationwide as the result of a psychological spillover effect from the defaulted issuer.

Leading examples of such refinancing programs include the creation of the Project Finance Agency in New York State to bail out the defaulted New York State Urban Development Corporation through additional appropriations, mortgage transfers, and state aid, and the establishment of the Municipal Assistance Corporation for the City of New York for a similar purpose and financed in similar ways. This lead time for "refinancing" provided by such security mechanisms as the "layered effect" is unique to American state and local government; corporate America really has no similar way out in the event of bankruptcy. Indeed, the resiliency of municipal governments is highlighted by the fine record of repayments subsequent to municipal defaults during the Depression years.

The "Layered Effect" in Practice

The City University of New York, both its Senior and Community Colleges, provide landmark examples of how the "layered effect" works in practice. Referring to the 6 tiers of bond security discussed earlier and using the data compiled on coverage of the two special tiers of security analyzed in the preceding sections, a potential default scenario on CUNY's bonds and its effect on the payment of the debt service would be as follows.

1. If the City failed to pay its entire share of the debt service on both the Senior and Community College bonds (50 percent of the total debt service), the State would step in and take from the $434 million in per capita State aid annually apportioned to New York City an amount equal to the City's portion of the debt service. This sum would be about $16 million for the Senior Colleges and $11 million for the Community Colleges, for a total of $27 million. *The degree of coverage is, therefore, obviously extensive.*

It is especially important to note that payments for the debt service on CUNY's obligations have a prior lien on State per capita aid to New York City above certain major City agencies, including the Municipal Assistance Corporation (MAC) for the City of New York.

2. *If State per capita aid was not appropriated, bond payments would be made from tuition and fee income.* With the imposition of tuition, coverage on the Senior College bonds jumped from 1.8× (times) to 3.2×, and coverage on the Community College bonds increased from only .78× to 2.2×.

In reality, then, financing the operations of the City University does not have a first claim on certain large amounts of the University's own operating income. *Interestingly, and as a result, the City University could completely cease operations, and the debt service on the bonds would contine to be paid for a number of years.*

3. If student enrollment dropped substantially and tuition and fees were not increased enough to pay the debt service on the bonds, then bond payments would be made from the debt service reserve fund. Unlike most instances, the debt service reserve fund, in this case, is in fact considered to be a tier of security because if it is used to any extent, the amount of monies used is subject to repayment into the fund by the State and the City in the following year. *Thus, the debt service reserve fund is not ultimately dependent on operating income, which may have been cut off entirely.*

4. If the debt service reserve fund is not sufficient or is used, and additional monies are not forthcoming, then the State has a "moral obligation" to replenish the fund for payment of the debt service on the bonds of the Community Colleges. Such an arrangement is the standard deficiency makeup provision, and *it takes a certain type of government official to risk impairing the entire credit standing of New York as well as that of its revenue authorities for failing to pay approximately $11 million.* In the case of New York State, it would be $11 million as compared to a total budget of almost $13 billion.

In summary, the common idea of keeping "theoria and praxis at their usual prudent distances from one another" may not hold in the case of a default scenario when the bond security is dependent on a "layered effect" of tiers of additional security.

Student Loan Revenue Bonds

The program, which enables students to borrow money for their education at a lower interest cost, has two basic types. Federally Insured Student Loans are those which are guaranteed by the Department of Health, Education and Welfare (HEW), and the Guaranteed Student Loan Program is guaranteed by either state agencies, private insurance, or other guarantors and is also eligible for additional insurance through HEW in the event of default, disability, bankruptcy, or death. Reimbursement from the federal government is for 80 to 100 percent of principal and interest based on the agency's default rate. This additional federal insurance may provide a second "layer" of security. The federal government also provides interest subsidies under both programs during the time that the payments on the loans are deferred. Bonds issued under both programs may have closed or open indentures, which may allow parity bonds to be issued, generally providing additional security.

Cash flow analysis is critical to evaluating the security of these bonds, especially the repayments made by students on their loans and their ability to make the debt service payments when they come due, as they relate to the maturity schedule of the bonds.

Notes to Appendix C

[1] Adapted from research completed by Stephen P. Rappaport at Thomson McKinnon Securities, Inc., in a report entitled *A New View of the City University of New York's Bonds,* Spring 1979.

[2] In mid-1979, New York State assumed a larger role in financing the City University of New York.

appendix D

The Case of New York City:
A Special Note

A century ago, James Bryce, government scholar of international renown, concluded in his three-volume treatise *The American Commonwealth* that the "one conspicuous failure of the United States" was the government of cities, and he argued further that the "vices of extravagance and mismanagement revealed themselves on the largest scale in New York City." In the wake of the New York City fiscal crisis of the 1970s, many financial analysts rendered the same remarkable verdict. Lost to many observers of the New York debacle was the City's problem in 1871: Europen bankers refused to extend it loans in light of its debt growth, and subsequently the trading of the City's bonds on the Berlin Stock Exchange was suspended. As a condition for additional loans to the City, New York bankers required that financial reforms be instituted and that audits of the City books be conducted. The City relented, and during that electoral year the Tweed Ring fell from power.

About 60 years later, in 1933, a similar fiscal crisis beset New York City, and on September 28 of that year *The New York Times* ran this headline: "Banks Agree to City Finance Plan." After a year of negotiations with Wall Street ficanciers in an effort to stave off default, the City concluded what was known as the 1933 Bankers Agreement with the nation's major banks, led by Thomas W. Lamont of J. P. Morgan Company. The City agreed to institute a seven-point austerity program in return for the refunding by the banks of its outstanding revenue bonds, which were issued against uncollected taxes.

It was against this backdrop that New York City skidded toward default again in the 1970s.

appendix E

The Municipal Assistance Corporation for the City of New York (MAC)

This book would be remiss if it did not include a brief description of the municipal financing vehicle that rescued New York City from its fiscal crisis of near bankruptcy in 1975. The Municipal Assistance Corporation for the City of New York (aptly dubbed "Big MAC") was created largely as a financing vehicle to refinance the City's outstanding debt obligations and issue additional debt, which totaled well into the billions, in the name of New York City, but without the backing of the City. The security behind MAC's municipal obligations, as will be discussed, was earmarked revenues for the City and certain taxes levied within the City. The lesson here is not that MAC may have been an undervalued municipal bond issuer because of the high coverage of its debt service, and it is not the simple fact that New York City was rescued from bankruptcy by the creation of MAC. The lesson lies in the fact that even in a potential and likely default scenario, the untapped and largely disguised resources inherent in the structure of the nation's public finance systems have the resiliency to turn a likely mammoth fiscal disaster into a much more stable financial situation within a relatively short time.

Background, Purposes, and Powers (MAC)*

The Corporation is a corporate governmental agency and instrumentality of the State constituting a public benefit corporation. The Corporation was created by State legislation adopted in June 1975 for the purpose of providing financing assistance and fiscal oversight for the City. To carry out such purpose, the Corporation was given the authority, among other things, to issue and sell bonds and notes, to pay or lend funds received from such sales to the City and to exchange the Corporation's obligations for those of the City. Between June 1975 and June 1978, the Corporation issued its obligations in accordance with these

* Adapted from various official statements.

purposes, and the City was provided with seasonal loans by the Federal government and long-term financing by certain City pension funds and the Corporation. The Control Board was established to oversee the financial affairs of the City.

By June 1978, the City had brought its operating budget into balance in accordance with State law and accomplished other budgetary and accounting objectives. Despite this progress, it became clear that further actions would be necessary to enable the City to finance itself. As a result, the Debt Issuance Plan was developed to provide necessary long-term financing to the City over the four fiscal years ending June 1982, during which time the City expects to follow a plan designed to bring its operating budget into balance in accordance with generally accepted accounting principles ("GAAP") and to enable it to regain necessary access to the public credit markets.

To enable the Corporation to fulfill its role in the Debt Issuance Plan, the State enacted legislation in 1978 that increased the amount of obligations which the Corporation may issue to $8.8 billion (excluding refunding obligations and short-term notes) and authorized the Corporation to issue its bonds and notes for several additional purposes and to pay or lend the proceeds to the City. Included in the additional purposes are (i) financing items permitted to be included in the City's capital budget, (ii) making available funds to reduce the City's requirements for State advances of State assistance moneys, (iii) financing payments to a reserve fund in connection with the Federal guarantee of obligations of the City, and (iv) assisting in financing the City's seasonal borrowing requirements.

The 1978 legislation extended the duration of the Control Board and modified its powers. In addition, the legislation required the Corporation to include in its bonds a covenant of the State that the State will not take certain actions, including any action that will substantially impair the authority of the Control Board to act in specified respects with regard to the City.

Debt service for obligations issued under the First General Bond Resolution is payable from funds paid into the Debt Service Fund from the special account in the State's Municipal Assistance Tax Fund, which is funded from revenues collected, less the State's charges for collection and administration, from the sales tax and, if necessary, the stock transfer tax. The net revenues from sales and stock transfer taxes which were collected by the State during the twelve months ended June 30, 1978 and March 31, 1979 amounted to $1,275 million and $1,398 million, respectively. Payments made to the Corporation from the Municipal Assistance Tax Fund are to be made quarterly and at such other times as the Corporation requests.

Debt service for obligations issued under the Second General Bond Resolution is payable from two sources: funds paid annually into the Debt Service Fund from the special account in the Municipal Assistance State Aid Fund, which is funded from per capita state aid otherwise payable by the State to the City, and, after satisfying the debt service requirements for obligations issued under the First General Bond Resolution as described above, funds paid quarterly from the Municipal Assistance Tax Fund. Per capita aid is subject to prior claims asserted by certain other State or City entities; however, no such claims have been asserted since the inception of the Corporation. Total per capita aid paid into the Municipal Assistance State Aid Fund on June 25, 1978, amounted to $434 million. An additional $49.3 million was paid into the Municipal Assistance State Aid Fund in October 1978.

Payment of the Bonds and Debt Service Coverage

The Corporation's revenues pledged to the payment of Second Resolution Bonds are derived from moneys that are paid to the Trustee, subject to annual appropriation by the State Legislature, from three sources: Per Capita Aid and (to the extent not needed to meet debt service, operating expenses and capital reserve funding requirements under the Corporation's First General Bond Resolution) the Sales Tax and the Stock Transfer Tax. "Per Capita Aid" consists of amounts that otherwise would have been payable to the City under the State law that provides for a general revenue sharing program applicable to localities throughout the State. The "Sales Tax" consists of a State sales tax imposed within the City, at the rate of 4%, on most retail and certain other sales. The "Stock Transfer Tax" consists of the State tax on the transfer of stocks and certain other securities. The Corporation has no taxing power.

Assuming that amounts available to the Corporation from Per Capita Aid, Sales Tax, and Stock Transfer Tax continue at present levels, Available Revenues for debt service on all outstanding Second Resolution Bonds, including the Series 15 Bonds, would be as follows:

	(Dollars in millions)	
	$ 980.0	Sales Tax (12 months ended March 31, 1979)
plus	387.3	Stock Transfer Tax (12 months ended March 31, 1979)
minus	5.5	operating expenses of the Corporation
minus	378.0	maximum annual debt service payments on currently outstanding First Resolution obligations (issuance test limits annual debt service to $425 million)
	$ 983.8	available tax revenues after provision for First Resolution obligations
plus	427.3	available Per Capita Aid (payable June 1979), net of $54.3 million of prior claims (none of which has been asserted since the inception of the Corporation)
	$1,411.1	Available Revenues
divided by	$ 354.1	maximum annual debt service payments on currently outstanding Second Resolution Bonds (including the Series 15 Bonds)
	3.99	Debt Service Coverage

Index

NOTE: Page numbers in *italics* indicate charts, figures, or tables.

DATE DUE

APR 7 1997			

DEMCO 38-297